mass media

FORCES IN OUR SOCIETY

mass media

FORCES IN OUR SOCIETY

edited by

FRANCIS AND LUDMILA VOELKER

St. Cloud State College

HARCOURT BRACE JOVANOVICH

New York   Chicago   San Francisco   Atlanta

ISBN: 0-15-555118-3

Library of Congress Catalog Card Number: 70-182342

Printed in the United States of America

ACKNOWLEDGMENTS

In addition to the individuals and companies cited in the text, the editors would like to thank those listed below for permission to use material in this book.

Cover photo: David Attie, New York

Part opening art: Petie Brigham, Roanoke, Va.

Page 55: Reprinted with the permission of Farrar, Straus and Giroux, Inc., from **The Pump House Gang** by Tom Wolfe, copyright © 1968 by Tom Wolfe, copyright © 1966 by the World Journal Tribune Corporation, copyright © 1964, 1965, 1966 by The New York Herald Tribune, Inc.

Page 81: © 1970 by The New York Times Company. Reprinted by permission.

Pages 99–107: Text portion reprinted by permission of **Esquire** magazine; © 1970 by Esquire, Inc. All art by R. Crumb except cartoon page 107, top left—Victor Moscoso.

Pages 138, 148: UPI

Page 151: IBM

Page 197: John Filo, **The Valley Daily News**, Tarentum, Pa.

Page 223: CBS News correspondent Walter Cronkite and **The CBS Evening News with Walter Cronkite**

Page 291: R. Derk, Urbana, Ill.

Page 327: Budd Yorkin–Norman Lear Tandem Productions

Page 343: Werner Wolff from Black Star

Page 378: Photo by Lawrence Ratzkin

Pages 390-91: Art by Benedict Umy, Esq.

preface

In the past few years we have witnessed considerable changes in the content and uses of the mass media, accompanied by an increased public awareness of the great influence they have on our lives. We have seen a national commission established to discover the effects of the mass media on the individual, to evaluate their role in bringing about social change, and to recommend what controls can or should be exerted on them. We have seen innovations in educational programs which utilize the media as both a method for teaching and a subject for study. And we have watched a generation of children grow up in a world that has been shaped by the increasingly pervasive mass media.

People are becoming more than just passive receivers of what the media offer; they are becoming media critics as well. It is to this trend toward intelligent appraisal of the media that this book is dedicated. The mass media today have such a great potential for good or ill that we cannot afford to accept their offerings unquestioningly. Critical and selective use of the mass media is essential.

The articles, excerpts, and visual materials presented in **Mass Media: Forces in Our Society,** most of which appeared in the late sixties and early seventies, give varied viewpoints on the contemporary mass media. The selections in Part 1 treat the broader implications of the media—their overall impact on our society and the possibilities for the future. Part 2 deals with the print and electronic media more specifically and covers a broad spectrum: magazines, photostudies, underground and overground newspapers, books, television, radio, popular music, and film. Finally, Part 3 looks at the media from the point of view of their three major roles—informer, entertainer, and persuader.

Besides serving as a text for courses on the mass media, this book is also suitable as a reader for composition courses. At the end of each section there are questions designed to stimulate discussion or serve as topics for composition; these are followed by bibliographies that direct the student to related materials. In addition, each section in Parts 2 and 3 concludes with a "mini–case study"—a collection of writings or visual materials dealing with a subject treated in that section. These mini–case studies can be used as a basis for writing or as a takeoff point for further research.

It is our hope that the selections in this book will help students to understand better the complex nature of the languages through which they communicate. We would like to express our appreciation to our many students of mass media and composition, present and past, who have been our inspiration in preparing this book. They have sharpened our awareness of the influence of the media upon their lives and our own, and have demonstrated that the study of the media can be a richly rewarding experience.

FRANCIS and LUDMILA VOELKER

contents

Preface
v

1 MASS COMMUNICATIONS: THEORIES AND PRACTICES
1

WESLEY C. CLARK, The Impact of Mass Communications in America   3
BEN H. BAGDIKIAN, How Communications May Shape Our Future
Environment   11
OTTO N. LARSEN, Posing the Problem of Effects   19
LEE LOEVINGER, The Ambiguous Mirror: The Reflective–Projective
Theory of Broadcasting and Mass Communications   24
HANS MAGNUS ENZENSBERGER, The Industrialization of the Mind   41
MARSHALL MCLUHAN, **from** Counterblast   51
EDMUND CARPENTER, The New Languages   56
NAT HENTOFF, Students as Media Critics: A New Course   71

STUDY QUESTIONS   76
BIBLIOGRAPHY FOR FURTHER STUDY   77

2 THE MEDIA   78

The Print Media   81

ROLAND E. WOLSELEY, The American Periodical Press and Its Impact   83
CLAY S. FELKER, Life Cycles in the Age of Magazines   91
"The Great Speckled Post": An Esquire Parody   98
ROLAND E. WOLSELEY, The Black Magazines   108
JULIO MITCHEL, The Silent Majority: Pictures Worth a Thousand Words   114
ART KUNKIN, What the Underground Press Is Trying to Tell Us   116
J. KIRK SALE, The Village Voice (You've Come a Long Way, Baby, But You Got Stuck There)   123
WALLACE E. STEGNER, The Book and the Great Community   132

MINI–CASE STUDY: DEATH OF A ROCK STAR   138

from THE NEW YORK TIMES, Janis Joplin Dies; Rock Star Was 27   139
from THE ST. CLOUD DAILY TIMES, Top Pop Singer Janis Joplin Is Found Dead   141
from NEWSWEEK MAGAZINE, "Singing Is Better Than Any Dope"   142
from LIFE MAGAZINE, Drugs and Death in the Run-Down World of Rock Music   144
from ROLLING STONE MAGAZINE, Janis Joplin   146
from ROLLING STONE MAGAZINE, Correspondence, Love Letters & Advice   147

STUDY QUESTIONS   148
BIBLIOGRAPHY FOR FURTHER STUDY   149

THE ELECTRONIC MEDIA   151

JOHN TEBBEL, TV and the Arts: The Prospect Before Us   153

WALT KELLY, **from** Pogo Primer for Parents   157

NAT HENTOFF, Participatory Television   158

ROBERT PAUL DYE, The Death of Silence   164

ROBERT A. ROSENSTONE, ''The Times They Are A-Changin' '': The
Music of Protest   168

JAMES W. THOMPSON, Media Means   177

from AVANT-GARDE MAGAZINE, Poetry by Computer   178

DENNIS HOPPER, Into the Issue of the Good Old Time Movie **vs.** the
Good Old Time   180

DAVID MOWAT, The Cinema's New Language   187

MINI—CASE STUDY: VIOLENCE AND THE ELECTRONIC MEDIA

197

from REPORT OF THE NATIONAL ADVISORY COMMISSION ON
CIVIL DISORDERS, The News Media and the Disorders   198

CHRISTOPHER EMMET, **from** The Media and the Assassinations   200

SOLOMON SIMONSON, **from** Violence in the Mass Media   201

NER LITTNER, **from** A Psychiatrist Looks at Television and
Violence   205

from REPORT TO THE NATIONAL COMMISSION ON THE
CAUSES AND PREVENTION OF VIOLENCE, **from** Mass Media
and Violence   210

CHARLES OSGOOD, WCBS Radio Commentary   214

STUDY QUESTIONS   215
BIBLIOGRAPHY FOR FURTHER STUDY   216

3 THE ROLES OF THE MEDIA

218

THE INFORMERS

223

WALTER CRONKITE, What It's Like to Broadcast News   225

IRVING E. FANG, It **Is** Your Business, Mr. Cronkite   233

ROBERT K. BAKER, Functions and Credibility   237

BURNS W. ROPER, Trends in Attitudes Toward Television and Other
Media: A Twelve-Year Review   249

WOODY KLEIN, The Racial Crisis in America: The News Media Respond to the New Challenge   255

MINI–CASE STUDY: AGNEW CHALLENGES THE NEWS MEDIA   263

Text of Agnew Speech on TV Network News   264

Excerpt from Transcript of Address by Agnew Extending Criticism of News Coverage to Press   270

The Editorial Cartoonists Respond . . .   271

NEIL HICKEY, In Defense of TV News: An Interview with Eric Sevareid   274

EDITH EFRON, There **Is** a Network News Bias   278

An editorial from THE NEW REPUBLIC, "Now Listen to This"   281

R. B. PITKIN, An Analysis of the News Media   283

LESTER BERNSTEIN, Does Agnew Tell It Straight?   285

STUDY QUESTIONS   288
BIBLIOGRAPHY FOR FURTHER STUDY   289

the entertainers   291

DESMOND SMITH, Pop Sex Among the Squares   293
JOHN CORRY, Television: Watching It   300
PETER HERMAN ADLER, Music: The Silent Stepchild   304
CHRIS HODENFIELD, The 60's Recollected: An Incisive Report   312
HENRY S. RESNIK, The Rock Pile   318
BARTON MIDWOOD, Fiction   323

MINI–CASE STUDY: CURRENT SOCIAL ISSUES AND THE ENTERTAINMENT MEDIA   327

PAUL D. ZIMMERMAN, The New Movies   328
DAVID DEMPSEY, Social Comment and TV Censorship   330
JOHN OLIVER KILLENS, "Our Struggle Is Not to Be White Men in Black Skin"   332
Letters from Listeners: KSJR/KSJN FM Radio, Collegeville, Minnesota   336

PETE SEEGER, King Henry   338
Comics Go Relevant   339

    STUDY QUESTIONS   341
    BIBLIOGRAPHY FOR FURTHER STUDY   342

THE PERSUADERS

343

JOSEPH T. KLAPPER, Basic Research in Persuasion and Motivation:
The Capability of Communications Media to Influence Opinions on
New Issues   345
DAVID HALBERSTAM, American Notes: Mr. Nixon Meets the Lan-
guage   348
STEPHANIE HARRINGTON, Enticers, 1970: On TV, Who Do They
Think You Are?   353
Visual Persuasion in the Media   358
from EBONY MAGAZINE, A Toddle Down "Sesame Street"   364
HUBERT H. HUMPHREY, TV: The Greatest Educational Tool   366
STEWART ALSOP, Radical Chic Is Dead   369
Reviews of Five Easy Pieces
    LIZ SMITH, from Cosmo Goes to the Movies   374
    CHRISTOPHER FLINDERS, from CIRCUS Movie Reviews   376

MINI—CASE STUDY: PERSUASION IN POLITICS

378

How Nixon Changed His TV Image: Interview with Roger E.
Ailes, President's TV Adviser   379
JOE MCGINNISS, from The Selling of the President 1968   383
PAUL E. SIGMUND, The Case for Humphrey   388
MURRAY KEMPTON, An Honorable Choice   390
BILL GARVIN, Mad's Guaranteed Effective All-Occasion Non-
Slanderous Political Smear Speech   392

    STUDY QUESTIONS   394
    BIBLIOGRAPHY FOR FURTHER STUDY   395

mass media

FORCES IN OUR SOCIETY

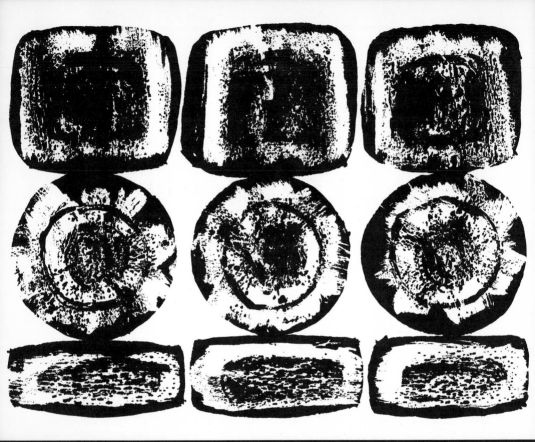

1 mass communications
theories and practices

We are surrounded by the mass media. Each year nearly 30,000 books are published in the United States. Ayer's **Directory** lists more than 9,500 periodicals published in our country, with an estimated 3 million copies sold daily. Over 30 million comic books are circulated each month by only seven of the comic book publishers. Ayer's **Directory** lists a total of over 11,000 papers, including underground publications. Every week about 45 million persons attend one of the 450 new movies produced annually. Over 290 million radios are tuned to 6,600 AM and FM stations, and over 48 million phonographs play over 10,000 new singles and LP's each year. In addition, Americans in 94 percent of the nation's households can view their 84.6 million television sets, selecting shows from the programing of 857 television stations.

The explosive growth of the mass media in the recent past has resulted in their becoming a natural part of the landscape of the seventies. However, each person needs to become aware of how they influence the shaping of his own being and the environment in which he lives.

The mass media are important forces in our society. They provide information and entertainment, and at the same time possess persuasive powers which have proved capable of effecting radical changes. The media do more than present ideas though; each medium also uniquely shapes what it presents. As Father John Culkin says:

Each medium has its own language, audience, methods of production, economics, and distribution. Each must be judged within these limits. The print media pose problems far different from the broadcast and image media. Movies differ from TV both in style and in distribution. Television and radio operate on channels belonging to the public and, therefore, have a different responsibility to that public than the strictly private enterprise products of print and film.*

Modern technology has radically altered the media. In a little over a decade we have progressed from the past tense of Edward R. Murrow's "You were there" to accompanying Apollo 12 on its historic moon mission. The fact that people the world over saw Neil Armstrong's first step on the moon may indeed have been the real "giant leap for mankind." Today, society's attention is focused on the present in light of the future, as contrasted with previous generations' concern with what Marshall McLuhan calls the "rear view mirror" concept of the present. Changes in the media have caused us to alter our time perspectives.

Many other changes evident today are at least partially attributable to the mass media. Young people's tendency to reject traditions and their concern for and involvement in international issues may be the result of the mass media environment, which has offered them a global view. They have participated in the national mourning for American leaders cut down by

* John M. Culkin, "Mass Media Study in the Schools," **Teaching English in Today's High Schools,** ed. Dwight L. Burton and John S. Simmons (New York: Holt, Rinehart and Winston, 1970), p. 439.

assassins as well as the funerals of elder statesmen like Eisenhower, Churchill, MacArthur, and DeGaulle. Oceans no longer divide us. Our young people's concern for ecological balance, which began with Rachel Carson's **Silent Spring** and grew as ecology received increasing attention from all media, became so strong that political and educational leaders could no longer ignore the issue. Political opinions have changed largely because the electronic media can provide seemingly uninterpreted news. Americans' viewing of real battles in living color contributed to President Johnson's decision to not seek reelection; a credibility gap had eroded into a chasm. In the sixties peace candidates experienced some successes at the polls, while at the same time a climate of violence passed over the country. It is difficult to imagine that these phenomena could have occurred without the mass media, and more especially without the electronic media.

The media have influenced entertainment and the arts as well. The camera, for example, has driven the poet and painter to do more with their pen and brush than simply picture reality. Disc jockeys and promotional campaigns have swayed the musical tastes of millions of listeners, while fan magazines have created cults. The viewer, listener, or reader is frequently unable to distinguish between information, entertainment, and persuasion. He may "read" ads for both information and entertainment and at the same time be persuaded. And finally, while critics often disparage the mass media, it must be remembered that the media have enormous appetites for new materials, making almost impossible demands on the creativity of writers and performers.

The selections in Part 1 attempt to explore the very complex nature of mass communications and their broad social and cultural implications.

the IMPACT

of mass
communications
in
america

by WESLEY C. CLARK

Wesley Clark, Dean of the School of Journalism at Syracuse University,
considers the impact of the media on society today
and discusses the important role they played in shaping America.

Most of the sins of America today are charged to mass communications.
In fact, whole academic disciplines have been built on this assumption.
The fact is that most of the sins credited to the mass media have been
committed by others and the real sins of the mass media, like their accomplishments, have gone unheralded. Let me explain.

The impact of mass communications in America has been persistent,
consistent, and with us for more than one hundred years now. The mass
media have changed the face of America, in some ways for the better and
in some ways for the worse, some obvious and some not so obvious. The
mass media have been given some credit for a great many of these changes,
but some are hardly credited to them at all, and yet it is they—the mass
media—who are largely responsible for much of the social legislation
which now affects your lives and mine.

The Impact of Mass Media in the Past

When people speak today of mass communications and of the mass media,
they think of audiences in terms of hundreds, and perhaps even thousands,

The Impact of Mass Communications in America: From *The Annals of the American Academy of Political and Social Science* (July, 1968). Reprinted by permission of Wesley Clark and the American Academy of Political and Social Science.

3

or millions. But one hundred years ago, when this country was more sparsely populated, circulations of newspapers were not in the millions. Nevertheless, the great newspapers and magazines which existed in those days were, by almost any standards, mass media, engaged in mass communications. They were directed to the masses. They were read by the masses, and, presumably, they had some effect on the masses.

For instance, Horace Greeley's *Tribune* never had a circulation of 300,000. But it was read throughout the United States, and the admonitions of Mr. Greeley were listened to and debated throughout the United States.

The mass media of those days were responsible for crystallizing the nation's opinions about the abolition of slavery and about the kinds of amendments to the Constitution which grew out of Abraham Lincoln's statement that all men are created equal. Without the newspapers' presentation of this point of view for ten or fifteen years, it is inconceivable that Lincoln would have made such a statement, and unlikely that the Civil War would have occurred when it did—and perhaps it might not have happened at all.

This is not to attribute to today's mass media and to the newspapers and magazines of the late nineteenth century all of the political and social changes which have come about in the American scene. The pulpit, the Chautauqua—that early-day version of television—and all of the other means of communication which were available in those days helped to

John A. Ruge. Copyright 1971 Saturday Review, Inc.

create this atmosphere. Nevertheless, no serious historian of the times can deny the important role of the mass media in changing America.

With this in mind, a look at history reveals a number of other things for which the mass media were largely responsible. The muckrakers of the late nineteenth century and early twentieth century—public figures such as Ida Tarbell, Lincoln Steffens, and others—were aided and abetted by newspapers and magazines across the land, and thus were largely responsible for the first early restrictions imposed upon business in this country. No Judge Landis could have come to the conclusion that the great monopoly of the Standard Oil Company should be broken up, had he not been so conditioned and so impressed by the press that such a decision was made easily possible. Nor can we deny the place of the nation's press in building the pressure which made it possible for the Congress of the United States to adopt the kind of legislation which eventually resulted in the Standard Oil cases getting into the courts. To be sure, Teddy Roosevelt and others were trustbusters in those days, but these were men who were coursing a sea of sentiment created by mass magazine and mass newspaper stories over a period of twenty or thirty years.

Although it is fashionable today for educators to pick on editors and newspapers and publishers as being opponents of the schools, such statements are merely self-serving defenses for academic politicians eager to get their hands on the public money. The fact is that not only during the last half of the nineteenth century and during this century, but back to the very beginnings of the press in this country, newspapers have consistently supported education. They have made possible the system of public education in this country. No reputable newspaper in the land at any time has been opposed to good education. They have, of course, been opposed to the abuses which educationists have imposed upon this system. They have been opposed to two Cadillacs for every superintendent of schools, and they have been opposed to the kind of under-the-table operations which go on in a great many school systems when it comes to purchasing school buildings and school furnishings.

The newspapers and magazines as protagonists of the schools have not acted out of sheer philanthropy. They had a serious purpose in this. They wanted educated people—people who could read and write—so that they would have more customers for their newspapers. And, in many instances, the newspaper has been the medium by which the young, the disadvantaged, and the illiterate have learned to read. Thus, the involvement of so many Negroes in athletics has made reading the sports pages in the newspapers a must for the young Negro. He wants to learn to read so that he can find out what his heroes, Wilt Chamberlain, Jim Brown, and Willy Mays, are doing. And this gives him a far higher motivation than can be given by any school teacher fresh out of a school of education. The fact is that, for more than two hundred years, newspapers, the basic media of the country, have pushed education to higher and higher levels.

Contemporary Mass Media's Effects on Society

This, perhaps, is ancient history. What are the mass media doing now, and what have they done recently, to change the face of America, or have they rather been merely carping critics of the changes which have come about?

One of the massive changes in the American scene has been the rise of the labor unions to positions of power. It is now apparent that the restrictions imposed upon business by various laws, and by the courts, have resulted in business' having little real power in the American politcal scene. It is also apparent that while government has risen to new heights of power and control, the only serious challenge to these powers is provided by the labor unions, who defy the government again and again, even when laws and sanctions have been reduced to a minimum.

How did this come about? It came about because for more than fifty years the press of this country, largely the newspapers, pleaded the cause of labor in a multitude of ways. They gave publicity to Sacco and Vanzetti, to Tom Moody, to all of the complaints against the crimes of management. They made folk heroes out of labor union leaders such as John L. Lewis of the United Mine Workers, Walter Reuther of the Congress of Industrial Organizations, Samuel Gompers of the American Federation of Labor, Eugene Debs of the American Railway Union, and a host of others. They created a climate which made it possible for legislators to pass, and for executive branches to approve, legislation favoring labor. This is apparent in the laws of both the federal and state governments. It is apparent in the executive branch of the government, and it is even apparent in the judicial branch of the government. There is no need to cite the host of administrative rules or the flux of Supreme Court decisions which bear out this point.

But, in a sense, these are the obvious things which grew out of the creation by the mass media of a climate of opinion favorable to social change in America. There are many obvious changes in which the mass media played a decisive, although unheralded, role.

Social historians of the present and recent American scene give little or no credit to the role of the mass media in making possible the Social Security Act. But then the fashionable social historian these days is one who apparently prefers a political point of view to a scholarly and serious approach to history. At any rate, in my reading of the histories of the last thirty or forty years in America, the impression comes through clear and strong that the Social Security Act and all its benefits and aids to mankind were the invention of the New Deal, of President Franklin D. Roosevelt and the little group of brain trusters who surrounded him. This is nonsense.

Franklin D. Roosevelt and the New Deal were merely the mechanism which put into being an American dream which had been sold to the American people for some seventy-five years by the great insurance companies; for during that time, insurance companies had preached the necessity for security in old age. "Make sure you have enough insurance to take care of your family." "Take out an annuity to take care of your old age." These are not new slogans; these are not Social Security slogans; these have been the slogans of insurance companies ever since life insurance and annuity insurance began to play a role in the United States.

Where was this message published? How did it come to the attention of the people? It came to the attention of the people through the advertisements of the Metropolitan Life Insurance Company and the other great insurance companies in the great mass media.

Again, Medicaid and Medicare are the result, not of the wild-eyed dreams of some politician, but of the mass propaganda of various insurance businesses, told through the media of the newspapers, the magazines, radio, and television, and drummed into the American people for the last twenty years.

With all of this propaganda, these persuasive methods, and with the climate of opinion thereby created, it would be incredible if politicians had not seized upon these slogans or ideas and incorporated them into their platforms and then into law.

There are a number of other areas in which the mass media have changed the face of America with the aid and active participation of politicians. Thus, for instance, the jewel in the crown of the Kennedy administration—the Peace Corps—is a direct development of the widespread interest of the mass communicators in the missionaries of America. For more than one hundred years, the role of the missionaries in bettering the lot of people in the underdeveloped areas was the subject of a great many articles and of books. The principal criticism of the missionaries came from the fact that they were engaged in selling Christianity abroad. And we have such plays as Somerset Maugham's *Rain* and the like which sharpened this criticism considerably. But there was no question in many people's minds that the missionaries had done a considerable amount of good in alleviating the ills of mankind in foreign countries. The Peace Corps, thus, was something that was difficult for any politician to deny, once the idea of a missionary society without God, or with a multitude of gods, was conceived.

Again, the mass media's gilding of the glories of private charity, in all of its aspects, made it difficult for any politician to deny that an increase in the scope of public welfare was necessary.

The Impact of Social Change on the Mass Media

The great media of mass communications do not stand alone, untouched by the other forces which are changing our society. They not only shape our society; they are shaped by it. And as society changes the mass media, so it, in turn, is changed by them.

The factors which have had the most effect in changing the nation are its increasing population, its increasing mobility, and the almost astronomical increase in the area of the public interest.

As more and more people have come to populate the nation and as their mobility has increased tremendously, the public interest has, of necessity, widened and broadened. Where once the disposal of waste was a private matter—the head of the household buried the waste in the backyard or fed it to the pigs—now waste is no longer a private matter, nor solely the concern of a town or a county, but has become a federal concern. Again, where once the wage contract between the employer and the employee was a private arrangement, now the federal government has stepped in and regulates such arrangements.

Confronted with these increases in population and in mobility and the consequent enormous increase in the areas of public interest, the media of mass communications have been swamped with an increase in news. For wherever the citizen and the public interest meet—in crime, in zoning, in food regulations, in labor matters, and in thousands of other places where the law and the people meet—these events must be reported if the people of the nation are to have the kind of information that they need in order to govern themselves properly.

In the face of the enormous and increasing need for news, the media of mass communications find themselves limited by the mind of man himself. It becomes a question of just how much time and attention he will devote to finding out about his environment through the mass media. Newspapers find that generally a man will devote thirty or forty minutes a day to reading the newspaper. Radio and television find that fifteen, or at most thirty, minutes comprise the outer limit of listening to or watching Huntley and Brinkley. In thirty or forty minutes, a man can read fifteen thousand to forty thousand words. In the same thirty minutes, he can listen to three thousand words, or about four newspaper columns.

This very fact tends to limit the amount of news which is published in the great newspapers and magazines, and limits even more severely the amount of news which is available through radio and television.

Higher Thresholds of Attention, Secrecy, and Political Centralization

Thus, newspapers everywhere have tended to raise the thresholds of their attention. Even so, thresholds of radio and television are even higher, and of necessity must be higher.

That this rise in the thresholds of attention of the mass communicators has had a profound influence on the structure of our government is suggested by two illustrations—one concerned with the courts, and the other concerned with the legislative and executive branches of the government.

A recent study of a county containing more than 400,000 people indicated that in a single month there were two thousand court cases of all kinds—federal, state, county, and municipal—all of them available for reporting by the mass media. The same study showed that the two daily newspapers which serve the county printed stories about less than sixty of these cases. In more populous areas, the figures would be even more astounding.

That the press does not report more court cases is due to the constant pressure to raise the thresholds of their attention. Thus, for most people, we have established an unofficial system of secret courts. The courts, the bar associations, and the legislatures are now trying to provide a court system whose secrecy is officially instead of unofficially sanctioned. And this is despite the fact that if the history of civilization proves nothing else, it proves that where secrecy cloaks the use of power it also cloaks the abuse of power. The consequence of this judicial secrecy, official and unofficial, is a growing distrust by people everywhere of the courts, the judiciary, the legal profession, and the mass media.

The impact of the rising thresholds of attention of the mass media upon the legislative and executive branches of the government is best illustrated by the great metropolitan area of New York City, where some twenty congressmen are elected every two years. These are United States Congressmen—not dog wardens or local constables—but twenty members of that august body which enacts the laws of the United States. Yet, in campaign after campaign, the New York City papers in years past, and I suspect even in this year, devote, in the six weeks preceding an election, as few as five hundred words to each congressional candidate and, unless the congressional candidate is a John Lindsay, hardly more than that. As a matter of fact, most New Yorkers are unaware of the congressional district in which they live or of the congressman who, presumably, represents them.

In these circumstances, it is not important to be an outstanding congressman or to represent a particular district well. But it is important to be a member of a winning political party and to ride on the coattails of that party. Thus, more and more, for the metropolitan congressmen, the question of survival depends, not upon their own efforts, but upon the efforts and the image presented by the leader of the party—in short, the President of the United States, or the governor of the state.

The concentration of political power in the hands of a few, coupled with an increase in secrecy, both official and unofficial, has set the stage for the greatest era of palace intrigue and political chicanery since Machiavelli wrote *The Prince*.

And as the arena of meaningful political action moves more and more toward Washington, and as secrecy cloaks the actions of more and more areas of government, the political man in America becomes more and more frustrated and tempted to forgo political action. Many men, for instance, express a fleeting interest in Elizabeth Taylor, or would express an interest in a woman of comparable dimensional beauty. But few devote hours each day to studying Miss Taylor. The reason is clear: they know there is no real possibility of persuading Miss Taylor to their way of thinking. And, of course, the Miss Taylors whom they do not know about engage their interest even less. To ask a political man to be informed through the mass media about government in depth and in detail when he has little or no chance to use the information to change the course of government is to ask too much.

By raising the thresholds of their attention to unprecedented heights, the mass media of communications have both simplified and complicated American life. They have simplified it by making it easy to concentrate upon a few great political leaders. They have complicated it by making it impossible for many individuals to be heard when the mechanisms of society impinge abrasively upon their rights and their lives. They have also complicated it to the extent that if individuals or groups have problems which need to be brought to the attention of the public, they must hire public relations counsel to make sure that the things that they need are brought to the attention of the public, or they must create some kind of a disturbance to make their needs known to the great mass media—or perhaps they must do both: hire public relations counsel to organize riots.

Summary

To summarize, then: mass communications and the mass media have played a major role in changing the face of America; they are playing a major role; they will continue to do so.

The mass media, by their very nature, by the limitations imposed upon them by man and by a changing society, are challenging the basic assumptions upon which this government was erected.

They have given us instant nationwide fashions and modes, and perhaps instant heroes, or nonheroes, both political and nonpolitical.

They have contributed substantially to the frustrations, political and otherwise, which beset the American populace.

But they have also, and in this lies the hope of America, paved the way for the great pieces of social legislation which have made this nation a better place in which to live.

They are, in fact, a somewhat paraphrased and modern version of the cadets of Gascogne: "the supporters of new homes, new names, and new splendors."

HOW COMMUNICATIONS MAY SHAPE OUR FUTURE ENVIRONMENT

by BEN H. BAGDIKIAN

In this article press critic Ben Bagdikian points out
how narrowly and thoughtlessly men have used the mass media
and speculates about the various potentials of mass communications,
especially the potential for bringing about desired social change.

In the near future the computer linked to electronic communications will probably alter personal and social life in ways comparable to the combined changes produced by the telephone, automobile and television in the last 90 years, but do it in the life-time of most of us.

It may change the shape of our cities by devising new ways to accomplish many transactions now done face-to-face, but not inherently involving personal closeness. It will probably make education a new force, not only in techniques, but in implementing what is already a compelling fact—that education must be a lifelong activity. It could even reconstitute the family as a tightly knit force by reducing the need to leave the home for largely impersonal acts. It could enlarge the aesthetic and intellectual horizons by making available to everyone in his home the culture and learning stored in distant places.

These forecasts are expressed in the subjunctive mood, the hiding place of all uncertain prophets. There are many "maybe's," not only because these are not completely predictable as technologies, but also because much depends on what society thinks about them, and today society isn't doing enough thinking about them.

We have usually behaved as though the march of technology is an act of nature that human beings cannot tamper with. It has become almost an article of national faith that the music for the procession of technical change must be played under an exclusive union contract by that ubiquitous trio, Mechanical Ingenuity, Mechanisms of the Marketplace and Individual Monetary Profit.

By leaving our environment to the tender mercies of this trinity, we have destroyed the greater water systems of the United States through pollution; we have contaminated our urban atmosphere to the point of threatening life; and we have permitted our inner cities to become horrid traps for the human animal. We may spend the rest of this century discovering whether we can recover from this careless delusion.

At the very least this tells us that human beings must take responsibility for what they do, whether they do it with their own hands or with brilliantly ingenious extensions of their hands. If we urge our adolescents to think ahead before they create little human beings, it shouldn't be an overwhelming task for adults to think ahead before they create little printed circuits.

In thinking about communications and the future, there are some truths that are obvious but often ignored, as obvious things frequently are.

The first is that new communications are agents of change, whether intentional or not. The telegraph and printing techniques in the early 19th century for the first time permitted human knowledge to travel faster than a running horse, and at the time this seemed mechanically fascinating and full of promise for convenience and profit. But if the early users had been told that their new gadgets would change the form of human government all over the world, they would have considered the idea ridiculous. Yet this is what happened.

In the 1950's and 1960's the transistor radio accelerated the world view among the uneducated populations in less developed countries by permitting cosmopolitan information to reach areas without good roads, vehicles or literacy. During this same period television in the developed countries has had revolutionary impacts we are just now appreciating. Novel channels of information carry messages to previously inert audiences and this produces profound change. We should stop being surprised.

Since such changes are inexorable, we need to ask how new techniques can best serve the individual and society. Mechanical efficiency and profit will always be important factors, but they cannot be the only ones. The real power in new technology does not lie in particular gadgets, but in the conceptions men have of their uses. The quality of life must be a part of this conception.

The second obvious truth is that we can use our techniques to meet large-scale social problems not ordinarily thought of as formal communication.

We can look back on our first 20 years of television and envision a more imaginative use of this new instrument. One of the great demographic upheavals of our time has occurred in this period. About 18 million rural people, most of them poorly educated to the point of semi-illiteracy, moved to urban centers. They now constitute an accumulation of despair and alienation that raises doubts whether our cities can survive and whether a democratic consensus is still possible.

A peculiar characteristic of this migration is that most of the adults involved probably would prefer to remain in farming if they did not face starvation and hopelessness.

We might have taken what amounts to about three years of city welfare for a family and loaned it to the same family while it was still in the countryside to buy enough arable land and equipment to become self-supporting. We might have augmented the limited county agent system with televised instruction for the farm family, not in spherical trigonometry or the history of the Hanseatic League, but in land use techniques, maintenance of farm equipment, repair of the home, farm management, literacy, how to fill out tax forms and other elementary arts of coping with the environment.

And what if we had taken the same view of those who migrated to the city, moving into an environment more strange to them than the cities of the 19th century were to the foreign immigrants?

What if we offered television instruction in solving their immediate personal problems, like how to read an installment loan contract, job information, how the local bus system works, how to shop in the city, how to maintain a city tenement, what the new and strange city laws were?

And what if we had provided televised instruction for the pre-school children of these migrants, so that they would not enter first grade to find the standard curriculum a total mystery?

It is easier to see these possibilities in retrospect, but at least it tells us that we have not been very imaginative in using our communications to solve practical problems.

The third truth is more difficult and involves the less precise dimension of individual and social needs in aesthetic, intellectual and emotional activity. We need to know more about this because in a short time we must make decisions affecting these needs.

For example, it seems likely that in the future our channels of communication may become an almost limitless resource. Where we now have a maximum of seven VHF television channels in our largest cities, in the future we may have any number of multiples of 20 to 24,000 TV channels in each community.

But the capacity of man to absorb information is not limitless, either intellectually or emotionally. We ought to consider what man needs and society requires. But we must do this without the illusion of looking for the universally perfect single program, since there is none, although our present mass media are largely based on the assumption that there is.

This introduces the philosophical dilemma we will never solve completely, but which we have to cope with: How do we use a social instrument for good as we see it without imposing uniformity and cultural dictatorship?

The need for variety and renewable decisions is not always recognized. Increasingly we hear during troubled times that what we need for survival is uniformity, regularity and order. But the human condition has infinite variety and in the relations among millions of individuals, there are unpredictable combinations of emotions, ideas and values. This human scene is forever creating new situations, and in order for society to survive, it must produce an unending supply of ideas in order to increase the odds that among them will be some that will fit the peculiar circumstances of each moment in history.

The New England Town Meeting that became obsolete when every citizen in the community could no longer fit in the same hall could come back, given large numbers of channels at very low cost, with a capacity for the citizen to respond.

In dealing with the new complexities in communication, we must guard against a mistake we made in the past of permitting access to our educational and communications facilities only to the very highly professionalized experts. We need experts, and we need standards of professionalism in many areas. But we must not let them monopolize the channels of communication.

The rise of the guitar and folk singing reflects the compelling need for nonprofessional communication. Much of hippie culture is a reaction to the exclusion of the individual amateur as a legitimate participant in culture. Without popular culture, High Culture becomes sterile and dies. Without free interchange among all minds, expertise becomes theology.

There is another reason we need to make many TV channels freely available. Dialogue between individuals and the quality of personal communication cannot easily be separated from our mass communications.

The value we put on individual freedom and the right of expression is embodied in our Bill of Rights. At the time this was ratified in 1788, there were only 4,000,000 people in the United States, 95 per cent of whom lived in rural areas where there was no settlement large enough to be called a town. A man presumably communed with his soul and his horse much of the time and with his family the rest. Only one in 20 knew how to read and write, but every time he met another human being, it was an event to be pondered and integrated into his experience. If a man felt the desire to speak to the rest of his community, he could tack a notice on the tavern wall or stand outside the Congregational Church on Sunday or climb on a stump on Saturday and by any of these personal acts communicate with a significant portion of his peers. If he talked to 50 people, he had made a very large impact on his community. Perhaps the whole community.

Today we are 200 million people and 72 million of us live in communities of over 50,000 population, a city size that didn't exist when our Constitution was written. Almost none of us commune with our horses any more, though we do with our souls on occasion, as when we are stalled in traffic or circling Kennedy airport. We still see our families, but only when it happens that all members in their separate outside circuits happen to orbit the dwelling place at the same time. If we feel like communicating with out fellow citizens, we can, if we wish, stand outside one of the 326,000 churches in the country, or get on a soapbox in a public park, but if we manage to speak to 50 people we are lucky and even then we have spoken to less than one-thousandth of one per cent of the people in a community. To make any impression at all we must either have professional access to the systems of mass communication, which is very difficult if not impossible for the ordinary citizen, or else do something spectacular like leap off a tall building or burn our draft card, which may be one reason people attempt to communicate that way.

The attempted withdrawal of a significant portion of our young leadership into hippie and other communities is a warning that something is seriously wrong. Among the reasons for this withdrawal is the one-way quality of mass communication, the implication that the listener or reader is a passive recipient, an empty sack being filled by somebody else's selection of goods.

We integrate new knowledge and experience by reacting to it, by receiving a message and influencing the next person by our response, so that we achieve one basic meaning of communication, which is a collaboration. One cause for hope in the future is that we shall probably have more two-way communications that will involve us in ways that could reduce the undifferentiated scraps of emotions and ideas that collect each evening in the base of our skulls.

It would make sense to reserve some of the many TV channels in every community as soapbox channels, for announcements, gripes or recitations of "Hiawatha." If this is done in neighborhoods, it is feasible that people will be able to respond from their homes in meaningful ways. They might signal applause or tell the performer that his lawn needs cutting.

This sounds strange to us because we know only the present conception of a small number of one-way communications channels serving very large areas. If your neighborhood had 50 channels of its own, it would not be so strange.

Similarly, we are not yet used to the combination of computer and communications channel, but this is already having an impact.

It is quite conceivable, for example, that in the not-too-distant future, the average home will have something like a teletypewriter connected with a computer that is connected with something like a television set that will be connected with every major library, newspaper, town hall, community center and mass access computer in the country.

By typing on the teletypewriter the individual in his home can send messages to particular people all over the world, without using the mails or his telephone. Or he can ask a computerized library for available materials on any given subject. Or his wife can ask for a visual display on the television screen of all children's raincoats in a certain size and price range, and when she sees the one she wants, she can signal and the store will send it to her. And at the moment that she orders it, the computer will instantly deduct the price from her bank account.

Men doing business will communicate this way with secretarial services, with other businessmen and with sources of information now considered so sophisticated that today only the largest corporations and research groups have them available.

The student can get programmed learning, being told what is correct and incorrect, and, more important, pursuing ideas and questions at his own pace and direction, going as deeply and as broadly as he wishes.

Because all this could replace transportation and face-to-face contact for largely impersonal transactions, there would be less need for dense population concentrations in cities. Home would be a more important place, with the need for communication drawing the individual into his home instead of its present tendency to pull him out of it.

If we are wise, we shall make this kind of facility plentiful, so that every neighborhood, every community, every school district will have many channels, often vacant, so that it becomes easy and inexpensive to circulate information, ask questions and get a response on the items of social and political need at the grass roots—communications that are now impossible in systems that have relatively few one-way channels addressing everyone in thousands of square miles.

It is difficult to comprehend the ability of the householder in Minneapolis to reach the files of the New York Public Library and get a printout of any document in its possession, at less cost and in less time than it would take for him to mail a query or drive to the local library.

But look back. When the telephone was first installed, it was a luxury for a few. There were four to 20 people sharing one line, and their combined line went to the local operator who recognized their voices and memorized the few numbers in town. You picked up the telephone, turned the crank and asked Mabel for Charlie Jones the plumber. If you had told this early user that in 1968 his telephone, in seconds, without his ever uttering a word, could connect with any one of 100 million other telephones all over North America, and with most of 100 million additional telephones all over the world, he would suspect you of being a premature user of LSD. He would have said that no telephone could have 200 million lines attached to it, that no operator could know 200 million numbers, and therefore the job of locating and identifying one phone out of 200 million was impractical. Yet today we take this for granted, and we acknowledge that to lack a telephone is to be forced to do things in a very inefficient way.

We cannot take this computerized development for granted. Nor is it an unmixed blessing. Even if it should reduce time spent in impersonal contacts and permit deeper personal relations, it would create a new problem that comes with great diversity—the need for some agreement on what the world looks like.

We need greater individuality, but we must maintain some degree of mutuality so that as we all grope toward the future, we do not misinterpret the desires and actions of others.

Rapid change is part of contemporary society, and it will be important that during this perpetual transformation we all have a high level of realistic information. In our times many societies have undergone radical change in a short period, going from the Stone Age to Coca Cola, from the 10th century to the 20th, from the dugout canoe to motorbikes, all in one generation. Some did it successfully, and some were destroyed by it.

The societies that navigated such changes successfully have generally had some mechanism that kept all segments of their society in touch with each other. Such societies saw the changes coming bit by bit, rather than as a large accumulation. Furthermore, people's motivations and aspirations were known to one another. Differing attitudes were less likely to be seen as malicious or insane, and the close communication led to greater sympathy.

The United States has been fragmenting its population geographically at an ominous rate since the end of World War II. We are separated today by race, by age, by income, by occupation, so that we know less and less about each other and our motivations are increasingly subject to misinterpretation.

Black and brown people tend to live in different kinds of places from white, or to be more exact, orange people. Black people have little idea what motivates orange people, and orange people find much of the behavior of black people incomprehensible.

The same is true of young people and older people. Young people accept the capacity for uninterrupted affluence, and the insanity of nuclear war, without the nagging reminders of those who lived through the Depression, World War II and the Cold War. The young have gone through high-pressure education since Sputnik and are intellectually quite different from their parents.

Blue collar workers are isolated from white collar workers. The affluent and the non-affluent look at the same phenomenon and react with opposite emotions.

Future society must provide not only a way to give each individual the greatest possible opportunity for personal fulfillment, but it must also give him insight into what motivates others.

It is ironic that, given the growing population of the world, what we call mass communications might—not necessarily will—but *might* permit us to see ourselves as individuals beyond anything possible since the growth of urban man. If it does not permit this, if all we get is a more efficient impersonality, then we shall have received a very bad bargain.

In Thornton Wilder's *Our Town,* Emily Webb goes to heaven where she sees all of life spread before her, and chooses to go back to earth for one day, on her 12th birthday, 14 years earlier. To her mother and father this is just another day in their lives, but to Emily it is the only day she has, and to the distracted, matter-of-fact manner of her mother she cries out:

"Oh, Mama, just look at me one minute as though you really saw me . . . just for a moment now we're all together . . . Let's look at one another."

We can hardly characterize our time today as heaven. But we know just enough about the working of our society to be able to see our past and vaguely what seems to be our future. What remains to be seen is whether we are wise enough to arrange a future world in which we can, like Emily Webb, in Grover's Corners, New Hampshire, "look at one another."

POSING THE PROBLEM OF EFFECTS

by OTTO N. LARSEN

In a paper prepared for the Media Task Force of the National Commission on the Causes and Prevention of Violence, sociology professor Otto Larsen discusses the frequently posed question of whether violence in the media has harmful effects on viewers' personalities and behavior.

The individual and social effects of mass communications must depend in some way upon: (1) the pattern of content offered by the mass media; (2) the opportunities for access to the media; and (3) the credibility attributed by audiences to media content.

Numerous studies from both commercial and academic research centers clearly support what has long been the contention of many concerned citizens about these elementary points: (1) the menu offered by the mass media is heavily saturated with violent content, including incidents of persons intentionally doing physical harm to one another; (2) more and more people have ready access to the media, with the average American spending between one-quarter and one-half of his waking day attending to the mass media; and (3) for most persons, but particularly for the poor in American society, television is perceived as the most credible and believable source of information on the reality of the world.

These points add up to a statement of one simple effect: *mass media portrayals of violence attract large audiences.* This also implies a much more troublesome question: If models for violent behavior are repeatedly

Posing the Problem of Effects: From *Mass Media and Violence,* A Report to the National Commission on the Causes and Prevention of Violence (November, 1969).

19

presented with few competing notions, and people, particularly children, repeatedly expose themselves to such materials, what could be a more favorable arrangement for learning *about* violence, if not learning *to do* violence? However, merely to ask this question is not enough. The abundance of violent media content, and the frequency of exposure to the same, do *not* suffice to prove that the mass media can modify attitudes or induce violent behavior.

When expressed in this manner, such questions can hardly be unequivocally answered. Indeed, many of the questions that concern us most intensely involve both fact and value-judgment. More than this, their answers depend on *relations between* different kinds of facts, connections between these relations, and certain value-judgments implicit in the thoughts of the questioner. It is not difficult, for example, to catalog the portrayals of violence on television. It is more difficult to relate such tabulations to personality and behavioral traits of viewers. It is still more difficult to show that such a relation is one of cause and effect, and if this can be established, the effects produced must still be evaluated. When any one of these steps

"As part of the new de-emphasis on violence, play up the line that he's fighting evil because he hates evil, instead of fighting evil because he loves to fight."

Sidney Harris. Copyright 1969 Saturday Review, Inc.

is omitted, basic policy decisions cannot readily be made about the desirability of continuing or changing the existing pattern of media performance.

Mass media, moreover, do not operate alone; they are embedded in a social system which has many other facets. Whatever may be their effects upon the members of their audience, these must be assessed in relation to the way *other* aspects of this larger system affect these same persons.

To speak meaningfully of the role of mass communications media in such critical concerns as the formation of personality, the induction of violent behavior, or in value formation, it is necessary to seek out and chart the main outlines of what is known *in general* about relevant processes of social learning. Because human personality is developed largely through a process of interaction in primary groups (such as the family), and because the various mass media can more or less simulate such primary interaction, they can play a real part in this process. Furthermore, they may do so unintentionally when they only seem to be entertaining or informing, because audience members are engaged in a process of "observational learning" and the mass media contribute to this through "symbolic modeling."

As a child matures physically, he also undergoes a process of social preparation for adult roles. Much of this preparation ordinarily takes place in the family, while some of it occurs in play groups and some of it involves formal education. It occurs all the time the child is awake and active, even when he and the persons with whom he interacts are not consciously concerned with shaping his character. He becomes a residue of what he has done and experienced, which in turn depends on his genetic endowment and the social heritage into which he was born.

As each child grows up, he has a wide range of skills to learn. He has values and customs to embrace, amend, or reject. He has to discover for himself what kind of world he lives in; he gets clues to this from the way others act toward things, toward each other, and toward him. He has to discover who and what he is, and how his identity relates him to the world; again his clues come from the interactions of others with him. He has to find out where he will be going in life, how he will go, who will accompany him, and how they can get together.

It would be surprising indeed if in our society the ubiquitous mass media did *not* play some part in this complex process. And yet until recently, not only has the potential involvement of mass media been relatively neglected, but even the fact that the process is social has sometimes been forgotten.

The mass media enter into this process mainly by providing material for "observational learning," defined as "imitation" in experimental psychology and as "identification" in personality theory. The common denominator for all three terms is a recognition that human beings in certain circumstances tend to reproduce the actions, attitudes, or emotions they perceive in other persons. These other persons may either be live or symbolized models (e.g., a character in a story). As knowledge of the principles of observational learning accumulates, more can be said about *how* groups shape the personalities of their members. The clearer our understanding of these mechanisms, the firmer the ground on which to base statements about the possible effects of symbolized groups, such as those depicted in a television drama.

If the content of mass communications is being widely discussed, perhaps this indicates that it has other effects. One contention is that symbolic violence, whether portraying fantasy or reality, will arouse aggression or increase aggressive behavior, hardening persons to human pain and suffering and leading them to accept violence as a way of life and as a solution to personal and social problems. Another school of thought contends that such exposure has precisely the opposite effect. This view holds that exposure to violence will allow the media user to discharge in fantasy what he might otherwise act out. Thus, watching *Gunsmoke* or reading a *Superman* comic will provide a safe and harmless outlet for human frustrations and aggressive-hostile impulses in much the same manner as hitting a punching bag. A third position holds that violent content has little or no effect. Proponents of this view suggest that in a controlled and relatively secure society, the passive recipient can vicariously live bravely and dangerously through the video hero with no enduring impact on his feeling, attitudes, or behavior in life.

It is, of course the first point of view which has aroused the concern and interest of vast sectors of the general public. However, little is accomplished if one merely notes the presence of undesirable features of some communication medium or art form, and then lets his aversion to both be transmuted into an assumption that the one disliked thing must be caused by the other. Much criticism of the mass media, and especially television, seems to reflect this kind of non-sequitur. This is unnecessary. There are research findings which afford a more objective basis for assessing the situation.

To understand the full implications of the research, it is important to keep in mind just how recent man's experience is with the pervasive presence of mass media. Even now, a decade into the space age, the majority of the world's human beings are illiterate. In our own advanced society, many citizens have first-hand memories of the pre-television and pre-radio era. Some can even remember a childhood in which there was no such thing as a movie theater. Daily newspapers, in fact, have been around for a mere five generations. Since mass communications are so relatively new, it is not surprising that men are not agreed as to the social impact of the various media.

Despite their tender age, mass communications have indeed become a pervasive aspect of our way of life. The media form the core of our leisure time activities, and television is the heart of this core. For the average American, mass media usage occupies almost as much time as does work, and for some, appreciably *more* time is devoted to mass communications. For children, television alone occupies almost as much time as school in their first sixteen years of life. Time-expenditure data by themselves do not prove any of the charges leveled against the media, nor do such data validate the praise the media have received. It is clear that the controversy over the effects of television is unlikely to be the only result of this deluge.

The fact that time devoted to one activity cannot be used in some other way means that the large amount of time allocated by Americans to mass communications must have entailed some redirection of their lives. Although casual radio listening can be done in conjunction with other (presumably inattentive) activities, and newspapers can be read on the commuter train, the mass media must in general have displaced other pursuits.

There are more direct and less incidental ways in which exposure to the mass media could influence persons, and these may have either immediate or long-range impact. Immediate effects include the emotional reactions of a person while he is viewing, listening, or reading, and the ensuing repercussions of these in defensive reactions, fatigue, excitement, dreams, and so on. The long-range effects concern the learning that is produced: both the content (vocabulary, items of information, beliefs) and the strengthening or weakening of personality traits, such as aggressiveness, passivity, and the like. Beyond the psychological level, concern must also be directed to the impact of the media on interpersonal relations, the development of norms, and the acquisition of values. The possibility of a change in behavior without a change in values must also be considered.

These are some of the dimensions of the effects of mass media violence that must be coped with. As with most significant social issues, seemingly straightforward questions become, upon analysis, acutely challenging and do not yield simple solutions. Thus, the following guideline must be set up: when we ask about the effects of the mass media, we must not phrase the question simply in terms of whether the media have an effect; rather, we seek to know under what conditions, how much, and what kind of effect the media are likely to have within specified populations.

We do not underestimate the enormity of the task, nor the necessity of its continuing pursuit. The impact of television in America is difficult to measure because very few people remain unexposed to it, and those few tend to act differently, in ways that pre-date the television era. One solution is to study the way television and other mass media fit into the life cycles of those who use them, without hoping for a comparison group of non-users. We all breathe air, after all, and the unavailability of a control group of non-breathers does not preclude our learning what air does for us.

The Ambiguous Mirror

The Ambiguous Mirror

the
reflective–projective
theory
of
broadcasting
and
mass communications

by LEE LOEVINGER

Former FCC Commissioner Lee Loevinger
examines some major theories
of mass communications
and broadcasting.
He then sets forth his own theory, which emphasizes the importance of the
individual's self-image in determining the impact of the media.*

In contemporary society more people spend more time in communication than in any other waking activity. If there ever was a period when man spent more time manipulating physical objects rather than symbols it is irretrievably past for us. Even in our organization of work we now have more white collar than blue collar workers, and our leisure time activities have long since become predominantly vicarious and communicative rather than manipulative and participant. However, communications is a very broad concept that includes such diverse activities as talking, from gossiping to lecturing, reading and writing, including reading and writing of

* Loevinger's fellow commissioner Kenneth Cox disagreed; he did not regard self-image as crucial and felt it was likely that the broadcast media would become effective tools for achieving social goals. See Kenneth A. Cox, "Can Broadcasting Help Achieve Social Reform?" *Journal of Broadcasting*, XII (Spring, 1968), 117–30.

The Ambiguous Mirror: The Reflective-Projective Theory of Broadcasting and Mass Communications: From *Journal of Broadcasting*, vol. 12, no. 2 (Spring, 1968). Copyright 1968 by the Association for Professional Broadcasting Education. Reprinted by permission.

numbers and figures, scanning newspapers and magazines, perusing books, chatting on the telephone, attending the theater, listening to radio, and watching television.

Mass communication, particularly radio and television, is usually the focus of current attention. It has become such a widespread and ubiquitous phenomenon that communication about mass communication has become a mass production enterprise itself. One can scarcely read a newspaper or magazine today without encountering a critique of the mass media in one aspect or another and one cannot listen long to radio without hearing some comment about television. However, when we search the literature for data or scholarship what we find is not impressive. There are innumerable critics of the mass media, especially broadcasting, a few objective observers, and almost no working scientists. Indeed the comments and arguments about broadcasting in general and television in particular are at least as stereotyped as the programs.

The most common comment on broadcasting is derogatory criticism. The characteristic comment is that television represents a wonderful potential and a miserable reality.[1] This is almost always based on either the critic's own subjective views or upon material gathered in response to a general invitation to readers of a particular column or journal to send their views in a letter to the columnist or editor. While all these people are surely entitled to hold any views they like and to express them freely, it must be clear that neither the critics nor their pen pals necessarily represent the public. The correspondence received by a particular critic, or even a particular magazine or newspaper, is not a "survey" in any scientific sense. To take such a sampling and report it as a "survey" is roughly equivalent to reporting the results of a survey taken on the steps of St. Peter's in Rome on Sunday morning regarding attitudes towards Christian Science, or reporting the views of a random sample found in the lobby of the Cairo Hilton as to the character or popularity of Moshe Dayan. Those who want to engage in such an exercise have a perfect right to do so, but the results cannot be taken seriously by anyone familiar with survey research or scientific method in general.

The most scientific investigation conducted to date of public attitudes towards television is still the Steiner study published in 1963. The findings were summarized by Lazarsfeld in these terms:

Dr. Steiner . . . found that a large number of respondents felt ambivalent about their amount of [television] viewing. They were ready to say that television is both relaxing and a waste of time.

[1] "So wonderful a potential, so miserable a reality" is given as the summary of "a reader survey" by the television critic of the *Christian Science Monitor*. (August 18, 1967, p. 9.) The views of the professional critics can be epitomized by a quotation from Bernie Harrison, television critic of the *Washington Star:* "I've been trying to find one critic who wrote something good, or even polite, about the new season of TV series." (September 21, 1967, p. B 13.)

Their other leisure activities were not surrounded by such a haze of doubt; reading is elevating, playing golf is wholesome, and sitting in a bar is clearly wrong. Among the better-educated, he found a number of respondents who stated frankly that they felt they watched more than they should.[2]

Interestingly enough, this conclusion is corroborated by a 1965 ITA study of the attitudes of managerial and professional classes in Great Britain toward television. The study concluded that these classes

by virtue of their educational and occupational background, tend more than the other social grades to have views about the meaningful use of time. They begin with reservations about television and the reservations are all the more likely to swell into irritation when they are themselves weak enough, as they see it, to be drawn into spending a good deal of time watching entertainment on television. They feel that television ought to have a tremendous potential for "good," in the sense of spreading knowledge and enlightenment, though it also seems clear that in having this concept of television they are thinking of the good it ought to be doing to *other* people rather than to themselves.[3]

There are a few other studies, mostly reported in the periodical literature, and some general theoretical analyses of mass communication, but there is no mass of empirical data from which we can derive any systematic view of functional theory of mass communications. There is, of course, a vast body of literature to be found under various library classifications beginning with the term "communications." However, these fall into three major classifications, each of which involves an entirely different frame of reference on an essentially different subject matter.

Communications Theories

When considering communications theory we must first distinguish among the engineering or technical, the economic, and the semantic frames of reference. The engineering or technical frame of reference encompasses what is now known as "information theory" and has to do with the modes and instruments of encoding, transmitting, and decoding messages of all kinds. This may involve an analysis of the physical means utilized (the electronic devices); the psychological processes involved; or consideration of linguistic and other symbols as means of encoding and decoding information. Economic analysis has to do, of course, with the financial as-

[2] Gary A. Steiner, *The People Look at Television.* New York: Alfred A. Knopf, 1963, p. 411.

[3] *ITV 1966.* A Guide to Independent Television, published by ITA, London, 1966, p. 25.

pects of mass communications. The semantic aspect of mass communications is the one that is most discussed and least understood. This is the one that has to do with the meaning and significance of what is communicated, and it is this aspect with which the critics, and most of the theory builders, are concerned.

From an examination of the literature it seems to me that there have been five major theories about the semantic function of broadcasting. The first view of broadcasting was that it was a remarkable and somewhat unbelievable technology that had specialized uses and would affect the public mainly as a hobby. This *hobby theory* of broadcasting was widely held from about the time of World War I until the early 1930's. Although the hobby theory of broadcasting is clearly out-dated, it is still recalled fondly by those of us who used to wind coils on old Quaker Oats boxes, made condensers, or capacitors as they are now called, from wax paper and tin foil, and used galena crystals as rectifiers.

In the early 1930's a great battle was fought between broadcasters and newspaper publishers over the right of broadcasting to transmit news.[4] The details are now only of historical interest and the outcome is well known. For many years after that, and up to the present time, broadcasting has been thought by many to derive its social significance from its effectiveness as a journalistic medium.[5] On occasion I have said that the *journalistic function* of broadcasting was its most important role.[6] A Roper survey indicating that more people look to television as a source of news than to newspapers, and that a substantial number rely on radio, gives support to this view.[7] Nevertheless, the journalistic theory of broadcasting seems to be more a normative view expressing what is thought to be the socially most important activity of the medium rather than an empirical view based on evidence encompassing all the functions broadcasting performs for its audience.

The "Social Reform" Theory

A third view that has gained some currency is the *social reform view* of broadcasting. This is the view held by people who see broadcasting as an immensely popular medium of communication, having a potentially vast influence and therefore offering an irresistible opportunity to achieve

[4] Mitchell V. Charnley, *News by Radio.* New York: Macmillan, 1948, p. 5 et seq.

[5] For a recent and very literate statement of the journalistic theory by a sophisticated and distinguished mind, see Raymond Swing, "Radio: The Languishing Giant," *Saturday Review,* August 12, 1967, p. 51.

[6] Lee Loevinger, "The Role of Law in Broadcasting," *Journal of Broadcasting,* VIII:2:133–126 at 121 (Spring, 1964).

[7] Burns W. Roper, *Emerging Profiles of Television and Other Mass Media: Public Attitudes 1959–1967.* A report by the president of Roper Research Associates on five national studies, April 5, 1967. (Published by the Television Information Office.)

a variety of social goals and ideals. This is the official attitude in many countries, particularly those of the Communist world. In this country there are those who see broadcasting, particularly television, as a means of doing quickly and easily what home, school, and church have been trying to do slowly and painfully for many years. This is the basic philosophy of those who feel that the FCC should exercise greater influence or control over broadcast programming.

The argument for government control of programming—whether extensive or limited—is usually ostensibly based upon the limitations of the spectrum and the consequent limitation of licensed broadcasting facilities. However it is noteworthy that those who are most eager to set official program standards are also among those who support most strongly the limitation of channels of mass communication on the grounds of harmful competition with existing broadcasting facilities. Both the doctrine of the Carroll case[8] and the rationale of the present CATV regulations[9] are based upon limiting the channels of mass communication in order to protect presently licensed enterprises. Regardless of whether such protection is justified, these legal rules make nonsense of the argument that program control is necessary or warranted because spectrum limitations impose an artificial scarcity on station assignments. So long as we are unwilling to permit the public to get as much broadcasting service as technology can provide, we cannot rationally say that technology imposes limitations requiring us to exercise control of programs because of technological limitations. Thus the social reform theory rests on the values and assumptions of its advocates rather than on an empirical foundation. In any event, whether or not broadcasting, and particularly television, is adapted to or capable of doing the work of social reform which some would have it undertake remains a question which is not answered merely by postulating the desirability of ideals to be achieved. The social reform theory needs a good deal more empirical investigation as well as philosophical analysis before it can provide a solid basis for acceptance.

McLuhan's "Sense-Extension" Theory

A fourth theory of mass communication is the *sense-extension theory* of Marshall McLuhan. This has become one of the most widely discussed theories of mass communication. It may be overstating the case to say that McLuhan presents a theory, since he is not a scientist and his ideas

[8] *Carroll Broadcasting Co. v. FCC*, 258 F2d 440, 17 RR 2066 (CA DC 1958). Also see *Southwest Operating Co. v. FCC*, 351 F2d 834 (CA DC 1965); James E. Meeks, "Economic Entry Controls in FCC Licensing: The Carroll Case Reappraised," 52 *Iowa Law Review* 236 (October, 1966).

[9] See *Regulation of CATV Systems*—Memorandum Opinion and Order on petition for reconsideration, 6 FCC2d 309, 330 (1967) (esp. dissenting opinion); *Fetzer Cable Vision*, et al., 6 FCC2d 845, 857 (1967) (dissenting opinion).

are expressed more as a series of disorganized observations than as a philosophical system. The widespread interest and popularity of McLuhan's publications really suggests the paucity of original thinking in this field.[10] Nevertheless the insights that McLuhan contributes are sufficiently supported by observation to warrant attention. His significant views may be summarized by some excerpts from his books:

Printing from movable type created a quite unexpected new environment—it created the PUBLIC. Manuscript technology did not have the intensity or power of extension necessary to create publics on a national scale. What we have called "nations" in recent centuries did not, and could not, precede the advent of Gutenberg technology any more than they can survive the advent of electric circuitry with its power of totally involving all people in all other people.[11]

.   .   .

Print, in turning the vernaculars into mass media, or closed systems, created the uniform centralizing forces of modern nationalism.[12]

.   .   .

[Individualism] is a meaningless principle where the uniform processing of minds by the habit of reading the printed word has not occurred. In a word, individualism . . . and self-expression, alike assumes a prior technology of homogenous citizens. This scabrous paradox has haunted literate men in every age.[13]

.   .   .

Print created national uniformity and government centralism, but also individualism and opposition to government as such.[14]

.   .   .

[I]n operational and practical fact, the medium is the message. This is merely to say that the personal and social consequences of any medium—that is of any extension of ourselves—result from the new scale that is introduced into our affairs by each extension of ourselves, or by any new technology.[15]

---

[10] Charles S. Steinberg, "The McLuhan Myth," *Television Quarterly,* 6:7 (Summer, 1967).

[11] Marshall McLuhan, *The Gutenberg Galaxy.* Toronto: University of Toronto Press, 1962. The quotation is from the summary in the facing page to the prologue in the first U.S.A. edition.

[12] *Ibid.,* p. 199.

[13] *Ibid.,* p. 209.

[14] *Ibid.,* p. 235.

[15] Marshall McLuhan, *Understanding Media: The Extensions of Man.* New York: McGraw-Hill Book Company, 1964. New York: Signet ed., 1966, p. 23. [Copyright © 1964 by Marshall McLuhan. Used with permission of McGraw-Hill Book Company.]

.   .   .

[T]he medium is the message because it is the medium that shapes and controls the scale and form of human association and action. . . . For any medium has the power of imposing its own assumption on the unwary. . . . [O]ur human senses, of which all media are extensions, are also fixed charges on our personal energies, and . . . they also configure the awareness and experience of each one of us. . . .[16]

.   .   .

There have been countless . . . men who know nothing about the form of any medium whatever. They imagine that a more earnest tone and a more austere theme would pull up the level of the book, the press, the movie and TV. They are wrong to a farcical degree. They have only to try out their theory for fifty consecutive words in the mass medium of the English language. . . . Suppose we were to try for a few sentences to raise the level of our daily English conversation by a series of sober and serious sentiments? Would this be a way of getting at the problems of improving the medium?[17]

.   .   .

[T]he critics of program "content" have talked nonsense about "TV violence." The spokesmen of censorious views are typical semi-literate book-oriented individuals who have no competence in the grammars of newspaper, or radio, or of film, but who look askew and askance at all non-book media. The simplest question about any psychic aspect throws these people into a panic of uncertainty. Vehemence of projection of a single isolated attitude they mistake for moral vigilance. Once these censors became aware that in all cases "the medium is the message" or the basic source of effects, they would turn to suppression of media as such, instead of seeking "content" control. Their current assumption that content or programming is the factor that influences outlook and action is derived from the book medium, with its sharp cleavage between form and content.[18]

.   .   .

Each new technology creates an environment that is itself regarded as corrupt and degrading. Yet the new one turns its predecessor into an art form. When writing was new, Plato transformed the old oral dialogue into an art form. When printing was new the Middle Ages became an art form. "The Elizabethan world view" was a view of the Middle Ages. And the industrial age turned the Renaissance into an art form . . . the electric age taught us how to see the entire process of mechanization as an art process.[19]

[16] *Ibid.*, pp. 24, 30, 35.
[17] *Ibid.*, p. 187.
[18] *Ibid.*, p. 274.
[19] *Ibid.*, p. ix.

Stephenson's "Play Theory"

An entirely different view of mass communications has been offered by William Stephenson, a behavioral scientist, under the name of "the *play theory* of mass communication."[20] Stephenson distinguishes play from work, with play being activity that is self-sufficient and pursued for the pleasure in it, while work is activity involving effort for a purpose regarded as gainful and to produce goods, services, ideas, or other ulterior objectives. He distinguishes between social control, which comprises the devices society employs to establish involuntary categorical imperatives and secure conformity, from what he calls "convergent selectivity," which is the relative freedom of individual choice among alternatives.

Stephenson shows how his theories explain otherwise unnoticed or inexplicable phenomena. For example, he concludes that people read newspapers primarily for pleasure rather than information. As evidence he notes the fact that people read most avidly what they already know about. They go to a football or baseball game, then read about it in the newspaper. People look first in the newspaper to read events they have been involved in and already know about. Furthermore, we all read accounts of the same thing over and over again. This is because newspaper reading is play and involves the reader in projection, or self-identification as a story teller. Thus newspaper reading is an example of convergent selectivity, or voluntary activity, rather than of social control. Similarly the mass media, plays, art, and the theater generally offer opportunity for convergent selectivity, or communication pleasure, rather than work, which is communication effort or pain. Mass communication, he says, is best understood as being manipulated by its audiences, who thoroughly enjoy what they are being offered for the first time in man's history. The media are not manipulating or oppressing their audiences, and they should not make work out of what should be pleasure. Says Stephenson:

> Social scientists have been busy, since the beginnings of mass communication research, trying to prove that the mass media have been sinful where they should have been good. The media have been looked at through the eyes of morality when, instead, what was required was a fresh glance at people existing in their own right for the first time. It is my thesis that the daily withdrawal of people into the mass media in their after hours is a step in the existential direction, that is, a matter of subjectivity which invites freedom where there had been little or none before.[21]

> •   •   •

> The fill of mass communication is not a flight from reality, escapism, or the like; nor is it debasing or seducing the masses as the

[20] William Stephenson, *The Play Theory of Mass Communication.* Chicago: University of Chicago Press, 1967.
[21] *Ibid.,* p. 45.

critics suppose. Rather it is seen as a buffer against conditions which would otherwise be anxiety producing. Without question a constant barrage of political propaganda would find few listeners or viewers, or, if it found many, would arouse deep anxieties in an unsettled world.[22]

.   .   .

The process of developing national character is no doubt basically rooted in social controls . . . , in which church, home, school, work, and all else mediate. But national character is also what a nation *thinks* of itself, as something to talk about, to sustain ongoing social or national conditions. It is best regarded as communication-pleasure, which has little effect on anything but gives self-satisfaction all around.[23]

It follows from this that separation of the elite from the culture at large creates a separatist culture within a country which bodes no one any good. What is most required for a national culture is something for everyone to talk about. The daily "fill" is far more important than the education of professionals. This is how social culture and character is formed, in songs, gossip, sports, dances, competition, or whatever is required to give people communication pleasure. Stephenson concludes that ". . . mass communication . . . should serve two purposes. It should suggest how best to maximize the communication-pleasure in the world. It should also show how far autonomy for the individual can be achieved in spite of the weight of social controls against him."[24]

Evaluation of These Theories

Each of these theories has some element of validity in it. After all, theories are simply conceptual schemes that enable us to see and relate the various aspects of phenomena under examination. Theories enable us to understand observations and to predict and make reasonable inferences beyond observation. In this sense theories are not true or untrue but more or less useful. Each of the theories, hobby, journalistic, social reform, sense extension, and play, points to an aspect of mass communications by broadcasting that has some significance. The journalistic and social reform theories focus on the medium and its message. The hobby, sense extension, and play theories focus on the audience and its reaction to the medium. However, none of these theories is entirely adequate to account for empirical data that can easily be observed. There are at least half a dozen observable and important facts about broadcasting that I think must be encompassed and explained by any mass communications theory before it may be accepted as adequate:

[22] *Ibid.*, p. 49.
[23] *Ibid.*, p. 91.
[24] *Ibid.*, p. 205.

First, broadcasting is extremely popular with the public and attracts a larger audience than any other mass medium in history, both relatively and in absolute numbers. In some individual cases both radio and television seem to be truly addictive. *Second,* the appeal of American-type broadcasting is universal. Even though much of our programming, such as TV westerns, is indigenous, it is popular throughout the world. Similarly American popular music has captured much of the world radio audience. Where state-controlled broadcasting systems have sought to use broadcasting for propaganda or educational purposes—and the difference is of interest to scholars rather than to audiences—they have been forced either by lack of audience or by competition from pirate, outside, or commercial stations to show more American or American-type programming, that is primarily entertaining. This has been the case in countries as diverse as Britain, Holland, Yugoslavia, Russia, and Japan. *Third,* during a period of increasing population, prosperity, and literacy, newspapers have not increased in number, and have declined in overall economic strength and competitive vitality, in Britain as well as in America, while reasonably reliable reports indicate that the general public relies more on television than on newspapers as a source of news.[25] Broadcasting now performs the journalistic function for most of the public part of the time and for much of the public most of the time. *Fourth,* broadcasting, especially television, arouses strong emotional reactions in most of those who either watch or listen and discuss it. In my experience, no other subject, not even religion, arouses such quick and violent emotional responses from people. *Fifth,* broadcasting, particularly television, is largely rejected or denigrated by intellectuals, and those who consider themselves intellectuals. Indeed, it is scarcely regarded as respectable to write or speak in public about television without deprecating its low intellectual estate. *Sixth,* broadcasting has become a part of ordinary living in contemporary society in a way that no other mass medium or art form has approached. Television or radio are in the home, in the car, in the office, on the beach, on the street, and constantly in company with the majority of the population. Broadcasting is about as ubiquitous as printing and for some people is a far more intimate and constant companion. The theater, pictorial art, and either contemporary or classical literature are none of them a part of everyday living for most people; they are not really an element of our communal experience. Not even the newspapers are a component of our common

[25] Burns W. Roper, *Emerging Profiles of Television and Other Mass Media: Public Attitudes 1959–1967.* A report by the president of Roper Research Associates on five national studies, April 5, 1967, p. 7 et seq. Also see A. H. Raskin, "What's Wrong with American Newspapers?" *New York Times Magazine,* June 11, 1967, p. 28; John Tebbel, "Britain's Chronic Press Crisis," *Saturday Review,* July 8, 1967, p. 49; Henry Raymont, "4 Chicago Newspapers Are Fighting Desperately to Regain Lost Readers," *New York Times,* September 5, 1967, p. 38. Mr. Raskin says, inter alia: "There is disturbing skepticism among large groups of readers, including many of the best educated and most intellectually alive, about whether what they read in their newspapers is either true or relevant."

culture in the sense that broadcasting has become. Any theory of broadcasting as mass communication must be consistent with and adequate to explain at least these data. Testing the five theories mentioned on this basis shows that none of them is wholly adequate.

The hobby theory is, of course, clearly outdated and is really quite inadequate to explain any of the observed data. The journalistic theory is somewhat more relevant and is at least consistent with the popularity of broadcasting, its journalistic function, and, possibly, its place as a cultural component. However, the journalistic theory is not consistent with the universality of broadcasting programs, with the emotional involvement of the audience, or with the attitude of intellectuals toward the medium. The journalistic theory is partially empirical, but is also in part a normative judgment as to the function that broadcasting should be performing rather than an empirical conclusion as to the function that it actually does perform or the need that it does meet. By its own terms, the journalistic theory is an incomplete account of broadcasting as mass communication.

The social reform theory explains the emotional involvement of those who either attack or defend broadcasting, as well as the attitude of the intellectual elite toward television. However, the social reform theory is not at all consistent with the popularity of broadcasting, with its universality, with its journalistic function, or with its observable role as a cultural component. The social reform theory must be judged to have very little empirical basis and to be almost wholly a normative ideal.

The sense-extension theory of McLuhan seeks to be empirical rather than normative and is consistent with the popularity of broadcasting, its universality, and its role as a cultural component. McLuhan explains the emotional involvement of the television audience by saying it is a "cool" medium which conveys little information and so requires audience participation to provide the links necessary to complete the message. I find this unconvincing because the theory strains the observable facts and simply does not apply to radio. Further, the McLuhan theory is neither consistent with nor adequate to explain the journalistic function of broadcasting or the attitude of the intellectual group generally. The play theory of Stephenson, similarly, is empirical and descriptive rather than normative. It is quite consistent with the popularity of broadcasting, with its universality and with its journalistic function. However, the play theory is not adequate to explain the emotional involvement of the audience, the attitude of the intellectual elite, or the place of broadcasting as a cultural component.

The "Reflective-Projective Theory"

A broader theory which seems to encompass all of the aspects of broadcasting mentioned, as well as others, is what I call the *reflective-projective theory* of broadcasting and mass communication. This theory postulates that mass communications are best understood as mirrors of society that reflect an ambiguous image in which each observer projects or sees his own vision of himself and society. This theory not only explains the observable facts about broadcasting better than the other theories but also differentiates the social and the individual aspects of the semantic significance of mass communications, which the other theories do not.

It is apparent that mass media reflect various images of society but not of the individual. However, broadcasting is not a simple, plane mirror but rather a telescopic mirror reflecting an image of what is distant and concentrating and focusing on points in a vast universe. Broadcasting is an electronic mirror that reflects a vague and ambiguous image of what is behind it, as well as of what is in front of it. While the mirror can pick out points and aspects of society, it cannot create a culture or project an image that does not reflect something already existing in some form in society. Further, the mirror can project an accurate or a distorted image and it can reflect an image that is very vague and ambiguous or one that is more clearly defined. These are matters of degree and there is always a significant amount of ambiguity in the image projected.

The ambiguous mirror of broadcasting obviously reflects not a single image but a variety of images of society, as it is turned toward one or another sector or aspects of society. As with a telescope or camera, the broadcasting mirror may be focused broadly or narrowly. So the reflective-projective theory, unlike the earlier theories, takes account of and allows for the variety of broadcasting. Educational television and what is now called "public broadcasting" help to present a broader, and therefore more complete, reflection of society. However, this theory also warns us not to expect too much of educational television or public broadcasting. They can supplement and expand the broadcasting image, but, like conventional broadcasting, so long as they are mass media they can perform only a reflective-projective function and are most unlikely to become instruments of social reform or great public enlightenment.[26]

[26] See Howard K. Smith, "Don't Expect Too Much from Public Television," *Washington Star,* October 1, 1967. Mr. Smith, an experienced broadcaster and social observer, says, "People who understand television but little, . . . are premature and hyperbolic in seeing a new age of wonders about to open. . . . Criticizing the fare on commercial TV is without doubt America's chief popular avocation, ... But for an exercise Americans indulge in so much, it is odd how ill thought out are their assumptions. There is not going to be any hegira away from commercial to public TV. There is nothing magic in public TV that is going to increase the quality of genius or imagination in our nation." I have supported and do support the establishment of a corporation for public broadcasting, not on the grounds that commercial broadcasting is deficient or has failed but on the grounds that the proposal will promote diversity, provide a potential for innovation and excellence, and afford the public a wider choice in broadcasting. See letter to Senator John O. Pastore in *Hearings* before the Subcommittee on Communications of the Committee on Commerce, U.S. Senate, 90th Congress, 1st Session, on S. 1160, The Public Television Act of 1967, Serial 90–4, p. 678.

This view is consistent with observation of national differences in broadcasting patterns. A substantial element of violence in American television reflects a tolerance and taste for violence in American society. This is somewhat offensive to Europeans, who have a different attitude toward violence and there is less of violence in European broadcast programming. On the other hand, European television has fewer sex and religious taboos than American television and this corresponds to European attitudes, which are looser in these fields than American attitudes. Basically all mass media are censored by the public since they lose their status as *mass* media if they become too offensive or uninteresting to a large segment of the public.[27]

While the mass media reflect various images of society, the audience is composed of individuals, each of whom views the media as an individual. The members of the audience project or see in the media their own visions or images, in the same manner that an individual projects his own ideas into the inkblots of the Rorschach test or the pictures of the Thematic Apperception Test, commonly used by psychologists.[28] Projection is a process that has been well known in psychology for many years. Essentially it consists of an observer attributing his own attitudes, ideas, or feelings to the perceptions he receives from the environment. There is some element of this in all perception. Perception itself is both selective and interpretative, as we never see all the details of any scene and necessarily interpret or impose preconceived patterns on our sensations when we perceive anything as having meaning. All media, including those exalted by the term "art," offer selected sensations which provide the basis for individual interpretations that vary with intellectual, emotional, and sensory responses. What is pure story-telling to one may be allegory or metaphor to another. Well known examples are such classics as *Gulliver's Travels, Alice in Wonderland,* and *Don Quixote.* However, it is not only literary classics that have this mixed narrative-allegorical-metaphorical quality. A recent sociological study of television comments:

Television series such as *Bonanza,* and *The Virginian,* and most popular films and fiction are in reality morality plays, that show how a hero confronts a moral dilemma and how he finally makes a moral choice. These dilemmas are often quite contemporary and controversial; I have seen *Bonanza,* one of the most popular TV programs, deal with questions of racial intolerance and intermarriage, albeit in a 19th-century Western setting. Programs like

27 See Wilbur Schramm, *Mass Media and National Development.* Stanford, Calif.: Stanford University Press and UNESCO, 1964. Basically Schramm argues that mass media cannot proceed far in advance of other social developments that relate to and support the media with an internal national culture.

28 Although there is some dispute among psychologists as to the effectiveness of the Rorschach inkblot test as a clinical diagnostic tool, there is no disagreement as to the phenomenon of projection and the fact that this response is elicited by the inkblot test. See Patricia McBroom, "The Rorschach Tested," *Science News,* 92:182 (August 19, 1967).

The Law and Mr. Jones, East Side/West Side, and *The Defenders* have discussed pertinent social issues in contemporary settings, although they have been less popular from a rating standpoint. And even the innocuous family situation comedies such as *Ozzie and Harriet* deal occasionally with ethical problems encountered on a neighborhood level; for example, how to help the socially isolated child or the unhappy neighbor. Although the schools argue that they are the major transmitter of society's moral values, the mass media offer a great deal more content on this topic.[29]

Thus broadcasting is an electronic mirror reflecting an ambiguous image of its environment in which the audience sees its vision of society. This view explains the several aspects of broadcasting that have been noted above. It also points to another fact which is of substantial significance. In the field of communications media, technology reverses psychology in order of development. The technologically most advanced media are psychologically the most elementary and primitive. Psychologically man has advanced from simple sensation to perception, and then to abstraction which is expressed in gestures, sounds, symbols, verbal signs, and, finally, developed language. Technologically, hieroglyphics were the first form of writing, and we have progressed from them to more sophisticated signs, to alphabet writing, to printing, followed by books and periodicals, and then through the electronic media from the telegraph to the telephone to radio and through the movies to television. The most highly abstract of the technological media is alpha-numeric writing which requires considerable effort and interpretation by the reader. Speech conveyed by telephone or radio is understood more easily and is a psychological regression from the abstraction of printed language to the more elemental level of oral language. Finally, television is a medium which, contrary to the theories of McLuhan, conveys the most information in the most literal form by giving us oral language combined with visual perception and requiring the least effort to interpret the abstractions. Thus television is a multichannel communication which is more elemental and therefore has greater immediacy and impact than other media.

This theory fully explains the aspects of broadcasting mentioned above. Broadcasting is popular and universal because it is elemental, responsive to popular taste, and gives the audience a sense of contact with the world around it which is greater than that provided by any other medium. Broadcasting is increasingly performing the journalistic function for the public not because it is superior by any abstract intellectual standards but because it is immediate, personal, and comprehensive. Television views of a scene may be and often are better than personal observation, in their ability to focus telescopically on details of interest, in their ability to move from place to place, and in their ability to select the scenes of action and

[29] Herbert J. Gans, "The Mass Media as an Educational Institution," *Television Quarterly,* 6:20–37 at 22 (Spring, 1967).

interest. Television and radio duplicate and overlap each other to a great extent, but apparently television has the greater popularity because its multichannel communication with the audience conveys a sense of greater involvement and a closer apprehension of reality.

The reflective-projective theory makes it easy to understand why people are so strongly attached to and upset by broadcasting and react so emotionally to it. It is because each projects his own ego into what he sees or hears and is frequently dissatisfied when he finds the picture unflattering. This reaction can easily be verified by a simple experiment. Take a picture of any individual with an ordinary camera and then ask him, or her, whether the picture is altogether attractive and pleasing. Virtually no one, man or woman, is ever wholly pleased with a picture or reflection of himself. When it is possible to blame the photographer or someone else, that is the easiest course and therefore most frequently followed. On the other hand, people are fascinated by pictures and are invariably more interested in pictures in which they appear than in pictures of others. Another empirical verification is the relationship between people and mirrors. Almost no one can resist at least a glance into a mirror no matter how often and how recently he has inspected his own reflection. Thus the mirror theory of broadcasting explains not only the emotional involvement of the audience but also the popular appeal and universality of the medium.

The reflective-projective theory also explains the democratic paradox that in the field of mass communications the greater the appeal to the mass the more alienated the majority of intellectuals seems to become. Most of those who articulate the demand for democracy and service to the public interest, and who are accustomed to influence policy and social action in this manner, are of an intellectual elite. Such leaders think of democracy as a system in which *they* define the public interest and the public is persuaded to accept or acquiesce in leadership views. But in fact the public wants to see its *own* image in the mass media mirrors, not the image of intellectual leaders. Consequently when the public gets what it wants from the mass media this incurs the wrath of an intellectual elite and the slings and arrows of outraged critics who have been demanding service to the public . . . but who have been expecting their own rather than the public's views and tastes.

Finally, the reflective-projective theory is wholly consistent with the observation that broadcasting has become an important component of contemporary culture. A nation or a community is not formed by lines on a map or even by geographical unity or natural boundaries, as we are learning anew each day. A nation or a community is formed by common interests, ideas, and culture—by a common image or vision of itself. But to have a common image or vision there must be one that is seen, understood, and accepted by most of the people, not merely by a minority or by an elite. This requires that the social image reflected in the media mirrors be one that truly reflects the mass.

The common interest in entertainment, sports, news, and even advertising is likely to be more universally understood and effective in providing common ties of association and conversation than more esoteric and aesthetic material. It seems probable that a television showing of the World Series or of a popular western or other entertainment show will do more to promote a sense of national unity than a lecture on morality by some nationally known clergyman or a performance of *Hamlet* starring some great Shakespearean player. A family is not formed by recollections of a prettily posed, neatly dressed, tinted studio shot of the group on grandmother's birthday. A family is formed by shared experiences of skinned knees, trips to the doctor, hurried meals, mended pants, and all the million and one mundane commonplaces, hardships, and irritations of everyday living together. Perhaps the smudged, commonplace, homely, slightly unattractive picture that we get of ourselves from our mass media is providing us with a common image and a common cultural bond that we could not get from a more elegant and more attractive portrait.

In analyzing the role of mass media, or any other social phenomena, we must distinguish the judgments expressed in empirical and normative theories. Empirical theories are those which are purely descriptive and seek to explain and harmonize observed facts. Normative theories are those which set norms or standards and imply obligations to conform. Of course we need both. However, the first task is to understand before we undertake to judge. It is silly to condemn a camel for having a hump and praise a horse for having a straight back, or condemn a horse for requiring frequent drinks of water and praise a camel for his ability to travel without water. These characteristics are simple facts of existence and are not rationally the basis for either praise or blame. These are things for which normative standards are irrelevant and the only reasonable course is to observe and understand. Once we observe and understand the nature of camels and horses we can then decide the use to which each is best put.

When we understand broadcasting it appears that the mission for which it is best fitted is the creation of a common contemporary culture and a sense of national (and perhaps international) unity. This also appears to be the function which now most needs to be performed. The creation of a common national culture embodying a spirit of national unity must surely rank as a foremost need of the present era. Of course, national unity does not require or imply unanimity of views on all issues or suppression of dissent. It does imply a common bond or mood as well as agreement on some basic ideas and principles. Indeed, national agreement on support of basic American constitutional principles is essential if dissent and its free expression are to survive.

On the other hand, the medium that provides the common denominator to promote national unity and community culture is not necessarily the one that can also provide general adult education, social reform, or even news and information, although these may be provided in some degree in the process of creating and disseminating a national culture. We should remember that Shakespeare in his day was a popular entertainer who wrote fanciful and escapist stories about royalty and nobility, about wars and violence, and not about the common people and ordinary experience.

Even among our mass media there are differences in the ability to perform the function of unification and common culture building. Magazines to an outstanding degree, and even newspapers, are written and published for particular groups and classes of society. Evidence of this is proudly paraded by the publishers in their analyses of the income and educational status of readers. Evidence of this can readily be observed by comparing such newspapers as the *New York Times* and the *Wall Street Journal* with the *New York Daily News,* and by comparing the *New Yorker* with *True Story* magazine. Even more obvious stratification is evident in magazines which appeal to particular ethnic or religious groups as well as those with specific vocational and economic specialization. In contrast, broadcasting is relatively universal and equally available to all members of the public. One can hardly imagine an underprivileged slum dweller buying a copy of *Fortune.* However, the poor, the middle class, and the rich are about equally exposed to news of business and finance given on television news summaries or transmitted by the implicit message of popular entertainment.

It appears that much of the dissatisfaction that is voiced with broadcasting media is really an expression of basic dissatisfaction with society. To a large extent in past history the intellectual elite have lived in a separate world from the great mass of people and have neither confronted the mass or mass views and tastes nor sought to impose their own views and tastes upon the mass, except with respect to a few political issues. Broadcasting, as a universal medium, changes this. To the degree that the intellectual elite pay attention to radio and television they inescapably confront mass tastes and desires. That this does not satisfy their own standards is not only to be expected but, indeed, is inherent in the very nature of things. It is also socially useful to have the elite thus exposed to mass culture.

What we urgently need today is a larger concept of community—to see the community of which we are part not merely as a town, city, metropolitan area, or state, but as a country, a unified, civilized, orderly national society.[30] This is an image that cannot be created by art, but that must grow in the minds and hearts of men. We cannot say with certainty just what will nourish and what will poison its growth. Yet it does appear that the growth of a unified and cohesive national community will be promoted by the presentation of highly popular programs on mass media, especially broadcasting. Our survival as a free nation may depend upon development of a truly common culture. That is a task worthy of any medium.

---

[30] See Jefferson B. Fordham, *A Larger Concept of Community.* Baton Rouge: Louisiana State University Press, 1956.

THE
INDUSTRIALIZATION
OF THE
MIND

by HANS MAGNUS ENZENSBERGER

This article by the German poet and philosopher Hans Enzensberger takes a very pessimistic view of the effects of the mass media on the individual. Enzensberger sees the media as tools of "the mind-making industry," a multifaceted movement toward increased regimentation and exploitation of the human mind.

All of us, no matter how irresolute we are, like to think that we reign supreme in our own awareness, that we are masters of what our minds accept or reject. Since the Soul is not much mentioned any more, except by priests, poets and pop musicians, the last refuge a man can take from the catastrophic world at large seems to be his mind. Where else can he expect to withstand the daily siege, if not within himself? Even under the conditions of totalitarian rule, where no one can fancy any more that his home is his castle, the mind of the individual is considered a kind of last citadel and hotly defended, though this imaginary fortress may have been long since taken over by an ingenious enemy.[1]

No illusion is more stubbornly upheld than the sovereignty of the mind. It is a good example of the impact of philosophy on people who ignore it;

The Industrialization of the Mind: Reprinted by permission of Suhrkamp Verlag. Copyright © 1962 Suhrkamp Verlag Frankfurt am Main. The article first appeared in *Partisan Review,* vol. 36, no. 1 (Winter, 1969).

[1] This delusion became painfully apparent during the Nazi régime in Germany, when many intellectuals thought it sufficient to retreat into "inner emigration," a posture which turned out to mean giving in to the Nazis. There have been similar tendencies in Communist countries during the reign of Stalinism. See Czeslaw Milosz's excellent study, *The Captive Mind* (London, 1953).

for the idea that men can "make up their minds" individually and by themselves is essentially derived from the tenets of bourgeois philosophy: sec-
ondhand Descartes, run-down Husserl, armchair idealism; and all it
amounts to is a sort of metaphysical do-it-yourself.

We might do worse, I think, than dust off the admirably laconic statement which one of our classics has made more than a century ago:
"What is going on in our minds has always been, and will always be, a
product of society."[2] This is a comparatively recent insight. Though it is
valid for all human history ever since the division of labor came into being,
it could not be formulated before the times of Karl Marx. In a society
where communication was largely oral, the dependence of the pupil on the
teacher, the disciple on the master, the flock on the priest was taken for
granted. That the few thought and judged and decided for the many was a
matter of course and not a matter for investigation. Medieval man was
probably otherdirected to an extent which our sociology would be at a loss
to fathom. His mind was, to an enormous degree, fashioned and processed
from "without." But the business of teaching and of indoctrination was
perfectly straightforward and transparent—so transparent indeed that it
became invisible as a problem. Only when the processes which shape our
minds became opaque, enigmatic, inscrutable for the common man, only
with the advent of industrialization did the question of how our minds are
shaped arise in earnest.

The mind-making industry is really a product of the last hundred years.
It has developed at such a pace, and assumed such varied forms, that it
has outgrown our understanding and our control. Our current discussion
of the "media" seems to suffer from severe theoretical limitations. Newsprint, films, television, public relations tend to be evaluated separately, in
terms of their specific technologies, conditions and possibilities. Every
new branch of the industry starts off a new crop of theories.[3] Hardly anyone seems to be aware of the phenomenon as a whole: the industrialization
of the human mind. This is a process which cannot be understood by a
mere examination of its machinery.

Equally inadequate is the term *cultural industry* which has become common usage in Europe after World War II. It reflects, more than the scope
of the phenomenon itself, the social status of those who have tried to
analyse it: university professors and academic writers: people whom the

---

2 Karl Marx, *Die deutsche Ideologie*, I (Teil, 1845–46).

3 A good example is the current wave of McLuhanism. No matter how ingenious,
no matter how shrewd and fresh some of this author's observations may seem, his
understanding of media hardly deserves the name of a theory. His cheerful disregard of their social and political implications is pathetic. It is all too easy to see
why the slogan "The medium is the message" has met with unbounded enthusiasm on
the part of the media, since it does away, by a quick fix worthy of a card-sharp, with
the question of truth. Whether the message is a lie or not has become irrelevant,
since in the light of McLuhanism truth itself resides in the very existence of the
medium, no matter what it may convey: the proof of the network is in the network.
It is a pity that Goebbels has not lived to see this redemption of his *oeuvre*.

power elite has relegated to the reservations of what passes as "cultural life" and who consequently have resigned themselves to bear the unfortunate name of cultural critics. In other words, they are certified as harmless; they are supposed to think in terms of *Kultur* and not in terms of power.

Yet the vague and insufficient name *cultural industry* serves to remind us of a paradox inherent in all media work. Consciousness, however false, can be induced and reproduced by industrial means, but it cannot be industrially produced. It is a "social product" made up by people: its origin is the dialogue. No industrial process can replace the persons who generate it. And it is precisely this truism of which the archaic term "culture" tries, however vainly, to remind us. The mind industry is monstrous and difficult to understand because it does not, strictly speaking, produce anything. It is an intermediary, engaged only in production's secondary and tertiary derivatives, in transmission and infiltration, in the fungible aspect of what it multiplies and delivers to the customer.

The mind industry can take on anything, digest it, reproduce it and pour it out. Whatever our minds can conceive of is grist to its mill; nothing will leave it unadulterated: it is capable of turning any idea into a slogan and any work of the imagination into a hit. This is its overwhelming power, yet it is also its most vulnerable spot: it thrives on a stuff which it cannot manufacture by itself. It depends on the very substance it must fear most, and must suppress what it feeds on: the creative productivity of people. Hence the ambiguity of the term cultural industry, which takes at face value the claims of culture, in the ancient sense of the word, and the claims of an industrial process which has all but eaten it up. To insist on these claims would be naïve; to criticize the industry from the vantage point of a "liberal education" and to raise comfortable outcries against its vulgarity will neither change it nor revive the dead souls of culture: it will merely help to fortify the ghettoes of educational programs and to fill the backward, highbrow section of the Sunday papers. At the same time, the indictment of the mind industry on purely aesthetic grounds will tend to obscure its larger social and political meaning.

On the other extreme we find the ideological critics of the mind industry. Their attention is usually limited to its role as an instrument of straightforward or hidden political propaganda, and from the messages reproduced by it they try to distill the political content. More often than not, the underlying understanding of politics is extremely narrow, as if it were just a matter of taking sides in everyday contests of power. Just as in the case of the "cultural critic," this attitude cannot hope to catch up with the far-reaching effects of the industrialization of the mind, since it is a process which will abolish the distinction between private and public consciousness.

Thus, while radio, cinema, television, recording, advertising and public relations, new techniques of manipulation and propaganda, are being keenly discussed, each on its own terms, the mind industry, taken as a whole, is disregarded. Newsprint and publishing, its oldest and in many respects still its most interesting branch, hardly comes up for serious comment any longer, presumably because it lacks the appeal of technological novelty. Yet much of the analysis provided in Balzac's *Illusions perdues* is as pertinent today as it was a hundred years ago, as any copywriter from Hollywood who happens to know the book will testify. Other, more recent branches of the industry still remain largely unexplored: fashion and industrial design, the propagation of established religions and of esoteric cults, opinion polls, simulation and, last but not least, tourism, which can be considered as a mass medium in its own right.

Above all, however, we are not sufficiently aware of the fact that the full deployment of the mind industry still lies ahead. Up to now it has not managed to seize control of its most essential sphere, which is education. The industrialization of instruction, on all levels, has barely begun. While we still indulge in controversies over curricula, school systems, college and university reforms and shortages in the teaching professions, technological systems are being perfected which will make nonsense of all the adjustments we are now considering. The language laboratory and the short-circuit TV are only the forerunners of a fully industrialized educational system which will make use of increasingly centralized programming and of recent advances in the study of learning. In the process, education will become a mass medium, the most powerful of all, and a billion-dollar business.

Whether we realize it or not, the mind industry is growing faster than any other, not excluding armament. It has become the key industry of the twentieth century. Those who are concerned in the power game of today, political leaders, intelligence men and revolutionaries, have very well grasped this crucial fact. Whenever an industrially developed country is occupied or liberated today, whenever there is a coup d'état, a revolution or a counterrevolution, the crack police units, the paratroopers, the guerrilla fighters do not any longer descend on the main squares of the city or seize the centers of heavy industry, as in the nineteenth century, or symbolic sites like the royal palace: the new régime will instead take over, first of all, the radio and television stations, the telephone and telex exchanges and the printing presses. And after having entrenched itself, it will, by and large, leave alone those who manage the public services and the manufacturing industries, at least in the beginning, while all the functionaries who run the mind industry will be immediately replaced. In such extreme situations the industry's key position becomes quite clear.

There are four conditions which are necessary to its existence; briefly, they are as follows:

1. Enlightenment, in the broadest sense, is the philosophical prerequisite of the industrialization of the mind. It cannot get under way until the rule of theocracy, and with it people's faith in revelation and inspiration, in the Holy Book or the Holy Ghost as taught by the priesthood, is broken.

The mind industry presupposes independent minds, even when it is out to deprive them of their independence; this is another of its paradoxes. The last theocracy to vanish has been Tibet; ever since, the philosophical condition is met with throughout the world.

2. Politically, the industrialization of the mind presupposes the proclamation of human rights, of equality and liberty in particular. In Europe, this threshold has been passed by the French Revolution; in the Communist world, by the October Revolution; and in America, Asia and Africa, by the wars of liberation from colonial rule. Obviously, the industry does not depend on the realization of these rights; for most people, they have never been more than a pretense, or at best, a distant promise. On the contrary, it is just the margin between fiction and reality which provides the mind industry with its theater of operations. Consciousness, both individual and social, has become a political issue only from the moment when the conviction arose in people's minds that everyone should have a say in his own destiny as well as in that of society at large. From the same moment any authority had to justify itself in the eyes of those it would govern; coercion alone would no longer do the trick; he who ruled must persuade, lay claim to people's minds and change them, in an industrial age, by every industrial means at hand.

3. Economically, the mind industry cannot come of age unless a measure of primary accumulation has been achieved. A society which cannot provide the necessary surplus capital neither needs it, nor can afford it. During the first half of the nineteenth century in Western Europe, and under similar conditions in other parts of the world, which prevailed until fairly recently, peasants and workers lived at a level of bare subsistence. During this stage of economic development the fiction that the working class was able to determine the conditions of its own existence is meaningless; the proletariat is subjected by physical constraint and undisguised force. Archaic methods of manipulation, as used by the school and by the church, the law and the army, together with old customs and conventions, are quite sufficient for the ruling minority to maintain its position during the earlier stages of industrial development. As soon as the basic industries have been firmly established and the mass production of consumer goods is beginning to reach out to the majority of the population, the ruling classes will face a dilemma. More sophisticated methods of production demand a constantly rising standard of education, not only for the privileged but also for the masses. The immediate compulsion which kept the working class "in their place" will slowly decrease. Working hours are reduced, and the standard of living rises. Inevitably, people will become aware of their own situation; they can now afford the luxury of having a mind of their own. For the first time, they become conscious of themselves in any fuller than the most primitive and hazy sense of the word. In this process, enormous human energies are released, energies which inevitably threaten the established political and economic order. Today this revolu-

tionary process can be seen at work in a great number of emergent nations, where it has long been artificially retarded by imperialist powers; in these countries the political, if not the economic conditions for the development of mind industries can be realized overnight.[4]

4. Given a certain level of economic development, industrialization brings with it the last condition for the rise of a mind industry: the technology on which it depends. The first industrial uses of electricity were concerned with power and not with communications: the dynamo and the electrical motor preceded the amplifying valve and the film camera. There are economical reasons for this time lag: the foundations of radio, film, recording, television and computing techniques could not be laid before the advent of the mass production of commodities and the general availability of electrical power.

In our time the technological conditions for the industrialization of the mind exist anywhere on the planet. The same cannot be said for the political and economic prerequisites; however, it is only a matter of time until they will be met. The process is irreversible. Therefore all criticism of the mind industry which is abolitionist in its essence is inept and beside the point, since the idea of arresting and liquidating industrialization itself (which such criticism implies) is suicidal. There is a macabre irony to any such proposal, for it is indeed no longer a technical problem for our civilization to abolish itself. However, this is hardly what conservative critics have in mind when they complain about the loss of "values," the depravity of mass civilization and the degeneration of traditional culture by the media. The idea is, rather, to be away with all these nasty things, and to survive, as an elite of happy pundits, in the nicer comforts offered by a country house.

Nonetheless, the workings of the mind industry have been analysed, in part, over and over again, sometimes with great ingenuity and insight. So far as the capitalist countries are concerned the critics have leveled their attacks mainly against the newer media and commercial advertising. Conservatives and Marxists alike have been all too ready to deplore their venial side. It is an objection which hardly touches the heart of the matter. Apart from the fact that it is perhaps no more immoral to profit from the mass-production of news or symphonies than from the mass-production of soap and tires, objections of this kind overlook the very characteristics of the mind industry. Its more advanced sectors have long since ceased to sell any goods at all. With increasing technological maturity, the material substrata, paper or plastic or celluloid, tend to vanish. Only in the more old-fashioned offshoots of the business, as for example in the book trade, does the commodity aspect of the product play an important economic role. In this respect, a radio station has nothing in common with a match

---

[4] The importance of the transistor radio in the Algerian revolution has been emphasized by Frantz Fanon, and the role of television in the political life of Castro's Cuba is a matter of common knowledge.

factory. With the disappearance of the material substratum the product becomes more and more abstract, and the industry depends less and less on selling it to its customers. If you buy a book, you pay for it in terms of its real cost of production; if you pick up a magazine, you pay only a fraction thereof; if you tune in on a radio or television program, you get it virtually free; direct advertising and political propaganda is something nobody buys—on the contrary, it is crammed down our throats. The products of the mind industry can no longer be understood in terms of a sellers' and buyers' market, or in terms of production costs: they are, as it were, priceless. The capitalist exploitation of the media is accidental and not intrinsic; to concentrate on their commercialization is to miss the point and to overlook the specific service which the mind industry performs for modern societies. This service is essentially the same all over the world, no matter how the industry is operated: under state, public or private management, within a capitalist or a socialist economy, on a profit or nonprofit basis. The mind industry's main business and concern is not to sell its product: it is to "sell" the existing order, to perpetuate the prevailing pattern of man's domination by man, no matter who runs the society, and by what means. Its main task is to expand and train our consciousness—in order to exploit it.

Since "immaterial exploitation" is not a familiar concept, it might be well to explain its meaning. Classical Marxism has defined very clearly the material exploitation to which the working classes have been subjected ever since the industrial revolution. In its crudest form, it is a characteristic of the period of the primary accumulation of capital. This holds true even for Socialist countries, as is evident from the example of Stalinist Russia and the early stages of the development of Red China. As soon as the bases of industrialization are laid, however, it becomes clear that material exploitation alone is insufficient to guarantee the continuity of the system. When the production of goods expands beyond the most immediate needs, the old proclamations of human rights, however watered down by the rhetoric of the establishment and however eclipsed by decades of hardship, famine, crises, forced labor and political terror, will now unfold their potential strength. It is in their very nature that, once proclaimed, they cannot be revoked. Again and again, people will try to take them at their face value and, eventually, to fight for their realization. Thus, ever since the great declarations of the eighteenth century, every rule of the few over the many, however organized, has faced the threat of revolution. Real democracy, as opposed to the formal façades of parliamentary democracy, does not exist anywhere in the world, but its ghost haunts every existing régime. Consequently, all the existing power structures must seek to obtain the consent, however passive, of their subjects. Even régimes which depend on the force of arms for their survival feel the need to justify themselves in the eyes of the world. Control of capital, of the means of production and of the armed forces is therefore no longer enough. The self-appointed elites who run modern societies must try to control people's minds. What each of us accepts or rejects, what we think and decide is now, here as well as in Vietnam, a matter of prime political concern: it would be too dangerous to leave these matters to ourselves. Material exploitation must camouflage itself in order to survive: immaterial exploitation has become its necessary corollary. The few cannot go on accumulating wealth unless they accumulate the power to manipulate the minds of the many. To expropriate manpower they have to expropriate the brain. What is being abolished in today's affluent societies, from Moscow to Los Angeles, is not exploitation, but our awareness of it.

It takes quite a lot of effort to maintain this state of affairs. There are alternatives to it. But since all of them would inevitably overthrow the prevailing powers, an entire industry is engaged in doing away with them, eliminating possible futures and reinforcing the present pattern of domination. There are several ways to achieve this end: on the one hand we find downright censorship, bans and a state monopoly on all the means of production of the mind industry; on the other hand, economic pressures, systematic distribution of "punishment and reward" and human engineering can do the job just as well and much more smoothly. The material pauperization of the last century is followed and replaced by the immaterial pauperization of today. Its most obvious manifestation is the decline in political options available to the citizen of the most advanced nations: a mass of political nobodies, over whose heads even collective suicide can be decreed, is opposed by an ever decreasing number of political moguls. That this state of affairs is readily accepted and voluntarily endured by the majority is the greatest achievement of the mind industry.

To describe its effects on present-day society is not, however, to describe its essence. The emergence of the textile industry has ruined the craftsman of India and caused widespread child labor in England, but these consequences do not necessarily follow from the existence of the mechanical loom. There is no more reason to suppose that the industrialization of the human mind must produce immaterial exploitation. It would even be fair to say that it will eventually, by its own logic, do away with the very results it has today. For this is the most fundamental of all its contradictions: in order to obtain consent, you have to grant a choice, no matter how marginal and deceptive; in order to harness the faculties of the human mind, you have to develop them, no matter how narrowly and how deformed. It may be a measure of the overwhelming power of the mind industry that none of us can escape its influence. Whether we like it or not, it enlists our participation in the system as a whole. But this participation may very well veer, one day, from the passive to the active, and turn out to threaten the very order it was supposed to uphold. The mind industry has a dynamic of its own which it cannot arrest, and it is not by chance but by necessity that in this movement there are currents which run contrary to its present mission of stabilizing the status quo. A corollary of its dialectical progress is that the mind industry, however closely supervised in its single operations, is never completely controllable as a whole. There are always leaks in it, cracks in the armor; no administration will ever trust it all the way.[5]

In order to exploit people's intellectual, moral and political faculties, you have got to develop them first. This is, as we have seen, the basic dilemma faced by today's media. When we turn our attention from the industry's consumers to its producers, the intellectuals, we find this dilemma aggravated and intensified. In terms of power, of course, there can be no question as to who runs the business. Certainly it is not the intellectuals who control the industrial establishment, but the establishment which controls them. There is precious little chance for the people who are productive to take over their means of production: this is just what the present structure is designed to prevent. However, even under present circumstances, the relationship is not without a certain ambiguity, since there is no way of running the mind industry without enlisting the services of at least a minority of men who can create something. To exclude them would be self-defeating. Of course, it is perfectly possible to use the whole stock of accumulated original work and have it adapted, diluted and processed for media use, and it may be well to remember that much of what purports to be new is in fact derivative. If we examine the harmonic and melodic structure of any popular song hit, it will most likely turn out to employ inventions of serious composers centuries ago. The same is true of the dramaturgical clichés of mediocre screenplays: watered down beyond recognition, they repeat traditional patterns taken from the drama and the novel of the past. In the long run, however, the parasitic use of inherited work is not sufficient to nourish the industry. However large a stock, you cannot sell out forever without replenishment; hence the need "to make it new," the media's dependence on men capable of innovation, in other words, on potential troublemakers. It is inherent in the process of creation that there is no way to predict its results. Consequently, intellectuals are, from the point of view of any power structure bent on its own perpetuation, a security risk. It takes consummate skill to "handle" them and to neutralize their subversive influence. All sorts of techniques, from the crudest to the most sophisticated, have been developed to this end: physical threat, blacklisting, moral and economic pressure on the one hand, overexposure, star-cult, cooptation into the power elite on the other, are the extremes of a whole gamut of manipulation. It would be worthwhile to write a manual analysing these techniques. They have one thing in common, and that is that they offer short-term, tactical answers to a problem which, in principle, cannot be resolved. This is an industry which has to rely, as its primary source, on the very minorities with whose elimination

---

[5] A good example of this instinctive sense of insecurity shared by the most entrenched political powers is offered by Senator Joseph McCarthy's lunatic crusade against Hollywood producers, actors and writers. Most of them had shown an abject loyalty to the demands of the industry throughout their career, and yet no abnegation of their talents could free them from suspicion. Much in the same way, Stalin never trusted even his most subservient trustees of the intellectual establishment.

it is entrusted: those whose aim it is to invent and produce *alternatives*. Unless it succeeds in exploiting and manipulating its producers, the mind industry cannot hope to exploit and manipulate its consumers. On the level of production even more than on the level of consumption, it has to deal with partners who are potential enemies. Engaged in the proliferation of human consciousness, the media proliferate their own contradictions.

Criticism of the mind industry which fails to recognize its central ambiguities is either idle or dangerous. It is a measure of their limitations that many media critics never seem to reflect on their own position, just as if their work were not itself a part of what it criticizes. The truth is that no one can nowadays express any opinion at all without making use of the industry, or rather, without being used by it.[6]

Anyone incapable of dialectical thinking is doomed as soon as he starts grappling with this subject. He will be trapped to a point where even retreat is no longer possible. There are many who feel revolted at the thought of entering a studio or negotiating with the slick executives who run the networks. They detest, or profess to detest, the very machinery of the industry, and would like to withdraw into some abode of refinement. Of course, no such refuge really exists. The seemingly exclusive is just another, slightly more expensive line of styling within the same giant industrial combine.

Let us rather try to draw the line between intellectual integrity and defeatism. To opt out of the mind industry, to refuse any dealings with it may well turn out to be a reactionary course. There is no hermitage left for those whose job is to speak out and to seek innovation. Retreat from the media will not even save the intellectual's precious soul from corruption. It might be a better idea to enter the dangerous game, to take and calculate our risks. Instead of innocence, we need determination. We must know very precisely the monster we are dealing with, and we must be continually on our guard to resist the overt or subtle pressures which are brought to bear on us.

The rapid development of the mind industry, its rise to a key position in modern society, has profoundly changed the role of the intellectual. He finds himself confronted with new threats and new opportunities. Whether he knows it or not, whether he likes it or not, he has become the accomplice of a huge industrial complex which depends for its survival on him, as he depends on it for his own. He must try, at any cost, to use it for his own purposes, which are incompatible with the purposes of the mind machine. What it upholds he must subvert. He may play it foul or straight, he may win or lose the game; but he would do well to remember that there is more at stake than his own fortune.

[6] Among those who blithely disregard this fact I would mention some European philosophers, for example Romano Guardini, Max Picard and Ortega y Gasset. In America, this essentially conservative stand has been emulated by Henry Miller and a number of Beat Generation writers.

FROM counterblast

by MARSHALL McLUHAN

In this brief selection, media theorizer Marshall McLuhan discusses some of the profound cultural changes that result from changes in man's means of communication.

Media are artificial extensions of sensory existence.

each an externalized species of the inner genus sensation. The cultural environment created by externalization of modes of sensation now favours the predominance of one sense or another. These species struggle through mutations in a desperate attempt at adaptation and survival.

Accidents foster an uneven rate of development of communication facilities. Circumstances fostering in one age painting, sculpture, music, may produce a bulwark against the effects of, say, printing. But the same bulwark may be quite useless before the impact of movies or TV.

Improvements in the means of communication are based on a shift from one sense to another. This involves a rapid refocusing of all previous experience. Any change in the means of communication produces a chain of revolutionary consequences at every level of culture and politics. Because of the complexity of this process, prediction and control are impossible.

John Donne and George Herbert transferred to the new printed page of the 17th century many effects which had previously been popular in the pictorial world of the later Middle Ages. For them print had made the visual arts recessive and quaint. In this century the sudden predominance of the graphic arts has made print recessive. We filter one past culture through the screen of others and of our own—a game we play with whole cultures and epochs as easily as we could previously combine phrases from two languages.

With writing comes inner speech, the dialogue with oneself—a result of translating the verbal into the visual (writing) and translating the visual into the verbal (reading)—a complex process for which we pay a heavy psychic and social price—the price, as James Joyce puts it, of ABCED-minded-ness. Literate man experiences an inner psychic withdrawal from his external senses which gives him a heavy psychic and social limp. But the rewards are very rich.

Today we experience in reverse, what pre-literate man faced with the advent of writing. Today we are, in a technical if not literary sense, post-literate. Literacy: a brief phase.

Aristotle described speech as the arrest of the flowing of thought. Today speech begins to look like an obsolete technology. The sounds we utter are structured in acoustic space by noise spaced in silence. What silence is to acoustic space, darkness is to visual space. Speech structures interpersonal distances. These distances aren't just physical, but emotional and cultural. We involuntarily raise our

voices when speaking to those who don't understand our language. Entering a silent house, we call
a name in a tone intended to extend throughout
that space.

Words are an orchestral harmony of touch, taste,
sight, sound. Writing is the abstraction of the visual
from this complex. With writing comes power: command over space.

Manuscript culture, based on parchment and the
scarcity of writing materials, made for a high degree
of memorization—the inevitable result of the scarcity
of manuscripts, the slowness of reading them and
the difficulty of referring to them. Everybody leaned
heavily on oral means for the intake of information.
Publication of a poem meant its oral delivery by the
author. Teachers gave out texts, commented on
variants and discussed the figures of speech, wit
and decorum of the author phrase by phrase. This
involved providing etymologies of the words, the history of their various meanings and their social back-
grounds and implications. Each student, therefore,
made his own grammar, his own dictionary, rhetoric
and commonplace book. Such was the practice in
classrooms even in Shakespeare's day, a century
after the invention of printing.

But, so far as the classroom was concerned, printing was decisive. Uniform texts became available
along with grammars and dictionaries, not only of
Latin but of Greek, Hebrew, and the vernacular
tongues. Print made not only many more past texts
available, but also large quantities of chronicle and
historical matter which the medieval classroom
could not possibly have found time to copy or discuss. From the point of view of previous education,
this made a shambles. The flow of information
shifted from wit, memory, and oral dialectics to
multilingual erudition. When the main channel of
information became the printed page, the critical
powers of the young couldn't be trained in the same

way. Print isolated the reader. The student who had formerly recited the lecture in a group and had then joined another group to discuss and dispute the points of the lecture was now alone with a text. In the same way, print isolated cultures, each in its own vernacular frame, where before all learning was in a single tongue.

Yet 16th century prose still retained many of the rapidly shifting perspectives of multiple levels of tone and meaning characteristic of group speech. It took two centuries of print to create prose on the page which maintained the tone and perspective of a single speaker. The individual scholar, alone with his text, had to develop habits of self-reliance which we still associate with the virtues of book culture. More and more learning was left to the unassisted industry of the individual. People were consumed by an "immoderate hydroptic thirst for humane learning and languages," in Donne's phrase, which went along with the first discovery of the smooth speed-ways of the printed page. No more stuttering pilgrimages through the crabbed columns of manuscript abbreviations. But it was a long time before people got to be at home with print. And by that time the newspaper page layout had begun to disturb the precarious equilibrium of 18th century book culture. The format of the 19th century newspaper page was like a dozen book pages set on a single sheet. The telegraph made this format the instantaneous global cross-section of a single day. This was no longer the book. Nor could the book stand up to this new cultural form born out of technology. The book tried to swallow this rival: Joyce in **Ulysses,** Eliot in **The Waste Land**—non-narrative epics which incorporate the newspaper art form.

The newspaper was merely the first of a quick succession of new information channels which challenged the cultural balance. But only the artists of our time have met or understood this challenge. With the arrival of print, Erasmus and his humanist colleagues saw exactly what had to be done in the classroom—and did it at once. But with the arrival of the press, nothing was done to accommodate its new modes of perception to an obsolete curriculum.

Education must always concentrate its resources at the point of major information intake. But from what sources do growing minds nowadays acquire most factual data and how much critical awareness is conferred at these points? It's a commentary on our extreme cultural lag that when we think of criticism of information flow we still use only the concept of book culture, namely, how much trust can be reposed in the words of the message. Yet the bias of each medium of communication is far more distorting than the deliberate lie.

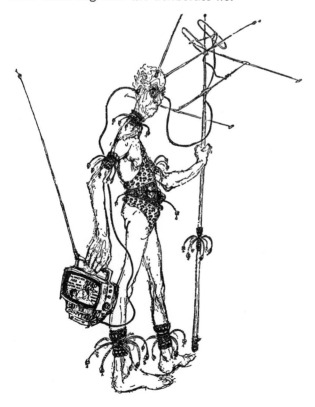

What if He Is Right?

Tom Wolfe

THE NEW LANGUAGES

by EDMUND CARPENTER

In this selection anthropologist Edmund Carpenter treats media as "languages" for expressing ideas and emotions. He compares the lineality, causality, and chronology of the old media with the simultaneity of the new, concluding that each has valuable uses.

> *Brain of the New World,*
> *What a task is thine,*
> *To formulate the modern*
> *. . . to recast poems, churches, art*
>
> WHITMAN

English is a mass medium. All languages are mass media. The new mass media—film, radio, TV—are new languages, their grammars as yet unknown. Each codifies reality differently; each conceals a unique metaphysics. Linguists tell us it's possible to say anything in any language if you use enough words or images, but there's rarely time; the natural course is for a culture to exploit its media biases.

Writing, for example, didn't record oral language; it was a new language, which the spoken word came to imitate. Writing encouraged an analytical mode of thinking with emphasis upon lineality. Oral languages tended to be polysynthetic, composed of great, tight conglomerates, like twisted knots, within which images were juxtaposed, inseparably fused; written communications consisted of little words chronologically ordered. Subject became distinct from verb, adjective from noun, thus separating actor from action, essence from form. Where preliterate man imposed form diffidently, temporarily—for such transitory forms lived but temporarily on the tip of his tongue, in the living situation—the printed word was inflexible, permanent, in touch with eternity: it embalmed truth for posterity.

This embalming process froze language, eliminated the art of ambiguity,

The New Languages: From *Explorations in Communication* by Edmund Carpenter and Marshall McLuhan. Copyright © 1960 by Beacon Press. Reprinted by permission of Beacon Press.

made puns "the lowest form of wit," destroyed word linkages. The word became a static symbol, applicable to and separate from that which it symbolized. It now belonged to the objective world; it could be seen. Now came the distinction between being and meaning, the dispute as to whether the Eucharist *was* or only *signified* the body of the Sacrifice. The word became a neutral symbol, no longer an inextricable part of a creative process.

Gutenberg completed the process. The manuscript page with pictures, colors, correlation between symbol and space, gave way to uniform type, the black-and-white page, read silently, alone. The format of the book favored lineal expression, for the argument ran like a thread from cover to cover: subject to verb to object, sentence to sentence, paragraph to paragraph, chapter to chapter, carefully structured from beginning to end, with value embedded in the climax. This was not true of great poetry and drama, which retained multi-perspective, but it was true of most books, particularly texts, histories, autobiographies, novels. Events were arranged chronologically and hence, it was assumed, causally; relationship, not being, was valued. The author became an *authority;* his data were serious, that is, *serially* organized. Such data, if sequentially ordered and printed, conveyed value and truth; arranged any other way, they were suspect.

The newspaper format brought an end to book culture. It offers short, discrete articles that give important facts first and then taper off to incidental details, which may be, and often are, eliminated by the make-up man. The fact that reporters cannot control the length of their articles means that, in writing them, emphasis can't be placed on structure, at least in the traditional linear sense, with climax or conclusion at the end. Everything has to be captured in the headline; from there it goes down the pyramid to incidentals. In fact there is often more in the headline than in the article; occasionally, no article at all accompanies the banner headline.

The position and size of articles on the front page are determined by interest and importance, not content. Unrelated reports from Moscow, Sarawak, London, and Ittipik are juxtaposed; time and space, as separate concepts, are destroyed and the *here* and *now* presented as a single Gestalt. Subway readers consume everything on the front page, then turn to page 2 to read, in incidental order, continuations. A Toronto banner headline ran: TOWNSEND TO MARRY PRINCESS; directly beneath this was a second headline: *Fabian Says This May Not Be Sex Crime.* This went unnoticed by eyes and minds conditioned to consider each newspaper item in isolation.

Such a format lends itself to simultaneity, not chronology or lineality. Items abstracted from a total situation aren't arranged in causal sequence, but presented holistically, as raw experience. The front page is a cosmic *Finnegans Wake.*

The disorder of the newspaper throws the reader into a producer role. The reader has to process the news himself; he has to co-create, to cooperate in the creation of the work. The newspaper format calls for the direct participation of the consumer.

In magazines, where a writer more frequently controls the length of his article, he can, if he wishes, organize it in traditional style, but the majority don't. An increasingly popular presentation is the printed symposium, which is little more than collected opinions, pro and con. The magazine format as a whole opposes lineality; its pictures lack tenses. In *Life,* extremes are juxtaposed: space ships and prehistoric monsters, Flemish monasteries and dope addicts. It creates a sense of urgency and uncertainty: the next page is unpredictable. One encounters rapidly a riot in Teheran, a Hollywood marriage, the wonders of the Eisenhower administration, a two-headed calf, a party on Jones beach, all sandwiched between ads. The eye takes in the page as a whole (readers may pretend this isn't so, but the success of advertising suggests it is), and the page—indeed, the whole magazine—becomes a single Gestalt where association, though not causal, is often lifelike.

The same is true of the other new languages. Both radio and TV offer short, unrelated programs, interrupted between and within by commercials. I say "interrupted," being myself an anachronism of book culture, but my children don't regard them as interruptions, as breaking continuity. Rather, they regard them as part of a whole, and their reaction is neither one of annoyance nor one of indifference. The ideal news broadcast has half a dozen speakers from as many parts of the world on as many subjects. The London correspondent doesn't comment on what the Washington correspondent has just said; he hasn't even heard him.

The child is right in not regarding commercials as interruptions. For the only time anyone smiles on TV is in commercials. The rest of life, in news broadcasts and soap operas, is presented as so horrible that the only way to get through life is to buy this product: then you'll smile. Aesop never wrote a clearer fable. It's heaven and hell brought up to date: Hell in the headline, Heaven in the ad. Without the other, neither has meaning.

There's pattern in these new media—not line, but knot; not lineality or causality or chronology, nothing that leads to a desired climax; but a Gordian knot without antecedents or results, containing within itself carefully selected elements, juxtaposed, inseparably fused; a knot that can't be untied to give the long, thin cord of lineality.

This is especially true of ads that never present an ordered, sequential, rational argument but simply present the product associated with desirable things or attitudes. Thus Coca-Cola is shown held by a beautiful blonde, who sits in a Cadillac, surrounded by bronze, muscular admirers, with the sun shining overhead. By repetition these elements become associated, in our minds, into a pattern of sufficient cohesion so that one element can magically evoke the others. If we think of ads as designed solely to sell products, we miss their main effect: to increase pleasure in the consumption of the product. Coca-Cola is far more than a cooling drink; the consumer participates, vicariously, in a much larger experience. In Africa, in Melanesia, to drink a Coke is to participate in the American way of life.

Of the new languages, TV comes closest to drama and ritual. It combines music and art, language and gesture, rhetoric and color. It favors simultaneity of visual and auditory images. Cameras focus not on speakers but on persons spoken to or about; the audience *hears* the accuser but *watches* the accused. In a single impression it hears the prosecutor, watches the trembling hands of the big-town crook, and sees the look of moral indignation on Senator Tobey's face. This is real drama, in process, with the outcome uncertain. Print can't do this; it has a different bias.

Books and movies only pretend uncertainty, but live TV retains this vital aspect of life. Seen on TV, the fire in the 1952 Democratic Convention threatened briefly to become a conflagration; seen on newsreel, it was history, without potentiality.

The absence of uncertainty is no handicap to other media, if they are properly used, for their biases are different. Thus it's clear from the beginning that Hamlet is a doomed man, but, far from detracting in interest, this heightens the sense of tragedy.

Now, one of the results of the time-space duality that developed in Western culture, principally from the Renaissance on, was a separation within the arts. Music, which created symbols in time, and graphic art, which created symbols in space, became separate pursuits, and men gifted in one rarely pursued the other. Dance and ritual, which inherently combined them, fell in popularity. Only in drama did they remain united.

It is significant that of the four new media, the three most recent are dramatic media, particularly TV, which combines language, music, art, dance. They don't, however, exercise the same freedom with time that the stage dares practice. An intricate plot, employing flash backs, multiple time perspectives and overlays, intelligible on the stage, would mystify on the screen. The audience has no time to think back, to establish relations between early hints and subsequent discoveries. The picture passes before the eyes too quickly; there are no intervals in which to take stock of what has happened and make conjectures of what is going to happen. The observer is in a more passive state, less interested in subtleties. Both TV and film are nearer to narrative and depend much more upon the episodic. An intricate time construction can be done in film, but in fact rarely is. The soliloquies of *Richard III* belong on the stage; the film audience was unprepared for them. On stage Ophelia's death was described by three separate groups: one hears the announcement and watches the reactions simultaneously. On film the camera flatly shows her drowned where "a willow lies aslant a brook."

Media differences such as these mean that it's not simply a question of communicating a single idea in different ways but that a given idea or insight belongs primarily, though not exclusively, to one medium, and can be gained or communicated best through that medium.

Thus the book was ideally suited for discussing evolution and progress. Both belonged, almost exclusively, to book culture. Like a book, the idea of progress was an abstracting, organizing principle for the interpretation and comprehension of the incredibly complicated record of human experience. The sequence of events was believed to have a direction, to follow a given course along an axis of time; it was held that civilization, like the reader's eye (in J. B. Bury's words), "has moved, is moving, and will move in a desirable direction. Knowledge will advance, and with that advance, reason and decency must increasingly prevail among men." Here we see the three main elements of book lineality: the line, the point moving along that line, and its movement toward a desirable goal.

The Western conception of a definite moment in the present, of the present as a definite moment or a definite point, so important in book-dominated languages, is absent, to my knowledge, in oral languages. Absent as well, in oral societies, are such animating and controlling ideas as Western individualism and three-dimensional perspective, both related to this conception of the definite moment, and both nourished, probably bred, by book culture.

Each medium selects its ideas. TV is a tiny box into which people are crowded and must live; film gives us the wide world. With its huge screen, film is perfectly suited for social drama, Civil War panoramas, the sea, land erosion, Cecil B. DeMille spectaculars. In contrast, the TV screen has room for two, at the most three, faces, comfortably. TV is closer to stage, yet different. Paddy Chayefsky writes:

The theatre audience is far away from the actual action of the drama. They cannot see the silent reactions of the players. They must be told in a loud voice what is going on. The plot movement from one scene to another must be marked, rather than gently shaded as is required in television. In television, however, you can dig into the most humble, ordinary relationships; the relationship of bourgeois children to their mother, of middle-class husband to his wife, of white-collar father to his secretary—in short, the relationships of the people. We relate to each other in an incredibly complicated manner. There is far more exciting drama in the reasons why a man gets married than in why he murders someone. The man who is unhappy in his job, the wife who thinks of a lover, the girl who wants to get into television, your father, your mother, sister, brothers, cousins, friends—all these are better subjects for drama than Iago. What makes a man ambitious? Why does a girl always try to steal her kid sister's boy friends? Why does your uncle attend his annual class reunion faithfully every year? Why do you always find it depressing to visit your father? These are the substances of good television drama; and the deeper you probe into and examine the twisted, semi-formed complexes of emotional entanglements, the more exciting your writing becomes.[1]

[1] *Television Plays*, New York, Simon and Schuster, 1955, pp. 176–78.

This is the primary reason, I believe, why Greek drama is more readily adapted to TV than to film. The boxed-in quality of live TV lends itself to static literary tragedy with greater ease than does the elastic, energetic, expandable movie. Guthrie's recent movie of *Oedipus* favored the panoramic shot rather than the selective eye. It consisted of a succession of tableaux, a series of elaborate, unnatural poses. The effect was of congested groups of people moving in tight formation as though they had trained for it by living for days together in a self-service elevator. With the lines, "I grieve for the City, and for myself and you . . . and walk through endless ways of thought," the inexorable tragedy moved to its horrible "come to realize" climax as though everyone were stepping on everyone else's feet.

The tight, necessary conventions of live TV were more sympathetic to Sophocles in the Aluminium Hour's *Antigone*. Restrictions of space are imposed on TV as on the Greek stage by the size and inflexibility of the studio. Squeezed by physical limitations, the producer was forced to expand the viewer's imagination with ingenious devices.

When T. S. Eliot adapted *Murder in the Cathedral* for film, he noted a difference in realism between cinema and stage:

Cinema, even where fantasy is introduced, is much more realistic than the stage. Especially in an historical picture, the setting, the costume, and the way of life represented have to be accurate. Even a minor anachronism is intolerable. On the stage much more can be overlooked or forgiven; and indeed, an excessive care for accuracy of historical detail can become burdensome and distracting. In watching a stage performance, the member of the audience is in direct contact with the actor playing a part. In looking at a film, we are much more passive; as audience, we contribute less. We are seized with the illusion that we are observing an actual event, or at least a series of photographs of the actual event; and nothing must be allowed to break this illusion. Hence the precise attention to detail.[2]

If two men are on a stage in a theatre, the dramatist is obliged to motivate their presence; he has to account for their existing on the stage at all. Whereas if a camera is following a figure down a street or is turned to any object whatever, there is no need for a reason to be provided. Its grammar contains that power of statement of motivation, no matter what it looks at.

In the theatre, the spectator sees the enacted scene as a whole in space, always seeing the whole of the space. The stage may present only one corner of a large hall, but that corner is always totally visible all through the scene. And the spectator always sees that scene from a fixed, unchanging distance and from an angle of vision that doesn't change. Perspective

[2] George Hoellering and T. S. Eliot, *Film of Murder in the Cathedral,* New York, Harcourt Brace Jovanovich, 1952, p. vi; London, Faber & Faber, 1952.

may change from scene to scene, but within one scene it remains constant. Distance never varies.

But in film and TV, distance and angle constantly shift. The same scene is shown in multiple perspective and focus. The viewer sees it from here, there, then over here; finally he is drawn inexorably into it, becomes part of it. He ceases to be a spectator. Balázs writes:

Although we sit in our seats, we do not see Romeo and Juliet from there. We look up into Juliet's balcony with Romeo's eyes and look down on Romeo with Juliet's. Our eye and with it our conscious-ness is identified with the characters in the film, we look at the world out of their eyes and have no angle of vision of our own. We walk amid crowds, ride, fly, or fall with the hero and if one character looks into the other's eyes, he looks into our eyes from the screen, for, our eyes are in the camera and become identical with the gaze of the characters. They see with our eyes. Herein lies the psychological act of identification. Nothing like this "identifi-cation" has ever occurred as the effect of any other system of art and it is here that the film manifests its absolute artistic novelty.

Not only can we see, in the isolated "shots" of a scene, the very atoms of life and their innermost secrets revealed at close quarters, but we can do so without any of the intimate secrecy being lost, as always happens in the exposure of a stage performance or of a painting. The new theme which the new means of expression of film art revealed was not a hurricane at sea or the eruption of a volcano: it was perhaps a solitary tear slowly welling up in the corner of a human eye.

Not to speak does not mean that one has nothing to say. Those who do not speak may be brimming over with emotions which can be expressed only in forms and pictures, in gesture and play of feature. The man of visual culture uses these not as substitutes for words, as a deaf-mute uses his fingers.[3]

The gestures of visual man are not intended to convey concepts that can be expressed in words, but inner experiences, nonrational emotions, which would still remain unexpressed when everything that can be told has been told. Such emotions lie in the deepest levels. They cannot be approached by words that are mere reflections of concepts, any more than musical experiences can be expressed in rational concepts. Facial expres-sion is a human experience rendered immediately visible without the in-termediary of words. It is Turgenev's "living truth of the human face."

Printing rendered illegible the faces of men. So much could be read from paper that the method of conveying meaning by facial expression fell into

[3] Béla Balázs, *Theory of Film*, New York, Roy Publishers, 1953, pp. 48, 31, 40; London, Denis Dobson, 1952.

desuetude. The press grew to be the main bridge over which the more remote interhuman spiritual exchanges took place; the immediate, the personal, the inner, died. There was no longer need for the subtler means of expression provided by the body. The face became immobile; the inner life, still. Wells that dry up are wells from which no water is dipped.

Just as radio helped bring back inflection in speech, so film and TV are aiding us in the recovery of gesture and facial awareness—a rich, colorful language, conveying moods and emotions, happenings and characters, even thoughts, none of which could be properly packaged in words. If film had remained silent for another decade, how much faster this change might have been!

Feeding the product of one medium through another medium creates a new product. When Hollywood buys a novel, it buys a title and the publicity associated with it: nothing more. Nor should it.

Each of the four versions of the *Caine Mutiny*—book, play, movie, TV—had a different hero: Willie Keith, the lawyer Greenwald, the United States Navy, and Captain Queeg, respectively. Media and audience biases were clear. Thus the book told, in lengthy detail, of the growth and making of Ensign William Keith, American man, while the movie camera with its colorful shots of ships and sea, unconsciously favored the Navy as hero, a bias supported by the fact the Navy cooperated with the movie makers. Because of stage limitations, the play was confined, except for the last scene, to the courtroom, and favored the defense counsel as hero. The TV show, aimed at a mass audience, emphasized patriotism, authority, allegiance. More important, the cast was reduced to the principals and the plot to its principles; the real moral problem—the refusal of subordinates to assist an incompetent, unpopular superior—was clear, whereas in the book it was lost under detail, in the film under scenery. Finally, the New York play, with its audience slanted toward Expense Account patronage—Mr. Sampson, Western Sales Manager for the Cavity Drill Company—became a morality play with Willie Keith, innocent American youth, torn between two influences: Keefer, clever author but moral cripple, and Greenwald, equally brilliant but reliable, a businessman's intellectual. Greenwald saves Willie's soul.

The film *Moby Dick* was in many ways an improvement on the book, primarily because of its explicitness. For *Moby Dick* is one of those admittedly great classics, like *Robinson Crusoe* or Kafka's *Trial,* whose plot and situation, as distilled apart from the book by time and familiarity, are actually much more imposing than the written book itself. It's the drama of Ahab's defiance rather than Melville's uncharted leviathan meanderings that is the greatness of *Moby Dick*. On film, instead of laborious tacks through leagues of discursive interruptions, the most vivid descriptions of whales and whaling become part of the action. On film, the viewer was constantly aboard ship: each scene an instantaneous shot of whaling life, an effect achieved in the book only by illusion, by constant, detailed reference. From start to finish, all the action of the film served to develop what was most central to the theme—a man's magnificent and blasphemous pride in attempting to destroy the brutal, unreasoning force that maims him and turns man-made order into chaos. Unlike the book, the film gave a spare, hard, compelling dramatization, free of self-conscious symbolism.

Current confusion over the respective roles of the new media comes largely from a misconception of their function. They are art-forms, not substitutes for human contact. Insofar as they attempt to usurp speech and personal, living relations, they harm. This, of course, has long been one of the problems of book culture, at least during the time of its monopoly of Western middle-class thought. But this was never a legitimate function of books, nor of any other medium. Whenever a medium goes claim jumping, trying to work areas where it is ill-suited, conflicts occur with other media, or, more accurately, between the vested interests controlling each. But, when media simply exploit their own formats, they become complementary and cross-fertile.

Some people who have no one around talk to cats, and you can hear their voices in the next room, and they sound silly, because the cat won't answer, but that suffices to maintain the illusion that their world is made up of living people, while it is not. Mechanized mass media reverse this: now mechanical cats talk to humans. There's no genuine feedback.

This charge is often leveled by academicians at the new media, but it holds equally for print. The open-mouthed, glaze-eyed TV spectator is merely the successor of the passive, silent, lonely reader whose head moved back and forth like a shuttlecock.

When we read, another person thinks for us: we merely repeat his mental process. The greater part of the work of thought is done for us. This is why it relieves us to take up a book after being occupied by our own thoughts. In reading, the mind is only the playground for another's ideas. People who spend most of their lives in reading often lose the

capacity for thinking, just as those who always ride forget how to walk. Some people read themselves stupid. Chaplin did a wonderful take-off of this in *City Lights,* when he stood up on a chair to eat the endless confetti that he mistook for spaghetti.

Eliot remarks: "It is often those writers whom we are lucky enough to know whose books we can ignore; and the better we know them personally, the less need we may feel to read what they write."

Frank O'Connor highlights a basic distinction between oral and written traditions:

"By the hokies, there was a man in this place one time by name of Ned Sullivan, and he had a queer thing happen to him late one night and he coming up the Valley Road from Durlas." This is how a folk story begins, or should begin. . . . Yet that is how no printed short story should begin, because such a story seems tame when you remove it from its warm nest by the cottage fire, from the sense of an audience with its interjections, and the feeling of terror at what may lurk in the darkness outside.

Face-to-face discourse is not as selective, abstract, nor explicit as any mechanical medium; it probably comes closer to communicating an unabridged situation than any of them, and, insofar as it exploits the give-take of dynamic relationship, it's clearly the most indispensably human one.

Of course, there can be personal involvement in the other media. When Richardson's *Pamela* was serialized in 1741, it aroused such interest that in one English town, upon receipt of the last installment, the church bell announced that virtue had been rewarded. Radio stations have reported receiving quantities of baby clothes and bassinets when, in a soap opera, a heroine had a baby. One of the commonest phrases used by devoted listeners to daytime serials is that they "visited with" Aunt Jenny or Big Sister. BBC and *News Chronicle* report cases of women viewers who kneel before TV sets to kiss male announcers good night.

Each medium, if its bias is properly exploited, reveals and communicates a unique aspect of reality, of truth. Each offers a different perspective, a way of seeing an otherwise hidden dimension of reality. It's not a question of one reality being true, the others distortions. One allows us to see from here, another from there, a third from still another perspective; taken together they give us a more complete whole, a greater truth. New essentials are brought to the fore, including those made invisible by the "blinders" of old languages.

This is why the preservation of book culture is as important as the development of TV. This is why new languages, instead of destroying old ones, serve as a stimulant to them. Only monopoly is destroyed. When actor-collector Edward G. Robinson was battling actor-collector Vincent Price on art on TV's *$64,000 Challenge,* he was asked how the quiz had affected his life; he answered petulantly, "Instead of looking at the pictures in my art books, I now have to read them." Print, along with all old languages, including speech, has profited enormously from the development of the new media. "The more the arts develop," writes E. M. Forster, "the more they depend on each other for definition. We will borrow from painting first and call it pattern. Later we will borrow from music and call it rhythm."

The appearance of a new medium often frees older media for creative effort. They no longer have to serve the interests of power and profit. Elia Kazan, discussing the American theatre, says:

> Take 1900–1920. The theatre flourished all over the country. It had no competition. The box office boomed. The top original fare it had to offer was *The Girl of the Golden West*. Its bow to culture was fusty productions of Shakespeare. . . . Came the moving pictures. The theatre had to be better or go under. It got better. It got so spectacularly better so fast that in 1920–1930 you wouldn't have recognized it. Perhaps it was an accident that Eugene O'Neill appeared at that moment—but it was no accident that in that moment of strange competition, the theatre had room for him. Because it was disrupted and hard pressed, it made room for his experiments, his unheard-of subjects, his passion, his power. There was room for him to grow to his full stature. And there was freedom for the talents that came after his.[4]

Yet a new language is rarely welcomed by the old. The oral tradition distrusted writing, manuscript culture was contemptuous of printing, book culture hated the press, that "slag-heap of hellish passions," as one 19th century scholar called it. A father, protesting to a Boston newspaper about crime and scandal, said he would rather see his children "in their graves while pure in innocence, than dwelling with pleasure upon these reports, which have grown so bold."

What really disturbed book-oriented people wasn't the sensationalism of the newspaper, but its nonlineal format, its nonlineal codifications of experience. The motto of conservative academicians became: *Hold that line!*

A new language lets us see with the fresh, sharp eyes of the child; it offers the pure joy of discovery. I was recently told a story about a Polish couple who, though long resident in Toronto, retained many of the customs of their homeland. Their son despaired of ever getting his father to buy a suit cut in style or getting his mother to take an interest in Canadian life. Then he bought them a TV set, and in a matter of months a major change took place. One evening the mother remarked that "Edith Piaf is the latest thing on Broadway," and the father appeared in "the kind of suit executives wear on TV." For years the father had passed this same suit

[4] "Writers and Motion Pictures," *The Atlantic Monthly*, 199, 1957, p. 69.

in store windows and seen it both in advertisements and on living men, but not until he saw it on TV did it become meaningful. This same statement goes for all media: each offers a unique presentation of reality, which when new has a freshness and clarity that is extraordinarily powerful.

This is especially true of TV. We say, "We have a radio" but "We have television"—as if something had happened to us. It's no longer "The skin you love to touch" but "The Nylon that loves to touch you." We don't watch TV; it watches us: it guides us. Magazines and newspapers no longer convey "information" but offer ways of seeing things. They have abandoned realism as too easy: they substitute themselves for realism. *Life* is totally advertisements: its articles package and sell emotions and ideas just as its paid ads sell commodities.

Several years ago, a group of us at the University of Toronto undertook the following experiment: 136 students were divided, on the basis of their over-all academic standing of the previous year, into four equal groups who either (1) heard and saw a lecture delivered in a TV studio, (2) heard and saw this same lecture on a TV screen, (3) heard it over the radio, or (4) read it in manuscript. Thus there were, in the CBC studios, four controlled groups who simultaneously received a single lecture and then immediately wrote an identical examination to test both understanding and retention of content. Later the experiment was repeated, using three similar groups; this time the same lecture was (1) delivered in a classroom, (2) presented as a film (using the kinescope) in a small theatre, and (3) again read in print. The actual mechanics of the experiment were relatively simple, but the problem of writing the script for the lecture led to a consideration of the resources and limitations of the dramatic forms involved.

It immediately became apparent that no matter how the script was written and the show produced, it would be slanted in various ways for and against each of the media involved; no show could be produced that did not contain these biases, and the only real common denominator was the simultaneity of presentation. For each communication channel codifies reality differently and thus influences, to a surprising degree, the content of the message communicated. A medium is not simply an envelope that carries any letter; it is itself a major part of that message. We therefore decided not to exploit the full resources of any one medium, but to try to chart a middle-of-the-road course between all of them.

The lecture that was finally produced dealt with linguistic codifications of reality and metaphysical concepts underlying grammatical systems. It was chosen because it concerned a field in which few students could be expected to have prior knowledge; moreover, it offered opportunities for the use of gesture. The cameras moved throughout the lecture, and took close-ups where relevant. No other visual aids were used, nor were shots taken of the audience while the lecture was in progress. Instead, the cameras simply focused on the speaker for 27 minutes.

The first difference we found between a classroom and a TV lecture was the brevity of the latter. The classroom lecture, if not ideally, at least in practice, sets a slower pace. It's verbose, repetitive. It allows for greater elaboration and permits the lecturer to take up several *related* points. TV, however, is stripped right down; there's less time for qualifications or alternative interpretations and only time enough for *one* point. (Into 27 minutes we put the meat of a two-hour classroom lecture.) The ideal TV speaker states his point and then brings out different facets of it by a variety of illustrations. But the classroom lecturer is less subtle and, to the agony of the better students, repeats and repeats his identical points in the hope, perhaps, that ultimately no student will miss them, or perhaps simply because he is dull. Teachers have had captive audiences for so long that few are equipped to compete for attention via the new media.

The next major difference noted was the abstracting role of each medium, beginning with print. Edmund M. Morgan, Harvard Law Professor, writes:

One who forms his opinion from the reading of any record alone is prone to err, because the printed page fails to produce the impression or convey the idea which the spoken word produced or conveyed. The writer has read charges to the jury which he had previously heard delivered, and has been amazed to see an oral deliverance which indicated a strong bias appear on the printed page as an ideally impartial exposition. He has seen an appellate court solemnly declare the testimony of a witness to be especially clear and convincing which the trial judge had orally characterized as the most abject perjury.[5]

Selectivity of print and radio are perhaps obvious enough, but we are less conscious of it in TV, partly because we have already been conditioned to it by the shorthand of film. Balázs writes:

A man hurries to a railway station to take leave of his beloved. We see him on the platform. We cannot see the train, but the questing eyes of the man show us that his beloved is already seated in the train. We see only a close-up of the man's face, we see it twitch as if startled and then strips of light and shadow, light and shadow flit across it in quickening rhythm. Then tears gather in the eyes and that ends the scene. We are expected to know what happened and today we do know, but when I first saw this film in Berlin, I did not at once understand the end of this scene. Soon, however, everyone knew what had happened: the train had started and it was the lamps in its compartment which had thrown their light on the man's face as they glided past ever faster and faster.[6]

[5] G. Louis Joughin and Edmund M. Morgan, *The Legacy of Sacco and Vanzetti*, New York, Harcourt Brace Jovanovich, 1948, p. 34.

[6] Béla Balázs, *op. cit.*, pp. 35–36.

As in a movie theatre, only the screen is illuminated, and, on it, only points of immediate relevance are portrayed; everything else is eliminated. This explicitness makes TV not only personal but forceful. That's why stage hands in a TV studio watch the show over floor monitors, rather than watch the actual performance before their eyes.

The script of the lecture, timed for radio, proved too long for TV. Visual aids and gestures on TV not only allow the elimination of certain words, but require a unique script. The ideal radio delivery stresses pitch and intonation to make up for the absence of the visual. That flat, broken speech in "sidewalk interviews" is the speech of a person untrained in radio delivery.

The results of the examination showed that TV had won, followed by lecture, film, radio, and finally print. Eight months later the test was read-ministered to the bulk of the students who had taken it the first time. Again it was found that there were significant differences between the groups exposed to different media, and these differences were the same as those on the first test, save for the studio group, an uncertain group because of the chaos of the lecture conditions, which had moved from last to second place. Finally, two years later, the experiment was repeated, with major modifications, using students at Ryerson Institute. Marshall McLuhan reports:

In this repeat performance, pains were taken to allow each medium full play of its possibilities with reference to the subject, just as in the earlier experiment each medium was neutralized as much as possible. Only the mimeograph form remained the same in each experiment. Here we added a printed form in which an imaginative typographical layout was followed. The lecturer used the blackboard and permitted discussion. Radio and TV employed dramatization, sound effects and graphics. In the examination, radio easily topped TV. Yet, as in the first experiment, both radio and TV manifested a decisive advantage over the lecture and written forms. As a conveyor both of ideas and information, TV was, in this second experiment, apparently enfeebled by the deployment of its dramatic resources, whereas radio benefited from such lavishness. "Technology is explicitness," writes Lyman Bryson. Are both radio and TV more explicit than writing or lecture? Would a greater explicitness, if inherent in these media, account for the ease with which they top other modes of performance?[7]

Announcement of the results of the first experiment evoked considerable interest. Advertising agencies circulated the results with the comment that here, at last, was scientific proof of the superiority of TV. This was unfortunate and missed the main point, for the results didn't indicate the superiority of one medium over others. They merely directed attention

[7] From a personal communication to the author.

toward differences between them, differences so great as to be of kind rather than degree. Some CBC officials were furious, not because TV won, but because print lost.

The problem has been falsely seen as democracy *vs.* the mass media. But the mass media *are* democracy. The book itself was the first mechanical mass medium. What is really being asked, of course, is: can books' monopoly of knowledge survive the challenge of the new languages? The answer is: no. What should be asked is: what can print do better than any other medium and is that worth doing?

Students as Media Critics: A New Course

by NAT HENTOFF

In this article from **Evergreen Review** Nat Hentoff points out the need for independent monitoring and criticism of the media and suggests how the media student can make worthwhile contributions in this area.

I have been an obsessive reader of newspapers almost since I could read. And quite early on I began to wonder why newspapers never criticized each other. Or hardly ever. In Boston, where I grew up, the *Globe* would miss or goof an important story, but the paper's dereliction would go unnoticed in the *Traveler*. I moved to New York and saw that process of mutual self-protection at work in this city. I've talked to reporters around the country, and it's the same almost everywhere.

There have been some correctives through the years, notably A. J. Liebling's "The Wayward Press" in *The New Yorker*. Reading Liebling taught me more about the morphology of newspapers—and their failings—than I've learned from any other source. When Liebling died, the press was again almost immune to criticism. The weekly "press" sections in *Time* and *Newsweek* are severely limited as to space, and seldom dig deep or long enough into any particular instance of press misfeasance, obtuseness, or just plain

Students as Media Critics: A New Course: From *Evergreen Review* (November, 1969). Reprinted by permission of Nat Hentoff.

slumber. The professional journalism publications are, by and large, gray and cautious. An exception from time to time is *The Columbia Journalism Review,* but its circulation and impact are limited. For relatively brief periods, WCBS in New York monitored the press, including the magazines —first with Don Hollenbeck and later with Charles Collingwood. These were tart, incisive, knowledgeable essays, but the audience ratings were comparatively low, and so the series was dropped.

In television too, stations and networks do not criticize, do not expose each other. And, except for Jack Gould of the *Times,* Robert Lewis Shayon of *The Saturday Review,* and an exceedingly small group of other writers, the level of newspaper and magazine criticism of television is of an order of ingenuousness and laziness that hardly causes anxiety in network board rooms. As a matter of fact, the best television criticism in the country can be found in the opinions of Nicholas Johnson, a member of the FCC, but those opinions are, to say the least, not given wide currency in newspapers or on television. A brilliant, twenty-six-page statement by Johnson in the case of the complaints against WBAI for having Julius Lester on the air received, as I recall, only four paragraphs in the remote fastnesses of the back pages of the *Times.*

Because of a contentious resistance to vacuums in communications—or near-vacuums—I wrote a regular column of press criticism for *The Village Voice* for some ten years. Since I was usually the only game in town, I would get all kinds of leads from reporters about stories they wanted to cover for their papers and couldn't, about whole areas of vital news in the city that were left untouched by the dailies. And doing my own legwork and telephone checking, I found scores of instances of press distortion and omission. But it is impossible for one man to be anywhere near as comprehensive a critic of the press as necessary. Especially now. The populace at large, according to a recent Louis Harris survey, have "a strong trust in the nation's press," and in television as well. The latter—Tom Jefferson save us all—is "the public's favorite source of news."

The public, moreover, considers itself, according to Harris, "better informed today than they were five years ago." How "informed" do you think the public really is about the Black Panthers, about the Justice Department's war on dissent, about the thrust toward "preventive detention," about the Dickensian nature of the lower criminal courts throughout the country, about the manifold and convoluted conflicts of interest among congressmen, about the specific ways in which huge corporations influence legislation and governmental executive appointments, about the appalling ways in which the schools are failing nearly all children, about the revolutions to come in Latin America and Asia, about the stunning laxness of Federal "regulatory" agencies, about the continuous contempt for "the public interest" in municipal governments and state legislatures? And on and on and on.

It has never been more essential that the media be monitored and corrected and that stories and developments ignored by them be reported. Some of this, of course, is being done—by I. F. Stone, by Andrew Kopkind, and James Ridgeway, by *Ramparts,* by Liberation News Service, by the Newsreel, by various underground papers, by WBAI. But nowhere is there a place devoted entirely to the monitoring of the media, in all its forms.

Such a place is in operation now at New York University's Graduate School of Education. It's only a beginning, but hopefully it will grow, and hopefully similar centers will start in other colleges and universities. At NYU, where I'm now an adjunct professor, whatever that may prove to mean, I am starting with ten graduate students. There will be no lectures, no regular classroom meetings. We may not all meet together more than once or twice during the semester, and that probably in a local bar. I'll be in contact with individual students as they feel the need arises, but weeks may go by before I hear from some of them.

The ten students will be monitoring the media. One or more may focus on *The New York Times,* checking out the stories it runs and the stories it does not run. Others will be examining and comparing the network television news strips. And others will look into magazine reporting or will pursue reportorial interests of their own while noting how much of what they find is unknown to the media. The students themselves will decide the forms in which they'll present their findings. I expect some articles will result and, if they're substantial enough, they'll appear in this and in other magazines. Eventually, a series of broadcasts on the media can be coordinated and produced by the students on WBAI. I would also expect that the publications of the university itself will be under scrutiny.

The possibilities in the years ahead are without limit. I would like, for example, to see a team of students do extended reportage on the schools— all kinds of schools—with a depth of detail and analysis that is alien to, let us say, *The New York Times'* educational reporting. And it has been years since the quality of the judiciary in the New York City courts has been seriously and systematically examined. How did they become judges? On the basis of what qualifications? How much do they really know of— let alone empathize with—constitutional law? What is their "judicial temperament"? What do they know of the prisoners before them? What are the differences in sentences for the same crime? What are the effects of these sentences on a man's family?

How much internal democracy is there in particular unions? What do insurance compaines do besides sell insurance? What are their patterns of investments? Who *are* the trustees of various universities and what are the interconnections between *their* interests and the ways in which the universities invest their funds? And how much about these stories—and so many more—do you see in the daily papers and on television? And if not, why not?

What we're starting to do at NYU can so easily be done anywhere else. New buildings are not required. Nor are rigid credential criteria necessary for those faculty who will be resource people for the students. I mean credentials in the customary academic sense. There has been a good deal of rhetoric about introducing professionals from the outside into university life, and this is certainly one area in which only they make educational sense. On a part-time basis, people like Murray Kempton, Andy Kopkind, I. F. Stone, Ralph Nader, Ben Bagdikian, and others can set up basing points for monitoring the media at other universities. There are several former FCC members—Clifford Durr comes to mind—who would be exceptionally useful in terms of radio and television.

Nor need these basing points be limited to colleges and universities. This is a pursuit which would surely interest sizable numbers of high school students and, if they are not bound by arbitrary rules of procedure, they are likely to astonish both themselves and their teachers by the capacity for independent research they reveal as they look into how the newspapers and television stations in their cities function and do not function. As the concept of monitoring the media spreads into the secondary schools, there would finally be a widespread pre-college stimulus for the emergence of large numbers of people who will have been self-trained to read the press and to watch television critically and comparatively.

Centers for monitoring the media would also give support to those newspapermen who would like to vent their frustrations in a wider context than mutual commiseration sessions at bars. Many would volunteer information to such centers—usually with the proviso that their names not be used. And it's also possible that with proliferating independent criticism of the media in schools, newspapermen in some cities will be encouraged to start their own journals in which the objects of the muckraking will be the papers where they work. Just such a publication, the *Chicago Journalism Review,* is already in vigorous operation. It provides a persistently revealing dissection of the regular Chicago press, as well as television stations, and should be both a model and a conscience-prod to newspapermen in other cities. (*Chicago Journalism Review,* 11 East Hubbard Street, Chicago, Illinois 60611. Five dollars a year.)

Equally needed, maybe more so, are independent publications in which television personnel can disclose in detail the restrictions under which they work. And I mean the employees of "educational" as well as commercial stations. In all media, and television more than others, there are infinitely diverse forms of censorship and self-censorship. But as of now, the viewer has no way of becoming aware of how these pressures effectively limit what he is allowed to see. For one example, only after the Smothers Brothers had been fired by CBS, was it revealed that seventy-five percent of their shows during their last season had been censored in one way or another. Those who watched the series had no idea of what had been going on. No words had been blipped out. But whole sequences had been forbidden—two interviews with Dr. Spock, for instance—and innocuous "filler" material had been inserted instead.

In how many cities does the local Red Squad and the FBI have access to all raw coverage of demonstrations and marches? Quite a few, according to information I've been given from inside television newsrooms. But the general public does not know that. Who decides which guests are too "controversial" to appear on local and network talk shows? What are the criteria? Do you know? I don't. But I'm certain lists of the proscribed do exist.

Nor have I seen a carefully researched analysis in any city of the comparative news coverage of television stations and newspapers. How many stations simply take their leads from the morning paper? How much and what kinds of investigative reportage is there on local television? What stories do both newspapers and television miss? How do the combined media cover student rebellions in a given city? To what extent, if any, are student views given equitable expression? When, as is so often the case, the television station and the newspaper are under the same ownership, what kinds of stories and sources are omitted from both media?

As you can see, I have barely sketched the potential range for centers which would monitor the media. Six months or so from now, I'll report on what we've been doing at NYU. If there are any similar media probes going on elsewhere in the country, I'd like to know about them. There is no reason why there should not be hundreds—thousands—of A. J. Lieblings throughout this country. And, among them, teachers—from elementary school on up.

And that's my final point, for now. These centers ought not to be only for those who themselves intend to be reporters, analysts, makers of documentaries. A basically self-directed course in monitoring the media is, it seems to me, essential for anyone in this society who wants to know what the hell's going on. And that includes teachers, professional radicals, radical professionals, all kinds of activists. And, for that matter, even the passive voter.

Last April, a speaker at a meeting in New York of the American Newspaper Publishers Association complained of signs that some among the public were becoming quite hostile to the media. This augury, he said, appeared to reflect an "uninformed and even distrustful public." It is because more and more people are becoming aware of how uninformed they are that they are now increasingly distrustful of all those media which purportedly have been "informing" them all along.

The growth of this therapeutic distrust can be the foundation for much more intensified monitoring of the media to come.

STUDY QUESTIONS

1. In his essay Wesley C. Clark discusses the mass media as playing an important role in social change. Examine the current media. Do you see evidence that the media, as Clark says, shape our society? Are the contemporary media, in turn, being shaped by social changes? Examine a current social issue in light of (1) the media's role in bringing it to public attention and affecting public attitudes toward it, and (2) the effects it has had on the media.

2. Bagdikian looks to the changes that will result from the communications of the future, while Carpenter, McLuhan, and Enzensberger discuss changes that are now occurring. Can you name some of the changes in attitudes and customs that have resulted directly from changes in communications? What about new developments in education? Changes in personal and social relationships? Have the media changed each other? What is the relationship between the novel and the film? Between poetry and music?

3. Enzensberger does not view McLuhan's theories very favorably. However, many parallels can be found in the thinking of these two men. What, essentially, does each man say about the mass media and their effect upon our culture?

4. The reflective-projective theory that Loevinger proposes views the mass media as "mirrors of society that reflect an ambiguous image in which each observer projects or sees his own vision of himself and society." Thus, the audience is a key factor in change resulting from communication. Another FCC Commissioner, Kenneth A. Cox, places more emphasis on the role of the media. He says that "the media can build on existing society and can consciously and significantly influence it."* From your observation of the media today, do you see any conscious attempts by editors, writers, producers, directors, etc. to change society? Does it seem that the success of such attempts depends upon the audience's prior acceptance or rejection of the idea? How do these views relate to Larsen's concerns about violence in the media?

5. Edmund Carpenter says that "each medium, if its bias is properly exploited, reveals and communicates a unique aspect of reality, of truth." McLuhan also spoke of each medium having a particular bias. Think of a book you have read that has also been made into a movie. Do the differences in the two versions seem to stem from intrinsic biases of the two media? Does the book communicate things that the movie cannot, and vice versa?

6. The Commission on Freedom of the Press claimed that our society needs a "truthful, comprehensive, and intelligent account of the day's events in a context which gives them meaning." Hentoff says that these needs are not always satisfied in the media. Follow his suggestion and monitor one of the media serving your area to see whether the public has full access to information about all segments of the community.

---

* Kenneth A. Cox, "Can Broadcasting Help Achieve Social Reform?" *Journal of Broadcasting,* XII (Spring, 1968), 125.

BIBLIOGRAPHY FOR FURTHER STUDY

Agee, Warren K., ed. *Mass Media in a Free Society.* Lawrence, Kansas: The University Press of Kansas, 1969.

Bogart, Leo. "Mass Media in the Year 2000." *Gazette,* XIII (November 3, 1967), 221–35.

Carpenter, Edmund, and Ken Heyman. *They Became What They Beheld.* New York: Outerbridge & Dienstfrey, 1970.

Cox, Kenneth A. "Can Broadcasting Help Achieve Social Reform?" *Journal of Broadcasting,* XII (Spring, 1968), 117–30.

Duffy, Dennis. *Marshall McLuhan.* Toronto: The Canadian Publishers, 1969.

Edwards, Verne, E., Jr. *Journalism in a Free Society.* Dubuque, Iowa: Wm. C. Brown Company, 1970.

Emery, Edwin, Phillip H. Ault, and Warren K. Agee. *Introduction to Mass Communications.* 2nd ed. New York: Dodd, Mead & Company, 1965.

Gerald, James Edward. *The Social Responsibility of the Press.* Minneapolis: University of Minnesota Press, 1963.

Goldberg, Toby. "A Selective Bibliography of the Writings of and about Marshall McLuhan." *Journal of Broadcasting,* XII (Spring, 1968), 179–82.

Hall, Edward T. *The Silent Language.* New York: Doubleday, 1959.

Hall, Stuart, and Paddy Whannel. *The Popular Arts.* New York: Pantheon Books, 1965.

Harrison, Randall. "Nonverbal Communication: Explorations into Time, Space, Action and Object." In J. Campbell and H. Hepler, eds., *Dimensions in Communication.* Belmont, California: Wadsworth Publishing Company, 1965.

Klapper, Joseph T. *The Effects of Mass Communication.* New York: The Free Press of Glencoe, Inc., 1960.

Larsen, Otto N., ed. *Violence and the Mass Media.* New York: Harper & Row, 1968.

Leigh, Robert D., ed. *A Free and Responsible Press.* A Report of the Commission on Freedom of the Press. Chicago: University of Chicago Press, 1947.

McLuhan, Marshall. *Counterblast.* New York: Harcourt Brace Jovanovich, 1969.

————. *Understanding Media.* New York: McGraw-Hill, 1964.

————, and Quentin Fiore. *The Medium Is the Massage.* New York: Bantam Books, 1967.

Peterson, Theodore, Jay W. Jensen, and William L. Rivers. *The Mass Media and Modern Society.* New York: Holt, Rinehart and Winston, 1965.

"Playboy Interview: Marshall McLuhan." *Playboy,* XVI (March, 1969), 53 ff.

Schramm, Wilbur and William Rivers. *Responsibility in Mass Communication.* Rev. ed. New York: Harper & Row, 1969.

Seldes, Gilbert. *The New Mass Media: Challenge to a Free Society.* Washington, D.C.: Public Affairs Press, 1968.

Stephenson, William. *The Play Theory of Mass Communication.* Chicago: The University of Chicago Press, 1967.

Wolfe, Tom. "What If He Is Right?" *The Pump House Gang.* New York: Farrar, Straus & Giroux, 1968, pp. 135–70.

Worsnop, Richard L. "Competing Media." *Editorial Research Reports,* II (July 18, 1969), 533–54.

2^{THE}MEDIA

In the introduction to Part 1 we noted that each medium uniquely shapes what it presents. In other words, the means of communication is an intrinsic part of the message conveyed. (Marshall McLuhan goes so far as to say that the medium **is** the message.) Thus the nature of a society is profoundly affected by the types of media that are prevalent in it. From the time of Gutenberg until the twentieth century, print was predominant. This meant that messages appeared in a spatial context (on the printed page) and that the visual sense was emphasized. Today these orientations are changing; we are experiencing a virtual revolution in communications. Walter Ong writes that "a new age is upon us, and its shift from sight-emphasis to increased sound-emphasis spans this entire area from the diffusion of the word to the exploration of one's surroundings."*

This shift from sight to sound has occurred largely because of the development of electronic media. Ong describes some of the implications of these new media:

In their whole trend, modern developments in communications, while they have not slighted the visual, have given more play to the oral-aural, which a purely typographical culture had reduced to a record minimum in human life. The sequence of the development running from silent print through audiovisual telegraph to the completely aural radio is an obvious instance of increasing aural dominance. Even television belongs partially in this visual-to-aural series, being only equivocally a regression to visualism. For the visual element in television is severely limited. The amount of detail feasible on a television screen is far less than that visible on a movie screen and not remotely comparable to that tolerable and easily discernible in photographs. Details on television have to be filled in aurally, by explicit vocal explanation or by suggestion through music and sound effects. Silent television is hardly an engaging prospect.†

This emphasis on the aural sense is not the only implication of the electronic media; they are shaping our messages in many other ways as well. For instance, in his article "The New Languages," Edmund Carpenter referred to print as an "embalming process" and described the printed message as inflexible and permanent. In contrast, the electronic media, with their messages comprised partially of sound, cannot communicate with such precision. Rational thought is giving way to multi-sensory perception. The TV generation tends to respond to a communication with "I feel" rather than "I know."

But the media do not operate in isolation; they are also shaped by each other. The newer media have not only become alternatives to print but have also caused the print media to change. For instance, the immediacy and urgency of interviews conducted on radio and television probably inspired the intimate, question-and-answer interviews that are becoming increasingly

* Walter J. Ong, **The Barbarian Within** (New York: Macmillan, 1962), p. 225.
† **Ibid.**

popular in the print media. The electronic media have also broadened people's attitudes toward books and have increased the variety of ways in which literature can be experienced. No longer is a book considered an object to be preserved in libraries. A poem is no longer merely set on a printed page; it may now be read aloud—often by the poet himself—and conceived as a media "production."

The print media also influence the electronic. For example, the magazine format has been adopted by some television news programs. One very significant change—which can be at least partially attributed to the influence of the print media—is in the audiences the media attempt to attract. One tends to associate the print media with small, selective audiences and the electronic media with mass audiences, but this distinction seems to be blurring. The broadcast networks and commercial film industries have recently been adopting a marketing approach that is traditionally associated with the print media: aiming their programs and films at small, homogeneous audiences rather than at the masses. For example, radio stations direct their programing toward one segment of a small community, some even making such fine distinctions as early versus late teens. Experimental and art films now compete with films which were designed to fit a formula attractive to wide audiences. The steady diet of escapism offered on commercial television is now spiced with shows with socially significant themes. Although films like **The Sound of Music** and television shows like **Petticoat Junction** are still in the majority, a viewer now has access to quality productions that draw a relatively small audience. **Easy Rider** did not enjoy the broad appeal of **Love Story,** but it served a significant segment of the film-going audience.

Part 2 deals with the technical and physical potentials and limitations of the print and electronic media. In reading the selections, the media student should keep in mind not only the differences between the print and electronic media but the implications of these differences. It is impossible to make an accurate evaluation of a communication without considering the characteristics of the medium through which it was presented.

Major Market Obstacles

Accord on Agricultural Preferences and
Commonwealth Sugar Producers Seen

The Print Media

storation of Cuts in

e Sharing Also

res New Levies

FRANK LYNN

to The New York Times

, May 12—Governor

said today that ad-

ate taxes would be

to finance new state

rochial schools and

including New York

ernor said he favored

state aid in both

added that the Legis-

ld have to make the

on, including the one

axes to increase to

added aid.

tional aid would be

million in the cur-

year for parochial

d about $75-million

on of cuts that had

in revenue-sharing

calities.

illion for City

kefeller's linking of

chial school and

ring aid was viewed

islators as apparent-

npt to put pressure

can legislators who

nt additional paro-

aid into supporting

the localities.

would receive about

of the restored

ring funds.

rnor also indicated

conference that he

publican legislative

ıld make the final

on which of the

on in taxes pro-

e New York City

ld be authorized by

ure.

kefeller said flatly

ouncil leaders would

ted to the discus-

tax package, and

uestions on wheth-

indsay would par-

By ANTHONY LEWIS
Special to The New York Times

BRUSSELS, Thursday, May 13—The negotiations on enlargement of the Common Market made major progress early today that brought final agreement into view.

The foreign ministers of the six members and the British negotiator, Geoffrey Rippon, settled two key issues:

First, Commonwealth sugar producers will get assurances of access to the enlarged community to sell their sugar. This agreement was subject to consultation with the countries concerned.

Second, Britain will be allowed to adjust gradually to the community's agricultural system, with its internal market preferences.

Agreement on those technical issues meant something much broader than the complicated details. It signaled a long political advance toward Britain's acceptance in a united Western Europe.

The way is now clear for Prime Minister Heath and President Pompidou to meet next week in an extremely hopeful atmosphere. Those favoring British entry wanted a negotiating breakthrough before the leaders' meeting, and now they have it.

There remains one issue on which Britain and the Six are not agreed or even approaching a solution. That is the right of New Zealand to sell her butter and cheese, much of which now goes to Britain, in the Community after Britain joins. New

Continued on Page 7, Column 1

$85.3-Million fo

Is Attached to M

and Sent to the

ACTION HAILED

Last-Minute Swi

Victory to Force

Ford, G.O.P.

By MARJORIE
Special to The New Y

WASHINGTON,

In a stunning rev

earlier stand, the

today to revive the

sial supersonic tra

gram.

A series of last-r

switches provided

197 margin by w

favoring the airline

life, at least tempo

project that both hou

gress halted less

months ago.

"We had it beat u

few minutes," Rep

Silvio O. Conte, Re

Massachusetts, said

The $85.3-million

liner was attached t

mental money bill,

House then passed.

fight now shifts to

where the outlook is

Hailing the Hou

President Nixon issu

ment strongly urgin

ate to vote the same

Many Jobs L

The President rea

earlier pledge that

will not be committ

duction until all env

concerns have been

satisfied." Fear that

would have an adve

upon the environme

factor in its earlier

The effort to rescu

gram, kept low-key

House Unit Agrees on Bill
For New Welfare System

By WARREN WEAVER Jr.
Special to The New York Times

WASHINGTON, May 12—The House Ways and Means Committee completed action today on an $8.8-billion bill that would completely revise the nation's much-criticized welfare system and make significant changes in Medicare and Social Security.

The major provisions of the bill would do the following:

¶Establish an income floor for poor families, $2,400 for a family of four, to be paid entirely from Federal funds. Such benefits would also go to the working poor but would taper off as their income increased.

¶Have the Federal government over a three-year period take over the adult welfare programs that aid the aged,

CITY ASKS CONTROL
OF SCHOOL BUDGET

Council Sends Bill to Albany
on Matter of Spending—
Board Attacks Measure

By EDWARD RANZAL

A bill that would permit the

The American Periodical Press and Its Impact

by ROLAND E. WOLSELEY

Journalism Professor Roland Wolseley discusses magazines in the United States, reaffirming that they are an important medium today. He considers both the impact of particular magazines and the impact of the magazine industry as a whole.

While this article was being written the world of the periodical press in the U.S.A. was the maker of front-page news. One of the country's oldest and most famous magazines, *The Saturday Evening Post,* died of malnutrition, i.e., of lack of advertising revenue. At its death, almost its 150th birthday anniversary, it had more than three million subscribers and newsstand buyers; a few months before it had in excess of six million, but half the subscription list was dropped in an economy move that was unsuccessful.

Too much circulation is a disease from which a number of American magazines have suffered in the past two decades. On the surface it appears to be a paradoxical situation. Generally speaking, in all print journalism it has for years been the rule that the higher the circulation the higher the advertising rate and consequently the greater the income. This formula still is followed, by and large. But an enormously expensive magazine to manufacture and distribute by the millions of copies each week (in recent years every other week), as was the *Post* and as were such other giants of circulation that succumbed at mid-century (*Collier's, Coronet, American,* and *Woman's Home Companion* were among them) must enlarge the formula to include 'if costs of production and distribution are kept in ratio'.

Once, too, magazines and newspapers could take for granted that if they offered an advertiser the readers he wanted they could count on him to buy the space to reach those readers. But today there is a new type of competitor: broadcasting, and particularly television. It can tell an ad-

The American Periodical Press and Its Impact: From *Gazette,* International Journal of the Science of the Press, vol. 15 (1969). Reprinted by permission.

vertiser that he can reach the mass of the people through television sets, of which in the U.S. there now are more in use than there are motor cars or telephones. Since television's arrival as an advertising competitor, two decades ago, magazines of mass circulation have had problems.

All this about the failure of widely-known American magazines may leave the impression that the periodical press is in an unhealthy state. But this conclusion has no basis in fact. On the contrary, the health of this industry as a whole is sound. The animal kingdom was not destroyed, centuries ago, when the dinosaurs, and almost all other huge animals, died out. Similarly, some of the giant magazines have not been able to adjust to new competition, new tastes, new climates of opinion, and a changing economic order. But there are at least 20,000 periodicals in the U.S.A., and the handful of huge-circulation publications is only a small, if widely-publicized, minority.

To understand the American periodical press and its impact it is necessary to see it whole. Only a few generalizations can be made about the entire industry, for it is in many segments. In fact, neither the industry itself nor the public at which it is aimed agrees on what that industry includes. To most Americans the word *magazine* (the term *periodical* is not much used) connotes a publication, weekly or monthly, intended either for all persons, as is *The Reader's Digest,* or for a large portion of the population, as is *McCall's* or *Ladies' Home Journal,* both multi-million circulation periodicals for women. And many persons employed in this consumer or general area of magazinedom take the same narrow view. In fact, the most widely used reports and studies of the industry usually cover only the consumer books (in the jargon of the publishing business a magazine often is called a *book,* to the utter confusion of outsiders), as if the thousands of small periodicals did not count. This situation came about, of course, because the bulk of the dollar investment in advertising space is in the consumer area: these magazines have been the big money makers. Actually the majority of the consumer magazines do not have large circulations despite their broad content.

Just what kind of publication the others are considered by the owners of the consumer magazines is not clear. Those others exist, just the same, and are far greater numerically and in the long run have a different and perhaps greater impact.

Depending upon how you count them, the consumer magazines may number as few as three and as many as 900. Perhaps *The Reader's Digest,* with 27,000,000 circulation, is the only true American consumer magazine left. The figure 900 is reached by including those that attempt to reach a wide public. The majority have small circulation and little advertising. They print trivia. They include sensational, sexy adventure magazines for boys and men; various fan publications for the worshippers of cinema idols, sports stars, and other entertainers; various collections of thin articles about hobbies; and numerous attempts to catch the teen-agers' coins with magazines telling the girls how to apply cosmetics and the boys how to become a professional football player.

The remaining 19,100 are for the most part the actual core of the magazine press. That figure, in round numbers, includes about 10,000 known as industrial periodicals but more commonly called house organs or company magazines, and are ignored by the entrepreneurs in the business because they do not accept advertising and are given to readers, who are employees of a company, its customers, its dealers, or its prospects. Also in the 19,100 are 2,500 business magazines, that is, commercially-published periodicals catering to the business world and ranging from the austere *Fortune,* published by Time Inc., to the highly specialized *Roads and Streets,* issued by the Reuben H. Donnelley Corp., which has 17 others equally specialized. And it also includes about 400 published by associations, embracing the *National Geographic* and the *Journal of the American Medical Association,* two of the most profitable enterprises in the business.

To these can be added about 1,500 that deal with religion, 300 magazines of education at different levels, 200 about labor, and the remaining thousands that are devoted to such subjects as science, specialized sports, all of the arts, and various juvenilia.

In America, it appears, if three or more people get together their first act is to form a committee and their second is to launch a publication; generally it is a magazine.

The periodical press in the U.S. therefore is overwhelmingly composed of specialized journals. Yet those who trace the press's current fortunes insist upon judging it by the fate of a minority of large periodicals hardly typical of the entire industry.

The situation is made even more complicated by the realization by some of the larger publishing companies that issue consumer magazines that the specialized field is a less risky one and that a mixture of operations is desirable. Cowles Communications, Inc., for example, is a widely diversified firm that issues several mass magazines (including *Look* and *Family Circle,* with 7,750,000 and 6,000,000 circulation, respectively) but also has a clutch of business periodicals which it calls 'Magazines for Industry'; these include *Candy Marketer, Food & Drug Packaging, Bottling Industry,* and nine others. Another large firm, Condé Nast, is best known for its popular *Vogue, Mademoiselle,* and *Glamour.* But only insiders realize that it also issues *Analog,* a science fiction periodical, and *House and Garden,* whose function is obvious from its title. Similarly, the Hearst firm, one of the ancients of American magazine journalism, has *Good Housekeeping* as well as *Motor* and *American Druggist,* among others, in its group of more than a dozen.

The picture of the industry must include certain trends. One relates to advertising. In each of the past four years the gross income from advertising has exceeded one billion dollars. Year by year the intake was higher. Actually it is more, for those who do the adding include mainly the consumer magazines. But at the same time the number of pages of advertising sold has decreased, the decline in 1968 from 1967 amounting to 2 per cent, for example. There has been some question about the soundness of an industry where such a situation exists. But it is a debatable situation and of concern, perhaps, largely to businessmen who insist on quantity, who measure success by numbers: number of subscribers, number of readers, number of advertisers, numbers of pages of it sold, and numbers of dollars brought in. They are so fascinated by numbers that they neglect quality and fail to see the danger of the numbers game, as did *The Saturday Evening Post* and several other magazines, before it is too late. Within the bitterly competitive consumer magazine business however, the worry about losses in amounts of advertising sold is justified, if for no other reason than that buyers of general advertising space tend to place their orders with periodicals already swollen with copy. They give little thought to any obligation to support a publication that may be in temporary distress so as to keep competition alive, if not a voice heard. In other words, the successful publication becomes still more successful and its rivals are killed off by advertisers who flock to the leader.

The worshippers of numbers stand in strong contrast to one of the great American editors, Frederick Lewis Allen, who was at the helm of *Harper's,* for many years a leading serious magazine. Writing in his magazine in 1950, Allen said: 'Our circulation . . . is a practically microscopic figure when set alongside the circulations of the monster slicks and digests. But it includes so many people who write, speak, teach, edit, manage, and govern that we may perhaps be permitted to remind you that the ignition system is a very small part of an automobile.'

The American periodical press is an industry which is fundamentally sound so long as printed communication is vital and has not been replaced by electronic means of communication. It also is a highly segmented and diversified industry. Few generalizations therefore can be made about its impact as a whole. Easier to point out are the effects of the various types of periodicals. The main obstacle to a clear, broad answer is that tools or techniques for the measurement of effect or influence still are rudimentary. Some progress has been made in noting the effect of single elements that can be isolated: certain advertisements of specific articles, for example, but little reliably beyond that. Some studies have been made which indicate effects within the segments, however, and these can be put on the record for what they may be worth.

The impact of the American periodical press also has been technological and social. The large, mass-circulation magazines have influenced the smaller magazines, which in many instances seek to imitate their appearance and to emulate the high quality of their printing, layout, and make-up. They also have influenced magazines around the world. Europe, for example, is given to publishing magazines resembling *Life* and *Look,* and almost no heavily industrialized country is without its imitator of *Time* (*The Link* in India, *Elseviers* in the Netherlands, *Tiempo* in Mexico, *Der Spiegel* in Germany, and *L'Express* in France, for example).

The social effect has to do with the discharge or failure to discharge its social responsibilities. These responsibilities the magazine press shares with all communications media, printed or electronic. They include the obligation, in a political democracy such as is the U.S.A., to provide the people with a fair presentation of facts, with honestly held opinions, and with truthful advertising. All but the subsidized periodicals hold—or seek to hold—to these goals within a certain framework: that of the business order, the private initiative, profit-making system.

As business institutions, commercial magazines, consumer and specialized alike, have influenced the progress of the business world by stimulating the desires for products and services on the part of readers through advertising and editorial content. This result has in turn affected the living standards of readers, influencing their decisions about how they dress, what they eat, and how they use their spare time. The enormous consumption of cosmetics by American girls and women is in part due to the years of commodity advertising in magazines for those readers. The sale of motor cars is heavily influenced by the advertising and special editorial content about new models.

What might be considered the official concept of the influence of the general magazines has come from the Magazine Advertising Bureau of the U.S.A. Placed first among general effects is the shaping of public opinion. 'The national magazine does not have the spot news function of either the newspaper or the radio,' MAB said. 'But being edited with deliberation, it is read with equal deliberation, and therefore has the unique ability to form a *mature* public opinion, nationally.' It also is a reflector of American life or what the owners think is American life. Said the MAB: 'Life is not the daily headlines of the newspaper, nor is it the artificial dramatics thrown out daily, hourly by radio. The solid values of the lives of millions of American families are reported by the national magazine, unsensationally but vividly and accurately, in articles and fiction, in pictures and illustrations.' The contrast with television, even sharper, might have been added.

James Playsted Wood, a magazine official and writer of several books on periodicals, reminds us that the magazine is read more persistently than any other medium, is less perishable, and is read attentively. It provokes results, receives reactions. Much magazine material later goes into books and motion pictures; reprints are made.

'The character of a given magazine limits its audience,' he says, 'thus, to some extent, the spread of its influence, its educational force, its persuasion to belief, and possibility to individual or social action.'

Wood properly qualifies his generalization by using the word *given*. The effects of the comic magazines are unlike those of the literary, and within the specialized magazine world the effects of one technical journal only in a superficial way resemble those of another.

Led by *The Reader's Digest,* condensed material and pocket-size magazines have stimulated popularized reading by the middle-class public, have spread certain social positions and attitudes, and have increased demand for short, quickly-read publications. The digest made the portable magazine among the most popular of those published, one of them being of world influence.

With magazines of seven and eight million circulation setting the pace, the women's group, with which may be associated the service and shelter books (*Woman's Day* representing service, with its many recipes, and *Better Homes,* the shelter group) has been principally responsible for influence wielded by advertising departments on homes and families of the middle class. They have to some extent standardized housekeeping tools, widened the variety of cookery, introduced or popularized certain habits, such as more frequent bathing and shaving, use of deodorants, and hair coloring, and called attention to books, motion pictures, and art works, considerably broadening their effect. Not a minor result has been the introduction of fictional stereotypes; most heroes and heroines of fiction in women's magazines seldom are realistic, although there is a trend away from that in a few. Consumer magazines try to exert influence through their advertising and editorial policies. *Esquire* in 1968, after the assassinations of Dr. Martin Luther King, Jr. and Senator Robert F. Kennedy, adopted a policy of accepting no gun advertising of any kind. This decision came after a campaign against gun advertising launched by *Advertising Age,* a business weekly. *McCall's,* with a circulation of more than eight million, on the day of Senator Kennedy's assassination, stopped its presses and inserted a two-page editorial calling on its women readers to support stronger gun control legislation, help stop excessive violence on broadcasting programs and in films, boycott certain toys, and follow other policies.

The confession magazine, more and more an imitator of the slick ones in content, has had a changing influence. In its early days it played a psychological role: it offered spiritual release for uneducated or immature readers (whether adults or adolescents) enabling them to experience adventures of the more daring and unorthodox without personal risks. Now, except for a surviving group offering stories of sex adventures and crime detection, it is achieving on its own economic level a standardization in reader habits and practices similar to the women's slicks.

The circulation and advertising leaders among men's magazines have turned away to some extent from tales of wartime bravery to tales of bedroom exploits, holding as admirable man's sexual domination of women and gratification of his dreams of wealth, power, and comfort. They encourage their readers to a hedonistic philosophy of life and to be primarily patrons of entertainment.

The religious magazines, less given than they once were to regularizing moral concepts, now are influencing their readers to apply their religious principles to social concerns as well as to personal conduct. Some have helped bring social movements into existence, such as the civil rights groups, and mustered support for social legislation in various areas of human activity: conscientious objection to war, better housing, and employment opportunities for minorities, for example.

American literary magazines have started movements, erected critical standards, and founded schools of criticism, introduced new writers, maintained the following of older ones, and provided an outlet for work not marketable to the public through general or consumer periodicals.

Magazines for juveniles have had definite effects, since their readers are in formative years. A youngster's heroes once were provided almost solely by books and magazines; today radio, television, cinema, and recordings also have strong influence, perhaps stronger. The religious juvenile publications have built concepts of right and wrong in human conduct and of individual responsibility at home and in the church or temple. They have aroused loyalties. The secular juveniles in more recent times have been simplified versions of magazines for grown-ups. Their effect has been at once to create little adults and to encourage youthful independence and also standardization of mores among adolescents. The comics have appealed to childish imaginations so effectively, and with so much questionable content, that they have been treated as social phenomena to be studied as seriously as are educational practices.

The effects of specialized magazines are vertical rather than horizontal. A clothing publication or a food magazine affects the profession, industry, business, or other group it serves by conveying news created by the group, evaluating trends within, providing an outlet for ideas, and stimulating business through advertising. Business periodicals have taken dramatic stands to correct what they consider evils. The company magazine (house organ, as often dubbed) has established itself as a bulwark or dam against ideas that its publishers deem undesirable or has helped to stimulate business.

These influences and effects have not escaped criticism. The adverse critics say that the magazines, particularly the consumer type, are too much inclined to give the public what it wants, they deprive the public of the fullest knowledge of facts and ideas; through advertising content they stimulate desires for possessions that cannot be gratified by the average reader's income. Nor is that all the criticism. The critics go on to say that the periodicals present only conventional or ultra-conservative viewpoints, that they evade their duty to provide leadership in solving social problems, that they are time-wasting, distracting the reader from more valuable uses of his leisure, and that they knuckle in to advertisers.

The favorable critics, on the other hand, counter that magazines have helped produce the high standard of living in the U.S.A. through their advertising content, have helped to stimulate mass consumption of goods and, thereby, mass production; have therefore contributed toward the lowering of the cost of living; that they have merchandised, as one proponent has put it, new ideas; and that they have played a part of importance in every national crisis, whether it be flood, war, depression, or recovery from such disasters.

As with so many arguments, this collection is not a clear case for either pro or con. To begin with, most critics of either side are talking exclusively about the consumer magazine, and, as usual, overlooking all the rest, which as we know are in the U.S.A. fifty times as numerous, and in some instances just as influential. Accepting the consumer scope, some parts of each set of criticisms may be accepted as true.

A business society such as that of the U.S.A. prevents the majority of the magazines, consumer or specialized, from fulfilling the role of the institution wholly devoted to the welfare of society as are, for example, the church, school, and the professions of medicine and nursing. It is left for the periodical press to play a part short of full devotion to the commonweal.

in the age of magazines

by CLAY S. FELKER

In this selection the editor of **New York Magazine,** Clay Felker, stresses the importance of the editor in establishing the personality and policies of a publication

At times the rise and fall of magazines has the fascination of classic Greek dramas, with fates seemingly pre-ordained and unsusceptible to the best efforts of intelligent men.

There appears to be an almost inexorable life cycle of American magazines that follows the pattern of humans: a clamorous youth eager to be noticed; vigorous, productive, middle-age marked by an easy-to-define editorial line; and a long slow decline, in which efforts at revival are sporadic and tragically doomed.

Magazines follow this kind of human life cycle probably because they are so peculiarly and stubbornly personal products. Magazines are, after all, something more than editorial formulas fleshed out by hack writers, syndicated columnists, computerized typesetters, and a blind adherence to budgetary projections.

A key fact about magazines, unlike newspapers, broadcast networks, and most other corporate forms of information, is that one man can influence every idea, every layout, every word that appears in print.

It would be humanly impossible for the contents of every daily newspaper to be edited by a single individual, and the same goes for the daily output of a radio or television station, but even within a complex operation such as a weekly newsmagazine, the editor, if he wishes (and he usually does), can control every one of the pieces that make up the editorial jigsaw for that week. In fact, a magazine that does not reflect the personality of a single individual will flounder editorially because it

Life Cycles in the Age of Magazines: Reprinted from *The Antioch Review,* vol. 29, no. 1 (Spring, 1969), by permission of the editors.

will soon find it impossible to maintain a consistent direction, giving the reader a coherent point of view to examine the universe of that particular publication.

This is not to deprecate the significance of the editorial formula of a magazine, but to say that as times change and editors give way to new men, the editorial formula for a given magazine will alter markedly. This has been strikingly evident in such archetypical formula magazines as *Time* (a weekly digest of the news) where the top editors have placed their own personally distinctive stamp on the weekly product. At *Time,* where the managing editor is the editorial chief, the newly appointed Henry Gruenwald is already producing a magazine significantly different from his predecessor Otto Fuerbringer's version of that formula. *Harper's* magazine under Willie Morris has a different tone and range of interests than John Fisher's *Harper's,* just as William Shawn's *New Yorker* of today varies greatly from that of Harold Ross's time. These magazines, and others, survive with varying degrees of success, seemingly depending on how well a particular editor develops the formula within the prevailing spirit and needs of the moment.

One of the problems in the successful publishing of a magazine is that both men and formulas become obsolete. The most striking example is that of the mass, general-circulation magazine. Of the four giants, *Colliers* (which rose to prominence on concerned examinations of national problems and on the short story), the *Saturday Evening Post* (designed for rural America), *Life* (the week's news in pictures), and *Look* (a pictorial and textual examination of major issues and personalities), two have died and two are facing trouble.

The Machine in the Garden

Technological advances both gave birth to national magazines and altered their relevance, changing all magazines in the process and killing some because of it.

The growth of the railroads, linked with the extension of the rural free mail service, the development of the steam-driven rotary press and advances in engraving, gave rise to the mass national magazine (these factors also nourished newspapers), but when radio and later television arrived, it meant that nothing would ever be the same.

The short story, which was a staple of so many magazines of mass or limited circulation, was superseded by dramas and situation comedies in the broadcast media, which also had the advantage of sound and motion. Thus the end of that function of *Colliers* and the *Saturday Evening Post.*

Now that 50 million people nightly see news in pictures on the Huntley-Brinkley and Cronkite newscasts, *Life's* role in presenting the news in pictures has been undermined, and with the spread and improvement of color television, both *Look* and *Life* have had formula trouble, severely compounded by other factors such as the rapid rise in the cost of printing and distribution—which places large-sized publications at a major economic disadvantage relative to so-called "standard" or *Time*-size magazines. The costs can be as much as 40 per cent higher for the production of a large-sized magazine, which is often more than the margin of profit; however, *Life* and *Look,* as picture magazines, need the large page size for effective display.

Equally important has been the change in the interests and the need of readers. As the national population shifted from the farms to the cities, the function of the *Saturday Evening Post* was vitiated. And as problems in the cities became of major importance to the people living in them, since the cities were unable to efficiently absorb the huge inflows of population, the journalistic focus changed from national to local, a shift which led to the development of regional editions of national magazines, and the rise of the "city magazine." *Life* now has 133 regional editions, *Look* 75, and there are close to 70 city magazines.

In general, the dominant fact of the post-war publishing market has been a sharp rise in population, income and education, creating the opportunity for specialty magazines, which can do a more efficient job for a particular segment of the American market than can a mass-circulation, general, national magazine. These changes have caused political and philosophical shifts in the national culture, which in turn have dictated new publishing and editorial directions, some of which have been brilliantly captured by the right editor for the right time, e.g. Hugh Hefner, whose *Playboy* is a handbook for the new hedonism, and Helen Gurley Brown, whose version of *Cosmopolitan* took half a step forward to be candid about how to get a man.

Above all, the successful editors of today realize that since television is the medium of the lowest common denominator (which has unbeatable advantages in immediacy, sound, and motion), print must be for the educated and affluent elite, providing something that can not be put on the home TV set. Moreover, magazines which have attempted to compete with television on the basis of total audience have usually failed, although *Life* and the *Reader's Digest* are still in the game.

Captains of Industry

Norman Cousins and the late Jack Kominsky (publisher of the *Saturday Review*) responded to the fragmented interests of the new educated and affluent masses by providing regular supplements on Hi-Fi, Travel, Science, Education, Records and Music, etc., skillfully striking an acceptable balance for a handful of diverse audiences.

At *Esquire,* Arnold Gingrich as publisher and Harold Hayes as editor successfully employ a subtle, sophisticated formula for a literate and active, Upwardly Mobile audience, depending on constant surprise, and unique writing and visual talents. It is worth noting that the greatness of Gingrich as an editor was demonstrated by a feat that probably no other editor of his time accomplished: the successful rescue of his own magazine. Other magazines have been saved by new editors being brought in, but Gingrich engineered a major editorial shift after years of early success with a somewhat different formula. As other magazines like *Holiday, Sports Illustrated,* and finally *Playboy* moved in on the travel, sports, and sex interests of the booming post-war upper-income market, Gingrich went off on a solitary retreat, and came back with the strategy which resulted in *Esquire*'s exfoliation. This involved abandoning some of the baggage of the past (i.e. pin-ups) and providing editorial material of interest to better educated, socially aggressive male readers. He also repackaged the magazine, discovering a young Viennese designer, Henry Wolfe, whose magazine designs have proved to be among the most exciting and successful in the past generation. Although Gingrich is far from unknown, he has not received the attention and acclaim he deserves for being one of the major innovative forces in American magazines.

The managements of the *Atlantic* and *Harper's* found their audiences growing old and shrinking, and both found brilliant new men to provide personal editing of balanced general magazines for what is presumed to be the intellectual elite. The *Atlantic* seems to talk directly to one of the most interesting audiences in the country for any editor, the Eastern Establishment, and under Robert Manning, a former State Department official and London bureau chief for *Time,* the articles are most successful when they are explaining this audience, its policies and its actions, to itself. At *Harper's,* Willie Morris has shown that the old-fashioned role of the editor in developing a devoted corps of writers, then forging a unified point of view from their work, can create new excitement in a traditional monthly publication. His successful appeal to the socially conscious younger elite throughout the nation reflects his capacity to anticipate the emerging movements of the day.

The *New Yorker,* which sometimes bills itself in its widespread subscription campaign as an "island of sanity," seems to be the detached and urbane guide of the suburbanite and those in the rest of the country who want to know about New York. Under the long tenure of William Shawn, the dominant personality of that great magazine, the *New Yorker* has made the transition from a local magazine to a national and at times international magazine, reflecting the shift in political interest of Americans following World War II. Now, as interests shift again, Shawn is currently active developing younger writers, like Michael J. Arlen, whose interests reflect newer developments in the culture.

One of the most interesting developments is the battle of the newsweeklies, now being joined by the recently appointed Henry Gruenwald at *Time* and Osborne Elliott at *Newsweek*. As magazines that deal with the news, they cannot help but be aware of emerging interests, some of which provide them with opportunities and some of which cause them problems. Both magazines are using more pictures, particularly color sections, and both are increasingly using longer inside stories, which in form and function are the same as the articles in magazines such as *Esquire, Atlantic,* or *Harper's,* except that they are more directly related to the news. Perhaps most significant has been the change in focus of the cover stories from the institutionalized personality "profile" to the issue-oriented story. This reflects the egalitarian political trend (the Age of the Common Man, One-Man-One-Vote) and the growing idea that it's the system not the man that counts.

Editors can assign writers to cover these issue-oriented stories, and writers might enjoy doing them, but since writers by nature are highly individualistic, they resist being submerged in a system such as group journalism. Also, the competition for writing talent has increased greatly in recent years, so much so that any good writer can not only battle successfully for his own identity but can make a remarkably good living in the process. In order to hold their most talented reporters and writers, the newsmagazines have increasingly provided various forms of identification for them. But by-lines may not be enough. The retention of personal style may be the next incentive needed to keep first-rate writers.

It is one of the delightful paradoxes in publishing that in an increasingly institutionalized age the unique talents of the individual can make the difference between failure and success. An examination of the constant tension between formula and talent can reveal some of the aspects of this problem and the strategies for solving it that are available to different kinds of publications.

Captives of Industry

Since an editor must depend on his contributors to make his formula work, he must clearly understand how to insure a constant level of quality. To do this, he can reward his writers in several ways: with money, status, or ideological satisfaction. Depending on the type of magazine, he can usually give more of one of these kinds of reward than of the other two. The editors of *Time* and *Newsweek* can pay staff writers adequately, less per article than a free-lancer of equivalent talent can make, but the income is assured and regular. However, status awaits the writers for the *Atlantic* or *Harper's,* where they are clearly identified but not paid as much as they would get from the newsweeklies, or from *Playboy.* Ideological magazines —such as *Ramparts, The Nation* or the *New York Review*—as a group pay least of all, but if the writer has a political point to make, he can be attracted to these publications.

In magazines where the pay is high, there is greater editorial control than with magazines which pay less. Magazines that reward the writer with more status tend to edit less, preferring to allow the writer his personal style of expression. Ideological publications also allow most writers full personal expression, so long as it fits within the confines of the ideology, which is usually rigid, dogmatic, and monotypic. Moreover, the form of an article is often determined by the kind of magazine that prints it. High paying magazines, such as the *New Yorker,* can afford to support a writer for an extended period of research and reporting.

In magazines in which status is the chief incentive, the articles may be shorter, or rehashed from other material with which the writer is already familiar. The form will often be that of an essay which can be written off the top of the head, and very likely not the "new journalism" which requires what Tom Wolfe calls "saturation reporting." The essay form is also most customary in ideological publications.

One of the ingredients of the increased interest in such magazines as *Harper's* has been the payment, on occasion, to writers like Norman Mailer of up to $10,000 for special pieces of reporting, such as his articles on the political conventions and the march on the Pentagon, and these expenditures have been accompanied by the judicious hiring of a few staff writers. In this way a satisfactory blend of reporting and well-written essays can be achieved. It is no accident that *Esquire,* which has been paying its writers well for a long period of time, is one of the leaders in the creation of the "new journalism." Another fertile ground for the "new journalism" was of course the New York *Herald Tribune,* which paid its writers less than did the *Times,* but often rewarded them with more personal prestige by allowing them to develop their distinctive skills more rapidly and fully. Again, it is no accident that both Tom Wolfe and Jimmy Breslin developed as "new journalists" at the *Herald Tribune,* where they were edited less severely than writers at the *Times.* Former *Times*men like Gay Talese and David Halberstam actually developed as writers outside the *Times* editing system. (Both of these men now write for *Harper's.*)

What Are Patterns For?

Although writing is the *sine qua non* of any publication (any editor knows that the name of the greatest photographer on the cover will not sell magazines, but that the coupling of a good writer's name with the right subject will raise circulation), there remains the necessity for what Henry Luce has posited as getting the ideas off the page into the reader's mind. This means attractive layouts, which can excite a jaded and busy reader but do not violate the central direction of the magazine.

In an increasingly visual age, the resources for an appealing presentation of a magazine have become virtually a corporate necessity. In some situations the appropriate talent can be found in an editor who has been visually trained beyond his traditional literary skills; in others it can be found in one of those rare creatures, an educated art director who does not *impose* design on editorial content.

It seems obvious that a modern editor should have a full command of editorial techniques, but the curious fact is that few do. Even such a powerful journalistic form as the *Life*-style picture story is dying because of misuse and because it takes a long time for an editor to master the form. However, because of this increased demand for effective visual presentation, art directors have been given more and more prominence in the editorial process. Perhaps future editors will come from the classes of college-educated designers, rather than from literary or journalism programs which offer no visual training. Such shifts in the technical knowledge needed to run a publication may seem relatively unimportant, but the life cycles of magazines are enormously affected by such things. A magazine is an artistic expression of an editorial idea. Whether this collective vision is shared by enough readers and advertisers will dictate whether a magazine is a success.

One of the strangest characteristics of a number of successful editors (but certainly not all) is that they can be mysteriously uncommunicative. For example, their sub-editors won't always know what they are talking about or what is wanted from the staff. Yet in some (even stranger) way, that editor strongly shapes his magazine in his own image, and creates a dynamic spirit which transmits itself to the editorial contributors, the readers, and the business audience. As the saying goes, philosophy follows facts, and after something is done perhaps it can be rationalized brilliantly —sometimes even by the editor who himself initiated the policy blindly and intuitively, acting on his biases and prejudices, and not on a carefully thought-out plan. It is almost always that way, because there is never enough time in publishing any magazine, whether it is a fast-moving weekly or a seemingly more leisurely monthly. Deadlines are made to be crowded, and that is a journalistic fact of life.

So what the editor is doing most often is acting on knowledge and emotions already programmed into his behavior pattern. And by the time an editor assumes his role as chief arbiter of a particular editorial formula, his personality has been set, his formal education and other journalistic training have been accomplished. From then on he's primarily drawing on what is already there. He may be unconsciously right for the spirit of the moment, but after some years, his interpretation of the formula is no longer fresh, his ideas are worn out, his decision pattern has become a *cul de sac*. These are the factors that cause magazines to go through their rising and falling life cycles. Occasionally an editor with the constantly renewable curiosity and the unflagging inspirational capacity of a Luce or a Gingrich comes along and prolongs the cycle. The vitality of a magazine depends not on great publishing organizations, precision editorial formulas, vivid promotion, or high-powered salesmen but on the vitality of one man's editorial dream. It's the beginning and end of magazines.

The Great Speckled POST

AN

Esquire

PARODY

In his article Clay Felker pointed out that one of the problems in magazine publishing is that a successful formula may become obsolete. He gave the mass, general-circulation magazine as the prime example of this overreliance on formula and cited two such magazines that are in financial trouble and two that are now defunct. One of the latter is the Saturday Evening Post, which went out of business in January, 1969 after 148 years of publication. The following parody, which appeared in Esquire magazine two years after the demise of the Post, pokes fun at the Post's traditional philosophy and editorial policies by serving up a Post that never was—a mass-circulation magazine that has overhauled itself to "keep up with the times." The only remaining similarities are the revamped Benjamin Franklin image and the commercial pitch of the "Groovy Prizes" page—which offers a comment on the motivations that lie behind the mass magazines' current move toward relevance.

The Great Speckled
POST
TEE
HEE
VERY FUNNY, MR.SHOID
Oh Wow

In This Issue:

Articles

Black Is Ugly .... By Al Joesop
My Daddy Is Far-Out .... By Kim Agnew
The Underground Railroad Depot ....By Billy Joe McAllister
Karma Burns a Pig Branch Bank
   (Coast Vibes) .... By The Big Banger
Monosexual Response in Human
   Males..................... By Masters and Masters
The Debutantes' Ball (Groovy!) .... By Suzie Woozie
The Deflowered Child .... By D. D. Teeter
The Sweet Smell .... By Leon Feather
I Call On Jerry Rubin .... By Martin Pete
Why David Eisenhower Chose the Navy ....By Gene Maroon

FAITHFUL READERS OF THIS SPACE ARE NO DOUBT SURPRISED TO FIND MISSING OUR USUAL LISTING OF DUDES RESPONSIBLE FOR LAYING THE POST ON YOU EACH WEEK. IN THE GREAT COSMIC RE-ORDERING—AS THE UNIVERSE INHALES AND EXHALES IN CONTINUOUS SUCCESSION—HOW COOL WOULD IT LOOK IF WE WERE TO ENCOURAGE EGO-TRIPPING BY PRINTING NAMES AND POSITIONS (YECCH)? WE HAVE ASKED ALL OUR EDITORS TO BECOME DUES-PAYING MEMBERS OF THE GREAT SPECKLED POST COMMUNE AND HOG FARM. FROM HENCEFORTH, WE WILL OPERATE AS THOUGH WE WERE A PEOPLE'S DEMOCRACY. ALL EDITORIAL DECISIONS WILL BE MADE FOLLOWING OUR DAILY GROUP GROPE. OFF INDIVIDUALS! MAGAZINES BELONG TO THE PEOPLE—FIGURATIVELY SPEAKING. THIS AIN'T NO HYPE. ALL POWER TO THE PEOPLE, TO COIN A PHRASE.

MARTIN AKKERMAN
PHANTASMAGORIC EXECUTIVE PUBLISHER

This Week's Cover

Through our rapidly changing age, a single man's head has remained really together: Benjamin Franklin's. As the founder of this magazine, he knew where things were at. And he knew also where they were going. RIGHT ON! It's truly amazing to think that his *Poor Richard's Almanack* predated the *Whole Earth Catalog* by two centuries! (Poor Richard, you'll recall, was an ecology freak like you and me.)

This issue marks the emergence of a more "together" publication. As such, it is solider, heavier, and bosser. It is no "rip-off" or "sell-out" or "cop-out." It comes screaming up from the underground like this incredible electric flash of white light. Oh, wow, psychedelic! The purpose of THE GREAT SPECKLED POST remains the same as the old POST: to keep you hep to all the far-out groovies going down in Amerikan (sic) life. Each action-packed issue will be an acid test for the Amerikan (sic) Dream. In a phrase, here is where it's at.

This week's cover was turned out by Norman Stonewell, a name that should be familiar to with-it POST readers. Stonewell's "thing" is to faithfully render outasight scenes from Amerikan (sic) local color. Do your head a favor and take a look at the cover again. Groove on it for a few minutes. Doesn't it look as though it was an actual photograph! Don't you wish you could draw like that? Dynamite stuff, those Stonewell covers.

We hope you can relate to the POST's new "bag." We know we do. Look for it each week—you'll recognize it by the original Stonewell picture on each issue. These covers, incidentally, can be used to roll the biggest joints you've ever seen. They are suitable for framing—you can hang them up on the walls of your dormitory room or decorate the frat house with them.

POWER TO THE PEOPLE!

From The Editor

Dear gang,

In this issue you'll find great things for that head of yours. No mind rot here! There's plenty of lively writing and sparkling cartoons. Martin Pete, one of the best observers of the pop scene, the "counter-culture," checks in with a dynamite view of Jerry Rubin. If you don't know who Rubin is, well, here's your chance to get acquainted with one of the all-time heavy dudes. Also in this issue, you'll learn things you've never dug before about David Eisenhower, grandson of the President of the same last name. If you thought Dave was straight, well, hold on to those roach holders because the kid's a real freak! You'll also learn about the "vibes" involved in burning banks as well as the inside "dope" (heh heh) of a groovy rock festival (with an illustration guaranteed to "turn" you "on"). To close out your trip, our usual feature of nifty drawings, POST SCRIPTS. These little babies are funny food for your head. And legal! So let's get on with the show. Oh, wow! Farrrr-out. Like we said, Can you *dig* it?

Euphoria H. Christ

RAPPING OUT by Leon Feather

THE SWEET SMELL OF THE WOODSTOCK NATION

When the news came that an 18-year-old black brother had croaked after rumbling with the Hell's Angels at Altamont, I freaked. Later during that sad day (December 6, 1969) I made an entry in my diary: "Retired to Nirvana to be forgotten are the flowers of the Woodstock generation." No more, no less. Only my wife and maybe Herb Cayenne of the *Chronicle* know how heavily the karma came down on me that Christmas. Not since 1965 when such immortals as Nat Cole, Tadd Dameron, Red Nichols, Spencer Williams, and Denzil Best were all taken, inexplicably, by The Great Bandleader, was I on such a bum trip.

By then I believed the Woodstock Nation's good vibes to be as important to these United States as Roy Wilkins is important to the N.A.A.C.P. No more, no less. Friends of this column may remember that once I had reservations about Woodstock: Is a music festival that costs 2,500,000 capitalist smackers relevant in the Aquarian Age?, I asked. Was it groovy for promoter John Roberts to be both groovy *and* heir to the Polident fortune?, I asked. Couldn't those 500,-000 wienies and hamburgers consumed blindly the first day by the hippie-hordes have been liberated for the starving

Chicanos in New Mexico?, and so on. But this was mere pee-pee in an ocean of truth that washed over me. It was as if Sonny Terry had been made to see again, as if Tricky Sam Nanton were alive and blowing again. Allen Ginsberg, the nudist, bearded beatnik, called it "a major planetary event." and he was bang on. Paramhansa Himself couldn't

have climbed the spiritual peaks reached by me after the glory of Woodstock. I had come to *believe* in the counter-culture.

To this belief came the violence of Altamont and gradually, like one big cosmic kick in the shins, came the artistic and spiritual debacles of the summer festivals. Powder Ridge, Love Valley, Livingstone Parish and (may the pig stench drive us out of the Citadel of Honk) *Chicago*! How can I, who have watched for years the quiet dignity of the jazz greats, forgive the unclean dudes who rampaged through the Loop, turning over cars and messing up the Grant Park band shell just because they were tired of listening to Fat Water do their thing. How can *I* forgive the humpy nakeds who performed Dionysian unspeakables before the townsfolk of Middlefield, Conn.

Forget not that I have watched the finest minds of the Bebop generation be wasted away by the Hell Weed known as *kif* (who could afford acid or psilocybin back then?), but not once did I witness perversion or a public disgrace. No more, no less. It may be "hip" and "in" to "tear off crack in a public place" but to me an orgy is an orgy and *that* is a disgrace. Where have all the flowers gone?

COAST VIBES by The Big Banger

KARMA BURNS A PIG BRANCH BANK

The day began inauspiciously for Karma and Frankie Floyd, feeling they had to do something, their heads being all ----ed up. They had to get it together, so to speak, but it seems that they couldn't find their stash nowhere in the squashed brown San Francisco dawn. Follow me? Well, Karma was having something of a brain conjugation because, well, he changed his mind about lighting himself up, and also because he couldn't burn his draft card since he already had done that once. Anyway, Karma and Frankie Floyd finally found the dope and smoked it for breakfast. After that, feeling like two champions indeed, they decided to

go on down to Poco Vista and burn down a pig branch bank. That's the kind of freaks they were—bank burners. Living in California, they were always tempted since like there are 883,231 branch banks in the state. So one of them says to the other (I can't remember which), "It'll blow our minds, man, to go out and burn down a branch bank."

The freeway near Poco was loaded with brothers and sisters as well as a lot of pigs who were stoning and truncheoning them. Karma and Frankie ducked that scene and walked through the plate-glass door of the bank. "Light that mother, Frankie boy," purred ol' Karma.

"I can't," said the other. "Aw, you couldn't ball a groupie," Karma said as he lit the fuse. Then the pigs busted in and offed everybody except Frankie and Karma. Then Frankie Floyd started stompin' on the fuse so that it would go out. Karma whispered to Frankie, "How come you're tryin' to stomp out the fuse, Frankie?" Then Frankie's eyes narrowed fiercely and he whips back the lapel of his coat and there's a badge stickin' there. That meant that Frankie was an undercover pig which is why he stomped out the fuse and busted Karma. That bomb was no hype. What it was was a rip-off.

The Great Speckled **POST**

WHY DAVID EISENHOWER CHOSE THE NAVY

WHEN YOU PUT IT ALL TOGETHER, YOU GET AN ALTOGETHER DIFFERENT VIEW OF THE KID'S HEAD!

by Gene Maroon

David Eisenhower joins the Navy! Like an electric shock the news shot through all the groovy teen-age nightclubs and campus coffee shops. It had been expected, of course, that David would continue in the family tradition, joining the Army and working from within the system to effect needed reforms. Youth wanted to know what was "coming down" with David. So did I.

I thought I'd try to talk to David in person, like an interview, but I didn't particularly relate to that hassle. I mean, it would be just too much, all those hordes of teen-age admirers and all those Secret Service pigs, transparently disguised as teen-age admirers. Phooey to that.

Well, that left me uptight. So I dropped 600 milligrams of Bayer's Best in twelve ounces of Coca-Cola and just sat awhile grooving on it. It was like some crazy combination of Disneyland and the Green Bay Packers, pregnant with truth. I knew what I had to do. I had to see the ocean!

What is the Navy but a disease of the ocean—men like microbes in the immensity of the primeval waters. I looked at the ocean. I had no recollection of getting there, but, man, I was there. I was hip deep in the old mother soup, my loins awash with phosphorescence, the little fishes nibbling at my bare toes. I felt a somehow indescribable love for my brother and sister creatures, the fish,

David Eisenhower, the crabs, the sea slugs AND THEN THE ASPIRIN HIT ME, MILLIONS OF CRAWLY SLIMY HUNDRED-LEGGED MONSTERS PENETRATING ME WITH THEIR HATEFUL EYES, GREEN AND PURPLE OCTOPUSES HOOKED THEIR BLOODY BEAKS INTO MY TREMBLING FLESH OF GOD OH GOD I WAS ALL ALONE AND THE

"What—me relevant?"

SAND DOLLARS THE SEA URCHINS THE SHARKS THE DOGFISH THE SPOTTED GROUPERS BUT THE WORST WERE THE JELLYFISH! THEY GOT ME! THEY GOT ME!

I knew I'd have to do research. I could do that because the Maharishi had taught me to read back in 1967 when he was on tour with The Beach Boys. And I knew how to find the Public Library, because I used to shoot up on the third floor. It was but a hop and step to the reading room where they keep the pig newspapers. I asked for the file on David Eisenhower. Man, that was some file. I didn't know there was that much to read. The first thing I saw was an interview from a magazine where David had said:

"I won't resort to the nine-to-five routine of living."

"You watch the California movies where the jet set is in charge. It seems glamorous and exciting."

"I was at New York University looking around one morning, and the sheer hopelessness of breaking through any of those front-office people really struck me."

Wow! Hard stuff! Now I knew! This kid was no pig! He understood alienation, alternative structures, everything! No wonder he joined the Navy! This was a rebel kid, a true descendant of Jimmy Dean just like me. I grooved on this kid!

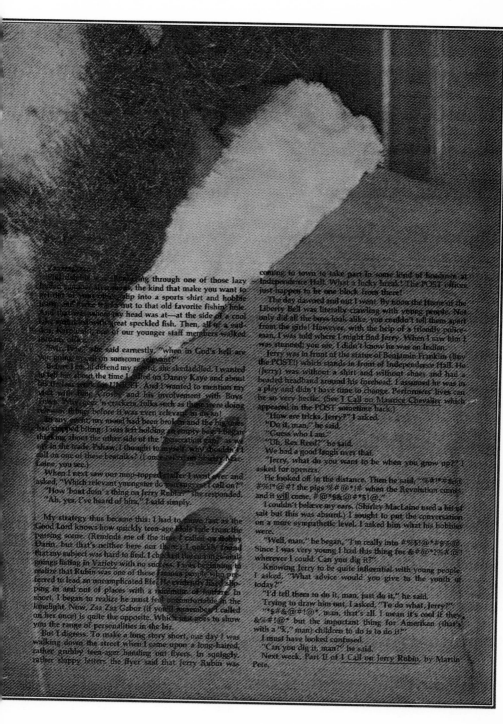

...relaxing through one of those lazy [   ] afternoons, the kind that make you want to pull on [   ] slip into a sports shirt and hobble [   ] out to that old favorite fishin' hole. And that's where my head was at—at the side of a cool lake stocked with great speckled fish. Then, all of a sudden, Kirtland, one of our younger staff members walked [   ].

"Mr. Post," she said earnestly, "when in God's hell are you going to call on someone relevant?"

Before I could defend my record, she skedaddled. I wanted to tell her about the time I called on Danny Kaye and about his [   ] work for UNICEF. And I wanted to mention my visit with Bing Crosby, and his involvement with Boys Town. Why, geez, crackers, folks such as these were doing relevant things before it was even relevant to do so!

At any event, my mood had been broken and the big ones had stopped biting. I was left holding an empty bag. I began thinking about the other side of the "generation gap" as we say in the trade. Pshaw, I thought to myself, why shouldn't I call on one of these beatniks? (I once called on Shirley MacLaine, you see.)

When I next saw our mop-topped staffer, I went over and asked, "Which relevant youngster do you suggest I call on?"

"How 'bout doin' a thing on Jerry Rubin," she responded.

"Ah, yes, I've heard of him," I said simply.

My strategy thus became this: I had to move fast as the Good Lord knows how quickly teen-age idols fade from the passing scene. (Reminds me of the time I called on Bobby Darin, but that's neither here nor there.) I quickly found that my subject was hard to find. I checked the comings-and-goings listing in Variety with no success. I was beginning to realize that Rubin was one of these famous people who preferred to lead an uncomplicated life. He evidently liked slipping in and out of places with a minimum of fanfare. In short, I began to realize he must feel uncomfortable in the limelight. Now, Zsa Zsa Gabor (if you'll remember I called on her once) is quite the opposite. Which just goes to show you the range of personalities in the biz.

But I digress. To make a long story short, one day I was walking down the street when I came upon a long-haired, rather grubby teen-ager handing out flyers. In squiggly, rather sloppy letters the flyer said that Jerry Rubin was

coming to town to take part in some kind of hoedown at Independence Hall. What a lucky break! The POST offices just happens to be one block from there!

The day dawned and out I went. By noon the Home of the Liberty Bell was literally crawling with young people. Not only did all the boys look alike, you couldn't tell them apart from the girls! However, with the help of a friendly policeman, I was told where I might find Jerry. When I saw him I was stunned; you see, I didn't know he was an Indian.

Jerry was in front of the statue of Benjamin Franklin (say the POST!) which stands in front of Independence Hall. He (Jerry) was without a shirt and without shoes and had a beaded headband around his forehead. I assumed he was in a play and didn't have time to change. Performers' lives can be so very hectic. (See I Call on Maurice Chevalier which appeared in the POST sometime back.)

"How are tricks, Jerry?" I asked.

"Do it, man," he said.

"Guess who I am."

"Uh, Rex Reed?" he said.

We had a good laugh over that.

"Jerry, what do you want to be when you grow up?" I asked for openers.

He looked off in the distance. Then he said, "%#!*#$%@ #%!*@#! the pigs %#@*!# when the Revolution comes, and it will come, #@*$&@#*$!@."

I couldn't believe my ears. (Shirley MacLaine used a bit of salt but this was absurd.) I sought to put the conversation on a more sympathetic level. I asked him what his hobbies were.

"Well, man," he began, "I'm really into #%$!@*#$%@. Since I was very young I had this thing for &#@*?%#@! wherever I could. Can you dig it?"

Knowing Jerry to be quite influential with young people, I asked, "What advice would you give to the youth of today?"

"I'd tell them to do it, man, just do it," he said.

Trying to draw him out, I asked, "To do what, Jerry?"

"$#&@#!@*, man, that's all. I mean it's cool if they, &%#!@* but the important thing for Amerikan (that's with a "k," man) children to do is to do it!"

I must have looked confused.

"Can you dig it, man?" he said.

Next week, Part II of I Call on Jerry Rubin, by Martin Pete.

There remain to this day communities in America where the kids look like they just stepped out of an R. Crumb comic book and the scenery fits Stanley Kubrick's conception of space. There are pockets of hazy euphoria where the head of a confirmed freak can forget Norman Rockwell's vision of modern Amerikan (sic) life. Don't believe what slick magazines tell you are bases of tranquillity. We know nine places that are hassle-free. They include Taos, New Mexico, Max Yasgur's Farm, North Beach in Frisco, the East Village, Sunset Strip, Goddard College, the Altamont racetrack, Spahn Ranch, and Big Sur. Dig you later.

Post Scripts

"It's a dog-eat-dog world."

"Dat's life. kid!"

THE BLACK MAGAZINES

by ROLAND E. WOLSELEY

In this article, Wolseley surveys the magazines that aim primarily at the black reader and points out the need for more publications written by and for blacks. He questions the purpose of current black magazines and their effect on their intended audiences.

Since *Freedom's Journal* was founded in 1827 as the first black publication in the United States, the journalism of the Negro people has been dominated by their newspapers. But the rise of the civil rights movement, the somewhat better coverage of the black community by white papers, the education now more readily obtainable by black citizens, and other causes have been bringing about the acceptance of the magazine as an important medium as well.

The new, re-segregating black society (the readers should substitute *Negro, Black, Afro-American,* or *non-Caucasian,* as desired, so there need be no arguments over nomenclature) will require many more specialized journals as well as the general periodicals it now possesses. White society for years has been giving the giants of magazinedom a hard time but supporting in increasingly large numbers various specialized publications. Among black readers the same trend to specialized magazines already can be noticed. Now available, for example, are the recently begun *Negro Heritage, Black Theatre, Urban West,* and *Soul Illustrated.*

As more black businesses are established—banks, investment houses, manufacturing firms—publications to serve their many interests are inevitable.

The world of religion has for a century or more issued dozens of magazines for black readers. Fraternal and other organizations have been pub-

The Black Magazines: From *The Quill* (May, 1969). Reprinted by permission.

lishing for years; one of the most important and influential periodicals in all Negro journalism is *The Crisis,* a monthly issued since 1910 by the National Association for the Advancement of Colored People. First edited by W.E.B. DuBois, its circulation has hovered around 80,000 in recent years; it fails to get the attention it deserves because it is passed over as merely the house organ of the NAACP, which is only one of its functions. Another has been to print the writings of some of black literature's most important writers: Langston Hughes, Paul Lawrence Dunbar, and James Baldwin, for instance.

The Negro magazine has been traced as far back as 1837, Frank W. Miles, one of the few historians of black magazines, reporting that the "first magazine to be both owned and edited by a Negro" was the *Mirror of Liberty,* a quarterly begun that year by David Ruggles. Owning, editing, and intention are important to black historians, some of whom rule out a periodical owned by whites but intended for black readers or edited by whites for blacks. Thus an even earlier magazine, *The National Reformer,* while edited by William Whipper, a Negro, was owned by the American Moral Reform Society, and so is not acceptable. The generally accepted first is *The African Methodist Episcopal Church Magazine,* founded in 1842. It, note, is specialized. The first general one is a Boston publication, *The Colored American,* begun in 1900.

All other general ones after that failed until *Ebony* and *Sepia* came into the field and today head the list. Behind them were several noble efforts, including *Our World, Bronze World,* and *Opportunity.* Since there is no limit to the possibilities for exploration of black history, culture, personalities, art, and the present condition of the Negro people, it is likely that the half dozen general magazines of today will flourish.

There are the four well-publicized Johnson Publishing Co. periodicals, led by *Ebony.* That picture monthly now is in the group of about 60 U.S. magazines that have more than one million circulation (it has 1,200,000). The other three are *Jet,* a peppy, vest-pocket-size weekly newsmagazine, shy on advertising but long on news nuggets; *Tan,* a sensational, somewhat squishy women's and confession book like *True Story* and *True Confessions* before they became service magazines for the workingman's wife, now a person of medium affluence; and *Negro Digest,* a money-losing maverick of the Johnson family because it is militant in behalf of the Negro whereas the others urge him to join what E. Franklin Frazier, the sociologist, once called the black bourgeoisie.

Although *Ebony* is John H. Johnson's best known publication, it was not his first. *Negro Digest,* which he began in 1942 after mortgaging his mother's furniture for $500, was followed by *Ebony* three years later, and then came the others, including two that did not pan out: *Hue,* for the small pocket or purse, was devoted largely to entertainment subjects, did well for a time, and then faded, having difficulty obtaining ads, as *Jet* still does; *Ebony International,* intended for English-reading Africans, lasted only a few issues, running into political and ideological complications.

Johnson now is a V.I.P. in the white Magazine Publishers Association (the black magazine firms have no organization of their own, as the Negro newspaper publishers have had for many years) but it took him almost two decades to gain recognition just as it took a long time for him to amass the advertising which now makes his publishing firm one of the most lucrative. It unquestionably is the dominant company in black magazine-dom and perhaps all Negro journalism.

Less widely known than the Johnson magazines but economically successful in a more modest way is another quartet, issued by the Good Publishing Co. in Fort Worth, Texas. Under the rule that the publisher must be black as well as the staff and readers these four may not qualify as Negro magazines, since George Levitan, the publisher, is white. Putting this technicality aside, they are four that must be noted. More given to exploitation of Negro emotionalism than exploration of Negro history and culture, these include *Sepia,* a monthly which attempts to rival *Ebony* but has one-twentieth of its circulation and far less advertising. Its companions are *Jive, Hep,* and *Bronze Thrills,* all lively and physically smaller than *Sepia,* which like *Ebony* is *Life-* or *Look*-size. They are monthlies and delight in printing realistic confession pieces with such titles as "A Den of Homosexuals" and "I Was a Nurse Abortionist" but also serious articles on the Negro in the Peace Corps and about the Riot Committee Report and the unrest in the colleges.

In recent years we have seen the rise of the magazine with the largest circulation among all black publications of this country: the ably-produced *Tuesday,* a four-year-old magazine supplement to white newspapers circulating in black neighborhoods, with a distribution of about 2,000,000. Physically resembling *This Week,* it is found in the Cleveland *Plain Dealer,* the Milwaukee *Journal,* the Chicago *Sun-Times,* and other large papers in Boston, Los Angeles, Detroit, and Philadelphia, among others, and puzzles whites who read these dailies and do not see *Tuesday* in their Sunday copy. That happens because it is sometimes inserted only in the copies that go to readers in the black part of the community. W. Leonard Evans, its editor and publisher, explained its philosophy in its third anniversary issue. He pointed out that the Negro income in the U.S. collectively represents $32,000,000,000. "We are poor individually, wealthy collectively," he wrote, and then presented the solution to the inequity:

The solution is simple enough, if men of good will and honest concern are willing to invest their time, their money, their talents and knowledge. And they must, for time is running out in our black communities (this was September, 1968) . . . *Tuesday,* for one, refuses to believe that despair is necessary. There must be hope for our people, our communities, our nation, our world. We believe these few ideas and proposals can help provide a solution. Once the black communities become economically profitable like others in our nation through the utilization of their creative and intellectual capacities then, and only then, will the true meaning of freedom be realized.

Tuesday is giving its readers a goal, attempting to create a particular image or at least something to which to aspire. It is difficult, however, to say what the black magazines as a group are saying or what image of himself or of other blacks the Negro reader is getting because the black periodical is much less standardized than is the black newspaper. In *Ebony* he is reflected as an aspirant to recognition by whites as being as capable as they in business, industry, sports, and the arts. He is portrayed as wanting *things*—swank cars, natural hair (or wigs), handsome suits and glamorous dresses, leisure for vacations, and other white middle class pleasures. The critics of the Johnson mass-appeal magazines (therefore excluding *Negro Digest*) accuse them of being too unrealistic, of building false hopes, of constructing a wonderland into which the black citizen really cannot hope to enter for many, many years. To be sure, Johnson's editors are changing this slightly; they are becoming more aware of the revolution now going on and they glorify personal success less than they did a decade ago, but it still is dominant. In edging into this new position they are running into new trouble. A reader in Isle of Palm, S.C., wrote this complaint:

". . . I'd like to protest the insults I receive every time I read it. Not an issue goes by but that you refer to the Caucasian race in the most insulting terms . . . Whitey, Charley and Honkie . . . ." He goes on to say that he feels "we are all Americans; not black, white, yellow or red" and accuses *Ebony* of preaching bigotry and violence.

A Canadian reader calls the magazine discriminatory because whites are excluded from it. "For you to be proud that you are a black man is just as wrong as for me to be proud I am a white man. We are men," he writes, adding: "You are the ones now giving importance to the coloring of the skin, the very crime you condemn the whites for."

In any of the four issued by the Good firm the image is of a superstitious young man or woman, intent on a good time, not too well educated and somewhat puzzled by life's every day problems. The Johnson reader has left the ghetto and the Good reader is perhaps on the fringe of the ghetto rebellion. He has many emotional and mental conflicts, it appears, and turns to *Bronze Thrills* or *Hep* for help or escape.

Beyond these popular-mass-aimed magazines are the specialized ones for hairdressers, businessmen, scholars, and others of particular purpose where there is no image-building but mainly service and information. As with so many other special sections of the magazine world, the black magazine industry has its own scholarly journals which rarely are seen by anyone except the few specialists themselves but influential nonetheless. These include the quarterlies called *Journal of Negro History, The Journal of Negro Education,* and *Phylon.* Similar in some ways but less objective is *Freedomways,* with a political and literary emphasis. All conform, more or less, to the physical pattern of the American scholarly journal.

Phylon, issued at Atlanta University, is somewhat more given to including literary as well as scholarly work. Like *The Crisis,* it was edited by W.E.B. DuBois, whose long activity in journalism is overlooked because of his noted career as a sociologist.

The *Journal of Negro Education* is 38 years old. Issued from Howard University, which sponsors others dealing with religion and the university's own life, it is produced by the Bureau of Educational Research. Less expensive than most such journals, it has the traditional purposes of these quiet, thick quarterlies and lists a large staff almost all of which, as is customary with these periodicals, is to lend prestige. Topping it is Charles H. Thompson, former dean of the Graduate School at Howard and founder and editor emeritus of the *Journal.*

The content is substantial, as is illustrated by the number dated Summer, 1968. The theme is race and equality in American education, with articles by Dr. Thompson; Robert L. Carter, the general counsel for the NAACP; Charles V. Willie, chairman of the sociology department at Syracuse; Lee S. Shulman, professor of educational psychology at Michigan State; John H. Fischer, president of Teachers College, and others from Harvard, Howard, Columbia, and Yeshiva.

A handful of new, small local weeklies or publish-when-we-cans, something like the white underground magazines, is entering the black journalistic scene. They can be placed in the magazine category as readily as the newspaper, even though printed on newsprint (so could the pioneering *Freedom's Journal,* for that matter). They are almost newsless tabloids, with long think pieces, and bear such names as *The Black Voice, Afros Expressions, The Plain Truth, The Liberated Voice,* and *The Ghetto Speaks.* Their number is unknown, for they come and go as subsidy permits. Often the more unrestrained call for violent revolution; all are given to sprawling generalizations about Negro affairs and rest their views on few facts.

These black underground publications are the lost souls and opportunities of Negro journalism. Unable or unwilling to become actual newspapers or magazines, which their communities usually need, they follow the easier formula of printing long magazine-type articles, lengthy editorials, and many free columns and much publicity from favorite causes. Little editing is done, the publications often are a typographical mishmash and reflect scarcely more than the prejudices of the non-journalists who usually are behind them. Unprofessional as they are, however, they are significant voices of dissent merely because they are vehicles. Since their crusades at times are justified, it is a pity that ineptness weakens them. So they disappear, remembered as well-meant but amateurish periodicals.

What is a pity—or maybe, depending upon what one thinks of their viewpoints, it is not—is that the readers in the ghetto are not being reached in any large numbers by these muckraking publications. What does the ghetto resident read in the way of magazines? Not much has been learned about that. From the few research studies made, it appears that the middle class Negro reads more or less the same white magazines as whites and to them adds perhaps two or three black periodicals: a general, consumer book; one provided by an organization to which he may give support, such as the NAACP; and possibly one of ideas about black culture. The ghetto resident reads few magazines of any color but if he comes from the revolutionary or militant group within it he may read one of the local weekly magazines of the underground type or perhaps a national monthly aimed at dissident blacks. If the ghetto resident reads a magazine at all it is likely, from his own group, to be *Ebony*.

As the swing toward separatism continues, the black publication, be it newspaper or magazine, is likely to flourish. If that swing should be reversed the turn to the black publication may be halted. But it seems unlikely that the probing of their past and the reporting of their present situation will leave the black people of America devoid of ongoing interest in their history and their culture. Because of their physical characteristics magazines may be able to satisfy that interest more effectively than any other medium.

The preceding three selections dealt largely
with the editorial content of magazines—but
the importance of visual content must not be
forgotten. Photography and graphic design
are playing an increasingly important role in
magazine articles (and, of course, in
advertisements). Magazines like LIFE and LOOK
frequently run articles composed primarily
of photographs, and it is not unusual for a
magazine to offer an entirely visual treatment
of a subject—as in this portion of Julio Mitchel's
pictorial essay on middle America, which
appeared in AVANT-GARDE magazine.

THE SILENT MAJORITY

****

PICTURES WORTH A THOUSAND WORDS

****

BY JULIO MITCHEL

What the Underground Press is trying to tell us

by ART KUNKIN

In this article Art Kunkin of the Los Angeles
Free Press discusses the underground
newspaper—a medium which, like the black
periodicals described by Wolseley, reaches
only a relatively small segment of society.
He feels the underground newspaper should
be brought above ground, arguing that the
freedom of the newspaper industry as a whole
is endangered if the underground press is
not accorded its full rights and privileges.

The people producing the Los Angeles *Free Press* do not feel "underground." July 1969 marked the beginning of the sixth year of continuous weekly publication for us. Our publication has recently been as large as 72 tabloid pages and we have a paid circulation of close to 90,000. (Yes, we are members of the Audit Bureau of Circulation.)

From a living room table in 1964, an initial $15 investment and a group of volunteers, we have grown to a full-time paid staff of more than 40 people occupying a two-story office building on a main street in Los Angeles.

What the Underground Press Is Trying to Tell Us: From *The Bulletin of the American Society of Newspaper Editors* (August, 1969). Reprinted by permission.

This growth, and the multiplicity of newspapers which began after the *Free Press,* is, in my opinion, due to the combination of the new offset technology plus the vacuum in modern American politics plus the creation of new community interest groups including black and brown minorities, college-educated urbanites and the new "youth class."

These groups were voiceless but desperately wanted voice.

They needed information and communication but the empty weekly neighborhood advertising shopper and the metropolitan daily with its ad pages surrounded by wire releases, high society sections and already established business and political entanglements would not and probably could never satisfy this journalistic vacuum.

This need for more community interchange called the "all-around" press into existence.

Newsweek reports that at the June 1969 Harvard graduation ceremony a moderate law graduate student, Meldon Levine, said, "For attempting to achieve the values which you have taught us to cherish, your response has been astounding. It has escalated from the presence of police on campuses to their use of clubs and gas. I have asked many of my classmates what they wanted me to say today. 'Talk with them about hypocrisy,' most of them said. 'Tell them they have broken the best heads in the country. . . . Tell them they have destroyed our confidence and lost our respect.' "

I do not want to belabor a point by underscoring how the great majority of conventional press coverage and editorial comment has contributed to this loss of respect, this sense of hypocrisy which makes the young people feel like foreigners in their own native land.

Instead of the inaccurate phrase "underground press" it might be better to say "all-around press" because this recent journalistic phenomenon is truly all around. Modern offset printing technology has made it possible for almost anyone to produce his own "newspaper." As a result there are countless numbers of "people's newspapers" without official status in high schools, colleges, prisons, military units as well as in almost every city.

Just as everyone was worrying about the trend toward monopoly in the newspaper business, technology has made a democratic leap possible.

In any large city where web offset equipment is available for trade work, anyone with an expenditure of not much more than $100 can produce several thousand copies of a four- or eight-page tabloid because the traditional cost of typesetting can be entirely eliminated or made negligible.

A typewriter with carbon ribbon can produce usable justified or unjustified type and, in some cases, "all-around" editors have chosen or been forced to produce pages of handwritten copy which the offset press reproduces as handily as the best typography.

And if a high school student, a prisoner at San Quentin or an Army private does not have access to a large web-fed offset, there is always the ubiquitous office duplicator—a printing press better than anything around one hundred years ago.

There is a new spirit in journalism, a do-it-yourself attitude. There is undoubtedly much amateurishness in many of the new papers, even in those that manage to sustain themselves beyond a few issues, but it is a vital amateurishness in the spirit of the pamphleteering journalism of the American Revolution of 1776. The "all-around" papers may be irreverent but they are not irrelevant.

The paste-up page ready for offset duplication is a collage which invites spontaneous treatment. In the hands of a young editor who is not bound by tradition there can be surprising results.

Last year I was a scheduled speaker at an Editors' Conference sponsored by the California Newspaper Publishers Association at Stanford University and sat in on the preceding session on modern newspaper layout.

The speaker had prepared a slide lecture to demonstrate that a newspaper page could be attractively laid out in massive blocks with no rules and lots of white space around pictures. This, the speaker said, was 20th-century layout. It was very dull, however well meaning.

When I was to speak, I said that it might be helpful for continuity of the conference if I began my remarks by speaking about the form and design of the Los Angeles *Free Press*. I held up individual pages of the *Freep* as examples of experimentation with offset technology. We then got into a vigorous discussion about the use of collage techniques for illustrations, satirical headlines, split-fountain color, full-page photographs and drawings as front pages.

We spoke about visual underlays behind type, the application of modern art principles and Dada to newspaper design, and the way that the modern publications audience, conceptualizing space, time and history differently from any other audience in the past, expects its editors to be creative artists and not simply interpretative organizers of words.

When the first issue of the *Free Press* appeared, probably the majority of those who saw it did not understand what it was doing and did not expect the paper to have a long life. The growth of the paper has been a process of educating the community in the new journalism while the community was educating the new writers and editors about what they wanted.

In 1964 the paper immediately began coverage of civil rights groups, peace groups and the local manifestations of the Berkeley Free Speech Movement. Six months after the paper began, we were deep in the controversies over the psychedelic revolution and President Kennedy's assassination.

We printed viewpoints on every side, making sure that the dissenters, critics and activists had a chance to say their thing in their own words. Very early, the policy of non-editorializing and being a writer's newspaper developed. Everyone who wanted had, and has, a chance to present his viewpoint on any important community development, as long as there was a fair presentation of facts and an adequate literary style.

Unlike the N.Y. *Village Voice,* which had been in existence for nine years when the *Free Press* began, I did not want the *Freep* to become a newspaper partisan to the liberal wing of the Democratic Party. I felt that such identification, or any party identification, would needlessly limit readers to partisans when what was most needed in the community and country was dialogue and debate, not party loyalty.

Typical of the ranging interest of even the early *Freep,* the first birthday issue was devoted to a commemoration of the death that week of the builder of the Watts Towers, Simon Rodia. The other newspapers in Los Angeles devoted a few pitiful inches to the life and death of this great untutored local artist who had created the greatest sculptural achievement of the 20th century.

The *Free Press,* on the other hand, drew on County Art Museum personnel, community leaders, poets, architects to do many pages on Rodia's achievement, observing that the drive of old Sam for a personal life and personal creation despite all obstacles was a positive vision for the entire community. This was partially in answer to those who saw the *Free Press* only as a "downer," a chronicler of all the bad and evil manifestations of our society.

The political community did not take the *Freep* seriously until the Watts riots of 1965. Then, while other publications were counting the still-burning fires, the *Free Press* was publishing articles by members of the Watts community revealing the problems that had caused the uprising and examining the facts of the disturbance.

By this time there had been a year of uninterrupted weekly publication. People had come to appreciate that the paper was a picture frame that would fill up each week with whatever the community was doing in accordance with the ability of staff and nonstaff writers. The *Free Press* had, and has, such a reputation for publishing eyewitness reports, whether it be those of a high school student or a nationally known novelist, that we often have more "reporters" at the scene of a local event than the major newspapers.

Very early in the game, the five original newspapers (*East Village Other,* N.Y.; *Berkeley Barb,* Calif.; *The Paper,* Ann Arbor, Michigan; *The Fifth Estate,* Detroit, Michigan; and the L.A. *Free Press*) decided on a free exchange of articles and photographs except where the writer himself did not want that exchange to happen. This has been the basis for many new papers starting; until they generated their own energy, already typeset copy could be obtained by scissoring one of the existing papers. There are presently about 200 members of the Underground Press Syndicate.

A more recent innovation has been Liberation News Service, which for a small fee per month sends twice weekly mailings to all UPS papers as well as 600 college and high school papers. LNS has telex communication with some papers.

This matter could encompass an entire article but since I have been asked by a *Bulletin* editor to comment on this specifically, here are some summary thoughts:

a. The staff of the *Free Press* is often dismayed at the sexual content of much of our display advertising because this distracts from our journalistic efforts. However, if there is any basic principle to the paper, it is anti-censorship. We do not want to institute censorship except where survival itself seems to dictate.

b. It is a fact of life that the Supreme Court decisions which made this explicit type of advertising possible are part of the social and technological revolution of our time which makes the "all-around" press so all around.

c. Since many conventional businesses outside of the youth market do not advertise in the *Free Press* because of the presentation of controversial views, the sexually-oriented ads pay the bills.

d. These admittedly exploitative ads are morally no worse than the sleazy promotion of used-car sales, shoddy department store merchandise, harmful liquor and cigarette ads that almost every other publication in the U.S. accepts as a basis for financing. Those in glass houses shouldn't throw stones! (Somebody said that before, but I couldn't resist it.)

e. The sex advertisers attempt no pressure on the editorial policies of the paper. In contrast, the liberal businessmen who urge the *Free Press* to censor the sex ads as a condition for their advertising dollar have rarely supported a liberal publication adequately. At the first sign of criticism of a liberal group or politician, these liberal advertising dollars disappear. I doubt if any large newspaper maintains the complete detachment of editorial department from advertising that we do.

It is very obvious that mass media journalists use the "all-arounds" as a steady source for stories and inspiration in style. In that sense the establishment press is getting more "open."

The fact that mass media journalists also give us stories that their own organizations won't use shows that we are still *the* open press as contrasted to the closed press.

About two years ago, members of the Los Angeles *Free Press* staff had occasion to interview a group of Russian citizens touring Los Angeles. They said to us: "Despite what you are called, the *Free Press* is not underground. You have news vendors and coin machines throughout the city selling your paper. Now, in our country if a paper is underground those producing and distributing it are subject to arrest."

The Russians were, of course, fundamentally correct but yet, as they left, they said, "Please don't write up our conversation in your newspaper. You are obviously quarreling with your Establishment. If your State Department would see it, it might endanger the cultural exchange of visitors between our countries." In short, even the Russians could see the state of tension in which the "underground" press finds itself.

Unfortunately, in many cities throughout the country there are indications that in the next year conservative forces would like to push the nonconforming press into a truly underground status. There are a growing number of municipal prohibitions on distribution, gathering of news and so-called "obscenity" actions which, even if without merit, drain the financial resources of a small publication while the matter goes to court.

The *Free Press* itself, now one of the largest paid circulation community weeklies in the country, has had to go to court to demand that the Los Angeles police issue press credentials to its full-time paid reporters. After we beat down in court the "legal" argument that we didn't deserve press credentials because the city didn't approve of our advertising policies, the judge finally ruled against us because we did not regularly cover "police beat news" like fires and auto accidents.

The fact that the lack of press credentials is used as an excuse to exclude our reporters from press conferences called by city officials and is used to prevent us from crossing police lines at demonstrations was only given cursory attention. The American Civil Liberties Union has recently filed an appeal to a higher court on this matter.

Editor and Publisher magazine and other publications of American journalism have begun to take note of some of these problems but without comment. As a matter of fact, only a few chapters of Sigma Delta Chi have recently begun to protest the scandalous denial of press credentials to the *Free Press;* everyone else in journalism has remained silent including the major newspapers in Los Angeles.

I therefore ask these questions: How long can the mainstream of American journalism observe this trend without expressing itself? Can some small, and some large, news publications be harassed, driven out of business, denied constitutional rights or be forced into a true underground status without endangering the free status of all other news publications?

Do members of the American Society of Newspaper Editors really believe that the so-called "underground" newspapers are so insignificant and so divorced from the basic functions of journalism that it does not matter if their activities are proscribed?

Some critics maintain that as the "all-arounds" get larger and have to maintain payroll records, etc., we are bound to become more conservative. I don't think this necessarily has to happen as long as there are young people around with full freedom to speak about editorial policy and responsive editors listening, as long as there is interchange between community and paper, as long as the papers keep to their job of observing and communicating the molecular process of social change and don't become party liners dedicated to one frozen point of view.

As *The Wall Street Journal* noted last year, the "underground" press is becoming politically oriented. It is increasingly clear to a lot of young people that the only way to stop the best heads from being broken is by changing the political leadership which puts the billy clubs into action.

The "all-around" press is going to play an important part in this democratic process of political change, and as this movement matures in the course of the next few elections, the recent victories of the so-called "law-and-order" candidates will seem like a passing puff of smoke.

The only thing the "all-around" press has to fear is being forced underground. And that will only happen if the good folk who operate inside the establishment press forget that no part of journalism is truly free if any part is fettered.

the village VOICE

(*You've come a long way, baby, But you got stuck there*)

by J. KIRK SALE

In the following excerpts from a longer article, J. Kirk Sale criticizes **The Village Voice**, an underground paper in its inception, for tenaciously holding to its original editorial policies rather than changing with the times, and thereby negating its purpose in the contemporary context.

Three things to keep in mind:

1. *The Village Voice* is the most successful weekly newspaper in the United States.

2. The editor of *The Village Voice* is Daniel Wolf, perceptive, cynical, quiet, aging, detached, noncrusading, fixed-liberal, old-bohemian.

3. *The Village Voice* is perceptive, cynical, quiet, aging, detached, noncrusading, fixed-liberal, old-bohemian.

You are what you edit.

Norman Mailer thought up the name. (Probably. There is a rival claim from a housewife in Scarsdale.) He put $5,000 into it at the start, another $10,000 by the end of the first year. He remains today one of the five co-owners. He is a friend of Dan Wolf's—his sister Barbara having been a childhood friend of Dan's wife, Rhoda—though the vicissitudes of age and fame and other preoccupations have made it a somewhat more attenuated friendship than in 1955 when Mailer dedicated *The Deer Park* to Dan and Mailer's then-wife Adele. Dan did not get stabbed.

The Village Voice (You've Come a Long Way, Baby, But You Got Stuck There): From *Evergreen Review* (December, 1969). Reprinted by permission of J. Kirk Sale.

Norman Mailer was also a columnist for the *Voice* in that first year. For three months and one week, thirteen issues. The column was originally entitled "Quickly, a column for slow readers" and was a way for Mailer to work out some ideas that were nudging his head. Not very good ones, as it turned out. The column was later called "The Hip and the Square," and it was the birthbed of the concept of hip that Mailer created, refined, put into the language, and in some way came to regret.

Norman Mailer quit after thirteen columns because the *Voice* was square, not hip. He wanted the paper to be, in the words of one of the editors at that time, "a kind of swinging New York *Enquirer*: cover the drug scene, the sex, the hard life of the new order of beats then coming into being in the Village and elsewhere." Or, as Mailer said in his last column: *"The Village Voice is remarkaby conservative for so young a paper, and deeply patriotic about all community affairs, etc., etc. . . . The Editor and Publisher . . . wish this newspaper to be more conservative, more Square— I wish it to be more Hip."* Mailer was, as usual, right. The *Voice* was square, patriotic, safe, liberal, and middle class. Still is. Only thing that's changed in fourteen years is that it has become enormously successful.

There have always been four Villages. The old-time Irish-Italian funeral-bank conservative business community. The high-rise-apartment professional uptown-by-day-fly-by-night squares. The creative successful brownstone-loft bohemians. And the hips. *The Village Voice* has always been the paper *of* that third community, directed *to* the second and third, *against* the first, and *apart* from the last.

Ed Fancher is the publisher of *The Village Voice*. He likes to say, essentially seriously, that "Greenwich Village is a state of mind." He's right, insofar as he means to describe the kind of people who read and like the *Voice*. They don't all live in the Village—55,199 of them live elsewhere, some in Burma, Peru, Tanzania, one fellow in Ceylon. What they all have in common is a left-liberalism within a right-bohemianism. They are the bo-libs. Bohemian-liberalism: bohemian, not hip, yip, digger, or beat; liberal, not radical, revolutionary, love-cultured, or anarchistic.

The bo-lib, born into the Lost Generation, is getting to be an old man. Probably owns his own brownstone, children in private school. Enjoys comforts from an age which respects its bohemians—respects them like crazy, as the old joke has it. The bo-lib came of age in wartime. Agonized, but did not suffer, through McCarthy I. Knew the cold war was wrong but accompanying prosperity didn't hurt. Saw zenith in Kennedy I. Grew to hate Vietnam, eventually. Love-hate with Kennedy II, love-puzzlement with McCarthy II. Fought for the coloreds, liked the Negroes, is now worried about the blacks. And the radicals.

The first amendment is the bo-lib's St. Christopher. (A rare Wolf editorial stated it: "A passion for democracy, faith in reason and tolerance, and an implacable opposition to violence and dehumanization.") Elective politics is his St. Valentine. (Wolf: "Our politics is very ordinary. We were called pinkos when we came out, but we were very middle-of-the-road, really. We were radical journalistically, perhaps, but never politically.") Urban man—white urban man—is his St. George. (Fancher: "We focused on the emergence of a new middle-class 'revolt of the urbs'—a struggle to organize to preserve parks and playgrounds, and the character of the community against arbitrary city planners and politically connected real estate interests.") Or perhaps they're not saints, after all.

Don't knock the bo-libs. They're important. So is their paper. In the decade and a half of its existence the *Voice* has been responsible for a lot of changes.

Like: The *Voice* made possible a new political style, the bo-lib style, represented best by John Lindsay and in a lesser way by Congressman Ed Koch. It recognized, nurtured, supported, and enteethed the Village Independent Democratic Club, aligned against the old-time Tammany Hall tiger, Carmine De Sapio, until it forced De Sapio out in 1963 and became something of a minor power in the city. The *Voice* recognized, supported, lionized, and propagated John Lindsay, and helped get him elected by drawing the bo-libs away from Abe Beame and to this new man with the new style. The *Voice* also saw in Bobby Kennedy elements of the bo-lib style, and he owed some part of his success to the bo-lib influence of the *Voice*.

Like: The *Voice* established a new literary journalistic style. Murray Kempton in his way, Seymour Krim to an extent, the *Herald Tribune* after its groping fashion, some of the smaller literary magazines all made attempts in the late fifties toward the New Journalism (personal, involved, introspective, biased) but it was the *Voice* in the early sixties which really developed that style and put it across. The success has since been emulated (each in its own way) by *New York Magazine, Esquire, The New Republic, Ramparts,* even *Life* and the *Saturday Evening Post* on occasion. And the *Voice* exemplars of the style—Nat Hentoff, Richard Goldstein, Stephanie Harrington, Jack Newfield, Joe Flaherty—have come to a new prominence. Not to mention non-*Voicers* who have picked up on it: Tom Wolfe, Andrew Kopkind, Rex Reed, Dick Schaap, and Norman Mailer.

Like: The *Voice* created a new generation of newspapers—the undergrounds—though neither likes to admit to the paternity. Still, the *Voice* was the first to prove you could make a success of a weekly paper that was *not* just a community bulletin board and chamber of commerce handout; that *was* concerned with breaking news, with giving larger dimensions to local stories, with being a sharp gadfly to the daily press, with freedom of expression. The Los Angeles *Free Press,* first of the undergrounds in 1963, said specifically that it would be the West Coast equivalent of the *Voice.* The *East Village Other,* in 1965, was very conscious of what it was being the other *to.* Even though the children grew up laughing at and despairing of the parent, of the family link there is no doubt.

Like: The *Voice* nurtured and promoted a new cultural style. Off-Broadway (and off-off Broadway, and so on) and underground movies (and under-underground, and so on). The *Voice* lavished attention on off-Broadway when it was just beginning and was virtually uncovered by other papers. The *Voice* originated and still gives the annual Obie (O.B., get it?) Awards for outstanding off-Broadway achievements. The two have grown together. Prosperously. Ditto, underground movies. Jonas Mekas, a cultist, fed the cult through his *Voice* column in his own special way ("*Yojimbo* is good. It is moral. It is clear. I have seen it four times. I could see it once more. But I was never really carried away by it."). Not all of what has come along in the wake of these two cultural dreadnoughts can be blamed on the *Voice*. But a lot can.

Like: The *Voice* served the uptown world as its antennae to the downtown scene. It was, to a degree still is, the cultural DEW line for the mass media's SAC. Mad. Ave., *Vogue* and the other culture-feeders, *The New York Times* and the news magazines, television networks, and even Hollywood and Seventh Avenue learned to read the *Voice* to find out what was *in,* what the new trend was, what the kids were thinking. Not that the *Voice* always knew, especially in later years, but that hardly mattered. Sufficient to pick up on the same things the *Voice* picked up on and quickly to suck them into the media maw, four-color them, Doyle-Dane them, Carsonize them. And send them across the land. The *Voice's* view of the scene, *mutatis mutandis,* became the Establishment's, and America's.

In its decade and a half, with accomplishments such as these, the *Voice* has proved itself a success. It now has a circulation of more than 127,000, up from 17,000 in 1960, 25,000 in 1963, 50,000 in 1966. The largest circulation of any weekly paper in the country, a larger circulation than many magazines, and a larger single-day circulation than ninety-five percent of the daily newspapers in the country. It claims to have the most consistently rapid circulation growth of any newspaper in the country. It has greater newsstand sales in New York City than *Time, Newsweek, The New Yorker, New York Magazine,* and *Cue,* among others. It has twenty-five full-time employees, thirty-four part-time, in its own triangular building jutting into Sheridan Square. It is bloated with ads, having sold over 1,700,000 lines of display advertising last year, 460,000 lines of classifieds. These days a plump seventy-two pages is standard.

The *Herald Tribune.* The *Daily Mirror.* The *World-Telegram and Sun.* The *Journal-American.* All have withered and died. The *Voice,* standing over their carcasses, lives on.

The *Voice* reader has been market-surveyed. He is, according to the paper's puff slogan, "a trend-maker." In fact he is 32.4 years old, has a median family income of $12,206 (35 percent make more than $15,000) and, the survey says, serves and uses alcohol in his home. 87.2 percent have some college education. 60 percent read *The New York Times,* 3.7 percent read *The Wall Street Journal,* 3.2 percent read *Ramparts.* 32.7 percent list drinking among their "hobbies and activities." 17.6 percent own Volkswagens, 0.4 percent Rolls-Royces. 52.2 percent are professional, 5.8 are housewives, 0.6 are unemployed. 28.3 percent are over 40, 57.3 are over 30. In short, bo-libs.

.   .   .

The first issue of *The Village Voice,* October 25, 1955, Vol. I, No. 1. "A WEEKLY NEWSPAPER DESIGNED TO BE READ." Five cents. Twelve pages. Lead: "VILLAGE TRUCKER SUES COLUMBIA" after being expelled for an article in school newspaper. Stories on music-makers in Washington Square Park, a New School speech, opening of a new department store, a poetry reading. The Village Square column by John Wilcock. "Editorial No. 1." Gilbert Seldes, Michael Harrington, Jerry Tallmer. Books 25 inches, art 18 inches, movies 28 inches, theater 48 inches, dance 6, photography 25, music 10. Fashions, restaurants, recipes. Classifieds ½ page. Advertising 20 percent. Circulation 2,500.

The *Voice* at midpoint, October 25, 1962, Vol. VIII, No. 1. "A WEEKLY NEWSPAPER OF GREENWICH VILLAGE." Ten cents. Twenty pages. Lead: "Are the Liberals Little Lost Sheep Gone Astray?" Stephanie Harrington (writing under the name Stephanie Gervis, before she married Michael Harrington) on the race in the 17th Congressional District. Stories on a critic of American newspapers, the UN reaction to the Meredith riot at Ole Miss, an open house at Greenwich Village Peace Center, an anti-Expressway rally, kennel club. The 359th Village Square column by Wilcock. No editorials. Letters 38 inches. Jane Kramer, Jonas Mekas, Michael Smith, Jules Feiffer. Books 0 inches, art 18 inches, movies 15 inches, theater 30, dance 0, photography 0, music 30, TV 18. Restaurants, nightclubs. Classifieds 2½ pages. Advertising 35 percent. Circulation 23,617.

The *Voice* in maturity, October 17, 1968, Vol. XIV, No. 1. "THE WEEKLY NEWSPAPER OF NEW YORK." Fifteen cents. Seventy-two pages. Lead: "A Prophet in His Own Country," Stephen Schlesinger[1] on James Farmer's congressional race in Brooklyn. Pictures of HHH in town. Stories on the Hatchett racial controversy at NYU, the New York teachers' strike, the threshold of pain, Biafran relief, corruption in the anti-poverty administration, articles from Peru and Mexico City. No more Wilcock. No editorials. Letters 52 inches. Steve Lerner, Nat Hentoff, Ross Wetzsteon, Andrew Sarris. Books 0 inches, art 32 inches, movies 55 inches, theater 250, dance 112, photography 40, music 80 inches (plus pop music 57), TV 40, cars 30, gossip 30. Fashions. Classifieds 8½ pages. Advertising 65 percent. Circulation 118,000.

There is no doubt that the *Voice* is a better newspaper today than it was in 1955. It is less parochial, less one-notey, less gray. Its writers are much sharper and freer, more personal and far-ranging. Its graphics,

[1] Yes, son of Arthur, Jr. Dan Wolf seems to have a penchant for using the sons and daughters of the famous: Sally [Murray] Kempton, Susan [Paul] Goodman, Michael [Dwight] Macdonald, Steve [Max] Lerner.

though still awkward, are more sophisticated and witty. Its reviews are not simply opinions but essays. Its fundamental concerns are deeper, more intelligent. But it is not as good as it should be.

The *Voice* is trapped in its bo-liberalism in a world exploding into radicalism. Its age—or Dan Wolf's age—is beginning to show. Ross Wetzsteon: "In the last two years we've become, well, more respectable."[2] Michael Harrington: "It takes a rational, sane political line—not like the undergrounds and the ultra left—which of course I find more congenial." Young staffer: "Two years ago, even last year maybe, there was a crusade. But not now. Now it's more like a lament."

Though the paper appears not to take an official line these days except at election time (it was for Mailer in the mayoral primaries), Dan Wolf can select the writers he finds congenial, mold them congenially, print them congenially. They, he, are down on much of the new world around them: Leary, drugs, Warhol, Rap Brown, Yippies, East Village. Paul Cowan attacks the underground press: "They transmit the forms of the demonstrations but no more than the slightest hint of their content." Richard Goldstein denigrates a book "on the same road as Burroughs, Ginsberg, and Beckett . . . because I find myself caring less and less about any new consciousness. (Do you get the feeling that even the Aquarian Age of literature will be a drag?)" And Feiffer bitterly draws a woolly-haired moustached youth saying: "I occupy buildings—raid files—scream obscenities—throw rocks—and call cops pigs—in an attempt to humanize this brutalized society."

The tone is becoming more and more establishmentarian. Why, even *The New York Review of Books* is more sympathetic. The *Voice* finds its place on the laps of the bo-libs, still. But the young seem to be reading it less and less. Or less and less avidly. Or less and less for what it has to say than for the services (movie listings, apartment ad) it has to offer. And not just the freaked young either.

Jeff Shero can speak for a certain segment of the young and concerned. Not without bias exactly—he's the editor of *Rat,* the psychedelic, angry, revolutionary underground published on the other side of town—but with a sharp intelligence.

I don't think it's sins of commissions so much as sins of omissions that's the trouble with the *Voice*. Like the twenty-one Panthers now in jail on these trumped-up charges. The *Voice* hasn't said a word about it, not one word. You see, they don't really know what's happening, where the action is. Like they care about this mayoralty

---

2 In its advertising as well as its reporting, Fancher has always been pretty stuffy about what he would accept, but the storm hit him recently when he banned a tasteful ad for a homosexual society. The gays picketed the *Voice* offices, the first time anyone can remember such an affront from any group. And the paper forgot to report it that week.

election, who beats who. It doesn't make any difference about an election, you know that—it's not going to change anything, this city is not going to change, and that's the important thing, really *changing* this city.

I read it from time to time, but I don't really think it's relevant to anything I'm concerned with. The writers there aren't interested in change. I read Newfield because I think he's honest, and Hentoff when he was attacking the press, that's good, but I feel that most of the people there are just pushing their own thing, out trying to hustle themselves, you know, and I don't especially trust them. This emphasis on personal journalism—I-was-there-so-it-must-be-more-accurate—well, it isn't more accurate than anything else.

I think what's happened is the *Voice* has grown old, along with its readers. Sure, it still gets one hundred thousand people reading it, but they're the same people who used to read it, most of them, only they're getting older.

Or to take another biased, interesting source, John Wilcock. He helped found the *Voice,* did a column there for eleven years, left in a row in February 1966. The blood is still bad between them. Very bad. But Wilcock's career since then has been in the undergrounds—*East Village Other,* Los Angeles *Free Press,* his own *Other Scenes*—and he has a valuable perspective:

The *Voice* is a liberal paper, and it's grown because the liberals have grown. It's very fashionable, it's been an "in" thing these last few years to be a liberal. But the *Voice* was never far out. It came out just after the McCarthy thing, you know, and people got the wrong idea about it, that it was this great communist paper and all that, but it never was.

Why, they were even embarrassed by my column, it made them uncomfortable. I was on to a lot of things they had never known about and didn't want to know about. Like drugs: I was the first person to talk about Leary, he was still up at Harvard then, but they didn't even want to talk about it, they were very scared of the drug thing. And Ed Sanders and the Fugs—they wouldn't even let me print the name of the Fugs at first, they said, "That's just Wilcock trying to be dirty again." I was on to things before they heard of them, and they wouldn't touch them till they became legitimized somehow, someone else picked them up and said they were OK.

And like the *Voice* prints two sides of everything, always having both points of view. Well, a lot of people out in the underground press feel there *aren't* two sides to every issue, you know, that there is one side that's *right* and that's what should be said. Like, are there really two sides on Vietnam? But the *Voice* will continue to have pieces on both sides because it's become respectable, doesn't want people accusing it of being biased and all that. It's become, really, a part of the establishment.

It's not only underground editors who feel the paper is somewhat out of date, a middle-aged matron in miniskirt. Many others in different parts of the political umbra do too. Take the establishment's own view. Here's a Lindsay aide:

The *Voice* isn't as important as it once was, five years ago, even three. I'd say there's been a decline in quality, it doesn't have the same local sources it used to have, so the political reporting isn't as good. Why, *New York Magazine* is consistently more interesting; they've got better sources in this city than anyone on the *Voice*. It's almost as if the *Voice* has stood still over the years, still back in 1965 or somewhere, while *New York* has gone on and developed new areas.

I'd have to say frankly that the *Voice* bores me, it bores people I know. I don't read it much anymore, except Flaherty, maybe, or Newfield. They're playing classical music and everyone else is listening to rock.

The *Voice* in the early sixties was a drummer for the youth, young kids out of college would read it. Not any more. And the writers—where are the thinking young writers today? A few years ago they'd all be writing for the *Voice,* now they're on the underground papers, or *New York Magazine,* or the radical press.

There's a feeling of, well, opulence about the *Voice*. It's not gritty like *Rat* and *EVO,* where you feel they still have a cause and are doing things rough. It's sitting back. It's too comfortable, too easy, now that they have it made. I don't think of the *Voice* as a young paper any more. It's more like middle-aged.

Or the attitude of a bright Village artist who's been reading the *Voice* for ten years, off and on. These days, mostly off.

I think the paper reached its peak in late 1966, early 1967, when everything was swinging for what I call the Establishment Left. Then they had Newfield's gossip column on politics, and they covered the anti-war movement which the dailies were ignoring, and McNeill was on to the hippies, and they had people really sympathetic to the black thing. And remember, it was practically the only other paper in town.

Well, things have changed now, and the *Voice* hasn't made the change along with the rest of us, I think. They got so damn successful right about then that they felt they must be doing something right, and they stopped there. Like those cryogenics people who freeze themselves when they're in top health so they can thaw out fifty years later, you know?

The *Voice* is still talking about anti-war demonstrators, only now they're against them, they don't like the crazies and the disruptors, the yippies and Hoffman and that crowd, don't like their "bad manners." They don't have anyone who goes over to the East Village anymore, so they don't know what the culture scene is over there, all they know is uptown and television. They're very uptight about the whole black thing—they go back and forth between printing you-better-watch-out-Whitey things you know they don't believe in and running seconds-before-the-apocalypse warnings from white guys who've been scared at some meeting.

And all the time the paper does this silly column about which Lindsay man pinched which Wagner lady's ass, and endless things about boxing, for Christ's sake, and reviews of some real nothing off-off-off-Broadway play in a loft, or how Michael Zwerin likes to ball in London or this dance girl likes to, I don't know *what* she does, in New York. I mean, there are serious things going on in our society, serious troubles and people wondering about serious answers, and the *Voice* tells us that boxing is in trouble.

They just don't have their head where it's at anymore.

Dan Wolf is fifty-two or fifty-three now. He's been through the years of struggle, and seen a lot of subgenerations come and go. He has looked at it all with the insight of cynicism, and it has wearied him, inevitably. His detachedness has reinforced his shyness now, pushing him a little farther back in his editorial chair. But he has made it, his paper has made it. Any wonder he should want to sit back now? Reflect on the vagaries of youth, the inexorable aging process? Gather around him men who are fat, sleek-headed men, and such as sleep o' nights? And wonder about the young with their lean and hungry looks?

The *Voice* has fought its battle. And won it, on its own terms. It is still an important paper—as much for what it was as for what it is—and you still have to read it. It has its loyal following. Its purpose, still. Its occasional brilliancies. But now it speaks for those whose revolutions have become doubts, whose hatreds have become merely distrusts, whose passions have become tempered interests.

You've come a long way, baby, but you got stuck there.

THE BOOK AND THE GREAT COMMUNITY

by WALLACE E. STEGNER

The following excerpt from Wallace Stegner's book **The Sound of Mountain Water** focuses on the role that books play in providing a sense of history. Stegner feels that this sense is lacking in today's cultural climate, partly because of the electronic media's emphasis on the present.

.　　　.　　　.

This is not the great age of books. They have been for a good while now drifting from the north before the breath of the media, and writers as well as librarians have been growing coats of protective hair. A rather small percentage of Americans read books, and many of those who do read, read nonbooks, or treat real books as if they were nonbooks. The paperback revolution that has made everything available has also tended to make everything expendable, like a used magazine. The American device of built-in obsolescence is operative even in literature. And there is always Marshall McLuhan, confidently predicting the Gutenberg Götterdämmerung, the end of print, with all that it has historically meant in terms of sequence, rationality, and tradition. If you are bent upon losing your head rather than keeping it, you do not need the alphabet.

Yet a librarian could be forgiven for thinking that the trouble is not too few books and too few readers, but too many of both. The presses of America alone turn out 25,000 titles a year, and what respectable library can confine itself to the books of its own nation? These days, if we read, we must read the world, and that will multiply the titles by a factor of six or eight, or ten. Assuming that not all of these are frivolous, or irrelevant to the concerns of educated Americans, and assuming that we have money to buy them and shelves to put them on, there is still the massive problem of selection. You can't preserve them all. Anyone who has had a stack card in the Library of Congress, and has pursued one single book through those labyrinthine miles of stacks, under streets and into annexes and through annexes of annexes, knows the nightmare of total inclusiveness. Then there is the problem of what to throw away, and when. One explosive science, biology, proliferates into print at so frenzied a pace that the mere abstracts of a mere month's articles fill a volume the size of a telephone book. Much of that, indispensable this year, is worthless next. Here the problem is not to store knowledge permanently, but to store it briefly and then throw most of it away.

If we solve the difficulties of selection and space and money and disposal, there is still the problem of retrieval, and that multiplies as readers do. Only 15 percent of Americans read books, but that 15 percent equals 30

"Women's lib! Women's lib! Everything now is women's lib!
Let's hope they last longer than pollution did!"

"Yes, it has redeeming social value, Mr. Barnes.
Unfortunately, it has no redeeming commercial value."

million people. Watch the bedlam activity in a great metropolitan library such as the New York Public, and you conclude that your notion of the librarian as ruminative, tranquil, rubbersoled, quietly dusty, gently helpful, needs revision. These people are required every day to build a great haystack in which, ever afterward, they will be able to find every single needle.

But if those were the only difficulties attending the preservation and distribution of books, no one would be dismayed. They may be eased by decentralization, miniaturization, standardized cataloging procedures, computerized retrieval, and other means; and if they cannot be completely solved, that should not bother us. Neither can any other real problem. What is harder for a book-centered generation or a book-centered intellectual class to cope with is the contemporary cultural climate that increasingly disregards the book and depreciates the traditions it reflects.

This climate, described and in fact celebrated by McLuhan, may be, as he thinks, a function of the mass media. In its neglect of print in favor of the image, and in its growing neglect of the eye in favor of the ear, it very probably is. The image is immediate, it needs no complicated symbolic system such as words to communicate its message; and the ear is at least as immediate as the image, and increasingly appealed to. You will find plenty of American homes without bookshelves, but few without a television set, a radio, and probably a stereo. But in its general rejection of the conventional, its emphasis on the present and distrust of the past, its faith in the spontaneous, innovative, and impromptu, as well as in its lively inventiveness, the generation raised on the media is only extending to the limit, and perhaps to absurdity, tendencies that have always been distinctly American, and that in fact have traditionally distinguished western nations from the nations of the East.

.   .   .

The Commission for the Year 2000, looking into present and future for the American Academy of Arts and Sciences, remarks that "a sense of historical time is absent from American thought." We have not only looked with suspicion on the dead hand of the past, we have been unwilling to admit that we cannot make the most profound social changes by a simple act of will or law. Instant Reform is as American a product as instant coffee. We have been as willing to legislate morality, or try to, as we have been to tear down obsolete buildings or retool plants. Thus contemporary dissenters show a family resemblance to the dissenters who left England for Holland in the 17th Century, and left Holland for America, and left the Atlantic colonies (or Nauvoo, to bring the parallel closer home) for the wilderness. In repudiating their heritage they assert it, for it is a heritage of questioning and rebellion. The Haight-Ashbury district, the capital of the Flower People, has its relationship not only to all bohemians, but to the Massachusetts Bay Colony, mad as that comparison seems.

No young person respects history as much as do people who have lived a little of it. "Why do you care where you came from or what your ancestors did?" a girl asked me when I was trying to explain to a group of students my reasons for writing a somewhat personal history book, *Wolf Willow*. "Isn't it what you *are* that matters? *Now?*"

Now. It is a big word with the young, almost as big a word as wow. Between them, those two words seem sometimes to comprehend the responses of a whole generation. Television's greatest hour, the show that above all others satisfied the demand for instantness as well as violent sensation, was Jack Ruby's shooting of Lee Harvey Oswald. The characteristic modern art form is the happening, which can't be programmed or repeated, but only joined in, participated in. Musicians celebrate silence over sound, or noise over music. Painters assert accident over design, a fiercely pure nonart over any sort of technique or manipulation. Pop artists transfer real objects into the art frame with so little organization or change that as Wright Morris suggests, the result differs hardly at all from window dressing. And the Berlin artist who exhibited himself as "a perfect living total work of art" was not thinking of himself as the complex end-product of biological, historical, and cultural forces, and still less as a creator or maker. He was thinking of himself as a happening. He would be right at home in San Francisco.

There is an obvious reason why the young have been able to seize power from the old in this generation as they have not been able to in the past, and the reason is not the media. The young now simply outnumber us, they find they can outvote us as the immigrant Irish found, about 1870, that they could outvote the Boston Yankees. They can not only outvote us, they can outbuy us, outmarch us, outshout us, and in general handle us. They are wooed by advertisers and politicians, they put the fear of God into university administrations, they challenge parents and police.

. . . In 1970, more than half [of all Americans were under 25]. Possessed of the power of numbers, they have naturally learned to exercise it. And it is easy for a generation coming of age in a time of bitter social crisis, and having a somewhat inadequate knowledge of history, to think that it invented idealism and commitment. It is easy to discard elderly counsels along with elderly error and timidity and failure. To trust no one over 30 becomes not only a declaration of personal independence but a moral imperative. Iconoclasm can become as compulsive as any other form of conventional behavior, and the voice of the young hormone is sometimes mistaken for the voice of God. The elders, outvoted, disregarded, held in contempt, watch this youth revolution from the sidelines, dismayed and aghast. Or else they try to join it, adopting cosmetically young ideas and some version of Carnaby Street costume or Haight-Ashbury hairdo, in order to get rich from it or win its votes.

I have said that the majority of Americans read no books at all. The youth who trusts no one over 30 may, since he is often an intellectual of sorts, but he does not read the books his elders admire. He reads in some counter-tradition, Zen or otherwise, and quotes from the Tibetan Book of the Dead, or he reads his own kind, books written in the spirit of intransigent modernity—purified of moral taboos, conventional "taste," traditional techniques, and sometimes coherence. Time, a traditional means of order, is melted down into the simultaneity of solipsism or the drugged consciousness. Form means nothing—what is admired is anything that turns the reader on, and this may be better done by irrational than by formal means. Greek rationalism sets as Afro-Asian mysticism rises, and words that were coined to convey meanings are made to serve as substitutes for strobe lights and over-amplified guitars. The virtue of anything—art, costume, life-style, sexual habits, entertainment, conversation—inheres in its novelty, its capacity to shock or titillate, and its promotion of states of ecstasy.

All of which only reminds an elder with some historical sense of Robert Frost's remark that there are no new ways to be new.

Nevertheless the elder must reserve judgment. This generation is probably as good as other generations, and will make its own contributions. But it cannot long continue the pretense that it is breaking entirely with the Establishment and the past. It will have to rediscover history, it will have to reestablish contact with the tradition it aspires to alter drastically or to destroy. Above all, it will have to acknowledge the absurdity of its cult of total individual freedom. The irresponsible individual "doing his thing" without reference to other individuals or to society is neither new or viable. Neither is the activist bent upon instant and total reform by means which amount to threat and coercion. Anarchy, pursued very long, is a form of suicide both individual and social.

For no risk, as Josiah Royce once said, is ever private or individual, and no accomplishment is merely personal. What saves us at any level of human life is union, mutual responsibility, what St. Paul called charity. The detached individual, Royce wrote,

> is an essentially lost being. That ethical truth lies at the basis of the Pauline doctrine of original sin. It lies also at the basis of the pessimism with which the ancient southern Buddhism of the original founder of that faith . . . viewed the life of man. The essence of the life of the detached individual is, as Gotama Buddha said, an unquenchable desire for bliss, a desire which hastens to enjoyment, and in enjoyment pines to feel desire. Train such a detached individual by some form of high civilized cultivation, and you merely show him what Paul called "the law." The law thus shown he hereupon finds to be in opposition to his selfwill. Sin, as the Pauline phrase has it, "revives."

The Buddha, unlike some of his contemporary western followers, found the salvation of the detached individual to lie in the resignation of all desires. Our own tradition pushes us toward the more dynamic solution of an organized and indoctrinated social interdependence, St. Paul's "charity." More of that human bond than he knows remains in the dropout who has "had" this civilization and wants no more of it. More of it than he would admit survives in the activist bent upon tearing down the imperfect political and social structure and erecting a perfect society where it stood. More of it than he imagines motivates the hippie who believes he has emancipated himself into total freedom and the life of pure sensation. Except for a few minor matters such as Christian faith and chastity, he is a dim copy of St. Francis of Assisi.

So there is virtue in the creation of a great library, even in a time which questions or repudiates so much of the tradition, which has made a specialty of the nonbook, which has cultivated instant communication and has taken speed-reading courses that will let it read *Hamlet* in 12 minutes—if it hasn't already read *Hamlet* in comic book form. Bright as the media are, they have little memory and little thought: their most thoughtful programs are likely to take the form of the open-end discussion, a form as inconclusive and random as the happening. Thought is neither instant nor noisy, and it is not very often tribal or communal in the fashion admired by McLuhan. It thrives best in solitude, in quiet and in the company of the past, the great community of recorded human experience. That recorded experience is essential whether one hopes to reassert some aspect of it, or attack it. "Like giants," Robert Frost said, "we are always hurling experience ahead of us to pave the future with against the day when we may want to strike a line of purpose across it for somewhere."

DEATH OF A ROCK STAR

The death of popular rock singer Janis Joplin provides an interesting example of the diversity that exists among the print media. The immediate news accounts differ from the later magazine stories largely because of the time pressure under which they were written. But the kind of coverage was also determined by the readership of each medium. For instance, while most newspapers reported Miss Joplin's death with a single article, **Rolling Stone** magazine devoted most of its October 29, 1970, issue to her life, death, and music, and then in the following issue printed a number of letters from readers about Janis.

Janis Joplin Dies; Rock Star Was 27

by REUTERS

HOLLYWOOD, Oct. 4—Janis Joplin, the rock singer, was found dead in her Hollywood apartment tonight. She was 27 years old.

The cause of death was not immediately determined, but the police said she apparently died of an overdose of drugs. They said she had been dead for about two hours when she was found shortly after 10 P.M.

Miss Joplin was the second noted American pop singer to die in less than three weeks. Jimi Hendrix, 27, died in London Sept. 18 after taking nine strong sleeping tablets.

Totally Involved

She would stand before her audience, microphone in hand, long red hair flailing, her raspy voice shrieking in rock mutations of black country blues. Pellets of sweat flew from her contorted face and glittered in the beam of footlights. Janis Joplin sang with more than her voice. Her involvement was total.

She lived that way, too. The girl from Port Arthur, Tex., who moved into stardom by way of the San Francisco rock upsurge, talked openly of the Southern Comfort she drank and of the joys of being inebriated. With the same abandon that she sang, she drove her Porsche through the hills of San Francisco, a fast looking car, decorated with psychedelic butterflies.

Once a reporter asked her what she wanted out of life [and she replied, "Staying] stoned, staying happy and having a good time. I'm doing just what I want with my life, enjoying it."

"When I get scared and worried," she said at the time, "I tell myself, 'Janis, just have a good time.' So I juice up real good and that's just what I have."

By that time she was riding the crest of rock popularity, having soared into prominence with her rendition of "Love Is Like a Ball and Chain" at the 1967 Monterey Rock Festival. The song, said one critic, "was wrenched out of some deep dark nether region of her Texas soul."

Back home in Port Arthur she had been a misfit. "I read, I painted, I didn't hate niggers," she once recalled. "Man, those people back home hurt me. It makes me happy to know I'm making it and they're back there, plumbers just like they were."

She tried college several times, and a job as a computer programmer. She collected Leadbelly and Bessie Smith records, but she never really sang professionally until June of 1966. An old friend, Travis Rivers, had formed a band in San Francisco called Big Brother and the Holding Company. He sent for her and once again she left Port Arthur, this time for the Haight Ashbury section of San Francisco.

It was June of that year and the band was playing the Avalon, a ballroom. She had just arrived and the ambiance of the flailing, gyrating, burgeoning "youth scene" of San Francisco was heady.

"I couldn't believe it, all that rhythm and power," she said.

I got stoned just feeling it, like it was the best dope in the world. It was so sensual, so vibrant, loud, crazy. I couldn't stay still; I had never danced when I sang, but there I was moving and jumping. I couldn't hear myself, so I sang louder and louder. By the end I was wild. . . .

There followed performances at the Psychedelic Supermarket in Boston, the Kinetic Playground in Chicago, the Whisky A-Go-Go in Los Angeles and the Fillmore East in New York. There was "Cheap Thrills," the album that sold more than a million copies. And there was Miss Joplin screaming, "Take another piece of my heart, baby."

There were big money and rock festivals. And the tempo of her private life kept pace with the driving songs. The Southern Comfort distillery gave her a fur coat in recognition of the publicity she gave the company by drinking from a bottle at her concerts.

Her home in San Francisco was decorated in Rococo bordello style. She shared it with a dog named George and a Siamese fighting fish named Charley whose aquarium was a wine bottle.

Her behavior was explosive. In November, 1969, she was arrested after a concert in Tampa, Fla., for screaming obscenities at a policeman in the audience. She was temperamental and demanded the same dedication of her backup musicians as she herself gave. She split from the Holding Company and formed her own band, the Janis Joplin Full Tilt Boogie Band.

And there were those who said that neither her voice nor her health could stand the demands she made upon them, on stage and off. Her answer: "Maybe I won't last as long as other singers, but I think you can destroy your now worrying about tomorrow."

from THE ST. CLOUD *Daily Times*

Top Pop Singer Janis Joplin Is Found Dead

HOLLYWOOD (UPI)—Singer Janis Joplin, whose husky, near-shouting vocal style propelled her to the top of the pop charts, was found dead at her apartment late Sunday.

Her body was found wedged between a bed and nightstand by one of the members of her group, "Janis Joplin Full Tilt Boogie Band." She was clad in a short nightgown.

Sgt. Ed Sanchez of the Hollywood Police Department said the singer had "numerous hypodermic needle marks on her left forearm." Some appeared to be covered over by makeup but were from 2 to 14 days old, he said. No drugs or narcotic paraphernalia was found in the room.

Sanchez said an autopsy would be performed to determine the cause of death.

Miss Joplin, 27, shot to the top of the recording world shortly after her appearance at the 1967 Monterey Pop Festival. At the time she was with "Big Brother and the Holding Company," a San Francisco rock group which had a large Western following. She left Big Brother in 1968 to form her own group.

Miss Joplin drank "Southern Comfort" by the quart while on stage and her fans would bring her scores of bottles of the liquor.

Her two biggest hits, "Piece of My Heart" and "Ball and Chain" came while she was with Big Brother on their "Cheap Thrills" album.

The oldest child of a refinery executive in Port Arthur, Tex., she ran away from home at the age of 17. She began singing professionally in clubs near the University of Texas at Austin and it was there she started her "white" blues style, which she called "cosmic."

Heavily influenced by negro singers Otis Redding and Bessie Smith, nearly all her songs were of rural blues origin.

She had been in the Los Angeles area since Aug. 24 recording a new album. Her body was discovered by guitarist John Cooke who said she failed to show up for a date.

It was the second death in the pop singing world in two weeks. Singer-guitarist Jimi Hendrix died of an overdose of drugs in London Sept. 18.

FROM **Newsweek** MAGAZINE

"SINGING IS BETTER

by HUBERT SAAL

Janis Joplin sang the blues, a black man's music, even though she was white, because she was born with ready-made grief inside her. No matter how she tried, no matter what the anodyne, she could not quiet her devils. One song she sang summed up her life: the "Kozmic Blues."

She was something to see and hear. She couldn't have held back if she tried. "I'd rather not sing than sing quiet," she said. She sounded her barbaric yawp into a mike plugged into the world. She never hesitated to sacrifice the beautiful tone for the raw power of emotion, for the animal sounds that accompanied the animal sensual grace of her passionate body. Visibly flesh, she came across as pure feeling. "Look at me, man," she once said. "I'm selling my heart."

At least the stage channeled her abandon. "Singing is better than any dope," she said. But offstage her appetites went unchecked, for alcohol and men and fast cars. "Whatever you need get it now," she used to say. "The other way you end up old and who needs it?" She never sang anything she didn't feel. The lyrics of one song on her unfinished album go: "A woman left lonely/Will grow tired of waiting/She'll do crazy things/On lonely occasions."[1] Last week in a Los Angeles motel littered with liquor bottles she was found dead at 27 from an overdose of heroin. Drugs had proved, if not better, stronger than singing.

Less than three weeks before, the brilliantly original blues guitarist Jimi Hendrix died a miserable death, choking on his own vomit in a London hotel after taking nine sleeping pills. There were striking parallels between Janis and Jimi, even if she was female and white and he was male and black. They were both 27, and they had achieved sudden prominence together at the now-legendary Monterey Pop Festival in 1967. Hendrix also embodied sexuality on stage—he could play his guitar between his legs, with his teeth,

---

THAN ANY DOPE"

flat on his back, kissing, caressing and sometimes in the end smashing it to smithereens. He could also play it straight, flying fingers venting a sur-realistic imagination, never more effective than when he closed the Wood-stock Festival with an anguished version of "The Star-Spangled Banner."

. . .

Janis Joplin was cremated last week and her ashes scattered along the Pacific. She leaves behind a contradictory recollection of an aggressively shy, coarsely sweet, belligerently vulnerable child-woman, not pretty, but beautiful when she sang, who even after years of practice still tripped over the obscenities tumbling from her mouth, who wore jangling bracelets, kooky dresses and floppy hats, and who almost literally sang her heart out as fervently as any black woman from the Mississippi Delta.

Superstar: Janis's friends called her Pearl. She liked that. She thought it was closer to what she was. She'd had no choice in her name when she was born in Port Arthur, Texas. "In high school, do you know they once threw things at me in the hall? I don't know why. I was strange, sure. It was like the whole environment turned on me, as if the trees said, go home. They hurt me in Port Arthur." She got out and made her way eventually to San Francisco during the incredible beginnings of the acid-rock groups. Then she sang "Ball and Chain" at Monterey —where Jimi Hendrix set fire to his guitar—and she was suddenly in one great incandescence a superstar. She played the part, overeating, overdressing, overdrinking, overeverything. "I love being a star more than life itself," she said.

Janis liked it when someone wrote how sexy her breasts were. "She'd been called many things," says a friend, "but never desirable. Before, she was kind of a pig, never bathed or dressed. Now she was like a little girl playing dress up, crying out to be pretty, to be loved."

"Have you ever been loved?" she asked a friend after a concert in Michigan. "I haven't. I only feel it on stage. I'm going to write a song about making love to 25,000 people in a concert and then going back to my room alone." Sensitive and smart, she was in a fundamental sense anti-intellectual. "You can fill your life up with ideas and go home alone," she said. "When I sing, I'm just feeling that love and lust and warm-touching thing inside your body that everybody digs."

FROM **LIFE** MAGAZINE

Drugs and death in the run-down world of rock music

by ALBERT GOLDMAN

First, it was Jimi Hendrix, rock's flamboyant superstar, snuffed out last month at 27, dead on arrival at a London hospital. The cause? Suffocation from vomiting while unconscious from sleeping pills. Accidental overdose? Suicide? The coroner could not say.

Then it was Janis Joplin, rock's greatest soul belter, also 27, found dead on the floor of a Los Angeles motel room last week, fresh needle marks on her left arm, a red balloon filled with a white powder stashed in her trash can. Coroner's finding: overdose of drugs.

Why should a young man and woman of such energy and talent, endorsed with immense success, imperil their lives with dope? If you were drawn even for a moment into Jimi Hendrix's breathless quest for life, his urgent headlong pursuit not simply of pleasure but of the most elusive and exotic states of mind and soul, you would know that his death was an inevitable product of his life. Hendrix once sent someone a bag of cocaine with a high-flown note inscribed in flowery script: "Within I grace thee with wings. O lovely and true Birds of Heavenly Snow and Crystals. Fly my love as you have before. Pleasures are only steps and this . . . just one more." That was the rhetoric of his life and it swept him along heedless of dangers that made his mere existence a daily miracle. It sent him flickering among the candles and bottles and fuming incense of his nocturnal day, it moved him to sniff cocaine and drop acid and drink wine all in a row, like the chord changes in a tune on which he was improvising.

Janis Joplin was possessed by a very different demon. She doted on the image of the hard-drinking, hard-living, hard-loving red-hot mama. She gloried in self-destruction, tearing out her throat with every song, brandishing a bottle of Southern Comfort on the stage, turning rock-solid blues like **Ball and Chain** into screaming, wailing nightmares. "Sure I could take better care of my health," she once said. "It might add a few years—but what the hell!"

The reckless lives of both Jimi Hendrix, a poor black, and Janis Joplin, a middle-class Southern white, are not unique within the context of our myths of art, show business, the jazz genius, the existential hero. Hendrix and Joplin had the additional pressure, as the king and queen of rock, of ruling over a crumbling kingdom. Since the peak year of 1967, when they flashed on the scene, rock has run down badly. This year of 1970 has seen the most lavish outlays ever made in the history of the pop recording business; yet hardly a star has come up with anything that could match his previous records. The rock festival has degenerated into a grotesque tragicomedy peopled by swindling promoters, gate-crashing kids, club-wielding cops and money-mad stars.

The world that once adored those innocent boys, the Beatles, which decked itself with flowers, practiced transcendental meditation, came together in the joyous Woodstock festival, danced wildly and spoke gently of love and peace—that beguiling world now lies broken. The rock culture has become the drug culture. Convinced that everything is fraud, feasting on films that feed their paranoia, feeling helpless and betrayed, huddled together, thousands of ordinary kids are a set-up for the pusher. What they are addicted to ultimately is not drugs but dreams.

So many of these kids seem indifferent to life. Where they once enhanced their looks and asserted their careless vitality through gay psychedelic plumage, they now shuffle around in drab, raggedy, dead men's clothes. Instead of exulting in the physical joys of dancing, the sensuous pleasures of love, the whole sensorium of rock music, most of the kids I see in the college classes I teach, at the rock concerts, or hanging out in the East Village seem depressed and apathetic, reckless about dropping, popping or smoking anything that promises a momentary high.

It is within the context of this New Depression that the deaths of the rock stars must be pondered. When I talked recently to friends of Jimi Hendrix and Janis Joplin, they painted almost identical pictures of the two stars during their last days. Both appeared to be groping for a new phase. Already past the frenzy of sudden fame, wise to the make-believe in their own legends, aware that both they and rock had lost the spark, both performers were trying to prepare new songs with new bands to reaffirm their status as superstars. It seems likely that the transition proved too much for them. After a brief high ride on the hot blast of the great years, the sudden chill of change, of reality, must have been deadly.

ROLLING STONE

Janis Joplin

When Janis Joplin failed to show up at Sunset Sound Studios by 6 PM, Paul Rothschild, her producer, gave in to the strange "flashing" he had been feeling all day and sent John Cooke, a road manager for the Full Tilt Boogie Band, over to the Landmark Motor Hotel to see why she wasn't answering her phone. "I'd never worried about her before," Rothschild said, "although she'd been late lots of times. It was usually that she stopped to buy a pair of pants or some chick thing like that." October 4th was a Sunday however, and there were few places to go, even in Hollywood. Even for Janis.

The Landmark is a big stucco building on Franklin Avenue. It is convenient to the sound studios on Sunset Blvd. and near the offices of the record companies and music publishers. It is painted a garish "sunburst orange" and "bear brown" (according to the man at the desk), and it is the favorite motel for visiting performers. The lobby has large plastic plants and some vaguely psychedelic designs on its walls, but the motel's attraction is its tolerance. The guy behind the desk remembered, laughing, the time a guest called to complain about the noise from a series of rooms where members of the Jefferson Airplane were having a party. "The guy who complained was thrown out," he said. It was Janis' kind of place.

When John Cooke got there it was almost 7 PM. He noticed Janis' car in the lot, and that the drapes in her first floor room were drawn. She didn't answer her door when he knocked, or even when he banged and yelled. He spoke to the manager, Jack Hagy, who agreed that they should go into the room. Janis was lying wedged between the bed and a nightstand, wearing a short nightgown. Her lips were bloody when they turned her over, and her nose was broken. She had $4.50 clutched in one hand.

Cooke called a doctor, then phoned Janis' attorney, Robert Gordon. Gordon claims he went over the room carefully but found no narcotics or drug paraphernalia. The police were called. When they arrived at around 9 PM, they too found no drugs or "works." But they told reporters Janis had "fresh needle marks on her arm, 10 to 14 of them, on her left arm."

By the time the 11 PM newscaster had finished his brief report, phone calls were already spreading wild rumors—Janis had been killed by some jealous guy, by a dealer, even by the CIA; Janis had done herself in because of some guy, because she thought she was fading, because she'd always been self-destructive. Each new theory had its "informed" proponents, and each was equally groundless.

The confusion was not helped by Los Angeles County Coroner Thomas Noguchi's preliminary report, issued the following morning. It said she "died of an overdose of drugs," but did not specify *what* drugs—alcohol, sleeping pills or something harder.

Gordon, understandably, tried to counteract many of the bizarre rumors and soften the edge of some of the wilder headlines by saying that he felt the drug inferences were unfounded and that Janis had died in much the way Jimi Hendrix had—from an overdose of sleeping pills, followed, in her case, by a fall from the bed.

By Tuesday, however Noguchi reported that Janis, who was 27, had in fact injected heroin into her left arm several hours before she died, and that it was an overdose that killed her. He said an inquest will be held, and that "behavioral scientists" would try to determine if the OD was "intentional."

When questioned about the facial injuries, police said they'd "ruled out the possibility of violence. She could have broken her nose when she collapsed," one detective said. The odd

amount of money in her hand remains a mystery, however, and will feed the imaginations of the people who *must* account in some tangible way for her death. At present, the explanations range from "it was change for a bag"—a bag of heroin goes for about $15 in Los Angeles these days—to grotesques about "change for a call for help" (but the phone in her room, as in most motel and hotel rooms, did not require change).

Reports on Janis' mood in the last weeks of her life do not help much either. They are perhaps appropriately contradictory. Superstars just fade, but culture heroines die hard.

FROM

CORRESPONDENCE, LOVE LETTERS & ADVICE

ROLLING STONE MAGAZINE

A couple of words for Janis Joplin. Man, I love her.

OPEL STU
BAKERSFIELD, CALIF.

I wish we could have listened to you ages more; maybe you could have taught us what to do. Damn, we're so slow, maybe we never would have understood and maybe you were right to free yourself from us, who had trapped you in your loneliness.

I don't think we meant it. We bought the records and saw all those concerts and shouted out our love from the seats we pushed aside to get closer to you. We loved you, Janis, but you sang so lonely up there we just couldn't believe you'd ever be anything else. A lot of us clung tighter to our love after we knew you for those hours you showed us: Didn't anyone ever hold you closer, lady blue?

If we were to talk about the best, maybe a little loneliness died in us

all, with you. I'd take it back, much more than my share of it, if you'd come back too, but liberty and death is yours forever.

SEAN KILTY
BOSTON

Man, in the end, who is really smarter —Elvis Presley and Tom Jones, or hard dopers like Jimi and Brian and Janis?

JACK
TORONTO

Don't you think you owe it to print articles and pictures of what drugs *really* are like, and what they can do? I'm sick of seeing friends get so incoherent and foggy that they go dribbling spit all over. For God's sake, help these people by telling the truth. Life isn't all that bad, life is a natural high the way it is.

KATHY AMELIA T.
SKOKIE, ILL.

THE PRINT MEDIA

STUDY QUESTIONS

1. In "The American Periodical Press and Its Impact," Wolseley says that the magazine is a reflector of life as it really is or a reflector of the publisher's idea of what life is. Do you see some problems that might arise if there are discrepancies between the two? Can you think of a current magazine in which such discrepancies are apparent?

2. How do the goals of a general magazine differ from those of a specialized one? Which type of magazine do you think might have a greater influence upon society? What factors do you have to consider in answering this question?

3. Can you find evidence in magazines today that would support Wolseley's conclusion that most magazines do not fully serve the public?

4. Felker calls attention to the fact that the development of the electronic media has forced changes upon the print media. Can you give some examples? What do you think of Felker's statement that print must be for the "educated and affluent elite"? Do you think this is true today?

5. Felker shows that the editor of a periodical is an important force in its success or failure. Can you think of any magazines that clearly reflect an editor's personal philosophy? Examine the contents of a periodical in depth. Do some elements of the magazine suggest that the editor is trying to convey a particular message? In how many aspects of the magazine do you see his philosophy? How strongly does he push his view?

6. In "The Black Magazine," Wolseley points out that more than any other medium, the magazine may be able to help the Negro in his search for his place in society. Can the same be said of other groups in society—militants, artists, intellectuals, youth? Discuss. How does the underground press which Kunkin describes serve this function?

7. Examine various underground newspapers. What functions do they perform? How are these functions different from those of the traditional, establishment press? How do various undergrounds differ among themselves? If you can find back issues, how do the newspapers today differ from their original concept? If it is available to you, compare the Los Angeles **Free Press** today with Kunkin's description (in August 1969) of its goals. Consider what Sale points out—that there is danger in an underground paper's becoming "establishment," that **The Village Voice,** for example, is "liberal" while the "world is exploding into radicalism."

8. Have the periodical press and the electronic media made the book outmoded? Stegner is pessimistic about America's cultural climate if the tendency to overlook the traditional media in favor of newer media continues.

Do we need books? What can books do that cannot be accomplished by the other print media? By the electronic media?

9. What place does the printed word have in communication? If the subtitle of Julio Mitchel's photographic essay is correct, pictures are worth a thousand words. Examine some of the pictorial and graphic material in the print media. Does it supplement the print material or, like "The Silent Majority," make its own comment? How does the printed picture differ from the moving picture?

BIBLIOGRAPHY FOR FURTHER STUDY

Abel, Bob. "The City Slickers." *Columbia Journalism Review,* VII (Spring, 1968), 11–18.

Antupit, Samuel N. "Laid Out and Laid Waste: On the Visual Violation of American Magazines." *Antioch Review,* XXIX (Spring, 1969), 57–66.

"Blues for Janis." *Time,* XCVI (October 19, 1970), 54.

Chandler, Otis. "Newspapers and the Revolution." *Seminar* (September, 1969), 12–14.

Consumer Magazine and Farm Publication Rates and Data. Skokie, Ill.: Standard Rate and Data Service, Inc., published monthly.

Directory: Newspapers and Periodicals. Philadelphia: N. W. Ayer & Son, published annually.

Duncan, C. J. "The Changing Market for Serious 'Books.'" *Publishers' Weekly,* CXCVIII (September 21, 1970), 188–90.

Editor & Publisher International Year Book. New York: Editor & Publisher, published annually.

Gent, George. "Death of Janis Joplin Attributed to Accidental Heroin Overdose." *The New York Times* (October 6, 1970), 50, cols. 2 and 3.

"Janis Joplin." *The East Village Other* (October 13, 1970), 11.

Kornbluth, Jesse. "This Place of Entertainment Has No Fire Exit: The Underground Press and How It Went." *Antioch Review,* XXIX (Spring, 1969), 91–99.

Literary Market Place: The Business Directory of American Publishing. New York: Bowker, published annually.

Locke, W. N. "Selling Books in Libraries." *College and Research Libraries,* XXX (January, 1969), 39–44.

McCann, Richard. "Prescription for the Post: Diet for Health." *Grassroots Editor,* X (January–February, 1969), 12–14.

Newspaper Rates and Data. Skokie, Ill.: Standard Rate and Data Service, published monthly.

Peterson, Theodore. *Magazines in the Twentieth Century.* 2nd ed. Urbana: The University of Illinois Press, 1964.

Reston, James. *The Artillery of the Press.* New York: Harper & Row, 1967.

Ridgeway, James. "The *Ramparts* Story." *The New York Times Magazine* (April 20, 1969), 36.

Roth, Joel A. "Publishing's Multi-media Future." *Book Production Industry,* XLIV (December, 1968), 35–39.

Steinem, Gloria. "What 'Playboy' Doesn't Know About Women Could Fill a Book." *McCall's,* XCVIII (October, 1970), 76–77, 139–40.

Talese, Gay. *The Kingdom and the Power.* New York: World Publishing Co., 1969.

Tebbel, John. "Magazines—New, Changing, Growing." *Saturday Review,* LII (February 8, 1969), 55–56.

Watson, Campbell. "627 Underground Newspapers: New Youth Press Laid to Vacuum." *Editor & Publisher,* CII (September 20, 1969), 12.

THE ELECTRONIC MEDIA

TV *and* *the* ARTS

The prospect before us

by JOHN TEBBEL

John Tebbel, Professor of Journalism at New York University,
cites the low cultural level of most programs on television
(the medium with the largest audience)
and argues for an alternative to commercial television.

We have reached the point in the development of television where the private monopoly in programing enjoyed by the networks has come into direct conflict with the public interest on a number of fronts. Nowhere, perhaps, has this conflict been sharper than on the cultural front. For years the medium has been under heavy attack by people who despise its cultural poverty, and recently there has also been a marked disaffection in the mass audience itself—a boredom with the product. No group is more bored than the young. College students who were glued to the tube as children now turn away from it. To use the most battered word of our times, they do not consider it relevant—politically, culturally, or any other way.

Even movies, upon which television has been relying so heavily, show signs of slipping in popularity. Motion picture audiences in this country are growing steadily younger, but the movies shown on television reflect, in general, the conventional middle-class and middle-aged values which have dominated movie exhibition in small towns for decades. The young prefer the kind of movies shown in art houses in cities and college communities; television does not dare show these films except occasionally and late—and even then, in cut versions—or on a UHF channel which has relatively little to lose. People who do watch movies on television are more and more irritated by the stupefying number of commercials, which often make the picture itself seem almost incidental.

As Jack Gould remarked recently in *The New York Times,*

much more direction and push from New York will be indicated to induce Hollywood to forget about formula stuff and use TV as a creative instrument in its own right. Sales-oriented executives, capable in their chosen field but largely numb in terms of venturous theater, still dominate too many decisions at the TV networks.

True, perhaps, but critics and resident intellectuals will likely be one with Nineveh and Tyre before TV is used "as a creative instrument in its own right" by those who presently control it. For television is a *mass* medium, in the truest sense of that abused phrase, and what television's critics sometimes forget is that the history of mass culture shows us that the more the base of a medium is broadened, the lower its cultural level will be. Television has the broadest base of any medium, and by and large, it rests at the lowest cultural level.

What else should we expect? For more than a decade, the critical litany has been that if television's entrepreneurs would only conceive of their medium in the lofty terms everyone envisioned when it first appeared as a factor in national life, everything would be fine. It is asserted repeatedly that the networks underestimate their audiences, that the ratings game is rigged and does not truly represent the national taste, and that programing

'I'll Select the Shows!'

more closely reflects the commercialism of the network operators than it does the cultural potential of the audience.

One could argue this question endlessly, and indeed that seems to be its fate. It is not difficult to cast doubts on the ratings business; sometimes the business obligingly casts doubts on itself. Nor is it hard to castigate much, or most, of what appears on television; no dead horse has ever been beaten more thoroughly. But had the Caesars given the ancient Romans chamber music instead of bread and circuses, there is no reason to believe that the cultural level of the populace would have been raised appreciably.

If the critics are right, they will have to explain why *Bonanza* was not only the number one show in America for so long, but quickly attained that status in every country where it was shown, in Europe and Asia alike. *Bonanza,* situation comedies of every stripe, audience participation games, daytime serials, old Hollywood movies, new Hollywood movies—all have one thing in common. They are mass entertainments, designed for a mass medium.

As long as television remains a private commercial enterprise instead of a government-sponsored institution, as it is almost everywhere else, it seems idle to condemn the network heads for programing what they know most people will look at, and therefore what these businessmen will be able to sell best. Surely the hope for the future does not lie in trying to persuade or force the networks to purvey something that would result in their economic suicide. Nor does it lie in government ownership or greater federal control. (Curiously, one hears and reads the same criticisms of television in Britain that are so common here.) Recent attempts to force the networks and individual stations to provide a diversity of programing on FM channels have met with failure, except in a handful of cases.

Would it not be more rational to accept the fact that there is a mass audience with concurrent tastes, to which commercial television is going to cater despite whatever vicissitudes of programing it may pass through as public taste fluctuates within a necessarily narrow range? Then would it not be better to proceed from that point and work out ways and means by which minority cultural tastes can be met and satisfied? Is there any valid reason why *Bonanza* cannot coexist with programing for a higher level of taste?

The consensus today seems to be that a viable alternative to commercial television must be provided, if the medium is to have any meaning beyond simple mass entertainment. As matters stand, music lovers cannot turn to it. What was once offered, holding so much promise, has virtually disappeared . . . . FM radio is the only resource for those who want serious music, and even there it is under commercial pressures that are presently diminishing its presence. Similarly, the balletomane finds dance represented only fleetingly in occasional "specials." Looking at art is a growing interest among Americans, as crowded galleries and museums testify, but it is

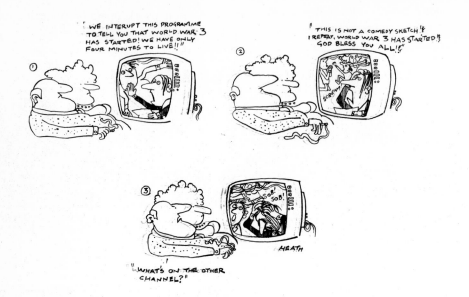

scarcely represented on television. Theater on the tube, which once held the most promise of all, has also been largely relegated to "specials," and many of these are of doubtful quality. Serious, young, creative playwrights no longer turn to television, as they did at its inception.

If we agree that a viable alternative is essential, two formidable questions arise: Who determines what is to be programed? And how is it to be financed?

The second question is the more difficult. Television is by far the most expensive of the media, and there is little reason to believe it will ever be less costly, except at the receiving end. The cost of experimenting, even of trying to establish the best alternative, has brought nearly every reform attempt to the brink of disaster.

In the case of the Ford Foundation–sponsored Public Broadcast Laboratory, one can see how hard it is going to be to answer both questions. The PBL was financed as a two-year experiment to extend and explore the range of viable alternatives to commercial television already being offered by National Educational Television; as such, it was able to use the facilities of NET stations around the country. It had some splendid plans. Yet, from the beginning it had to contend with a wide disparity of ideas, among everyone concerned, about what constituted good public broadcasting. The governing editorial board disagreed with the creative staff; the creative staff often disagreed with itself.

FROM

POGO PRIMER FOR PARENTS

by WALT KELLY

*T*here are a few things to practice not doing. Do not be afraid of your t.v. set. These things are probably here to stay. Do not be a-fraid of your child. He is not here to stay. He is a precious visitor. Do not wind your child up and set him to watch the t.v. unguided. Do not wind the t.v. set up and set it to watch your child. A machine is a bad sole companion. It needs help. You can help it. Love your child.

Reprinted from Walt Kelly, *Pogo Primer for Parents* (U.S. Department of Health, Education, and Welfare, 1961), p. 23.

Participatory
Television

by NAT HENTOFF

In this article Nat Hentoff speculates about whether
the individual television viewer will ever be able to have
an active voice in what is broadcast. He sees this as
possible through decentralization and through
localization of programing, but predicts strong
opposition from owners of commercial stations and
holders of cable television franchises.

*Television continues to strengthen its ranking as the medium most people
rely on for news and the medium they are most inclined to believe.*

WALTER D. SCOTT, Chairman of the Board, NBC

*. . . One basic assumption underlying the First Amendment's protection
of speech is that "the widest possible dissemination of information from
diverse and antagonistic sources is essential to the welfare of the public . . ."* Associated Press v. United States, *326 U.S. 1, 20 (1944).*

Nicholas Johnson, FCC

*What may puzzle the lay observer is the enormous energies and resources
which the broadcasting industry has invested in trying to question accessibility to the airways by the average citizen.*

Jack Gould, *New York Times*

Yes, television is the quickest—and often the most powerful—means of
persuasion. And yes, television does *not,* to say the least, provide "the
widest possible dissemination of information from diverse and antagonistic
sources." As Jack Gould has emphasized: "Television, to be blunt about
it, is basically a medium with a mind closed to the swiftly moving currents

Participatory Television: From *Evergreen Review* (October, 1969). Reprinted by
permission of Nat Hentoff.

of tomorrow. The networks have erected an electronic wall around the status quo."

Where is the television time for regular commentary by the Black Panthers, by the various wings of SDS, by Mexican-Americans, by Puerto Ricans, by poor whites—by you? On what station can black students present their own documentaries on their schools? Or white students? Or radical teachers? Or nonradical teachers?

Well, you see, this kind of programming just doesn't seem "suitable" to management. And television management is small and concentrated—and often quite distant. In the eleven largest cities of this country, not a single network-affiliated VHF (very high frequency) station is independently and locally owned. All of them are owned by the networks, newspapers, or multiple station owners.

For a more general picture of television's "independence": of the 496 commercial stations around the country, 160 are hooked up one way or another with newspapers. And there are 44 communities in which the only local paper controls the only local television station.

The folks who decide on programming for the commercial stations, urban and rural, already know what the Black Panthers and dissident students are all about. They've been "informed" by the newspapers who pay the salaries of many of them. That's all been covered, friend. No need to preempt Lucy for anything like *that*.

A few of the "educational" television stations are somewhat more open

*"Say, let's generate a little excitement around
here! What's on television?"*

to "diverse and antagonistic sources" of information. But not too diverse, and certainly not too antagonistic. And in any case, just as on commercial outlets, the station or the network decides who is to be heard and in what context.

That—along with concentration of ownership—is the essence of American television as an undemocratic activity. Jack Gould has put this very clearly: "The test of a communications medium, especially one dependent on survival through use of air waves that are public property, is a willingness and commitment to make its facilities available *to persons other than employees under its direct supervision.*"

Do you know of any station in this country with such willingness and commitment? Oh, a few UHF (ultra high frequency) stations occasionally make tentative moves in that direction, but there, too, the power to decide and control is the station's.

By contrast, as FCC member Nicholas Johnson has pointed out in *TV Guide,*

In Holland, any group that can get 15,000 persons to support its list of proposed programs is awarded free time on the Dutch Television Network for a monthly program. There is even an organization for tiny and often eccentric splinter groups without 15,000 supporters. If a similar experiment were conducted in this country, groups interested in electronic music, drag racing, handicrafts, camping, as well as the League of Women Voters, the National Association for the Advancement of Colored People, local school boards, theatre and drama associations, the Young Republicans (and who knows, even the Smothers Brothers), could obtain television time to broadcast programs prepared under their supervision.

But this won't happen here unless the extraordinary technological possibilities now beginning to become available through cable television are made accessible to the "average citizen." Present cable systems have the capacity to relay at least twenty separate channels to a home connected to the system. That number can eventually rise to fifty, and probably more. In addition, since these channels are distributed over a wired hookup from a central control point, a simple switching process can direct individual channels to specific small neighborhoods. Watts or Greenwich Village—or even smaller subdivisions—could have their own channels. Also, because reception is so much clearer on cable television, it's likely that as many as ninety percent of American homes will be hooked into a cable system within a decade.

The conditions, then, for decentralization of television are at hand. But, specifically, how can this be accomplished? And how much will it cost?

Television can be democratized, as the American Civil Liberties Union makes clear in a presentation to the FCC, by requiring cable television companies, "as a condition of franchising, . . . to provide separate and individual channels by geographic units of any reasonable size down to a thousand or fewer households." And these local units could then be hooked up regionally and nationally with other groups with similar interests and concerns. Watts and Bedford-Stuyvesant could share ideas and information. So could high school students in Los Angeles and New York.

It's easy to do. Cable television is like the telephone system with its 20,000 local "exchanges." The various geographic units that are possible in cable television can, as the ACLU has noted, "be interconnected in an unlimited variety of patterns." As for the cost, the ACLU proposes that cable television operate as "a common carrier, leasing channel time to all those who desire it at uniform, fair, and reasonable rates with the operator of the facility having no control over the intelligence which is carried through his channels." If these fees are carefully regulated by the FCC, there is no reason why the television screen cannot become as accessible to "the average citizen" as long-distance telephone service. And for those who can't afford any fees at all, the service should be made available without cost. These are *public* airwaves, right?

Nor need the price of equipment—cameras, lights, etc.—be prohibitive. Equipment can be rented. But why shouldn't it be obtained permanently, through government grants, for education, for job training, for community involvement in its own affairs? And why shouldn't some of it be given to local communities by the commercial stations and networks which have been prospering so long and so well from "free" television? Giving equipment will not only improve the "image" of commercial stations and networks but will also result in tax credits. (The ideal corporate gesture: a profitable benison.)

The potential ramifications of bringing democracy to television can just barely be conceived at present. Consider the learning possibilities, on all kinds of levels. From individual neighborhoods with access to their own channels—and with connections outside—there will emerge thousands of black, Puerto Rican, and Mexican-American commentators, reporters, engineers, lighting directors, and administrators. These, along with whites of the underclass (why not an Appalachian channel?), could not otherwise become active *participants* in television in so short a time.

Certainly many will then choose to make more money by working on the commercial stations which, by the way, will no longer be able to claim a paucity of "qualified" television professionals among the poor. Many others of the new professionals, however, will prefer to remain where they are, sharpening their techniques and their capacity for action on the basis of the knowledge they're acquiring by informing themselves as well as others.

And this knowledge will spread and grow in individual communities and through intercity hookups. Blacks, for example, no longer limited to

Huntley-Brinkley-Cronkite priorities for television news, will be finding—
and thereby making—their own news. Let us suppose, for one instance,
that a percentage of a particular neighborhood is not yet sufficiently
aroused by the state of its schools to change them. And let us suppose
another segment, though aware, feels impotent in terms of making those
changes. A neighborhood channel would *show* the schools in detail to the
first group. And it might have Rhody McCoy give a series of talks with
film clips to the second group about ways to get community control of
schools and about the educational directions Ocean Hill–Brownsville was
able to start exploring even when under siege.

This, and so much more, could happen on cable television in a stunning
liberation of the medium for all manner of groups and neighborhoods.
Decentralization of television is not only technically and economically
possible *now* but it's also entirely desirable in terms of any organic definition of what democracy ought to and can be.

So what's in the way? The commercial broadcasters and the owners of
cable systems. The latter would like to use as many as possible of their
twenty, or fifty, channels per city to make money. Much more money than
can be made by charging "common carrier" fees. Meanwhile, owners of
present commercial stations and networks want as little competition as
possible. They can't any longer hold back cable television but they are
intent on preventing cable systems from linking themselves together into
competing networks. And they certainly don't want hundreds, eventually
thousands, of thoroughly independent neighborhood channels chipping off
audience percentages and—much worse—making these local citizens highly
skeptical about anything they see on commercial television, the news in
particular.

Accordingly, commercial station owners and holders of cable system
franchises are trying to come to an agreement among themselves which
will keep the "electronic wall around the status quo" from being breached.
[In June, 1969], for example, a cartel arrangement was almost sealed. The
cable people would have agreed not to interconnect their facilities to form
networks. In return, local cable systems would have been allowed a greater
quantity and variety of time to sell than they now are allotted. Also part of
the agreement would have been a limitation of the number of channels in
each city. The proposal foundered. Partly, I suspect, because Jack Gould
exposed it in the *Times* as a plan which "would put the force of law behind
a package understanding on ground rules for competition, and allow those
already in the business to decide what constitutes adequate television
service for the public." Those already in the business will, of course, keep
trying to prevent the "average citizen" from having access to television in
any other way than as a passive consumer. They have strong allies in
Congress. But they can be defeated.

Such liberals as exist in Congress who do not own stock in newspaper-broadcasting combines ought to be filled in by interested constitutents on the need to keep cable television open to all the citizenry. And more effective as a source of counterpower against the broadcasting industry would be a national alliance to bring democracy to television. This is a clear, palpable issue around which could be organized those most directly and urgently concerned with breaking down that electronic wall—blacks, Puerto Ricans, Mexicans, students, radicals, liberals, Buckley conservatives, good government groups, the kind of labor unions being led by César Chavez and Leon Davis of the Hospital Workers' 1199. The list can go on and on. This alliance, once it gains some momentum, could bring real pressure for open television.

In the meantime, since individual citizens so seldom write to the FCC, even your single cymbal note of support can have weight. Particularly if you write to Nicholas Johnson, an authentic populist from Texas, the one man on the FCC most committed to the First Amendment and to actualizing democracy. His address is: Federal Communications Commission, Washington, D.C. 20554.

Johnson, in a concurring opinion, when the FCC dismissed the United Federation of Teachers' charges against WBAI-FM (and Julius Lester), wrote:

If truly free speech is to flourish in broadcasting, and if individual citizens are to be given rights of access to the media to exercise their First Amendment freedoms to any meaningful extent, then it is apparent to all that the public must seek its First Amendment champions among other than industry spokesmen.

And where else must it seek if not in itself?

THE DEATH OF SILENCE

by ROBERT PAUL DYE

In this article Robert Dye of the University of Hawaii describes how "screamer" stations limit the artistic potential of radio broadcasting.

Radio's funniest moment occurred on the *Jack Benny* program when a thief demanded from the great tightwad, "Your money or your life." The long silence that followed was more violently hysterical than any of the quick retorts that are the stock in trade of most comedians. Benny's use of silence, his great sense of timing, made him one of the most popular comics of this century. Benny, of course, was not the only radio artist who recognized that silence could be more effective than sound: silence followed the crash of Fibber McGee's closet, preceded McCarthy's responses to Bergen. The chillers became more chilling when there were moments of silence. Silence was used to make the romances erotic and the quiz shows suspenseful.

Radio has changed. The cacophony of today's radio has been dignified as "The Poetica of 'Top 40' "[1] by University of Oklahoma professor Sherman P. Lawton. Dr. Lawton tells us to "Face up to the fact that, like it or not, from the bowels of radio has come a new art form." The practitioners of the new art are the managers of the "screamer" stations, ". . . stations with an extreme foreground treatment, playing only the top tunes, with breathless and witless striplings making like carnival barkers."

The bible of the practitioners, Lawton tells us, is *The Nuts and Bolts of Radio,* authored by George Skinner and published by the Katz Agency.

[1] Sherman P. Lawton, "The Poetica of 'Top 40'," *Journal of Broadcasting,* IX:2 (Spring 1965), 123–128.

One of Mr. Skinner's prescriptions is that there should be no silence longer than a fifth of a second, from sign-on to sign-off *there shalt be continuous sound*. Lawton writes,

On two stations, which I consider the prototypes of the new art, news headlines are proclaimed in a style which can best be described as one well suited to be the second Annunciation. Then, quick segue music, overlapping with the headline that follows. And then, Bam, we might get a roll of drums.

It is curious that the elimination of silence, so long in symbiosis with sound, should be the major difference between the "new art" and old time radio. It was silence which made radio visual, it gave the listener time to imagine the faces, places and action suggested by sound. Silence, like the white space between magazine articles, signalled conclusions and promised beginnings. Silence served as comma, period and paragraph, just as those marks served to signal silence.

Not all radio is continuous sound. Competing with the screamers for popularity are the phone-in programs, an adaptation of two rural America

"Every now and then Roger likes to cut himself off from all media."

Joseph Farris. Copyright 1970 Saturday Review, Inc.

pastimes—listening in on the party line and speaking at the town meeting. This is reactionary programming, an attempt to again involve people in radio by providing a means for do-it-yourself programming. For the most part, the telephone programs are not planned, they happen. They appear to serve as an antidote and as an alternative to the screamers. However, on many stations the antidote and the alternative are more appearance than reality and Mr. Skinner's prescription that there shalt be continuous sound is obeyed.

The death of silence limits some types of aural communication, in some cases eliminates them. The meaningful reporting of Ed Murrow, the stirring rhetoric of Winston Churchill and the fireside chats of Franklin Roosevelt would not have been possible if radio had screamed in the Forties. When silence is prohibited so is drama and poetry. Men like Orson Welles and Archibald MacLeish are forever barred from using the "new art" for their art. Dialogue is also impossible: people just don't speak to each other without so much as a second of silence to signal meaning. Formerly, only stereotyped, fictional creations spoke without pause.

The talkers Ring Lardner satirized would have envied the screamers:

Well girlie you see how busy I have been and am liable to keep right on being busy as we are not going to let the grass grow under our feet but as soon as we have got this number placed we will get busy on another one as a couple like that will put me on Easy st. even if they don't go as big as we expect but even 25 grand is a big bunch of money and if a man could only turn out one hit a year and make that much out of it I would be on Easy st. and no more hammering on the old music box in some cabaret . . .[2]

But even Lardner's characters eventually had to breathe and lose the floor. The screamers, armed with years' worth of recorded sounds, instantly available and always repeatable, can chatter incessantly.

But unlike Ring Lardner, the screamers do not satirize monologue— they spoof it. They even spoof the commercials. Screamer stations have no sacred cows; at least they give that illusion. The screamers take nothing seriously, except themselves. What at first hearing appears to be pure play turns out to be pseudo-play and devoid of fun. What appears to be a playa- thon is really instant and constant spoof. Spoof is both the strength and the weakness of the screamers. It is a strength because spoofing is "in"— James Bond and his imitators. It is a weakness because spoofing is hypo- critical.

Spoof is described by David Sonstroem[3] as "surgery with a rubber

---

[2] Quoted in Constance Rourke, *American Humor* (Garden City: Doubleday, n.d.), 228.

[3] David Sonstroem, "An Animadversion upon Spoof," *The Midwest Quarterly,* VIII (Spring 1967), 239–246.

knife," as "a new kind of playful, ironic attitude toward the old conflict between good and evil." He says,

Spoof is not true to itself. It cheats at its own game. It only pretends to take life as a game, but then inadvertently lets earnest break in and govern it. Although pretending to be above and beyond it all, spoof cares, and cares very much. This unconscious hypocrisy lies at the root of all that I find objectionable in spoof, with its enchanting trick of protecting foolish fantasy by pretending to expose it.

The screamers are spoofers. They lack the courage to be moral and at the same time cannot deny the desire to be moral. The result is that the audience is cheated and deceived. It is neither shocked into moral consciousness, nor freed, for the moment, from moral considerations. It is mired in ambivalence, and the result is malaise.

Old time radio was not ambivalent, nor were its listeners. The residents of Allen's Alley did not spoof American society, they satirized it. The rise of Senator Claghorn hurried the demise of Senator Bilbo. And there was fun on old time radio, the kind of fun that comes from playing and results in laughter. The laughter from old time radio was in the home, not merely the studio. There were belly laughs from the listeners, not merely self-conscious giggles from Lawton's "witless striplings."

Radio developed an art that quickened all the senses. The screamers have developed a technique of monopolizing a single sense. Radio once allowed the listener to participate. The screamers force him into the role of observer. Radio once took life seriously. The screamers take only themselves seriously. Spoof is a degenerate form. It is not true to itself, it prohibits participation. Art is true to itself, it causes participation. The screams from the bowels of today's radio are not the birth cries of a new art form, but the death rattle of an old art medium. The death of silence is the death of sound broadcasting.

"THE TIMES THEY ARE A-CHANGIN'"

THE MUSIC OF PROTEST

by ROBERT A. ROSENSTONE

Robert Rosenstone, Associate Professor of History at the
California Institute of Technology, points out how popular
songs express the concerns of youth—their alienation,
their rebellion—and claims that music has helped to create
a youth subculture which questions some basic premises
of American life.

At the beginning of the 1960's, nobody took popular music very seriously. Adults only knew that rock n' roll, which had flooded the airwaves in the 1950's, had a strong beat and was terribly loud; it was generally believed that teen-agers alone had thick enough eardrums, or insensitive enough souls, to enjoy it. Certainly, no critics thought of a popular star like the writhing Elvis Presley as being in any way a serious artist. Such a teen-age idol was simply considered a manifestation of a subculture that the young happily and inevitably outgrew—and, any parent would have added, the sooner the better.

Today, the view of popular music has drastically changed. Some parents may still wonder about the "noise" that their children listen to, but impor-

"The Times They Are A-Changin' ": *The Music of Protest:* From *The Annals of the American Academy of Political and Social Science* (March, 1969). Reprinted by permission of Robert A. Rosenstone and the American Academy of Political and Social Science.

tant segments of American society have come to recognize popular musicians as real artists saying serious things.[1] An indication of this change can be seen in magazine attitudes. In 1964, the *Saturday Evening Post* derided the Beatles—recognized giants of modern popular music—as "corny," and *Reporter* claimed: "They have debased Rock 'n Roll to its ultimate absurdity." Three years later the *Saturday Review* solemnly discussed a new Beatles record as a "highly ironic declaration of disaffection" with modern society, while in 1968 *Life* devoted a whole, laudatory section to "The New Rock," calling it music "that challenges the joys and ills of the . . . . world."[2] Even in the intellectual community, popular music has found warm friends. Such sober journals as *The Listener, Columbia University Forum, New American Review,* and *Commentary* have sympathetically surveyed aspects of the "pop" scene, while in *The New York Review of Books*—a kind of house organ for American academia—composer Ned Rorem has declared that, at their best, the Beatles "compare with those composers from great eras of song: Monteverdi, Schumann, Poulenc."[3]

The reasons for such changes in attitude are not difficult to find: there is no doubt that popular music has become more complex, and at the same time more serious, than it ever was before. Musically, it has broken down some of the old forms in which it was for a long time straight-jacketed. With a wide-ranging eclecticism, popular music has adapted to itself a bewildering variety of musical traditions and instruments, from the classic

[1] The definition of "popular music" being used in this article is a broad one. It encompasses a multitude of styles, including folk, folk-rock, acid-rock, hard-rock, and blues, to give just a few names being used in the musical world today. It does so because the old musical classifications have been totally smashed and the forms now overlap in a way that makes meaningful distinction between them impossible. Though not every group or song referred to will have been popular in the sense of selling a million records, all of them are part of a broad, variegated scene termed "pop." Some of the groups, like Buffalo Springfield, Strawberry Alarm Clock, or the Byrds, have sold millions of records. Others, like the Fugs or Mothers of Invention, have never had a real hit, though they are played on radio stations allied to the "underground." Still, such groups do sell respectable numbers of records and do perform regularly at teen-age concerts, and thus must be considered part of the "pop" scene.

[2] *Saturday Evening Post,* Vol. 237, March 21, 1964, p. 30; *Reporter,* Vol. 30, Feb. 27, 1964, p. 18; *Saturday Review,* Vol. 50, August 19, 1967, p. 18; *Life,* Vol. 64, June 28, 1968, p. 51.

[3] "The Music of the Beatles," *New York Review of Books,* Jan. 15, 1968, pp. 23–27. See also "The New Music," *The Listener,* Vol. 78, August 3, 1967, pp. 129–130; *Columbia University Forum,* Fall 1967, pp. 16–22; *New American Review,* Vol. 1, April 1968, pp. 118–139; Ellen Willis, "The Sound of Bob Dylan," *Commentary,* Vol. 44, November 1967, pp. 71–80. Many of these articles deal with English as well as American popular groups, and, in fact, the music of the two countries cannot, in any meaningful sense, be separated. This article will only survey American musical groups, though a look at English music would reveal the prevalence of most of the themes explored here.

Indian sitar to the most recent electronic synthesizers favored by composers of "serious" concert music.

As the music has been revolutionized, so has the subject matter of the songs. In preceding decades, popular music was almost exclusively about love, and, in the words of poet Thomas Gunn, "a very limited kind [of love], constituting a sort of fag-end of the Petrarchan tradition."[4] The stories told in song were largely about lovers yearning for one another in some vaguely unreal world where nobody ever seemed to work or get married. All this changed in the 1960's. Suddenly, popular music began to deal with civil rights demonstrations and drug experiences, with interracial dating and war and explicit sexual encounters, with, in short, the real world in which people live. For perhaps the first time, popular songs became relevant to the lives of the teen-age audience that largely constitutes the record-buying public. The success of some of these works prompted others to be written, and the second half of the decade saw a full efflorescence of such topical songs, written by young people for their peers. It is these works which should be grouped under the label of "protest" songs of the 1960's, for, taken together, they provide a wide-ranging critique of American life. Listening to them, one can get a full-blown picture of the antipathy that the young song writers have toward many American institutions.

Serious concerns entered popular music early in the 1960's, when a great revival of folk singing spread out from college campuses, engulfed the mass media, and created a wave of new "pop" stars, the best known of whom was Joan Baez. Yet, though the concerns of these folk songs were often serious, they were hardly contemporary. Popular were numbers about organizing unions, which might date from the 1930's or the late nineteenth century, or about the trials of escaping Negro slaves, or celebrating the cause of the defeated Republicans in the Spanish Civil War. Occasionally, there was something like "Talking A-Bomb Blues," but this was the rare exception rather than the rule.[5]

A change of focus came when performers began to write their own songs, rather than relying on the traditional folk repertoire. Chief among them, and destined to become the best known, was Bob Dylan. Consciously modeling himself on that wandering minstrel of the 1930's, Woody Guthrie, Dylan began by writing songs that often had little to do with the contemporary environment. Rather, his early ballads like "Masters of War" echoed the leftist concerns and rhetoric of an earlier era. Yet, simultaneously, Dylan was beginning to write songs like "Blowin' in the Wind," "A Hard Rain's A-Gonna Fall," and "The Times They Are A-Changin'," which dealt with civil rights, nuclear war, and the changing world of youth that parents and educators were not prepared to understand. Acclaimed

---

[4] "The New Music," *loc. cit.*, p. 129.

[5] *Time*, Vol. 80, Nov. 23, 1962, pp. 54–60, gives a brief survey of the folk revival.

as the best of protest-song-writers, Dylan in mid-decade shifted gears, and in the song "My Back Pages," he denounced his former moral fervor. In an ironic chorus claiming that he was much younger than he had been, Dylan specifically made social problems the worry of sober, serious, older men; presumably, youths had more important things than injustice to think about. After that, any social comment by Dylan came encapsulated in a series of surrealistic images; for the most part, he escaped into worlds of aestheticism, psychedelic drugs, and personal love relationships. Apparently attempting to come to grips in art with his own personality, Dylan was content to forget about the problems of other men.[6]

The development of Dylan is important not only because he is the leading song writer, but also because it parallels the concerns of popular music in the 1960's. Starting out with traditional liberal positions on war, discrimination, segregation, and exploitation, song writers of the decade turned increasingly to descriptions of the private worlds of drugs, sexual experience, and personal freedom. Though social concerns have never entirely faded, the private realm has been increasingly seen as the only one in which people can lead meaningful lives. Now, at the end of the decade, the realms of social protest and private indulgence exist side by side in the popular music, with the latter perceived as the only viable alternative to the world described in the former songs.[7]

. . .

Though the times may be changing, the songsters are well aware that—despite their brave words and demands—there is plenty of strength left in the old social order. Obviously, they can see the war continuing, Negro demands not being met, and the continuing hostility of society toward their long hair, music, sexual behavior, and experimentation with drugs. Faced with these facts, the musicians must deal with the problem of how to live decently within the framework of the old society. Here they tend toward the world of private experience mentioned earlier in this article in connection with Dylan. Many of their songs are almost programs for youth's behavior in a world perceived as being unlivable.

The first element is to forget about the repressive society out there. As Sopwith Camel says, "Stamp out reality . . ./Before reality stamps out you."[8] Then it is imperative to forget about trying to understand the outside world rationally. In a typical anti-intellectual stance, the Byrds de-

---

[6] Willis, op. cit., gives a good analysis of his work. Though he is very quotable, there will, unfortunately, be no quotations from Dylan in this article because the author cannot afford the enormous fees required by Dylan's publisher for even the briefest of quotations.

[7] It must be pointed out that, in spite of the large amount of social criticism, most songs today are still about love, even those by groups such as Country Joe and the Fish, best known for their social satire.

[8] "Saga of the Low Down Let Down," The Sopwith Camel. Copyright by Great Honesty Music, Inc.

scribe such attempts as "scientific delirium madness."[9] Others combine a similar attitude with a strong measure of *carpe diem*. Spirit derides people who are "always asking" for "the reason" when they should be enjoying life, while H. P. Lovecraft admits that the bird is on the wing and states, "You need not know why."[10] What is important is that the moment be seized and life lived to the fullest. As Simon and Garfunkel say, one has to make the "moment last," and this is done best by those who open themselves fully to the pleasures of the world.[11]

The most frequent theme of the song writers is the call to freedom, the total freedom of the individual to "do his own thing." Peanut Butter Conspiracy carry this so far as to hope for a life that can be lived "free of time."[12] Circus Maximus and the Byrds—despite the fact that they are young men—long to recapture some lost freedom that they knew as children.[13] Such freedom can be almost solipsistic; Jimi Hendrix claims that even if the sun did not rise and the mountains fell into the sea, he would not care because he has his "own world to live through."[14] But for others, it can lead to brotherhood. As H. P. Lovecraft says, "C'mon people now, let's get together/Smile on your brother,/Try and love one another right now."[15]

A desire for freedom is certainly nothing new. What is different in the songs of the 1960's is the conviction that this freedom should be used by the individual in an extensive exploration of his own internal world. Central to the vision of the song writers is the idea that the mind must be opened and expanded if the truths of life are to be perceived. Thus, the importance of external reality is subordinated to that of a psychological, even a metaphysical, realm. The most extensive treatment of this subject is by the Amboy Dukes, who devote half of a long-playing record to it. Their theme is stated quite simply: "How happy life would be/If all mankind/Would take the time to journey to the center of the mind."[16] Like any mystical trip, what happens when one reaches the center of the mind is not easy to describe. Perhaps the best attempt is by the Iron Butterfly, who claim that an unconscious power will be released, flooding the individual with sensations and fusing him with a freedom of thought that will

[9] "Fifth Dimension," *Fifth Dimension.*
[10] "Topanga Window," *Spirit* (Ode, 212 44004); "Let's Get Together," *H. P. Lovecraft* (Phillips, 600-252).
[11] "Feeling Groovy," *Sounds of Silence.*
[12] "Time Is After You," *West Coast Love-In* (Vault, LP 113).
[13] "Lost Sea Shanty," *Circus Maximus* (Vanguard, 79260); "Going Back," *The Notorious Byrd Brothers.*
[14] "If 6 Was 9," *Axis* (Reprise, S 6281).
[15] H. P. Lovecraft, "Let's Get Together," *H. P. Lovecraft.* [Copyright 1963, Irving Music, Inc. (BMI). All rights reserved. Words and music by Chet Powers. Reprinted by permission.]
[16] "Journey to to the Center of the Mind," *Journey to the Center of the Mind* (Mainstream, S 6112). Copyright 1968 by Brent Music Corporation.

allow him to "see every thing." At this point, man will be blessed with the almost supernatural power of knowing "all."[17]

Such a journey is, of course, difficult to make. But youth has discovered a short cut to the mind's center, through the use of hallucinogenic drugs. Indeed, such journeys are almost inconceivable without hallucinogens, and the so-called "head songs" about drug experiences are the most prevalent of works that can be classified as "protest."[18] In this area, the songs carefully distinguish between "mind-expanding," nonaddictive marijuana and LSD, and hard, addictive drugs which destroy the body. Thus, the Velvet Underground and Love both tell of the dangers of heroin, while Canned Heat warn of methedrine use and the Fugs describe the problems of cocaine.[19] But none of the groups hesitate to recommend "grass" and "acid" trips as a prime way of opening oneself to the pleasures and beauties of the universe. As the Byrds claim in a typical "head song," drugs can free the individual from the narrow boundaries of the mundane world, allowing him to open his heart to the quiet joy and eternal love which pervade the whole universe.[20] Others find the reality of the drug experience more real than the day-to-day world, and some even hope for the possibility of staying "high" permanently. More frequent is the claim that "trips" are of lasting benefit because they improve the quality of life of an individual even after he "comes down."[21] The Peanut Butter Conspiracy, claiming that "everyone has a bomb" in his mind, even dream of some day turning the whole world on with drugs, thus solving mankind's plaguing problems by making the earth a loving place.[22] An extreme desire, perhaps, but one that would find much support among other musicians.

A Repressive Society

This, then is the portrait of America that emerges in the popular songs of the 1960's which can be labelled as "protest." It is, in the eyes of the song writers, a society which makes war on peoples abroad and acts repressively toward helpless minorities like Negroes, youth, and hippies at home. It is a land of people whose lives are devoid of feeling, love, and sexual pleasure.

[17] "Unconscious Power," *Heavy.*

[18] There are so many "head songs" that listing them would be an impossibly long task. Some of the most popular protest songs of the decade have been such works. They include Jefferson Airplane, "White Rabbit," *Surrealistic Pillow;* the Doors, "Light My Fire," *The Doors* (Elektra, EKS 74007); Strawberry Alarm Clock, "Incense and Peppermints," *Incense and Peppermints;* and the Byrds, "Eight Miles High," *Fifth Dimension.*

[19] "Heroin," *Velvet Underground;* "Signed D. C.," *Love* (Elektra, 74001); "Amphetamine Annie," *Boogie;* "Coming Down," *The Fugs.*

[20] "Fifth Dimension," *Fifth Dimension.*

[21] See Country Joe and the Fish, "Bass Strings," *Electric Music for the Mind and Body;* or United States of America, "Coming Down," *United States of America.*

[22] "Living, Loving Life," *Great Conspiracy.*

It is a country whose institutions are crumbling away, one which can presumably only be saved by a sort of cultural and spiritual revolution which the young themselves will lead.

Whether one agrees wholly, partly, or not at all with such a picture of the United States, the major elements of such a critical portrait are familiar enough. It is only in realizing that all this is being said in popular music, on records that sometimes sell a million copies to teen-agers, in songs that youngsters often dance to, that one comes to feel that something strange is happening today. Indeed, if parents fully understand what the youth are saying musically to one another, they must long for the simpler days of Elvis Presley and his blue suede shoes.

If the lyrics of the songs would disturb older people, the musical sound would do so even more. In fact, a good case could be made that the music itself expresses as much protest against the status quo as do the words. Performed in concert with electronic amplification on all instruments—or listened to at home at top volume—the music drowns the individual in waves of sound; sometimes it seems to be pulsating inside the listener. When coupled with a typical light show, where colors flash and swirl on huge screens, the music helps to provide an assault on the senses, creating an overwhelming personal experience of the kind that the songs advise people to seek. This sort of total experience is certainly a protest against the tepid, partial pleasures which other songs describe as the lot of bourgeois America.

Another aspect of the music which might be considered a kind of protest is the attempt of many groups to capture in sound the quality of a drug "trip," to try through melody, rhythm, and volume to—in the vernacular— "blow the mind" of the audience. Of course, youngsters often listen to such music while under the influence of hallucinogens. In such a state, the perceptive experience supposedly can have the quality of putting one in touch with regions of the mind and manifestations of the universe that can be felt in no other way. Such mysticism, such transcendental attitudes, are certainly a protest against a society in which reality is always pragmatic and truth instrumental.

To try to explain why the jingles and vapid love lyrics of popular music in the 1950's evolved into the social criticism and mystical vision of the 1960's is certainly not easy. Part of it is the fact that performers, who have always been young, started writing their own songs, out of their own life experiences, rather than accepting the commercial output of the older members of tin pan alley. But this does not explain the popularity of the new songs. Here one must look to the youthful audience, which decided it preferred buying works of the newer kind. For it was the commercial success of some of the new groups which opened the doors of the record companies to the many that flourish today.

Though one cannot make definitive judgments about this record-buying audience, some things seem clear. Certainly, it is true that with increasingly rapid social change, parents—and adults in general—have less and less that they can tell their children about the ways of the world, for adult life experiences are not very relevant to current social conditions. Similarly, institutions like the school and the press suffer from a kind of cultural lag that makes their viewpoints valueless for youth. Into the place of these traditional sources of information have stepped the youth themselves, and through such things as the "underground" press and popular music they are telling each other exactly what is happening. In this way, the music has achieved popularity—at least in part—because it telegraphs important messages to young people and helps to define and codify the mores and standards of their own subculture. A youngster may personally feel that there is no difference between his parents' drinking and his use of marijuana. Certainly, it is comforting to him when his friends feel the same way, and when popular songs selling millions of copies deliver the same message, there are even stronger sanctions for his "turning on." Thus, the lyrics of the music serve a functional role in the world of youth.

It is interesting to note that the popular music also puts youth in touch with serious, intellectual critiques of American life. Perhaps it starts only as a gut reaction in the song writers, but they have put into the music the ideas of many American social critics. Without reading Paul Goodman, David Riesman, C. Wright Mills, or Mary McCarthy, youngsters will know that life is a "rat race," that Americans are a "lonely crowd," that "white-collar" lives contain much frustration, and that the war in Vietnam is far from just. And they will have learned this from popular music, as well as from their own observation.

The other side of the coin from criticism of contemporary life is the search for personal experience, primarily of the "mind-expanding" sort. As is obvious by now, such expansion has nothing to do with the intellect, but is a spiritual phenomenon. Here a final critique is definitely implicit. Throughout the music—as in youth culture—there is the search for a kind of mystical unity, an ability to feel a oneness with the universe. This is what drugs are used for; this is what the total environment of the light and music shows is about; and this is what is sought in the sexual experience—often explicitly evident in the orgasmic grunts and moans of performers. Through the search for this unity, the music is implicitly condemning the fragmentation of the individual's life which is endemic in the modern world. The songsters are saying that it is wrong to compartmentalize work and play, wrong to cut men off from the natural rhythms of nature, wrong to stifle sex and love and play in favor of greater productivity, wrong to say man's spiritual needs can be filled by providing him with more material possessions.

This is obviously a criticism that can only be made by an affluent people, but these youth do represent the most affluent of all countries. And rather than wallow in their affluence, they have sensed and expressed much of the malaise that plagues our technological society. The charge may be made against them that they are really utopians, but the feeling increases today that we are in need of more utopian thinking and feeling. And while one might not wish to follow their prescriptions for the good life, they have caught something of the desire for freedom that all men feel. What could be more utopian and yet more inviting in its freedom than the hopeful picture which the Mothers of Invention paint of the future:

> There will come a time when everybody
> Who is lonely will be free . . .
> TO SING AND DANCE AND LOVE
> There will come a time when every evil
> That we know will be an evil
> WE CAN RISE ABOVE
> Who cares if hair is long or short
> Or sprayed or partly grayed . . .
> WE KNOW THAT HAIR
> AINT WHERE IT'S AT
> (There will come a time when you
> won't even be ashamed if you are fat!)
>
> Who cares if you're so poor
> You can't afford to buy a pair
> Of mod a-go go stretch elastic pants
> THERE WILL COME A TIME
> WHEN YOU CAN EVEN
> TAKE YOUR CLOTHES OFF WHEN
> YOU DANCE.[23]

[23] "Take Your Clothes Off When You Dance," *We're Only in It for the Money*. © 1968 Frank Zappa Music, Inc. All rights reserved. Reprinted by permission.

MEDIA MEANS

by JAMES W. THOMPSON

STRANGE,
how MEDIA MEANS,
Sitting mid-morning—
so clock announced
in a scream a six
stopped by a slap
on the back by a hand
designed to web
air space of stage—
in slum, a warm
significant personage
dignifies & "smoke"
makes supreme;
(as flames from several
7 day lights set such
objet d' art as Africa
affords the *connoisseur,*
this one a lover
not copious w/coin
of the realm
but replete w/taste,
to pulsate beneath
the naked sun of a
red 100 watt, beating
the trail of incense
which clouds its glare
in gentle gloom/
a Frankincense & Myrrh
perfume to match
the furred feeling
of the CASTRO,
contoured through use
and such abuse
as bodies meaning
to be heard extend) speaking
to Young Blacks
whom MEDIA has made
             B E L I E V E
that a Black Blues Chord
played by BLACKS
is an
A C I D   R O C K   T U N E
that White imitation
of a very black feeling/
I was forced to scream:
INTEGRATION IS DREADFUL
when you don't control
the media which makes
ZOMBIE/ISM a constant
condition.) IT SELLS IMAGES—
imitations of REAL
and REALITY imitates
             IT:
Black folks imitating
             white folks
                  who
                  imitate
                  THEM!

from AVANT-GARDE

POETRY BY COMPUTER

There must be some things a computer can't do, but—aside from pole vaulting—it's getting harder and harder to name them. And now the electronic monster is also a poet! Maybe a good one, even. What is poetry, anyway, or some kinds of poetry at least, but words strung together on a page to a musical, surprising, or otherwise interesting effect? And this a computer can do like crazy, producing in 10 minutes the normal life's work of its old-fashioned human counterpart. All it requires is an engineer to program its grammar and vocabulary and a man of taste to winnow its rhapsodic outpourings. The best of these outpourings, being uncontaminated by stylistic habits and conceits, comprise an ingenuous but really striking surrealism; and though the computer may not yet be the greatest of poets, it is certainly among the freshest and most original. Would you believe an anthology of the future featuring the works of IBM 360? Click.

The [poem below was] written by an IBM 360 assisted by IBM programs analyst Don Shea, who programed it for various verse forms and loaded it with random words and phrases from several modern poets. From the resultant 900-odd stanzas the following were selected and juxtaposed by Avant-Garde to emphasize the machine's genius for melodic and moving repetitions, as the same word or phrase recurs again and again in ever new and surprising contexts. Of course this arrangement is only one among thousands of possibilities, which suggests a role in the future for human poets, after all—computer-poem editors. Until, that is, IBM invents a way to program self-criticism and creates an electrical Keats. . . . Do you doubt it?

HEIRESS

THE HEIRESS ABOVE WRITHING MISTS
WALKS
THE NEXT ROOM BEYOND RUINED THE FUTURE
CERTAINLY USED TO LEAD
HERMITS FLOWERING THE TOUGHEST TINTED DISTANCES

TO REST HERMITS
TO FEEL
TO DIE
THE RED LOVE-CARS FIRST ENTERED

VERTICAL BLOSSOMS TAKE ENLARGING IN LOVE-CARS
TARNISHED EYELIDS OF STONE CRINGE EQUALLY IN THE FUTURE
THE OBSOLETE GOSSIP LIVES PRETENDING ROCKS, MOSS

TO BE ROCKS, MOSS
CURIOUS THE MOON BLUSHED

GLISTENING A FOOTSTEP BLUSHED
IT IS HIS POISON
THE GREEDIEST SPRING SNOW EXCITES

NOBODY BY SIMPLE SPRING SNOW
ALONE FLOATS
THE MOON ON THE TOUGHEST SEVEN TULIPS

SEVEN TULIPS KILLED LIGHT
THE TOUGHEST GOSSIP CRINGES
THE SEAL CANNOT BE
AFTER THE DOORWAY

BRIGHT THE HEIRESS ADMIRES TO DIE WATCHING
PUNGENT JOY KILLED WITHIN LOVE-CARS

INTO THE ISSUE OF THE GOOD OLD TIME MOVIE VS. THE GOOD OLD TIME

by DENNIS HOPPER

In his introduction to this essay, written in 1969, actor and director Dennis Hopper stated that a national magazine had invited him to write an article about movies and had then rejected it on the grounds that it was "an apologia for bad American movies." That was before he had the opportunity to make **Easy Rider,** in which he had a fairly free directorial hand. More recently Hopper has been more optimistic about the possibility of film becoming an art medium rather than an industry.

"Howdy! Rope 'em up." "Cut!" No good. Airplane. No good for sound. Airplane's gone. Good for sound. Roll 'em. Rolling speed. Buzzer. Clap board. Take six. Bang clank. Powder puff. Action. Dialogue. "Howdy! Rope 'em up."

(Cowboy throws rope out of frame. Director says "Cut! How'd it look?" Cameraman shrugs disinterestedly, shows us his shoulder. "It was all right." Shrugs again. Director: "Just all right?" Cameraman: "Mmm. It was good." Director: "Come on, man! How was it? Was it just good? The loop in the lasso—I mean did it make a circle? Did you see it go out of frame?" Cameraman: "Yeah, I saw it. Yeah it was—it was fine." Soundman yells: "It was good for sound!" The director decides it was great, it wasn't just good, it was WHAM BAM right on the MONEY!

It was great with a CAPITAL G! "Gee whiz!" says the little newspaper boy, "Shazam and no Captain Marvel?" and a great silence prevails, over dead water waiting for a waterfall.)

Movies are better than ever! Combining Good Citizenship With Good Movie-Making! Million-dollar low-budget fiasco, the million dollar baby!

"Fifteen million? What'd it gross?"

"I don't know."

"Must have made money, they're planning a twenty-five million dollar one."

"Let's hope so. Tours are our best seller this season. Kept us alive all summer. Yeah, they're no fools."

"Young man, we'd like you to know your underground film gave us as much pleasure as 'The Sound of Music.' "

No. Well who is? And who needs Disneyland-with-glass-sound-stages-so-people-can-watch Studios? Props? Heavy equipment? Thirty people on a crew? Three dollars and seventy five cents an hour for an old man who opens a door and sweeps cigarette butts off the floor and makes coffee (as a matter of fact great coffee), and when he dies (and believe me, he won't quit before), his son will take over and do the chore of opening and closing the door.

Big old-fashioned sound stages that cost them more to run and build sets on when the whole damn country's one big real place to utilize and film, and God's a great gaffer. Shoot natural light! Use lightweight reflectors!

"Bergman makes films with six on a crew. Wouldn't you?"

The talk goes on and on, but it's only a matter of time until somebody's going to do it. When it's only a matter of time, being patient helps. And I don't mean a patient like in a nuthouse.

[In 1960] there were fifty art theaters in the United States; now there are six thousand.

"They don't make money, those European films." Another Exec: "Yeah, you should see the bad ones."

Someone's smart over there in Europe. "America's where the money is," someone said about ten years ago. "How can we get into their market? We cannot compete on their level of film. Hey! I've got a great idea! Let's make art films. That's something they'll never think of!"

And of course we haven't yet.

Fifty theaters to six thousand in five years.

No American films for six thousand theaters.

"Oh well! Hmmm. You should see the bad ones."

The American Art Film cannot be an imitation of the European Art Film. Simple enough statement. Yes, it's simple enough, that statement. What's the answer? What's the question?

Bruce Connor, of all the so-called "underground movie-makers," is the most original talent. Bruce rarely shoots the film he edits. He takes quick cuts from many old movies and by juxtaposing them he makes much-more-than-interesting things happen. What a great idea for a major company to hire Connor. Turn him loose on the stockpile of films that lie decaying in the vaults of all the major studios, and make fresh films without the expense of shooting one foot of film. That's a multi-million-dollar idea. Have *you* had one lately?

The Sixteen Millimeter Film. The Sixteen Millimeter Film. Drinks flow. More talk into the night. More talk into the morning. More talk. Etcetera. Etcetera. Etcetera.

The Sixteen Millimeter Film Revolution. Is it possible? Oh, yes, it's absolutely possible. Oh, yes, honestly, it is absolutely possible. But not this way.

        Cocktail   Gingerale   Five Cents A Glass
        Ring Around The Rosey   Pocket Full Of Posey

A drag-down-around-the-corner approach to the cinema-come-lately American art film better known as the New American Film Society and still Better Known in the In Harper's Bazaar Vogue Top Top Top Mags as the lust-rious underground movie set Andy Warhol Gregory Markopolis Taylor Meade Superstars. Genius the lot, but at the moment not harmful to an industry that has made films and art with great character and direction, and money. As Cocteau said, "Even in disorder, there is order." I like their films, but I like all films. Warhol behaves like a man who has never seen a camera or movie. He behaves like the inventor, Tom Edison. He sets people in front of a stationary camera and asks them to stare blankly into the lens, or the Empire State Building appears and disappears. Warhol doesn't edit. He merely connects white leader together, which explains the appearing and disappearing, exposed under or underexposed, the total movie is eight hours. The underexposed part, one light-setting for the whole movie, is only three of those hours.

What ever happened to Baby Jane?

        It jumped up her petticoat and bit her on her
        Cocktail   Gingerale   Five Cents A Glass

Everyone can talk, drink, smoke, buy art, discuss 1930's musicals, and how movies, with the exception of those, haven't been good since the advent of sound, nothing good after Busby Berkley's at Warner Bros. in the Thirties.

"The second reel of Berkley's—oh, what's the name of that film? Just the second reel. Oh, you know the one—it was one of those Thirties' films —the one with the Piano Scene—great big piano keys and they all danced all over it. What a great scene! What the hell's the name of that movie?"

Out of a dark corner I hear:

"Where does Marlon come off making a million dollars a picture, and what is he doing with it?"

"Well. I'll have a drink. That should make me think of the name of that damn movie!"

"Dames!"

"What?"

"DAMES! That's the name of the movie!"

"Hell, you knew it all the time, you crazy galoot."

"Hey! Look at Andy's movie! It's getting close to where that light switches on, on top of the Empire State!"

It sure is, but not *that* way! What we need are good old American— and that's not to be confused with European—Art Films. But who delivers? Where do we find them? How much does it cost? Where do they get a quarter of a million dollars? What would they have to be to do it? Where do we go? It all depends on X Y Z, and no one seems to know the answer.

(But when the time comes, they'll appear.) America's where it can be done. Maybe the Europeans have a great start, because of government help. God forbid that happens here before the wealthy support the film! We all admire the Church for having given Michelangelo money to build his lasting work. But Greco and Goya and a lot of people were supported by patrons. Yes, I think that's the word. Patrons. Where are the Patrons? Patrons, if found and cornered, ask: "Why not get it from the Industry?"

It's a second- and third-generation industry. It's an industry.

Film is an art-form, an expensive art-form, it's the Sistine Chapel of the Twentieth Century, it's the best way to reach people. The artist, not the industry, must take the responsibility for the entire work. Michelangelo

"But I don't want to see a truthful
little film shot with a hand-held camera.
I want to see a big lying movie made
with the latest sophisticated equipment."

did less than one quarter of the Sistine Chapel; yet directed all work, stone by stone, mural by mural, on and on and on.

Patrons. Patrons. That's the word.

But where are the angels? Even the flesh? Better still, WHERE'S THE CASH?

But even better still, WHERE ARE THE PEOPLE TO GIVE THE CASH TO??? Not to worry. No, not to worry. They'll be here when it's their turn to change the balance of power in the good old American Way; then my generation will have its say. Our grandfathers and fathers made it what it is today, they invented it. Can we sustain it? Because we've lost it. Can we fill the movie-gap? And take back our invention? And surpass the Europeans? Yes, when that Individual comes to town. Remember him? The Individual? Well, then, when it's his turn. Yes, we'd better do it then. Or I'm going to die a very cranky Individual, and I won't be alone. It's time for a transition shot.

the cinema's new language

by DAVID MOWAT

As illustrated by the collage of magazine
covers to the left, various critical
commentaries on films are popular content
in magazines. In this article British film
critic David Mowat deals with the uses and
misuses of the new cinematic techniques.
Several of the new techniques he
discusses—such as frequent departure
from chronology and the use of
improvisation—recall the characteristics
of the electronic media that Edmund
Carpenter outlined in his "The New
Languages."

For those who liked their cinema new, with a tang of revolution about it,
the early 1960s were a blissful cinematic dawn. A hitherto plodding form
had suddenly learned to run, and the momentum was tremendous. New
vistas appeared in every direction. New names flashed—Truffaut, Malle,
Resnais, Godard, Fellini, Antonioni, Pasolini. New devices came to birth,
each almost a historical event: the still, the jump-cut, the hand-held
camera, shooting into the sun, improvisation. An unprecedented number
of directors began shooting their first features. Critics began talking excit-
edly about a new language.

Now, in the early '70s, the momentum of most of the great names above
seems diminished. A few others have appeared, and new areas (notably
in Eastern Europe) have opened up. But the air of excitement has lessened,
and much of the charisma has dwindled. Except for the partisans, most
would admit that many previously great directors have made bad films.

The Cinema's New Language: From *Encounter* (April, 1970). Reprinted by permission of *Encounter* and David Mowat.

Once spoken by an élite, the new language has become common property: devices once exciting are now too familiar to move us. This is inevitable: nothing remains new for long. But there is another problem—the misuse of the language, based on incomprehension. If the misuse cannot soon be halted, the language, however widely known, may become a pidgin dialect.

An unpatriotic suggestion, but perhaps English (and American) directors share some responsibility for the decline. In the early '60s, when things were simpler, and directors less frequently boarded planes, the difference between the English-speaking and Continental film was strongly marked. Simply expressed, the English film had a story, and did not take many liberties with it, whereas in the Continental offering the story had to compete with "artiness," tricks of style or whatever, and sometimes disappeared altogether. Of course if you liked "artiness" and found English products unimaginative you merely called the Continental films more visually expressive. Some liked "Style," the mood and shape imposed on the film by the director, others preferred "Content," or story. Most often the Continent provided the one and the English-speaking film the other. Now the distinction has largely disappeared: many English directors have taken to Style. But the result is often unsatisfactory, and the directors themselves just do not seem to match up to their Continental counterparts. As if in sympathy the Continental counterparts seem to be falling off too.

Why should this be? Perhaps one should try to see what may first have caused the rift, look at the big differences of the early 1960s. The Continental directors were then pre-eminent, beginning to be known internationally. Now for this international fame they had to pay—as they still do—a simple price: they had to subtitle. An English director has a potential unsubtitled audience of over three hundred million. Not so the Frenchman, Italian, or Swede; and to the U.S.A. (that giant of audiences) his language is gibberish. So he subtitled: he traded an ear for an eye—and in doing so he accomplished a truly cinematic transaction. As an international deaf-mute his gestures became more expressive: the language he used had to be eye-dominated. So the whole idea of the story came in for review. A story is usually told by mouth and heard by ear. If you are confined to a non-aural rendering, with a few lettered signs, you will probably begin to play down plot; instead you will concentrate on what can be seen, and develop from there. A character, instead of being a function of the story, becomes its perceiver. Instead of saying what happens to him you show what he sees; and what he sees is him. This simple formula the English film never grasped, when during the early '60s no English character's perceptions graced celluloid. And in the late '60s, when artiness was really in vogue, it had still not grasped this essential point: that the cinema is uniquely qualified to explore a character via his perceptions, via the quality of what he sees. English-speaking directors, not realising this, gave us *Poor Cow, Herostratus, Petulia,* which by any standards fell short of (say) *L'Eclisse, Muriel, Une Femme Mariée.* The stature of these last three is not a mystery: they were nourished with a different food, not the crumbs of a fast-staling "plot," but a genuinely cinematic diet of character and perception.

The key to the new language, I have suggested, is character. We see the limitation or potential of a character, and we observe his relationship with his environment. We observe his commitment or disengagement. If the shape of the film is the structure of his perception, its content is his inter-action with his environment.

This basic form can produce divergent results. In the Italian or "cool" school, the character's predicament is often the limitation of his own character. He is estranged from an environment he finds alien; or else through his own inertia he becomes aimless. This translated into the cin-ema becomes the slow . . . slow image: the tempo of life which is Anto-nioni's metronome, and which allows Pasolini his long, breathtaking stares. But if the Italians play it "cool," the French, with their irrepressible instinct for revolution (the editor's scissors are the modern guillotine) lean more to "bop." The hero's commitment leads him to action and triples the pace. Alternatively, disengaged, he is subject to the racing pulse of his con-science, in its turn spurred by the tempo of things around. Committed he rides fast and far; uncommitted, stationary, he is bombarded by a swirl of unpatterned events. Either way there is motion, and either way it de-rives from an element in his character—the factor of commitment.

The English film is not readily identified with either tradition. It likes the new language but does not bother to find a key. It is not original but eclectic, and if it likes a phrase of the new language it will seize it. But this is the director's whim, and is at the heart of the trouble. Our directors have not learned to take their points of departure from their characters. Thus unruly, over-zealous, the result is no new language but a tiresome gabble. While the film should start with character and proceed through perception to mood and style, it starts at once with its story, or (worse) with style itself, and the two, instead of being harmoniously related, wage a terrible war of attrition in which, in this mechanised age, the spectator is often the first casualty (see any of the English films mentioned above).

The recent work of Ingmar Bergman, one of the most prolific of modern film directors, seems currently to be suffering from too much hybridisation, personal paranoia and strenuous modishness to represent straightforwardly any portion of the new language. No one would deny, however, that in the 1950s, before the rush, some of his work was highly influential in changing the direction of the cinema. The film *Wild Strawberries,* for instance, made in 1955, shows clearly a character-form interaction that at the time contrib-uted much to the undoubted novelty and power of the work, which was to be crucial in building Bergman's international reputation. It was evident when it appeared that the film represented a strong contrast to much of the cinema of the time, and the difference is perhaps worth considering.

Wild Strawberries is not about a story, but about an old Professor. The perspective of visual characterisation rather than the reporting of events necessarily cuts down on action, reducing the scope of the film to an analysis of a single day. Compared with the high-selection of the traditional film, *Wild Strawberries* selects less, reveals more; it dwells; its rhythm becomes less and less the frenzied tempo of plot, more the leisured tempo of thought. Of course events still occur (no day would be entirely without them) but they are integrated, not cumulatively but as equivalent episodes revealing something of the mind of the leading character.

So much for the general approach of the film. Its form is a rather brilliant matching of its character-content. The Professor (Alf Sjöberg) is old: this is his predicament, and this provides the tension between himself and his environment. Being old he is drawn in two opposite directions: through memory, back to his youth; through fear, forward to his death. His present tense is the fulcrum balancing these opposites: it is defined by their polarity. His orientation, his present peace of mind, will depend on his coming to terms with both ideas. The form of the film illustrates this neatly: the present tense (the objective flow) of the film stops at four principal moments to admit alternately nightmare, memory, nightmare, memory—all of which we perceive from the old man's subjective point of view: we partake visually of his predicament.

In style the film resembles the character of the old man: moody, sombre, testy and rather edgily nostalgic. But the style is not imposed on the film by the director; rather he has abdicated his position in favour of his principal character: the latter, so to speak, "directs" the form and quality of the film.

Much of the eloquence of the film derives from the power of its "new language." Here, as so often, the alteration in technique which marks the divergence from tradition has much to do with tempo. The altered (slow) tempo is more analytic, more exploratory. By avoiding "story" and substituting character-linked episodes, a new, deeper, and certainly more visual rhythm has been achieved. Specifically time itself has been expanded: it has been qualified by the reverie (self-criticism) as well as by the projection, the fantasy of the future (fear of loneliness, death).

Antonioni, another of the most influential of modern directors, refines this procedure much further. As with Bergman, many of his films are integrated by the central character's predicament, which is again subjected to a visual analysis. To generalise, the predicament of the character is an estrangement from an intractable or uncongenial environment. Such an estrangement ("existential" if you will) leads to an aimless predicament. Life, without aim, is nonselective, non-orientated, and therefore experienced as a series of equivalent episodes without tension, often without words, and with much consequent emphasis on mood.

L'Eclisse (1962) confines itself to a rather shorter day than that of *Wild Strawberries*. The heroine (how perfectly Monica Vitti embodied the predicament) lacks orientation; again as with Bergman the form of the film is shaped to the quality of her perception; again the structure is suspense-less, a series of equivalent episodes. The human ant-hill of the fifteen minutes of the stock-exchange crisis only emphasises the torpid drift of the remainder of the film. This noisy overactive scene depicts just the quality of "action" which the director, via his heroine, is repudiating. The ending of the film is a pure, condensed illustration of this approach taken to an extreme. Estrangement from the activity of life has proceeded to the point where even human intercourse is excluded: instead we focus merely on a series of *things*. The usual perspective of the film-as-commentary, the film *about* things, has been replaced in favour of objects in their own right: the film *is* things.

Resnais is another director who is not interested in story-telling: the texture of his films is, however, very different from Antonioni's. The difference lies in the characters. Antonioni structures his films round characters whose predicament leads them towards an aimless contemplation of their environment. Resnais prefers to use characters whose predicament (often involving a form of trauma) centres on a conflict between their present existence and some past event. As with the Professor in *Wild Strawberries* the present is unstable ("critical" in the nuclear language—a key image for Resnais). A trauma in the past, reawakened by some present event, disturbs and disorientates the equilibrium. When this happens an urgent attempt is made to come to terms with the past, and this involves what psychologists call "perseveration," persistently working over the memory of an event in the hope of finding a reorientation for the present.

This formula occurs with such regularity in Resnais' films that it is tempting to suppose that the pattern coincides with his basic notion of the structure of a film; that when discussing a script with its author, he begins to cut the cloth of the material in accordance with the shape of this basic conception. Certainly his relationships with script-writers seem to produce very consistent results.

In *Hiroshima Mon Amour* (1959) two events, both traumatic, both flashpoints of conflict between opposing sides, stand in the past of two people of different lands who come together briefly in a love-affair. But there is little peace in this antipodal union. Their meeting reawakens in each the trauma that has scarred their past life. The fusion of the ideas of atomic destruction and of the punished liaison with the German cleaves the centre of the film. Their union leads to the specific disintegration of perception. The sovereignty of the present (as in all Resnais' major films) is threatened by the encroachment of the past. In terms of the "new language" the brilliant device evolved to evoke this schizoid condition is that of "intercutting," of moving in rapid consecutive shots from one place to another (Hiroshima : Nevers) or between the "now" and the "then" (1959:1945). From this tension the film takes its shape. Intercutting has replaced the flabby flashback (where a closeup of the hero's eyes dissolves mistily into reminiscence) with the slap in the face of adrenal memory. The past now defines, animates, qualifies the present. The film has ceased to be a moving present, leavened with digressions, and has become instead the violent conflict of opposing modes.

Last Year in Marienbad (1961) explored a similar predicament: the disturbed present due to trauma involving again the ideas of love and death. The unity of the film is the disunity of the mind; the form is the quality of memory, the attempt by the mind to orientate an episode of the past. In addition to the method of swift transition, other devices lend their assistance to evoke the nature of memory—discontinuity, distortion, stylisation, under- and over-exposure. These and other variations from the standard practice, distortions of the cinematic norm, show the evolution of new vocabulary in response to the desire to illustrate the quality of a predicament.

Once evolved, however, there is no guarantee that a language will be treated with respect, or even with sufficient understanding. Use of the devices mentioned above may earn a film the epithets "new," "experimental," "avant-garde." At a simple level they attract attention not functionally, but solely by virtue of their novelty. At the time of writing there may be as many as a hundred such devices of which (say) ten may be readily identified as clichés. From original appearance to cliché to unremarked inclusion in the new language are three easily taken steps. At cinema's present gallop they can be too easily and too thoughtlessly taken.

The device of intercutting, popularised by Resnais, may now perhaps claim to be almost the definite article of the new language. The unexpectedly fast cut from one shot to another causes a jerk in perception that may have an arresting impact. It is striking, "new" (little used before 1959) and easy to do (a pair of scissors suffices). Thus it is popular where immediacy, impact, novelty are required.

In Resnais' films the technique, as I have suggested, is related to a conflict integral to a character's predicament. As used by other directors, as a passport to novelty, it has become almost meaningless—devalued by reckless inflation. In Don Levy's *Herostratus* (1968), for instance, it is invoked, nominally, to show the quality of the character's "subconscious"—how a thousand fleeting impressions, many subliminal, interract in an individual's mind. This is fair—but arbitrary. In the first place it is a general truth, not specifically related to Max, the film's hero, and thus seems more casual than anything else. Admittedly, done with sufficient force, it is striking, but one searches in vain for the integration that character or predicament would provide. The subconscious is complex, but it is more than this—it is dynamic. It lives in a brain which belongs to a human being; it cannot be regarded independently of that human being, and of his desires, fears, etc. Clips of Hitler and Churchill newsreels are all very well and may have great emotive power for one who was then alive, to whom such events were contemporaneously accessible (such as the director of the film) and who thinks of Hitler and Churchill a great deal—but to Max (surely barely out of adolescence) they must remain arbitrary: he is not involved in them. His mood (despair, violence, sexual insecurity) cannot really incorporate material a quarter-of-a-century old. He may think about a stripper or a slaughter house (though their alternation seems rather pat) but Hitler at Nuremberg is less likely to occupy his mind than, say, the idea of nuclear war. Throughout the film one feels that an appeal is being made to our sense of novelty. The traditional film—that old Aunt Sally—is under attack, and the more urgent task of creating character is taking second place.

Then we get a film like Dick Lester's *Petulia* (1968), an attempt to grow Resnais in Hollywood which lands all too squarely in kooksville (lunchtime at Tiffany's, perhaps). Sure enough Petulia (Julie Christie) has had a trauma or two, which is apparently sufficient to lead her through a wild mosaic of present/past. But her character is so woolly (like Max: part cliché, part blur) that it can't underscore or support these intercutting fantasies. Once again, through the stylistic rainbow, a dreary plot emerges, decked with sentimental strings and a taste of fashionable violence, not to mention every prop of the leisured rich. (Fellini's *Giulietta degli Spiriti* must be largely responsible for this terrible vogue. All right, so we live in a gadget society: now tell us something else.) How much more interesting a black-and-white documentary of San Francisco would have been. Instead we have an example of the new language at its worst.

Both these films, of course, share one important feature: they are in colour. This, overriding many technical mannerisms, constitutes one of the most notable trends of the '60s, and may be responsible for profound formal differences whose influence should not be underestimated. Some of these may be worth considering.

The convention that dominated the 1950s almost certainly had its origin at the box-office. The entertainment film, the family film with its good box-office prospect could afford the luxury of colour (children always prefer it). The "serious" film, with its smaller (student, etc.) audience and expectation of lower returns, could not. This crude dichotomy allowed almost no exceptions, and nobody complained. Then, towards the end of the '50s, films which slightly overlapped existing forms broke fresh ground and challenged these hitherto absolute conventions. Louis Malle's *Zazie dans le Métro* was not *quite* a children's comedy. Michael Powell's *Peeping Tom* was more than *just* a glossy horror. In fact both films were pivotal: both directors (unquestionably brilliant film-makers) had shown how colour could escape from its normal decorative haunts.

The leap, however, was not so easy. Resnais, with enormous care, survived in *Muriel* (1963). Other directors with a taste for chromatic novelty did not do so well. The public for the next few years was treated to the extraordinary spectacle of almost every major film-maker falling on his face. Some (Antonioni perhaps) just broke a toe—others looked like being permanently crippled. Bergman, Fellini, Godard started producing trash (only partisans will disagree) and even peacemaker Malle seemed to stumble. Beside earlier monochromatic work these results simply lacked impact. Resnais, in an extraordinary coup, which was also a timely (quite unheeded) warning, returned with *La Guerre est Finie* (1966) to the more tractable medium. But the rush could not be stopped. The English director had to try his luck. Gradually the lessons were learned by some: Claude Lelouch and Agnes Varda apotheosised, glorified, even conquered colour. Joseph Losey showed that he ranked with his Continental counterparts by coming off unscarred in *Accident* (1967). The secret was in intuition—the timing—the pace which characterised his somnolent, summery Oxford, the genuine context of his characters.

What is the difference between colour and black-and-white? Was there more than a financial sense in the distinction quietly observed by the 1950s? Of the two alternatives, most will agree that black-and-white is the more compelling, urgent, direct, while colour is leisurely, rich, relaxing. Why? People customarily have not two but three eyes: two for the present (and they never *see* anything but the present) and the mind's eye, the inward eye, which focuses on past and future. The present is always with us, always around us. Unsifted, unsorted, it awaits our classification, while the mind's eye surveys not the ceaseless flow, but the classified, developed image tray of memory (stills or newsreels) or a projection of anticipations of the future (goal-directing, danger-avoiding). The mind's eye is concerned with orientating: it deals with material already selected, not constantly flooding in, and therefore entails greater urgency, necessary impact.

The next stage is subjective, and can appeal only to individual experience. Here is the hypothesis: the present tense is always in colour, the non-present in a modified form of colour. Test it by closing your eyes and reconstructing every colour of the room you are in. If the mind's eye comes short of a complete colour visualisation it necessarily modifies colour. Now modification can extend from (say) the restrained tones of Ektachrome as far back as black-and-white. But no further: without black-and-white (or an equivalent chromatic duality) there can be no image. Black-and-white, therefore—the extreme case of colour-modification—stands, I suggest, and is apprehended as the most obvious, most convenient symbol of modified colour. So it effectively depicts the field of the mind's eye.

Is this perhaps why black-and-white has been predominantly (almost exclusively until about 1963) associated with the "think" film and colour with the "sit-back-and-enjoy" film (the film that ends when you leave the cinema)? And is this perhaps the reason why most "think" directors using colour have stammered in the new language? Why the *Times* critic after seeing *The Red Desert* (1964) was suddenly moved to announce that "Mr. Antonioni" was not an intellectual? Irrelevant perhaps, but in black-and-white "Mr. Antonioni" would never have been unmasked. Significantly the *Times* critic, in 1963, could not fault *L'Eclisse*.

To come back to character, I would suggest, tentatively, that since a character's perception is so related to his thought, his mind, his inner eye, only black-and-white can approximate this on the screen: colour sears it. But there are two escape clauses—(*1*) if film colour is severely modified, and deliberately distanced away from technicolor, or (*2*) if colour (and its equivalent, living firmly in the present) is part of the character-picture. I think that Agnes Varda, alone, has achieved the secret in *Le Bonheur* (1965). Here the luxuriant use of colour perfectly characterises the sensual, happy, present-tense-with-a-vengeance world of the hero. The character is the colour, and *vice versa*. Who but a Continental director could achieve this formula?

A final point concerns another key concept of the new language: improvisation. Fashionable for would-be fashionable directors and "true" for those whose ears jar to set dialogue. Of course it's difficult. The question is—is it worth it at all? Unrestricted improvisation is impossible for technical reasons, to say nothing of affecting the unity of the film. Some degree of control is necessary, but the greater the inhibition the less true the improvisation can be. Set dialogue need not however be stale: Bonnie and Clyde's first encounter with C. W. Moss is as spellbinding a moment as any in the modern cinema. But two things can stale any film, bad dialogue or under-rehearsed actors. Preferring not to risk pitfalls, the director may opt for improvisation, not realising how tricky his route will still be. Improvisation is not magic. First of all any genuine improvisation will combine spontaneity of speech and action, and according to Film Rule No. 1 (decreed by human biology) in a straight fight the eye always beats the ear—movement kills words. Lelouch deals with the problem cleverly in *Un Homme et une Femme*. He sits his actors down at a table to eat, thus validly inhibiting movement, and he cuts down to filter, modifying colour, cutting out distraction. He gets away with this rather domestic improvisation which in its small way remains quite plausible (the actors naturally *want* to eat, order food, make small talk).

In the wake of this success a film like *Poor Cow* seems to approach improvisation as a modish technique rather than as a chance of letting the characters add to their own characterisation. One has the impression in this film of faked improvisation ("discuss the character of Dave . . ."), in which the freedom of improvisation is desired while the possible area is severely restricted—like saying "run around on this foot-square patch of ground." The consequence is all the negative results of improvisation—semi-audibility, artificiality, aimlessness of subject-matter—without any of the positive ones—unexpectedness, development, insight. In fact the final shots of the film (close-ups of Carol White, normally an excellent actress) suggest an amateur at her first improvisation class; they are embarrassing.

Don Levy succeeds slightly better in *Herostratus*. The actors have a wider area of choice, but the plot being what it is and two characters (Max and Farson) being at best types, at worst blurs, they seem to move within a field of oddly static idiocy. Both of them do try and shake off their seemingly existential air of being film-clichés (representing Violent Youth and Conventional Authority) but they seem bound with the chain of symbol to the structure of the silly plot. Of course they contradict and repeat themselves. By cutting down on his direction and leaving them relatively free, Don Levy has left them too literally "directionless." This is nowhere better illustrated than where Farson, in the breakfast in bed scene, begins walking round Max in a series of circles, apparently locomoted by carefully enunciated invective: lacking direction (both senses) he falls into a cliché of the amateur stage. What is said, too, is often hackneyed, and more mechanical than a set script. (If a stale script is dead, stale improvisation may be positively decomposed.) These actors must be further liberated before they can spread their wings: half-tied to plot and cliché-character they flap on the ground like wounded birds, uttering platitudes and making meaningless movements.

It is the Character versus Plot problem again. Abandon plot by all means, but do it honestly—don't have a half-plot. Brilliant and compelling films have been virtually plotless—*Il Posto, La Notte, L'Eclisse*. But they do—this is their triumphant quality—they do explore a character in depth and in detail. The director (a true sign of strength) has abdicated his individuality in working out the character-perception of his hero/heroine. Thus humble he has his techniques in his hand, and uses them, like a good cardplayer, appropriately; he does not throw down all his trumps at once. Control is a difficult thing: too much or too little can be fatal. It must be properly understood, properly exercised. Only when technical control, control over theme and character, has been fully achieved, can genuine freedom be reached and a language spoken truly.

MINI–CASE STUDY

VIOLENCE

AND

THE ELECTRONIC MEDIA

KENT STATE: MAY 5, 1970

The mini-case study for this section focuses on violence in the mass media, a subject that generated much discussion at the end of the 1960's. Two presidential commissions, the National Advisory Commission on Civil Disorders and the National Commission on the Causes and Prevention of Violence, explored the problem of whether the reporting of violent events generates further violence. These commissions examined all the media, but in this mini–case study we have chosen only selections dealing with the electronic media. The selections, which range from the opinions of a psychiatrist to reports submitted by the presidential commissions, represent various viewpoints on the way electronic media handle violence. For students interested in exploring the subject further, additional sources are listed in the bibliography at the end of this section.

THE NEWS MEDIA AND THE DISORDERS

Report of the
National Advisory Commission
on Civil Disorders

. . .

As the summer of 1967 progressed, we think Americans often began to associate more or less neutral sights and sounds (like a squad car with flashing red lights, a burning building, a suspect in police custody) with racial disorders, so that the appearance of any particular item, itself hardly inflammatory, set off a whole sequence of association with riot events. Moreover, the summer's news was not seen and heard in isolation. Events of these past few years—the Watts riot, other disorders, and the growing momentum of the civil rights movement—conditioned the responses of readers and viewers and heightened their reactions. What the public saw and read last summer thus produced emotional reactions and left vivid impressions not wholly attributable to the material itself.

Fear and apprehension of racial unrest and violence are deeply rooted in American society. They color and intensify reactions to news of racial trouble and threats of racial conflict. Those who report and disseminate news must be conscious of the background of anxieties and apprehension against which their stories are projected. This does not mean that the media should manage the news or tell less than the truth. Indeed, we believe that it would be imprudent and even dangerous to downplay coverage in the hope that censored reporting of inflammatory incidents somehow will diminish violence. Once a disturbance occurs, the word will spread independently of newspapers and television. To attempt to ignore these events or portray them as something other than what they are can only diminish confidence in the media and increase the effectiveness of those who monger rumors and the fears of those who listen.

The News Media and the Disorders: From the Report of the National Advisory Commission on Civil Disorders (Washington, D.C.; U.S. Government Printing Office, March 1, 1968).

But to be complete, the coverage must be representative. We suggest that the main failure of the media last summer was that the totality of its coverage was not as representative as it should have been to be accurate. We believe that to live up to their own professed standards, the media simply must exercise a higher degree of care and a greater level of sophistication than they have yet shown in this area—higher, perhaps, than the level ordinarily acceptable with other stories.

This is not "just another story." It should not be treated like one. Admittedly, some of what disturbs us about riot coverage last summer stems from circumstances beyond media control. But many of the inaccuracies of fact, tone, and mood were due to the failure of reporters and editors to ask tough enough questions about official reports and to apply the most rigorous standards possible in evaluating and presenting the news. Reporters and editors must be sure that descriptions and pictures of violence, and emotional or inflammatory sequences or articles, even though "true" in isolation, are really representative and do not convey an impression at odds with the overall reality of events. The media too often did not achieve this level of sophisticated, skeptical, careful news judgment during last summer's riots.

·   ·   ·

FROM

The Media and The Assassinations

by CHRISTOPHER EMMET

The distorted and counter-productive effects of much news media treatment of the [Robert] Kennedy assassination compounded the tragedy itself, just as they did in the case of Martin Luther King. The impact of most of the reporting and editorial comment, here and abroad, was to suggest that both tragedies were typical of America and therefore proved the "sickness of our society," the special nature of "American violence" and the guilt which all white Americans should feel over the assassination of three of the most prominent champions of Negro rights. A more likely explanation of the three murders is that there must exist in a nation of 200 million people tens of thousands of psychotic potential murderers whose unbalanced emotions and resentments are stimulated by the pace and change of modern life, emotions which may be activated by the effects of instant television. There also seems to be a contagious effect, which leads psychopaths or neurotics to imitate highly publicized acts of violence, just as it helps organized, cold-blooded revolutionary groups to exploit and imitate both the hysteria and the techniques revealed by the television pictures of the revolts in other countries. For example, the French students at the Sorbonne used the slogan, "This is our Berlin," referring to the Berlin riots against the Springer press after the wounding of Rudi Dutschke. Similarly, the German who shot Dutschke said his action was "inspired" (or more aptly, "triggered") by the murder of Dr. King.

This last conclusion was evidently shared by Robert Kennedy himself. In an article in the May 30 issue of *Le Figaro,* Romain Gary quoted Kennedy in a recent conversation as follows: "I know that there will be an attempt on my life sooner or later. Not so much for political reasons, but through contagion, through emulation." Kennedy added that the world was in a peculiarly sensitive mood for this sort of emulation. Although he did not say so, surely it must be obvious that this mood is stimulated by instant, worldwide, massive and often morbid news coverage.

.   .   .

The Media and the Assassinations: From *National Review* (July 30, 1968). Reprinted by permission of *National Review* and Christopher Emmet.

from

VIOLENCE

in the mass media

by SOLOMON SIMONSON

. . .

There is nothing more pretentious or misleading than the impression cast by some social critics to the effect that the American people were formed from the onset of our history into this mold of violence, that the cult of the gun governed our rise in power, that it is simply an extension of over-aggressiveness that manifests itself so cruelly and regularly upon our national consciousness.

The history of the content of the mass media in the last thirty years puts the lie to these notions. A comparison of the films of the thirties with those of the sixties indicates clearly that the "practical" gun has attained prominence only in recent years. The "western" was legendary, belonging to another time. And the "detective" story has indeed undergone great change from *The Thin Man* to Mike Hammer. Even the gangster melo-dramas culminated in ethical resolutions that were both true and reasonable. *Scarface, Public Enemy,* and *Little Caesar* depicted the ugliness of the central figures without recourse to false sentimentality. Paul Muni, James Cagney, and Edward G. Robinson were perceived as actors and not as embodiments of the criminals they portrayed so effectively. Their heroism was a result of their acting talents. The contrast to the sixties is striking. What began in this decade as James Bond spoofing has evolved into *A Fistful of Dollars, Bonnie and Clyde,* and violence for its own sake. Even the standards of mystery films have deteriorated from Hitchcock's *39 Steps* to his *Psycho.* And this has set a precedent for television:

In the film offerings of the earlier decades, there was a pretty simple diet of goodness in one person and badness in another so as to identify us with goodness unqualifiedly. The present adolescent

Violence in the Mass Media: From *Catholic World* (September, 1968). Reprinted by permission of *Catholic World* and Solomon Simonson.

reacts to what appears to be a more mature balance of badness-goodness in each person through more realistic drama, hence liberating him from the naive but possibly more wholesome identification that our earlier age maintained. There is "so much good in the worst of us" that the punishment of a sick creature or a charmer who commits a crime appears criminal. The effectiveness of the advocate who seeks forgiveness for his defendant's "natural" compulsions may stir viewers to emulation of the criminal charmer.

Some consider it rewarding to charm one's way to success, but the merit of imitating a criminal charmer is blind to ethical considerations. Guilt is discounted and wrongdoers are forgiven on the false assumptions of a mercy-morality, whereas in reality a new illusion is mirrored for new vanity.

Our weaknesses appear to us to be the mere consequence of a poor home, an uncontrollable urge, a mysterious "bad seed." Responsibility is disclaimed. The removal of the stereotypes of "good" and "bad" exposes the young viewers to people as people, not as groups or patterns of types. *The logical merit of de-stereotyping is worthless when secured at the cost of moral responsibility.*[1]

When we look at the acclaim that the Academy Awards have granted to some of the film industry's products and personnel, we see that we have taken a long downward trek from Bette Davis' *Dangerous* to Julie Christie's *Darling,* from the characterization of female impishness to nymphomania, from some deceitfulness to any utter lack of values. This seems clear when the majority of the films nominated for the best of the year in 1967 involved violence of one kind or another.[2]

The advertisers of the films have been making an effort to outdo the films themselves. Recently, the marquee of a theater on New York City's celebrated thoroughfare, Broadway, read as follows: "Taylor, Brando in *Reflections in a Golden Eye.* Lust, nudity, brutality, hatred, and insanity that culminate in murder" (*The Daily News*). What an insidious joining of forces of the press, the film, and the advertiser! Down the block, the picture *Devil's Angels* had this description on the marquee: "See every brutal torture known—bold, inconceivable, shocking, true—violence their god, lust their law." In the thirties, advertising still used the naive superlatives of colossal, stupendous, magnificent, memorable, and spectacular. When Humphrey Bogart played in *The Left Hand of God,* the advertisement for the film had a gun drawn into the letter "O" of the word God. It was sacrilegious, but not at all as horrendous as "violence their god."

Although television's violence is not of the Grand Guignol variety, a survey reveals that a modicum of violence is an integral part of more than seventy per cent of the programs in prime time. Now, it is questionable

---

[1] Simonson, S., *Crisis in Television,* chapter on Creating Cultural Disadvantage, pp. 44–45. New York: Living Books, 1966.

[2] As to the newspaper world's self-discipline, I can personally testify to having been a Judge of the Page One awards for many years, as having carefully avoided prizes to "violence" reporting.

*"In this film, Rod, we want to show the public that violence
is a lousy thing. Now beat that man to a pulp as if
you really meant it."*

whether such programing is truly representative of our times; consequently, it is impossible to defend, either on ethical or logical grounds, this use of the people's airwaves. Clearly, the people need protection from harassment and inundation with violence. But neither the F.C.C. nor the self-regulation of the industry is providing it. The F.C.C. will not "censor" and the "telegogs" will not interfere with "creative integrity."

But exercising responsibility is neither censorship nor interference. Mr. Cox and Mr. Johnson of the F.C.C. have shown signs of being prepared to act on behalf of the people, and the presidents of the networks have promised action. As a result, one of the networks, NBC, has ordered the elimination of violence from promotional material and opening teasers and has changed a basic policy directive from "violence only where justified" to "violence only when essential."

Promises—promises. After the death of Senator Kennedy, the networks courteously displaced shows of "violence" with quieter programs. It may be remembered, also, that out of respect for the death of Valerie Percy, the murdered daughter of Senator Percy of Illinois, CBS removed *Psycho* and substituted *Kings Go Forth* for its Friday night movie. (This happened to have been the evening of Yom Kippur—the holiest day of the Jewish calendar.) The programs of that night included bits of violence in *The Man from UNCLE, T.H.E. Cat, Twelve O'Clock High,* and a Milton Berle slapstick on the bitter play, *Who's Afraid of Virginia Woolfe. Psycho* caught up to the race by being scheduled later in the year. Sooner or later, promises notwithstanding, tragedies and awesome days notwithstanding, the "telegogs" go back to "business as usual." The addiction to violence will not be cured by promises. Nor will a shift of blame onto the audiences help the situation any. The standard attack of the "telegogs" has been that the people speak through the ratings and that shows of violence have done exceedingly well in the ratings. Drew Pearson wrote of "the American passion for televised crimes and violence," and the Attorney General of the United States, Mr. Clark, agreed with him on the June 9 program of *Issues and Answers,* that television gives people "what they want to see."

The fallacies involved in this position are legion:

1. Among the greatest audiences ever assembled for television programs were for the specials, *The Bridge on the River Kwai, Death of a Salesman, Peter Pan,* etc. These programs beat all their competition in the ratings. The highest attendance and income for any in film history was secured by nonviolent *The Sound of Music.*

2. The demand did not create a supply of these brilliantly styled films with moral insights and objectives. Neither the television nor the film industries continued "to give the people what they wanted to see."

3. In entertainment, it is a more acceptable truism to assert that "the supply creates the demand." Leisure time cries for fulfillment. When we are stimulated in any one direction, we tend to channel our tastes in that direction.

4. Even if the case were otherwise, and the people were responding favorably to shows of violence, the instruments of measuring preference, the ratings, are insufficient to tell the real preferences of people, particularly where the available programs may all be of a similar content and style.

5. Ratings do not inform us of the degree of interest in viewing a program, the composition of the audience, whether the person who is tuned in likes the program, etc.

6. The ratings provide even less evidence of public preferences when an entertainment program of any quality is set up in competition with an educational program or documentary. This would make for a particularly unfair judgment since the documentary or educational program is frequently produced without the technical skills and without the uses of the significant factors of interest that are necessary for good programing.

7. There is no excuse for excessive violence on television on the forthright moral ground that television is a home product and should be treated as a living room guest of an average family.

8. A final counter-question should be raised: Why give the public what it wishes? No one may claim the right to determine another's best interests, but we should resolve what is generally detrimental to the public interest irrespective of its wishes.

.   .   .

a psychiatrist

LOOKS

at television and violence

by NER LITTNER

.   .   .

I can summarize my own views of the effects of television violence as follows:

1. I believe that the vast amount of violence on television is *basically a reflection of the violent interests of the viewers;* it is a symptom, not a cause; it graphically portrays the violence in our souls. I doubt that it is a serious cause of much of it.

2. I do not believe that television violence, when *honestly portrayed,* engenders violence in viewers of any age who were not violent already; and I do not believe that it raises violent impulses to an uncontrollable pitch in those who are already violent. (I will discuss later what I mean by "honest" television.)

3. I do think, however, that for some who are already violently disposed, TV violence may provide a model, a *modus operandi,* when they choose to discharge their violent urges. However, a book, a newspaper, or a radio program may provide a violent person with the same type of detailed plan for the expression of his violence.

4. As far as *dishonest* television violence is concerned, I do think that exposure to repeated doses may possibly interfere, to a degree unmeasurable at present, with the normal development of impulse control in normal or disturbed children; but I do not think that "dishonest" television violence has any marked pathological impact on the average adult.

5. Instead of wasting their efforts on such red herrings as censorship,

A Psychiatrist Looks at Television and Violence: From *Television Quarterly* (Fall, 1969). Reprinted by permission.

violence, sex, or nudity, I think that both the viewing public and the television industry would be far better off if the television industry would devote its considerable talents and energies to creating conditions that would make it possible to develop and screen television shows specializing in such qualities as excellence, artistic value, creativity, originality, honesty, and integrity. If *these* were the hallmark of our television shows, we would not have to worry about possible censorship of their violence, sex, or nudity.

.   .   .   .

. . . let me discuss for a moment the whole subject of violence on television. There has been until recently an increasing trend to violence on television. I think that this is due to a variety of reasons:

1. We are, and always have been a violent nation. We live in an age of violence. Therefore, to a large degree the violence on television accurately reflects the violence of our times.

2. We are increasingly freer in our acceptance of freedom of expression. The public and the courts are showing greater tolerance of, and are more

"Keep your shirts on! I'll find you some violence."

Drawing by Whitney Darrow, Jr.; © 1969 The New Yorker Magazine, Inc.

liberal towards, what can be shown. In a similar way we are far more relaxed about displays of sex and morality. Therefore, more violence is being shown as part of this relaxation of censorship.

3. For some program directors and moviemakers, the showing of violence is a cheap way of producing something that may make money. Instead of relying on art, talent, or creativity, reliance is placed on violence for the sake of violence, of shock for the sake of shock. The shock effect of the violence is being used to sell the movie or the program.

4. Because the portrayal of obscenity is against the law, this sets a limit on the amount of sex that can be safely sneaked in. The portrayal of violence is not against the law and therefore can be used to the extent that audiences will accept it.

These are four reasons (there probably are many more) for the great use of violence on television programs. This is not to say that the showing of violence on television is necessarily bad. Actually, it can have decidedly positive effects on the viewing public, and particularly children. These *positive effects* include the following:

1. An appropriate display of violence tends to present the world as it really is, rather than as we wistfully wish it would be. It is unrealistic to leave it out when it is part of the scene. Therefore, when shown in appropriate amounts it can be of *educational* value.

2. It can also be of *mental health* value, if appropriately done. Like watching a bullfight or boxing match, it can help discharge indirectly various violent feelings of the viewer. This tends to keep the viewer's violent feelings from boiling over in more dangerous ways. Therefore, in appropriate amounts it can provide a safe catharsis.

On the other hand, the *negative effects* of viewing television include the following:

1. The child or adolescent has not yet settled on his typical behavior patterns for functioning. If exposed to a repetitive display of *violence as a television-approved method for solving problems,* the child may be encouraged in that direction, particularly if he already comes from a family setting where violence also is the way of settling difficulties. Therefore, there may be an encouragement towards immature methods of problem solving. When, in an attempt to show that crime does not pay, there is violent retribution, its main effect is still to teach violence as the way to solve problems.

2. The individual, whether child or adult, who already uses violent behavior as a solution, may find worked out for him on television a detailed *modus operandi.* Therefore, the violent viewer may use the detail of the television programs as a way of expressing his violence. Television does not cause juvenile delinquency, but it can contribute techniques for a child already delinquent.

3. If excessive doses of violence are presented on television, it may have sufficient of a shock effect to prevent it being used for catharsis. There is

a limit to how much viewing of violence can be used for a safe discharge.

The impact of repeated exposure to excessive violence depends on at least three factors: (a) the age of the viewer; (b) the maturity of the viewer; and (c) the way in which the violence is presented and packaged.

The Age of the Viewer

As I have already mentioned, the mature adult will be offended and disgusted by excessive or inappropriate displays of violence. Therefore he can ignore it or turn it off. The *normal adolescent (or the immature adult)* is in a different situation. The excessive display of violence may cause a sympathetic resonance of inner violent feelings in the adolescent to a degree that he cannot handle it. There is no socially acceptable way of discharging excessive violent feelings. Therefore the adolescent may have his normal attempts to come to peace with his violent and rebellious feeling jeopardized. The normal adolescent, unlike the normal adult, will also tend to be attracted to the violence rather than repelled. The *normal pre-adolescent child* may also be disturbed by excessive and inappropriate displays of violence. However, he probably will be less upset than the adolescent because he is not as concerned, as is the adolescent, with problems of violent rebellion against authority.

The Maturity of the Viewer

The more emotionally disturbed the viewer is, the more likely it is that he will have difficulty in managing stirred-up violent feelings.

Let us consider an extreme situation where an adolescent, immediately after seeing a TV program in which a juvenile delinquent violently rapes a girl, leaves the TV set and violently rapes the first girl he meets. For such a sequence of events to have occurred, one would have to say that the adolescent probably was seriously disturbed emotionally *before* he saw the TV program. It is highly unlikely that any program, no matter how violent, could have such an effect on a normal adolescent.

One also could not say that it was the viewing of the TV program that "caused" the adolescent to rape the girl. One could only say that the program had two effects. Its first was to *trigger* a previously existing emotional disorder. The traumatic effect of the program was but one of the many etiological factors which, coming together, resulted in the adolescent's violent action. The second effect would be to provide the disturbed adolescent with a *blueprint* for discharging his violent tensions. These violent tensions, of course, would probably have originated in violent problems within his own family, completely predating his ever seeing the TV program.

Violent television does not make children aggressive; rather, *the aggressive child turns to violent TV*. And, for that matter, TV does not make a child passive; rather, it is the passive child who chooses the TV.

The Way in Which the Violence Is Presented and Packaged

I. The television violence will be least traumatic if it is completely appropriate and realistic to the story in which it is contained;

II. The television violence will be most traumatic if it is presented dishonestly, if it is being used to sell the program, if it is contrived and inappropriate, if it is unrealistically focused on, if it is presented out of context—in other words, if it is violence for the sake of violence and if the television show is deliberately using violence and brutality to attract and hold a larger audience.

The reason why *dishonest* television violence can be traumatic to the normal child or adolescent is because he feels exploited and used. *He senses he is being taken advantage of.* This tends to reactivate any conflictual feelings he may have about being exploited by his own parents. These reactivated feelings add an additional traumatic impact. In addition, the inappropriateness of the violence makes it harder for the child to deal with it mentally.

·   ·   ·

FROM

MASS MEDIA AND VIOLENCE

Report to the National Commission on the
Causes and Prevention of Violence

The Two Worlds of Violence: Television and Reality

.　　.　　.

The norms for violence contained in the television world of violence are in
stark contrast to the norms espoused by a majority of Americans.[1] The
most notable contrasts bear upon the criteria which distinguish between
approved and disapproved violence. Legality is a primary criterion of
approved violence for the majority of adults and teens, while it is not in
the television world of violence. In the television world, violence is used
almost without restriction as successful means to individual ends. The
majority of adult and teenage Americans place severe restrictions on the
use of violence in such a manner. For example, low-level violence is approved as a means of punishment and control when a person is in a position
of authority or when he is sufficiently provoked. Severe violence, on the
other hand, can only be used as a means to law enforcement, or defense
of self, others, or property, when the situation clearly necessitates its use.

The norms for violence espoused by a majority of Americans are
virtually at polar opposites with those contained in the television world of
violence. There is an even greater disparity between the minority of adults
and teens who espouse norms of non-violence (persons who very rarely or
never approve of violence in any situation) and the television world's
norms for violence.

The least disparity between the television world and real world in norms

From *Mass Media and Violence,* a Report to the National Commission on the
Causes and Prevention of Violence (Washington, D.C.: U.S. Government Printing
Office, November, 1969).

[1] References to television programming or the TV world of violence are based
on the programs broadcast during the weeks of October 1–7 in 1967 and 1968
during prime-time hours 4 p.m. to 10 p.m. Monday through Friday and Sunday, and
8 a.m. to 11 a.m. and 7 p.m. to 10 p.m. on Saturday.

210

"But first this message. Any and all acts of violence in the following program are not to be construed as an advocacy of violence by this station."

for violence is found between the sizable minority of adults and teenagers who have been called the "violents." Their norms for violence are *less* restrictive than the majority of Americans', but are still *more* restrictive than implied norms in the television world.

The television world of violence does not accurately reflect the real world in many significant respects. The vast majority of all levels of violence experienced by adult and teenage Americans as victims, observers, and assailants occurs with persons who are friends or family members of the respondents.[2] In the television world, the majority of violence occurs between strangers. The most prevalent type of violence in the television world involves the use of a weapon; the great majority of adults and teenagers have never experienced this type of severe violence. The most common role in the television world of violence is the assailant, while the least common is the role of observer; in the actual world, the observer is most common and the assailant is the least common role.

The television world of violence is often set in a time and place other than contemporary America. Television may or may not inaccurately reflect the actual world of violence in the American past or in foreign countries; there is no evidence from present research which can prove or disprove this statement.

When comparing the actual and television worlds of violence, our concern lies with the kinds of implied norms that are projected by television. What can or do audiences, especially children, learn from short- and long-term exposure to the television world of violence and what are the behavioral implications of such learning?

[2] The great majority of homicides (94 percent) occur within racial groups and in only twelve percent of all homicides were the assailant and the victim strangers. One-quarter of all homicides involve family members, and twenty-eight percent involve close friends. For further information, see Marvin Wolfgang, *Patterns in Criminal Homicide,* Philadelphia, Pa.: University of Pennsylvania Press, 1948.

211

The Relationship of the Two Worlds of Violence

The viewing habits and preferences of American audiences are a vital link between the actual and television worlds of violence. One method of assessing the relationship between the two worlds is to compare the characteristics of those in our study sample who have been identified as "violents" with the characteristics of persons who use television as their primary mode of media entertainment. Characteristics of adult and teenage "violents" can also be compared with the characteristics of those who have strong preferences for media violence, especially on television.

Users of TV for Entertainment

Adults and teenagers were presented with a list of mass media (radio, newspapers, magazines, television, books, movies) and asked which one, if any, they most frequently choose when they wanted to relax and get away from daily tensions. The responses are presented in Table 1.

Table 1   Adult and teen media choices for entertainment or relaxation (in percent)

	ADULT	TEEN
Television	43	32
Books	19	22
Radio	12	26
Magazines	9	6
Newspapers	9	4
Movies	5	9
Other	1	1
None	2	
Total	100	100

Teenagers, in general, choose the electronic media (radio, television, and movies) more than adults. A larger percentage of adults choose television as the mass medium most frequently used for relaxation. Note that these figures do not represent all television users, but only those who prefer television as a method of relaxation.

The same demographic characteristics which best distinguished "violents" in norms for and experience with violence were used to describe groups who choose television.

The demographic subgroup of adults with the highest proportion of its members choosing television for relaxation is composed of adults (no difference between males and females) between the ages of eighteen and thirty-five having less than a college education. Age and education characteristics are the same both for this subgroup and the group of adult "violents."

The demographic group of teenagers with the highest proportion of its members choosing television for relaxation consists of males, between the ages of thirteen and fifteen, who are black. Common characteristics between this subgroup and the teenage "violents" are sex, race, and, to some extent, age.

The Approvers of Television Violence

Twenty-eight percent of the adults said they approved of the kind of violence portrayed on television. The group with the largest proportion approving of television violence is composed of males, from eighteen to thirty-five years of age, residing in metropolitan areas, and having less than a college education. This group contains the largest proportion of adult "violents" in terms of norms and experience with violence.

Fifty-three percent of the teenage respondents approved of the kind of violence portrayed on television. The group with the greatest proportion of approvers is made up of males, between the ages of thirteen and fifteen, living in metropolitan areas, who are black.

There is almost a complete overlap between this group of approvers and teenage "violents" both in terms of norms and experience with violence. Common characteristics are sex, race, and, to a large extent, age and residence.

Persons with a Strong Preference for Media Violence

Adult and teenage respondents were given a series of six paired alternatives, with each pair containing one violent media content choice and one non-violent choice. For each pair, the respondents were asked to pick the one that they would prefer. An analysis of the choices can be summarized into an index of overall preference for media violence.

Fifteen percent of the adult respondents express high media violence preference.[3] The demographic group with the largest proportion of its members having a high media violence preference consists of males, eighteen to thirty-five years of age, who have less than a college education. This group overlaps with adult "violents" in all respects except residence.

Thirty-three percent of the teenagers have a high media violence preference. The demographic group with the largest proportion of its membership having a high media violence preference consists of males between the ages of thirteen and fifteen. This group overlaps with teen "violents" with regard to sex and, to some extent, age, but not in terms of residence and race.

.   .   .

[3] A high media violence preference is defined as those persons who select four or more violent alternatives out of the six paired alternatives.

WCBS Radio Commentary

by CHARLES OSGOOD

To hate somebody, to hate them enough to kill them, you must first dehumanize them in your mind. Remember the cartoons of the Japanese and the Germans during World War II? Outrageous. Racist. But effective war propaganda means painting the enemy as something other than human. That way I can hate him. That is why racial and religious epithets are so evil. To call somebody a nigger or a kike or a spic or wop is to rob a human being of his humanity. It is a frame of hate, a form of murder.

GI's in Vietnam don't like to think about killing fathers, mothers, children. They talk about killing gooks. Yes they do.

We are in trouble these days and part of it, anyway, is our willingness to despise people by reducing them to non-humans. Peace protesters who deplore that process when they see it in Vietnam do it themselves when they call policemen pigs. No person there inside that uniform. Just a pig. Campus demonstrators acting in the name of love and peace and humanity bait the authorities, the police, the administrations of their schools with their insults, their cutting, accusing *up against the wall* masters of the four letter word. Oh how satisfying to curl one's lip and through clenched teeth let them have it. Tell them how you feel. Oh how wonderfully self-righteous. And how pleasing to stand before some dinner and talk about punks and hippies to write *off* protesting students that way. How comfortable to think that everything would be fine if it weren't for the bums or the effete snobs or whatever other dehumanizing name you want to use.

How easy to see the military, how easy to see the President of the United States as some kind of monster. It makes him easier to hate.

William Fulbright, the civilized Senator from Arkansas, doesn't do that. He disagrees very much with what Mr. Nixon is doing. But he told a newsman yesterday, "I have never doubted his intentions, but I very gravely doubt his ability to *achieve* those intentions."

The word is the father of the act. If we are going to avoid blood then we must learn soon to curb our tongues, to end this orgy of self-indulgence in words with warheads.

Carl Sandburg said it. "Look out how you use proud words. When you let proud words go, it is not easy to call them back. They wear long boots, hard boots. Look out how you use proud words."

WCBS Radio Commentary: Reprinted by permission of WCBS/Newsradio.

THE ELECTRONIC MEDIA

STUDY QUESTIONS

1. Tebbel recognizes that commerical television must produce programs for the mass audience in order to remain viable. He suggests that both the mass audience and those with "minority tastes" might be satisfied if an alternative to commercial television is provided. Study the television situation in your area. Is there any programing available that is not on a commercial network? What are the viewing habits of the people in your area? Do you think a network devoted to education and the arts is necessary?

2. Questions have been raised about television's ability to serve the real needs of people. Hentoff sees cable television as a way to give exposure to all elements of our society. What benefits do you think will accrue from increased use of CATV? If CATV is available in your area, analyze its programing. Does it serve its intended purpose?

3. Dye, in calling attention to the "death of silence," is really noting some basic changes in radio programing in recent years. What are the probable causes of these changes? What is radio's function today? Can radio still be considered an artistic medium?

4. Rosenstone says that the protest songs of the 1960's provide a critique of American life. Study some of the songs of the 1960's. What picture of American life do you get from those songs? Is it the same picture that you could get from looking at the motion pictures of that period? At magazines? Compare the songs of the sixties with today's popular songs. Are the protests the same? Are there differences in music? In lyrics?

5. Have the electronic media treated blacks fairly? Have they been concerned with the black struggle for equality? Or might the media perhaps be guilty of using the Negro cause to make themselves look better? What is the poet James W. Thompson saying about blacks and the media?

6. What is your reaction to the poetry by computer in this section? You may have once listened to computer-made music. Do you feel that more communication was being achieved when you were listening to computer-made sounds than when you were reading computer-arranged words? Does the fact that words connote preconceived ideas hamper your appreciation or understanding of the poem?

7. Dennis Hopper calls film "the Sistine Chapel of the Twentieth Century." Are movies this important to youth today? What are today's "youth" movies telling their audiences? Realism in movies reflected the mood of the late 1960's. What are contemporary films reflecting about our culture today? Or are they setting trends?

8. The film **Easy Rider,** which was directed by Dennis Hopper, achieved at least some of its success because it celebrated the individual. It also marked a shift in film making away from the industry to the individual producer and director. What implications does this have with regard to the role of film in setting cultural mores? In his article Hopper mentions the underground film. If you have seen an underground film, compare it with a commercial film, even one made by a new director like Hopper. Does anything happen to the artistry of a film when it is commercialized?

9. David Mowat observes that many films today are deemphasizing plot. What is replacing plot? What new techniques comprise the new film language?

10. Analyze a current film in terms of how the director used the elements of film language cited by Mowat. Would you classify the film you selected as a "think" film or a "sit back and enjoy" film?

11. What effects has television had on the movie industry? Do you see any evidence that television's accessibility has forced film to become a more artistic, cultural medium?

BIBLIOGRAPHY FOR FURTHER STUDY

Barnouw, Erik. *A History of Broadcasting in the United States: A Tower in Babel.* Vol. I—to 1933. New York: Oxford University Press, 1966.

———. *A History of Broadcasting in the United States: The Golden Web.* Vol. II—1933 to 1953. New York: Oxford University Press, 1968.

"Black TV: Its Problems and Promises," *Ebony,* XXIV (September, 1969), 88–90.

Bleum, A. William and Roger Manvell, eds. *The Progress in Television.* New York: Focal Press, 1967.

Bobker, Lee R. *Elements of Film.* New York: Harcourt Brace Jovanovich, 1969.

Borghesani, William H., Jr. "Who Is Going to Control Data Processing and Data Communications?" *Stores: Retailing's Own Magazine,* XL (September, 1967), 33–36.

Compton, Neil. "Television and Reality." *Commentary,* XLVI (September, 1968), 82–86.

Cox, Kenneth A. "Competition in and Among the Broadcasting, CATV, and Pay TV Industries." *Antitrust Bulletin,* XIII (Fall, 1968), 911–25.

Daley, Eliot A. "Is TV Brutalizing Your Child?" *Look,* XXXIII (December 2, 1969), 99–100.

Dawson, G. P. "How Dangerous is TV Violence?" *Parents' Magazine,* XLIV (October, 1969), 60–61, 73.

Eisen, Jonathan, ed. *The Age of Rock.* New York: Vintage Books, 1969.

Fyock, James A. "Content Analysis of Films: New Slant on an Old Technique." *Journalism Quarterly,* XLV (Winter, 1968), 687–91.

Geduld, Harry M., ed. *Film Makers on Film Making.* Bloomington: Indiana University Press, 1967.

Gerbner, G. "Cultural Indicators: The Case of Violence in Television Drama." *Annals of the American Academy of Political and Social Science* (March, 1970), 69–81.

Hazard, Patrick D., ed. *TV As Art.* Champaign, Illinois: National Council of Teachers of English, 1966.

Hickey, Neil. "What Television Should Be Doing to Safeguard Our Greatest Natural Resource—Our Children." *TV Guide,* XVII (November 29, 1969), 6–11.

Johnson, Nicholas. *How to Talk Back to Your Television Set.* New York: Bantam Books, 1970.

Kuhns, William. *The Electronic Gospel.* New York: Herder and Herder, 1969.

LaMarca, James. "FM's Two Faces—Yesterday's and Today's." *Media/Scope,* XII (January, 1968), 85–87.

Macy, John W., Jr. "The Critics of Television: A Positive Answer." *Vital Speeches,* XXXVI (February 15, 1970), 286–88.

Robinson, John P. "Television and Leisure Time: Yesterday, Today and (Maybe) Tomorrow." *Public Opinion Quarterly,* XXXIII (Summer, 1969), 210–22.

Rubin, Bernard. *Political Television.* Belmont, California: Wadsworth Publishing Co., 1967.

Schickel, Richard. "The Movies Are Now High Art." *The New York Times Magazine* (January 5, 1969), 32 ff.

Schillaci, Anthony. "Film as Environment." *Saturday Review,* LI (December 28, 1968), 8–12, 14, 60.

Steele, Robert Scott. *The Cataloging and Classification of Cinema Literature.* Metuchen, New Jersey: Scarecrow Press, 1967.

Summers, Robert E. and Harrison B. Summers. *Broadcasting and the Public.* Belmont, California: Wadsworth Publishing Co., 1966.

White, David Manning. *Sight, Sound, and Society: Motion Pictures and Television in America.* Boston: Beacon Press, 1968.

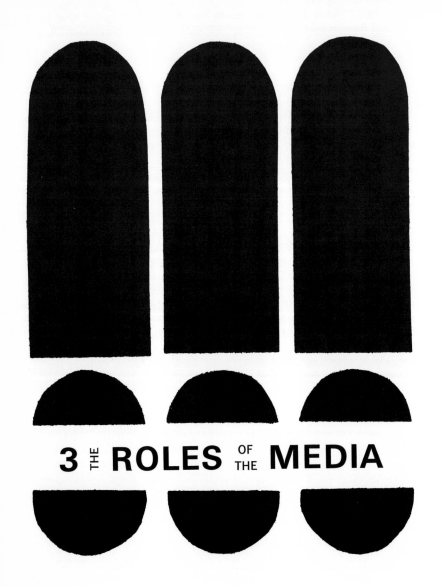

3 THE ROLES OF THE MEDIA

While Part 2 looked at the media from the point of view of their technical and physical potential, Part 3 examines them as they perform their basic roles as informer, entertainer, and persuader. We have a great dependence upon the media. C. Wright Mills, a media critic, claims that: "Very little of what we think we know of the social realities of the world have we found out firsthand. Most of 'the pictures in our heads' we have gained from these media."*

The three media roles are not isolated from one another. Although we will attempt to distinguish the roles for purposes of analysis, they are rarely fully separate. Nor should they be. For instance, without the persuasive function of advertising, many of the media that inform and entertain would cease to exist. This interdependence causes problems, for readers and listeners often fail to differentiate between editorial and advertising content. Pauline Kael notes that: "Television is blurring the distinction for all of us; we don't know what we're reacting to anymore, and, beyond that, it's becoming just about impossible to sort out the con from the truth because a successful con makes its lies come true."†

Any element of a medium may be playing a hidden role as well as its obvious one. While advertising is readily understood to be persuasive, the media content, while on the surface appearing to be entertaining or informative, may also be persuasive. Consider the sports magazine. Some readers would claim that the magazine's role is to entertain, just as the sport itself entertains. Others would maintain that the magazine's most important role is to inform us about amateur and professional sports, which often occupy significant economic and cultural positions in our lives. Both views are legitimate. However, it should be noted that the content of the magazine, while informing and entertaining the reader, is also promoting sports.

The front page of a newspaper also illustrates how the three roles are blended. In almost any daily newspaper today one can find human interest features, action lines, and pictures alongside the hard news. Perhaps this indicates our desire to be entertained as well as informed. In addition, one can find the generally acknowledged persuasive devices—editorials, columns, and letters—on the editorial page. However, it should be noted that persuasion may also appear in the guise of a news format. Front-page news stories often advocate a cause or a point of view. For example, an account of the conditions of a minority group may be intended to stimulate corrective measures by a legislative body, or a news story about the President may be the result of his deliberate generation of news in an attempt to change public opinion about a certain issue.

To educated, responsible members of a free society, the media's role as informer is perhaps their most significant one. It is essential that there be objective reporting of all issues and events. In 1947 the Commission on Freedom of the Press declared:

* C. Wright Mills, **The Power Elite** (New York: Oxford University Press, 1956), p. 311.
† Pauline Kael, "Numbing the Audience," **The New Yorker,** XLV (October 3, 1970), 74.

Today our society needs, first, a truthful, comprehensive, and intelligent account of the day's events in a context which gives them meaning; second, a forum for the exchange of comment and criticism; third, a means of projecting the opinions and attitudes of the groups in the society to one another; fourth, a method of presenting and clarifying the goals and values of the society; and fifth, a way of reaching every member of the society by the currents of information, thought, and feeling which the press supplies.*

In our present pluralistic society, these ideals are a challenge to the media. Representing the majority is not enough; blacks, radicals, reactionaries, youth, the aged, the poor—all must find their world represented accurately. ABC Correspondent Harry Reasoner says that we are the best informed mass citizenry in the history of the world†; yet many feel (like Nat Hentoff in his "Students as Media Critics") that the media are not successful in informing us about all segments of society.

Because of the variety of media, we are at least well informed in the sense of being able to obtain many different kinds of information. The type of information provided by a medium is largely determined by its primary function and by the size and nature of its audience. For example, the size of television's audience—55 million viewers for network news shows—requires that it present the news in a broader perspective than that of William Buckley's **National Review** or Art Kunkin's Los Angeles **Free Press.** Another difference among media is degree of immediacy. Radio and television can give live coverage of an event, while newspapers at best reach the public a few hours after the event. Days or weeks intervene between an event and a magazine's reporting of it; yet this delay affords the magazine the opportunity to provide background information, which is one of its most important functions. All media, regardless of their functions and their audience, attempt to provide more than just a reporting of events.

If a poll were taken, we would probably find that most people think the chief role of the mass media is entertainment. We are a nation of people who want to be entertained. In fact, we generally receive our information in a format which is at the same time entertaining, as illustrated by the magazine format of television news programs like **First Tuesday** and **Sixty Minutes** and the "light touches" on the evening news and even the weather report.

All media entertain to some extent—and entertainment in the media can be anything. It can be reality or fantasy. It can deepen one's awareness or it can insulate one from the real world; it can expand one's understanding of his fellow man or it can reinforce an already held stereotype. It can be a Marvel comic book or Tom Wolfe's "Radical Chic" in **New York** magazine, the "Top 40" or **La Traviata,** a situation comedy or a socially relevant drama.

* **A Free and Responsible Press,** Report of the Commission on Freedom of the Press (Chicago, 1947), pp. 20–21.
† Neil Hickey, "An Anchor Man Answers Some Questions," **TV Guide** (March 20, 1971), 7.

The more homogeneous the audience of a medium is, the greater are the medium's chances of satisfying all members of that audience. Perhaps the central problem faced by the mass media in their role as entertainer is the almost impossible task of satisfying the tastes of a wide audience. Television, in attempting to make its programs accessible to large masses, is less likely to provide culturally rich experiences than, say, an FM radio station. **New York** magazine (with its primarily local appeal) or the rock-oriented magazine **Circus** or an underground film better satisfies the needs of a specific audience than do media which are designed for mass audiences.

The final role to consider is the media as persuader. On the one hand, the media can be used to move an audience to a definite belief or action by a persuasive editorial or advertisement. On the other hand, if we think of "persuasion" in its broadest sense, the media can be used to persuade an audience to accept new information. (Here the role of persuasion overlaps the role of "informing through entertainment.") A good illustration is the successful **Sesame Street,** which uses persuasive techniques in its attempt to educate a previously neglected segment of the population.

Persuasion can take two forms. The message can be obvious, open, and forceful, as it is in political speeches or in hard-sell advertising for detergents and headache remedies. More important to recognize is the subtle type of persuasion, illustrated by the more sophisticated political commercials and by the deliberate use of the inner-city setting in **Sesame Street** to suggest a point of view. Attitudes about such things as families, morality, religion, technology, work, drugs, minorities, youth, politicians, and "cops" are greatly influenced by their treatment in the media; the extent of this influence is as yet unknown. Thus it is especially important that any media treatment of these subjects be viewed in the context of the interrelated roles they play.

THE INFORMERS

What it's like to broadcast news

by WALTER CRONKITE

CBS anchorman Walter Cronkite defends his profession by
citing the unique elements that make up a TV newscast and the
difficult demands made on the newscaster's judgment.
He holds that TV news reporting has largely positive effects on
society and argues for the TV newsman's freedom to report
all the news "and let the chips fall where they may."

When Vice President Agnew, in November 1969, unleashed his attack
upon the news media, he was following, albeit with unique linguistic and
philosophic departures, a long line of predecessors. Somewhere in the history of our Republic there may have been a high government official who
said he had been treated fairly by the press, but for the life of me, however,
I can't think of one.

Mr. Agnew's attacks, of course, were particularly alarming because of
their sustained virulence and intimidating nature. But the Vice President
was simply joining the chorus (or, seeing political opportunity, attempting
to lead it) of those who have appointed themselves critics of the television
medium. Well, I don't like everything I see on television either, but I am
frank to say I'm somewhat sick and mighty tired of broadcast journalism
being constantly dragged into the operating room and dissected, probed,
swabbed, and needled to see what makes it tick.

I'm tired of sociologists, psychologists, pathologists, educators, parents,
bureaucrats, politicians, and other special interest groups presuming to tell
us what is news or where our responsibilities lie.

Or perhaps I'm phrasing this wrong. It is not those who squeeze us
between their slides and hold us under their microscopes with whom my
patience has grown short. The society *should* understand the impact of
television upon it. There are aspects of it that need study so that the people
can cope with an entirely revolutionary means of communication. Those

who disagree with our news coverage have every right to criticize. We can hardly claim rights to a free press and free speech while begrudging those rights to our critics. Indeed, that would seem to be what some of them would like to do to us. So believing, it clearly cannot be the responsible critics or serious students of the TV phenomenon with whom I quarrel. I am provoked more by those in our craft who, like wide-eyed country yokels before the pitchman, are losing sight of the pea under the shell.

We must expose the demagogues who would undermine this nation's free media for personal or partisan political gain. That is news. And we should not withhold our cooperation from serious studies of the medium. But we must not permit these matters to divert us from our task, or confuse us as to what that task is.

I don't think it is any of our business what the moral, political, social, or economic effect of our reporting is. I say let's get on with the job of reporting the news—and let the chips fall where they may. I suggest we concentrate on doing our job of telling it like it is and not be diverted from that exalted task by the apoplectic apostles of alliteration.

Now, a fair portion of what we do is not done well. There are things we are not doing that we ought to do. There are challenges that we have not yet fully met. We are a long way from perfection. Our problems are immense, and they are new and unique.

A major problem is imposed by the clock. In an entire half-hour news broadcast we speak only as many words as there are on two-thirds of one page of a standard newspaper. Clearly, the stricture demands tightness of writing and editing, and selection, unknown in any other form of journalism. But look what we do with that time. There are twenty items in an average newscast—some but a paragraph long, true, but all with the essential information to provide at least a guide to our world that day.

"That's the trouble with a truly enlightened electorate."

Drawing by D. Fradon, © 1968 The New Yorker Magazine, Inc.

Film clips that, in a way available to no other daily medium, introduce our viewers to the people and the places that make the news; investigative reports (pocket documentaries) that expose weakness in our democratic fabric (not enough of these, but we're coming along), feature film reports that explore the byways of America and assure us that the whole world hasn't turned topsy-turvy; graphics that in a few seconds communicate a great deal of information; clearly identified analysis, or commentary, on the news—I think that is quite a package.

The transient, evanescent quality of our medium—the appearance and disappearance of our words and pictures at almost the same instant—imposes another of our severe problems. Most of us would agree that television's greatest asset is the ability to take the public to the scene—the launch of a spaceship, a Congressional hearing, a political convention, or a disaster (in some cases these are not mutually exclusive). Live coverage of such continuing, developing events presents the radio-television newsman with a challenge unlike any faced by the print reporter. The newspaper legman, rewrite man, and editor meet the pressure of deadlines and must make hard decisions fast and accurately. But multiply their problems and decisions a thousandfold and you scarcely have touched on the problems of the electronic journalist broadcasting live. Even with the most intensive coverage it still is difficult and frequently impossible to get all the facts and get all of them straight as a complex and occasionally violent story is breaking all around. We do have to fill in additional material on subsequent broadcasts, and there is the danger that not all the original audience is there for the fuller explanation.

When a television reporter, in the midst of the riot or the floor demonstration or the disaster, dictates his story, he is not talking to a rewrite man but directly to the audience. There is no editor standing between him and the reader. He will make mistakes, but his quotient for accuracy must be high or he is not long for this world of electronic journalism. We demand a lot of these on-the-scene television reporters. I for one think they are delivering in magnificent fashion.

Directors of an actuality broadcast, like newspaper photo editors, have several pictures displayed on the monitors before them. But they, unlike their print counterparts, do not have ten minutes, or five, or even one minute to select the picture their audience will see. Their decision is made in seconds. Theirs is a totally new craft in journalism, but they have imbued it with all the professionalism and sense of responsibility and integrity of the men of print. Of course we make mistakes, but how few are the errors compared to the fielding chances!

Our profession is encumbered, even as it is liberated, by the tools of our trade. It is a miracle—this transmission of pictures and voices through the air, the ability to take the whole world to the scene of a single event.

But our tools still are somewhat gross. Miniaturization and other developments eventually will solve our problem, but for the moment our cameras and our lights and our tape trucks and even our microphones are obtrusive. It is probably true that their presence can alter an event, and it probably also is true that they alter it even more than the presence of reporters with pad and pencil, although we try to minimize our visibility. But I think we should not be too hasty in adjudging this as always a bad thing. Is it not salutary that the government servant, the politician, the rioter, the miscreant knows that he is operating in the full glare of publicity, that the whole world is watching?

Consider political conventions. They have been a shambles of democratic malfunction since their inception, and printed reports through the years haven't had much effect in reforming them. But now that the voters have been taken to them by television, have sat through the sessions with the delegates and seen the political establishment operate to suppress rather than develop the democratic dialogue, there is a stronger reform movement than ever before, and the chances of success seem brighter.

I would suggest that the same is true of the race rioters and the student demonstrators, whatever the justice of the point they are trying to make. Of course they use television. Hasn't that always been the point of the demonstrator—to attract attention to his cause? But the *excesses* of the militants on ghetto streets and the nation's campuses, shown by television with almost boring repetition, tend to repel ᵣather than enlist support, and this is a lesson I hope and *believe* that rational leaders are learning.

Scarcely anyone would doubt that television news has expanded to an immeasurable dgree the knowledge of many people who either cannot or do not read. We have broadened the interests of another sizable group whose newspaper reading is confined to the headlines, sports, and comics. We are going into homes of the untutored, teaching underprivileged and disadvantaged who have never known a book. We are exposing them to a world they scarcely knew existed, and while advertisements and entertainment programing whet their thirst for a way of life they believe beyond them, we show them that there are people and movements, inside and outside the Establishment, that are trying to put the good things within their reach.

Without any intent to foster revolution, by simply doing our job as journalists with ordinary diligence and an extraordinary new medium, we have awakened a sleeping giant. No wonder we have simultaneously aroused the ire of those who are comfortable with the status quo. Many viewers happily settled in their easy chairs under picture windows that frame leafy boughs and flowering bushes and green grass resent our parading the black and bearded, the hungry and unwashed through their living rooms, reminding them that there is another side of America that demands their attention. It is human nature to avoid confronting the unpleasant. No one *wants* to hear that "our boys" are capable of war crimes, that our

elected officials are capable of deceit or worse. I think I can safely say
that there are few of us who want to report such things. But as professional
journalists we have no more discretion in whether to report or not to report
when confronted with the facts than does a doctor in deciding to remove
a gangrenous limb.

If it *happened,* the people are entitled to know. There is no condition
that can be imposed on that dictum without placing a barrier (censorship)
between the people and the truth—at once as fallible and corrupt as only
self-serving men can make it. The barrier can be built by government—
overtly by dictatorship or covertly with propaganda on the political stump,
harassment by subpoena, or abuse of the licensing power. Or the barrier
can be built by the news media themselves. If we permit our news judgment to be colored by godlike decisions as to what is good for our readers,
listeners, or viewers, we are building a barrier—no matter how pure our
motives. If we permit friendship with sources to slow our natural reflexes,
we also build a barrier. If we lack courage to face the criticism and consequences of our reporting, we build barriers.

But of all barriers that we might put between the people and the truth,
the most ill-considered is the one that some would erect to protect their
profits. In all media, under our precious free enterprise system, there are
those who believe performance can only be measured by circulation or
ratings. The newspaper business had its believers long before we were on
the scene. They practiced editing by readership survey. Weak-willed but
greedy publishers found out what their readers *wanted* to read and gave
it to them—a clear abdication of their duties as journalists and, I would
submit, a nail in the coffin of newspaper believability.

Today, before the drumfire assault of the hysterical Establishment and
the painful complaints of a frightened populace, there are many in our
business who believe we should tailor our news reports to console our critics.
They would have us report more good news and play down the war, revolution, social disturbance. There certainly is nothing wrong with good news.
In fact, by some people's lights we report quite a lot of it: an anti-pollution
bill through Congress, a report that the cost of living isn't going up as fast
as it was last month, settlement of a labor dispute, the announcement of a
medical breakthrough, plans for a new downtown building. There isn't
anything wrong either with the stories that tell us what is right about America, that reminds us that the virtues that made this nation strong still exist
and prosper despite the turmoil of change.

But when "give us the good news" becomes a euphemism for "don't give
us so much of that bad news"—and in our business one frequently means
the other—the danger signal must be hoisted.

It is possible that some news editors have enough time allotted by their
managements to cover all the significant news of their areas—much of it,
presumably, in the "bad" category—and still have time left over for a

"good news" item or two. But for many and certainly those at the network level, that is not the case. To crowd in the "happy" stories would mean crowding out material of significance. Some good-news advocates know this, and it is precisely what they want: to suppress the story of our changing society in the hope that if one ignores evil it will go away.

Others simply are tired of the constant strife. They would like a little relief from the daily budget of trouble that reminds them of the hard decisions they as citizens must face. But can't they see that pandering to the innocent seeking relief is to yield to those who would twist public opinion to control our destiny?

It is no coincidence that these manipulative methods parallel those adopted half a century ago by Russian revolutionaries also seeking the surest means to bend the population to their will. You will not find bad news in Russian newspapers or on broadcast media. There are no reports of riots, disturbances of public order, muggings or murders, train, plane, or auto wrecks. There are no manifestations of race prejudice, disciplinary problems in army ranks. There is no exposure of malfeasance in public office—other than that which the government chooses to exploit for its own political purposes. There is no dissent over national policy, no argument about the latest weapons system.

There is a lot of good news—factories making their quotas, happy life on the collective farm, successes of Soviet diplomacy, difficulties in the United States. The system works. Without free media—acerbic, muckraking, irreverent—the Soviet people are placid drones and the Soviet Establishment runs the country the way it wants it run.

Since it is hard to know the real motives in others' minds—indeed, it is hard sometimes to know our own motives—and since few are likely to admit that they would seek to suppress dissent from Establishment norms, it would be wrong to ascribe such Machiavellian connivance to the good-news advocates. The only trouble is that the other, more likely motive—profiting from the news by pandering to public taste—is almost as frightening. To seek the public's favor by presenting the news it wants to hear is to fail to understand the function of the media in a democracy. We are not in the business of winning popularity contests, and we are not in the entertainment business. It is not our job to please anyone except Diogenes.

The newsman's purpose is contrary to the goal of almost everyone else who shares the airwaves with us, and perhaps we should not be too harsh with those executives with the ultimate responsibility for station and network management. We are asking a great deal of them. For seventeen of the eighteen hours during an average broadcast day their job is to win friends and audience. They and we live on how successfully they do this difficult job.

But then we ask them to turn a deaf ear to the complaints of those dissatisfied with what we present in the remaining minutes of the day. We ask them to be professionally schizoid—and that would seem to be a lot to ask. But is it, really? After all, in another sense, as journalists we live this life of dual personality. There is not a man who can truthfully say that he does not harbor in his breast prejudice, bias, strong sentiments pro and con on some if not all the issues of the day.

Yet it is the distinguishing mark of the professional journalist that he can set aside these personal opinions in reporting the day's news. None of us succeeds in this task in all instances, but we know the assignment and the pitfalls, and we succeed far more often than we fail or than our critics would acknowledge. We have a missionary duty to try to teach this basic precept of our craft to those of our bosses who have not yet learned it. We in broadcasting, at least, cannot survive as a major news medium if we fail.

We were well on the way before the current wave of politically inspired criticism. In my twenty years in broadcasting I have seen more and more station owners taking courage from their news editors, tasting the heady fruit of respect that can be won by the fearless conveyer of the truth. Some years ago William Allen White wrote that "nothing fails so miserably as a cowardly newspaper." I suspect he spoke not only of commercial failure but of the greater failure: not winning the confidence of the people. A radio or television station also can fail this test of courage, and when it does its owner wins not a community's respect and gratitude but its contempt.

Broadcast management is going to need a stiff backbone in the days ahead—not only for its own well-being but for the good of us all. We are teetering on the brink of a communications crisis that could undermine the foundation of our democracy that is a free and responsible press. We all know the present economic background. We in radio and television with our greater impact and our numerous outlets have forced many of our print competitors out of business. It is a rare American city today that has more than one newspaper. And yet I think most of us will acknowledge that we are not an adequate substitute for the newspapers whose demise we have hastened. We cannot supply the wealth of detail the informed citizen needs to judge the performance of his city, county, or state. If we do our jobs thoroughly, however, we can be a superb monitor over the monopoly newspaper, assuring that it does not by plot, caprice, or inadvertence miss a major story.

We *can* be, that is, if we are left alone to perform that essential journalistic function. The trouble is that broadcast media are not free; they are government licensed. The power to make us conform is too great to lie forever dormant. The ax lies there temptingly for use by any enraged administration, Republican, Democrat, or Wallaceite. We are at the mercy of the whim of politicians and bureaucrats, and whether they choose to chop us down or not, the mere existence of their power is an intimidating and constraining threat.

So on one side there is a monopoly press that may or may not choose to present views other than those of the domineering majority, on the other side a vigorously competitive but federally regulated broadcast industry, most of whose time is spent currying popular—that is, majority—favor. This scarcely could be called a healthy situation. There is a real danger that the free flow of ideas, the vitality of minority views, even the dissent of recognized authorities could be stifled in such an atmosphere.

We newsmen, dedicated as we are to freedom of press and speech and the presentation of all viewpoints no matter how unpopular, must work together, regardless of our medium, to clear the air while there is still time. We must resist every new attempt at government control, intimidation, or harassment. And we must fight tenaciously to win through Congress and the courts guarantees that will free us forever from the present restrictions. We must stand together and bring the power of our professional organizations to bear against those publishers and broadcast managers who fail to understand the function of a free press. We must keep our own escutcheons so clean that no one who would challenge our integrity could hope to succeed.

If we do these things, we can preserve, and re-establish where it has faded, the confidence of the people whose freedom is so indivisibly linked with ours.

IT IS YOUR BUSINESS, MR. CRONKITE

by IRVING E. FANG

Dr. Irving Fang, Associate Professor in the School of Journalism
and Mass Communication at the University of Minnesota and
author of **Television Notes,** replies to Cronkite's article,
noting that the journalist should be concerned with the
consequences of his work.

Walter Cronkite, in a recent article adapted from a speech to the Sigma
Delta Chi national convention, stated, "I don't think it is any of our business what the moral, political, social, or economic effect of our reporting
is" ["What It's Like to Broadcast the News," *SR,* Dec. 12].

I disagree with Mr. Cronkite. It *is* the journalist's concern to consider
the consequences of his work, just as it is the physician's, the attorney's,
the minister's, the professor's, and indeed every professional man's concern.

Of course, Cronkite is not heedless of public reaction. If an obscenity
were part of an important news story (for example, what the Chicago
Seven were really saying in court), he would not repeat it on the air. Nor
would he repeat a blasphemy. Nor would he use pornography to illustrate
a national concern. No responsible journalist does these things, whether
or not they might be news.

The journalist operates as he does because society chooses that he do so.
Our society, based on the libertarian ideals of a democracy, chooses wisely
that journalists should, within certain bounds, "tell it like it is." Besides
obscenity, blasphemy, and pornography, news that lies out of bounds
includes certain military secrets, indefensible libels, matters of personal

privacy, and unsubstantiated rumor. While broad, the rights of free speech and freedom of the press are not absolute.

To the left and to the right of our democracy lie the censored societies. Lenin asked:

Why should freedom of speech and freedom of the press be allowed? Why should a government which is doing what it believes to be right allow itself to be criticized? It would not allow opposition by lethal weapons. Ideas are much more fatal things than guns. Why should any man be allowed to buy a printing press and disseminate pernicious opinions calculated to embarrass the government?

And Franco's former foreign minister, Alberto Martin Artajo, stated:

There are certain substantive freedoms derived from natural law— man's freedom to worship his God, to found a home, to educate his children, to work, and to act with self-respect and independence. These freedoms [in Spain] once succumbed to the action of license, as a result of the excess of other freedoms, like freedom of the press, of party, of trade unions, of strikes, which are not of the same nature and degree, because they are, so to speak, secondary freedoms, "adjective" freedoms, of a lower order. That is why the [Franco] regime has in some way repressed these other political freedoms, which, because they are secondary, must be the safeguard of the previous ones.

Some Americans can always be found who would like more restrictions on what may now be broadcast or printed. I have even heard this from a few men who make their living in the news business. (I am reluctant to call them journalists.) Vice President Agnew's Des Moines speech has less significance than the apparent support it received across the land. Many, many Americans honestly believe that television network news isn't telling it as it is. I sometimes ask for a show of hands in a college classroom to learn how many students believe that television newscasts, network and local, report news in an unbiased manner, without fear or favor. The voting usually runs 4 to 1 against the newscasters. The reasons vary. Some students, supporting the Vice President, see a liberal bias. Some students see a conservative, Establishment bias. Some students are convinced that broadcast journalists do not report news harmful to advertisers. And so on.

If such an erosion of faith exists among university students, who are among the most libertarian members of our society, can the journalist argue that it is not his business what the effect of his reporting is?

Let us look beyond journalism for a moment. When a society feels itself sufficiently threatened, it reacts. Lenin and Franco felt sufficiently threatened by freedom of speech and freedom of the press to crush them. If those

Americans who would restrict freedom of speech and freedom of the press take action, will the rest of America rise up in indignation or fury to stop them?

We hope so. We hope these freedoms matter to enough Americans. But should not the journalist be aware of the effect he is having? Should he not buttress his hope that most Americans value freedom of the press, even when the news is upsetting or grim or pleases their political opponents or undercuts their moral philosophy or appears to give aid and comfort to their nation's enemies? In short, news which shows us what we are, warts and all?

Mr. Cronkite may have expressed himself here more broadly than he intended. If he meant to argue that the journalist has a responsibility to report significant news, even if it upsets us, then he ought to have the support of all who regard the right to know as paramount.

The distinction between the journalist judging an individual story on its merits and the journalist ignoring the impact of news upon his audience is obviously far more than hairsplitting. To cite one example, riot news was once reported on television newscasts purely on its merits as news. But it soon became evident that the impact of riot news on television viewers—including the rioters themselves—was so great that television news departments trimmed their sails. Broadcast journalists had to make the effects of riot news their business. They did so voluntarily, behaving as responsible members of our society. To ignore the effects of this news would have been unacceptable, and everyone knew it.

In his article, Mr. Cronkite stated:

. . . I'm somewhat sick and mighty tired of broadcast journalism being constantly dragged into the operating room and dissected, probed, swabbed, and needled to see what makes it tick.

I'm tired of sociologists, psychologists, pathologists, educators, parents, bureaucrats, politicians, and other special interest groups presuming to tell us what is news or where our responsibilities lie.

He immediately qualified this by saying the researchers really have a right to research, "But we must not permit these matters to divert us from our task, or confuse us as to what that task is."

To his statement, I would say "Amen," if the journalists would undertake their own research instead. Who is better qualified to study journalism than the journalist? I don't mean every journalist should undertake a research project, any more than every lawyer does legal research and every physician does medical research. But some should, and others should support them. (To argue that journalism is merely a craft and not a profession is quibbling with definitions. Journalism is too powerful to ignore professional responsibilities.)

The networks and large television stations now have sales research departments. A few of the largest news departments also employ a "researcher" or two, usually a girl whose job it is to look things up and make telephone calls for information. That, plus some intelligently managed survey research for network election coverage and some polling, is about it for news operations, so far as I know.

Networks and large stations ought to engage in basic and applied mass communications research, using university facilities where needed. And the results of their research should influence their work. Other professions benefit from their own research. Why not journalism?

For example, I should like to see research on the effect of visual images on auditory news information. When film of a farmyard is used to illustrate a story about farm legislation, it is possible that the picture of a cow munching hay overwhelms what the newscaster is reporting. I don't know that this is so, but I venture to guess that neither does the news director who ordered the film shot.

If this rustic example sounds simple, there is more complex and sensitive research to be done, not only by sociologists and psychologists who often don't know the territory, but by trained and concerned television journalists. How can film of a riot or a demonstration or strike violence best be put into perspective (the viewer's perspective, not the newscaster's) by words? How can war coverage be improved in the only way that really matters—the information being imparted?

The list is long, maybe endless, and the questions are not trifling. If electronic journalism is to have the future we hope for, continued growth in freedom, the men who practice it must make it their business to analyze the effects of what they do upon the tens of millions of Americans who watch television newscasts daily.

FUNCTIONS AND CREDIBILITY

by ROBERT K. BAKER

Robert Baker, Co-Director of the Task Force
on Mass Media and Violence, notes the need
for credibility in the news media, particularly
since the media play the major role in
intergroup communication today.

*Those who make peaceful revolution impossible
will make violent revolution inevitable.*

JOHN F. KENNEDY

All social progress is laid to discontent.

ABRAHAM LINCOLN

Conflict is part of the crucible of change. It may yield progress or repression. But conflict is not a state of social equilibrium. Whether conflict is resolved by violence or cooperation will depend in part upon the actors' perceptions of the world about them. Providing an accurate perception of that world is the media's most important responsibility. Conflict may be resolved by force, but, in every conflict, there is a point short of the use of force that would be to the mutual advantage of the participants and society. Violence takes its toll on the victor, the vanquished, and the nation.

Conflict cannot be resolved rationally unless each participant has an accurate perception of the intentions and goals of others. Mutual trust must exist. Confidence must exist in the desire of each person to reach a nonviolent and mutually satisfactory accommodation of divergent interests.

Functions and Credibility: From *Mass Media and Violence,* a Report to the National Commission on the Causes and Prevention of Violence (Washington, D.C.: U.S. Government Printing Office, November, 1969).

And a rough equivalency must exist in the conflicting groups' perceptions of reality. The media cannot make the unwilling seek mutual accommodation, but they can make an extremist of the moderate. Regardless of their performance, the media will never be able to assure the non-violent resolution of conflict, but they can assure the violent resolution of conflict.

In our increasingly complex and urban society, interdependence has increased greatly and the need for cooperation between various groups has grown in direct proportion. The rate of change has grown geometrically and the requirement for information about this changing environment has expanded in a similar progression. At the same time, the individual's capacity to acquire knowledge through personal experience has increased only marginally, if at all. Similarly, his ability to communicate with others informally has increased only slightly, and is totally inadequate. Rational and non-violent readjustment to a changing society requires accurate information about our shifting environment.

The news media are the central institutions in the process of intergroup communication in this country. While face-to-face communication has an important role in intergroup communication and may serve a mediating role in the process of persuasion, to the extent that the news media are regarded as credible, they are the primary source of information.

Never before have the American news media been so defensive while being so successful. Today, more information is disseminated faster and more accurately than ever before. The standards of reporting and the sense of responsibility have improved measurably since the beginning of this century. But the changes in American society have been more than measurable; they have been radical. The issues, more numerous and complex, require greater sophistication and time to report adequately. The need for more and different kinds of information has mushroomed. The broadening of the political base and the growth of direct citizen participation in politics and institutional decision-making require not so much a larger flow of words as a more sophisticated treatment of information.

An apparent unwillingness by the journalism profession to analyze its utility in a rapidly evolving democratic society has resulted in a sometimes blind adherence to values developed in the latter half of the 19th century. Old practices have been abandoned only when the most contorted rationalizations have been unable to provide any support. Energy has been wasted on mischievous attempts to justify practices of the past and to explain why they are serviceable for the present. Little attention has been given to what will be needed in the next two decades.

When the layman inquires about today's practices, he is frequently told that "news is what I say it is and journalism is best left to journalists." This kind of arrogance does not lead to understanding between the public and the news media. If the media cannot communicate their own problems to the American people, there is little hope that they can function as a medium of communication among the several groups in society.

Have the media failed to achieve perfection or to perform the impossible? Walter Lippmann has written:

As social truth is organized today, the press is not constituted to furnish from one edition to the next the amount of knowledge which the democratic theory of public opinion demands. . . . When we expect it to supply such a body of truth, we employ a misleading standard of judgment. We misunderstand the limited nature of news, the illimitable complexity of society; we over-estimate our own endurance, public spirit, and all-round competence. We suppose an appetite for uninteresting truths which is not discovered by any honest analysis of our own tastes. . . . Unconsciously the theory sets up the single reader as theoretically incompetent, and puts upon the press the burden of accomplishing whatever representative government, industrial organization, and diplomacy have failed to accomplish. Acting upon everybody for thirty minutes in twenty-four hours, the press is asked to create a mystical force called "public opinion" that will take up the slack in public institutions.[1]

To suggest that the media cannot compensate for the defects of other institutions is quite different from urging that all is well.

The journalists do not have principal roles in making the news and have only limited power to determine what will be read, watched, or believed. But they do have the power to determine the relative availability, and non-availability, of millions of daily transactions, their mode of presentation, and the context in which they will be cast. While this view suggests that the responsibility for disaffection with the media should not be placed entirely on the profession and their employers, it also suggests that they stand in the best position to do something about it.

The inadequacy of traditional journalistic values is clearest in the case of television. It has not yet defined its role in the news communication system. A desire to be first with the news, linked with the logistical problems of providing pictures and action, plus an inherited show-business ethic, have imposed serious limitations on the medium. The heavy reliance of a majority of Americans for their news on a medium that is unwilling or unequipped to provide no more information than the front page of a newspaper has resulted in additional stress. The limited number of channels, television's relatively greater impact, and a preoccupation with pictures substantially increase the burdens of the medium. Finally, the requirement that television serve a truly mass audience and that it be licensed and subject to regulation by a Congressional agency has made it both more timid and more responsible than other media.

[1] Quoted by Robert E. Park, "The National History of the Newspaper," in *Mass Communications,* Wilbur Schramm, Ed. (Urbana: University of Illinois Press, 1960), p. 13.

Although the development and growth of radio and television news have generated some thought among the print media about their changing role, reorientation has been painful and slow.

As a result of changes in technology, financial and political organization, the educational level of the public and its shifting information needs, the forces of dislocation continue to operate on the news media. Technological developments could, within the next two decades, radically reconstitute the media.

The news media have vigorously urged the government to recognize the people's right to know. Harold Cross, a newspaper attorney, has summed up the argument:

Public business is the public's business. The people have a right to know. Freedom of information is their just heritage. Without that the citizens of a democracy have but changed their Kings.[2]

Lately, a similar argument has been used to meet a perceived threat of government intervention. Said Walter Cronkite:

When we fight for freedom of the press, we're not fighting for our rights to do something, we're fighting for the people's right to know. That's what freedom of the press is. It's not license to the press. It's freedom of the people to know. How do they think they're going to know? By putting television news or newspapers or any other news source under government control?[3]

The press vigorously asserts its rights to the access to government information and defends the first amendment on the ground that the people have a right to know. Rightly so. But if the people have a right to know, somebody has the obligation to inform them: an obligation to provide the accurate information necessary to rational decision-making and a rational response to a changing environment. That obligation devolves upon the news media.

A. Functions of the News Media

Again Walter Lippmann has said it best:

If the country is to be governed with the consent of the governed, then the government must arrive at opinions about what their governors want them to consent to. How do they do this? They do it by hearing the radio and reading in the newspapers what the corps of

[2] Harold Cross, *The People's Right to Know* (New York: Columbia University Press, 1956), p. xiii.
[3] Walter Cronkite, *"The Whole World Is Watching,"* Public Broadcast Laboratory, Broadcast Dec. 22, 1968, script p. 56.

Still Freedom's Bulwark

Roy Justus, The Minneapolis Star

correspondents tell them is going on in Washington and in the country at large and in the world. Here we perform an essential service . . . we do what every sovereign citizen is supposed to do, but has not the time or the interest to do for himself. This is our job. It is no mean calling, and we have a right to be proud of it and to be glad that it is our work.[4]

The purpose of communicating news should be to reduce uncertainty and to increase the probability that the audience will respond to conflict and change in a rational manner.

[4] Walter Lippmann, "The Job of the Washington Correspondent," *Atlantic,* January, 1960, p. 49.

Harold D. Lasswell suggested the media have three functions:

(1) *Surveillance* of the environment, disclosing threats and opportunities affecting the value position of the community and the component parts within it; (2) *correlation* of the components of society in making a response to the environment; and (3) *transmission* of the social inheritance.[5]

These are primary functions of the news media today.

Surveillance of the environment describes the collection and distribution of information about events both inside and outside a particular society. Roughly, it corresponds to what is popularly called "news." *Correlation* of the components of society to respond to the environment includes news analysis, news interpretation and editorials, and prescriptions for collective response to changing events in the environment. *Transmission* of culture includes messages designed to communicate the attitudes, norms, and values of the past and the information which is an integral part of these traditions. This third category is the educational function of the media.

In 1947, the Commission for a Free and Responsible Press set forth five goals for the press so it could discharge its obligation to provide the information the public has the right to know:

1. A truthful, comprehensive, and intelligent account of the day's events in a context which gives them meaning.

2. A forum for the exchange of comment and criticism.

3. A means of projecting the opinions and attitudes of the groups in the society to one another.

4. A method of presenting and clarifying the goals and values of society.

5. Full access to the day's intelligence.[6]

Although most of these suggestions drew on recommendations or ideas generated by editors and publishers, the media greeted the Commission's report with hostility and it received a rather general denunciation in columns and editorials and at professional meetings.

Perhaps most important to the non-violent resolution of social conflict are two much more specific objectives: 1) The news media should accurately communicate information between various conflicting groups within society and the circumstances surrounding the conflict; and 2) they must make the "marketplace of ideas," a fundamental rationale for the first amendment, a reality.

The news media cannot perform their important functions unless they have the public's confidence. Any decline in the credibility of formal

[5] Harold D. Lasswell, "The Structure and Function of Communication in Society," in Schramm, *op. cit.,* footnote 1, p. 130.

[6] Robert M. Hutchins, Chairman, *A Free and Responsible Press,* Commission on Freedom of the Press (Chicago: University of Chicago Press, 1947), pp. 20–21.

channels of communication will invariably result in the development of informal channels of communication. Under conditions of mild stress, such channels may serve moderately well to provide accurate intelligence on the surrounding environment, but it is impossible for such informal channels to serve the needs of the people in a democratic society as effectively as a free and responsible news media. Moreover, during periods of great stress, complete reliance on informal channels of communication can result, and has resulted, in a completed breakdown of social norms, and has produced irrational responses. The credibility of the media is a function of the perceptions of its audience, not "truthfulness" in some abstract, Olympian sense. The basic issue of media credibility today is whether the media are presenting a biased or distorted picture of the world through selective reporting, rather than a concern for fabrication of facts. Nevertheless, if the audience does not believe that the media are providing all relevant facts, it will rely on informal channels of communication and its own imagination to supply the perceived omissions, creating a substantial potential for distortion.

It therefore matters little whether the news media have favored one particular point of view over another. What does matter is the effect of media practices and values on the public's perception of the media's credibility, on the public's perception of reality, and the manner in which these practices and values might be changed to facilitate more effective communication of the information the public has a right to know. In some instances, an allegation of bias will be the result of deviation from some abstract concept of "truth"; as frequently, however, it will be the result of the media's failure to tell its audience what it would like to hear.

B. Credibility of the News Media

A crisis in confidence exists today between the American people and their news media. The magnitude of the problem is open to debate; its existence is not. Concern ranges from a high-level official at the *New York Times,* who believes that readers see the editorial policy of the *Times* controlling the content of news, to a western newspaper editor, committed to improving race relations, who believes his paper's standing and credibility in the white community have declined as a result of his commitment. It extends from the network news commentators, who hypothesize the public chose not to believe the scenes of disorder broadcast during the 1968 Democratic National Convention in Chicago, to the general manager of a midwestern metropolitan television station who has run over one hundred five-minute spots dealing with race relations and speculates that his station has alienated a significant part of its white audience.

The concern is not totally unfounded. In a recent issue of the *International Press Institute Bulletin* it was reported:

In the United States, where journalists have long enjoyed a special position compared with colleagues elsewhere, a disquieting develop-ment has been noted. . . . Newspapers, it appeared in surveys, were no longer trusted by their readers, who felt that they lie, manufacture news and sensationalize what they do report. . . . For the press of America and elsewhere, its own communication prob-lem of reestablishing the trust of the readers may prove harder to solve than the technical and economic problems which beset it.[7]

There is evidence that the news media have been developing a credibility problem, at least since the early 1960's. One study of a medium-sized California city found that respondents discounted, on the average, a third of what they read in the newspapers and a fifth of what they saw on tele-vision.[8] A 1963 study—two years before the Watts riots—showed that, among Los Angeles Negroes, only 32 percent felt the metropolitan dailies would give a black candidate coverage equal to that given a white oppo-nent; only 25 percent felt Negro churches and organizations had a chance equal to that of white organizations of getting publicity in the daily press; and 54 percent felt the daily press was not fair in treatment of race rela-tions issues.[9]

Yet there is little hard evidence of any widespread public belief that the facts provided by the media are false. The primary objection seems to be that the news media either omit important facts or slant the presentation of the facts they do report. In Chicago, for example, the evidence suggests that the objection was to the media's failure to provide adequate coverage of the provocations by the demonstrators toward the police, and some objection to network personnel who were perceived as critical of the police.[10]

For example, a survey in a large midwestern city conducted while the events of Chicago were still fresh in the public conscience found that among viewers interested in civil disorders: "Foremost, viewers desire more 'honest' coverage." Approximately 49 percent of the Negroes and 41 percent of the whites believed that television stations are hiding the "truth" in their coverage of rioting;

---

[7] *International Press Institute Bulletin,* January, 1969, p. 4. See also Norman Isaacs, "The New Credibility Gap—Readers vs. The Press," *American Society of Newspaper Editors Bulletin,* February, 1969, p. 1.

[8] Jack Lyle, *The News in Megalopolis* (San Francisco: Chandler, 1967), pp. 39–42.

[9] *Ibid.,* p. 171.

[10] Thomas Whiteside, "Corridor of Mirrors: The Television Editorial Process, Chicago," *Columbia Journalism Review* (Winter, 1968/69), pp. 35–54.

Commenting on his involvement in the events in Chicago, Walter Cronkite said, "I am ashamed of having become emotionally involved, if we are talking about on-air involvement, when our own man was beat up before our eyes on the floor of the convention. I became indignant, said there were a bunch of thugs out there I think on the floor. I shouldn't have. I think that's wrong." Broadcast Dec. 22, 1968, 8:30 p.m. edt, by the Public Broadcast Laboratory, script p. 43.

they desire that the coverage of rioting be more candid and the "truth" be told. In terms of specifics, one-half (52 percent) of the whites and one-third (36 percent) of Negroes request more "balanced" or "fair" news coverage. . . . In addition, some viewers maintain that stations are unfair in their coverage of riot situations because they focus solely on the sensational rather than balance it with the mundane. Thus, both Negroes and whites believe that stations should de-emphasize the sensational aspects of riot coverage or, in some cases, eliminate it entirely.[11]

C. The Importance of Being Credible

When the public does not believe the information they receive from the news media or thinks the media are omitting important facts, there will be increased reliance on less formal sources for information. Ordinarily, this means they ask their friends and neighbors, or worse, they supply the information from their own imaginations. The consequences of such a breakdown of formal channels of communication can be very serious.

Shortly after the bombing of Pearl Harbor, for example, the credibility of the media was seriously questioned by a large number of Americans, because, in part, they did not trust the source of much of the pertinent information—the Roosevelt administration—and because, in part, of the adoption of wartime censorship.

In their pioneer study of rumor, Allport and Postman analyzed more than 1,000 rumors from all parts of the country during World War II. Of these, almost 67 percent were categorized as "hostility (wedge-driving) rumors." These included such "news" as the Jews were evading the draft in massive numbers, American minority groups were impairing the war effort, and Negro servicemen were saving ice picks in preparation for revolt against the white community after their return home. Another 25 percent of the rumors were classified as "fear (bogy) rumors," e.g., the government is not telling the truth about the destruction of our fleet at Pearl Harbor or, in another instance, a collier was accidentally sunk near Cape Cod Canal and New Englanders believed that an American ship filled with Army nurses had been torpedoed, killing thousands of nurses.[12]

Similarly, almost any after-action report on the recent civil disorders will confirm that rumors run rampant during periods of great stress and almost invariably involve gross exaggerations. The direction of the exag-

[11] The Survey was commissioned by WFBM-TV at the direction of Eldon Campbell shortly after the assassination of Senator Kennedy and was performed by Frank N. Magid Associates. We appreciate the generosity and cooperation of Messrs. Campbell and Magid in making it available to us and discussing it with us. Unfortunately it was not completed in time for us to make more extensive use of it. Pp. 130–31.

[12] Gordon Allport and Leo Postman, *The Psychology of Rumor* (New York: Holt, Rinehart & Winston, 1947).

geration depends upon the community in which the rumors circulate. In the black community, for instance, rumors prevail about extreme police brutality or about camps like the concentration camps in Germany during World War II. In the white community, it is not uncommon to hear that Negroes are arming themselves to invade the white section of town.

The direction of distortion of information received through informal communication is almost invariably toward the group's preconceptions. In one series of experiments reported by Allport and Postman, they first showed one of twenty subjects a picture of people in a subway car. One person in the group was black and the rest were white. There appeared to be some dispute among them. A white man held a razor in his hand. The subject of the experiment viewed the picture and was asked to describe it to the next person; the second, to repeat the description to the third, and so on. In over half the experiments using white subjects, the final version had the Negro (instead of the white man) brandishing the razor. Among the possible explanations for this distortion, all were related to the subject's preconceptions about blacks:

Whether this ominous distortion reflects hatred and fear of Negroes we cannot definitely say. In some cases, these deeper emotions may be the assimilative factor at work. And yet the distortion may occur even in subjects who have no anti-Negro bias. It is an unthinking cultural stereotype that the Negro is hot tempered and addicted to the use of razors as weapons. The rumor, though mischievous, may reflect chiefly an assimilation of the story to verbal-clichés and conventional expectation.[13]

A review of the literature on rumor indicates that at least two conditions are prerequisite to their circulation: an event that generates anxiety—an event about which people feel some need to know—and a state of ambiguity concerning the facts surrounding that event.[14] The extreme case for these two conditions is a major event, such as the assassination of a prominent public figure, and non-coverage by any of the news media. These conditions can also exist where the event is reported and anxiety aroused but the message is characterized by a high degree of uncertainty. Such uncertainty can result either from the omission of significant facts or the lack of credibility of the communicating medium. Under these circumstances, the message recipient has considerable latitude to supply the missing information from his own imagination or adopt the speculations of others he receives through informal channels of communication. Such informal communications are popularly referred to as rumor.

[13] Gordon Allport and Leo Postman, "The Basic Psychology of Rumor," in *The Process and Effects of Mass Communication*, Wilbur Schramm, Ed. (Urbana: University of Illinois Press, 1955), p. 153.
[14] Tamotsu Shibutani, *Improvised News: A Sociological Study of Rumor* (Indianapolis: Bobbs-Merrill, 1966).

At the very least, rumors tend to reinforce present positions, and in most cases the recipient will move further toward one of the attitudinal extremes than if he had received the kind of full and fair account of significant facts a skilled journalist can provide.

In an era that demands the subjugation of our emotional attitudes about race, either a decline in credibility of the media or the failure of the media to meet the demand for information on issues of race relations will solidify rather than dissolve prejudice. The same is true in varying degrees on other issues, depending upon the strength of audience predispositions.

A full and credible presentation of the news also serves the interests of the news organization. The eventual impact of increasing polarization will reduce the media's ability to hold a mass audience. Through the process of selective exposure, people will tend to listen to those voices that agree with their special point of view.[15] Where the society is highly polarized, it will become increasingly difficult for the media to communicate effectively except by tailoring their presentation to the predisposition of particular audiences. What will develop is a series of media, each appealing to a small section on the continuum with strongly held and relatively homogeneous views. Under such circumstances, intergroup communication substantially decreases.

D. Credibility and Audience Bias

Accusations that the news media are biased are frequently the result of strong political, attitudinal, or behavioral convictions. Many of the same charges of bias, for example, are raised against the media from both extremes of the political spectrum. The charges made by the conservatives at the 1964 Republican convention, for instance, remind many observers of those made by liberal Democrats throughout the years.[16]

A 1960 study showed a much greater perception of political bias in the *Dallas News* among Catholic priests than among Baptist ministers. More significant, it found that, among *all* clergy, the perception of political bias increased if the individual thought the paper unfair to his religious group.[17] If the reader gives the newspaper low marks for accuracy or fairness on one subject, he is likely to apply it to others.[18]

[15] Lazarsfeld, Berelson, Gaudet, *The People's Choice* (New York: Columbia University Press, 1948); Cartwright, "Some Principles of Mass Persuasion: Selected Findings of Research on the Sale of United States War Bonds," *Human Relations,* II (1949), pp. 253–67; Starr & Hughes, "Report on an Educational Campaign: The Cincinnati Plan for the United Nations," *American Journal of Sociology* (1950), pp. 389–400; Cannel & MacDonald, "The Impact of Health News on Attitudes and Behavior," *Journalism Quarterly* (1956), pp. 315–23.

[16] Lyle, *op. cit.,* footnote 8, p. 171.

[17] *Ibid.,* pp. 44–45.

[18] James E. Brinton, *et al., The Newspaper and Its Public* (Stanford University, Institute for Communications Research, undated).

Further, experimental studies on attitude change also suggest this situation is general. Hovland and Sherif reported that respondents tended to distort the location of other points of view as a function of their own position on the continuum. Thus, those at either extreme tend to shift the midpoint toward themselves, thereby exaggerating the extremity of other positions as well as putting the objective neutral position "on the other side."[19] A member of the John Birch society, for example, may perceive former Chief Justice Earl Warren as a Communist, while students on the far left may regard Hubert Humphrey as an arch-conservative at best and a Fascist at worst. Clearly, strongly committed persons at either end of the spectrum will regard a newspaper that follows an objective and neutral course as biased and lacking in credibility.

The news media are inevitably bound by this paradox. Traditionally, they have attempted to extricate themselves by distinguishing between "news" and "editorial comment." More recently, a third category, "news analysis," has been added. Newsmen are increasingly recognizing that some degree of interpretation inheres in the very act of reporting, regardless of the medium. At a minimum, interpretation results from individual differences in physical perception and social and cultural background.

The news media will not be able to meet the communications needs of the country in the coming decades until they acknowledge—at least to themselves—that the old distinction between "news" and "editorial comment" is inadequate.

---

[19] Carl Hovland and Muzafer Sherif, *Social Judgment* (New Haven: Yale University Press, 1961).

TRENDS IN ATTITUDES TOWARD TELEVISION AND OTHER MEDIA

A twelve-year review

by BURNS W. ROPER

This report by the Roper Organization,
based on 1,993 interviews of
adult Americans conducted in 1971,
considers public attitudes over a
twelve-year period toward the news media
as comparative sources of information.

This study, conducted early in 1971, finds television held in high esteem by the American public. Twelve years ago, when the first study was conducted, television was vying with newspapers—leading in some respects but not in others.

Since 1959 television has steadily moved ahead as "the people's choice" among media. On almost every comparative rating, it is now as strong as or stronger than in 1968, when the last study was conducted. While people are not wholly uncritical of the medium, they continue to approve generally of their TV fare—both programs and commercials.

Despite the heat engendered by last Fall's election—with charges of news bias by television reporters and the press, and calls for investigation and regulation—the public remains wary of government regulation of television. New questions asked this year provide further insights into this.

Source of News

Since the first study, three questions comparing media have been asked before any questions focusing specifically on television.

The first question in every questionnaire has asked people where they get most of their news. Television leads today, as it has since 1963, and

Trends in Attitudes Toward Television and Other Media: A Twelve-Year Review: From *An Extended View of Public Attitudes Toward Television and Other Mass Media 1959–1971,* a report by The Roper Organization, Inc. Reprinted by permission.

it has kept, if not actually increased, the sizable lead over newspapers it attained in 1968.

"First, I'd like to ask you where you usually get most of your news about what's going on in the world today—from the newspapers or radio or television or magazines or talking to people or where?"

Source of most news	12/59 %	11/61 %	11/63 %	11/64 %	1/67 %	11/68 %	1/71 %
Television	51	52	55	58	64	59	60
Newspapers	57	57	53	56	55	49	48
Radio	34	34	29	26	28	25	23
Magazines	8	9	6	8	7	7	5
People	4	5	4	5	4	5	4
Don't know or no answer	1	3	3	3	2	3	1
Total mentions	154	157	147	153	158	145	140

Analysis of multiple responses	12/59 %	11/61 %	11/63 %	11/64 %	1/67 %	11/68 %	1/71 %
Television only	19	18	23	23	25	29	31
Newspapers only	21	19	21	20	18	19	21
Both newspapers and television (with or without other media)	26	27	24	28	30	25	22
Newspapers and other media but not television	10	11	8	8	7	6	5
Television and other media but not newspapers	6	7	8	6	8	5	7
Media other than television or newspapers	17	15	13	12	10	13	13
Don't know or no answer	1	3	3	3	2	3	1

Multiple answers are accepted to this question, in the belief that single answers should not be forced from people who rely on more than one medium. When, for no apparent reason, multiple answers dropped in 1968, it was suggested that more people may be relying on a single medium. This year's results give some substance to this speculation. Multiple answers have continued to drop.

The Relative Credibility of Media

Since the 1961 study, television has led steadily as the most believable news medium. By 1968, television had established a lead over newspapers of two to one. Nothing has happened since to narrow the margin. On the contrary, television's percentage has increased, while the figure for newspaper believability remained constant.

"If you got conflicting or different reports of the same news story from radio, television, the magazines and the newspapers, which of the four versions would you be most inclined to believe—the one on radio or television or magazines or newspapers?"

Most believable	12/59 %	11/61 %	11/63 %	11/64 %	1/67 %	11/68 %	1/71 %
Television	29	39	36	41	41	44	49
Newspapers	32	24	24	23	24	21	20
Radio	12	12	12	8	7	8	10
Magazines	10	10	10	10	8	11	9
Don't know or no answer	17	17	18	18	20	16	12

On the converse question, **least** believable medium, the "dip" for television registered in 1968 appears to have leveled off. Television was named by only one-fourth as many as named magazines and newspapers.

"Which of the four versions would you be least inclined to believe—the one on radio, television, magazines or newspapers?"

Least believable	12/59 %	11/61 %	11/63 %	11/64 %	1/67 %	11/68 %	1/71 %
Newspapers	24	28	30	28	25	28	32
Magazines	23	25	26	24	29	27	30
Radio	10	9	10	11	11	11	11
Television	9	7	7	6	5	9	8
Don't know or no answer	34	32	27	31	30	25	19

*"Who am I to question our government's policies? I'll tell you who I am! I'm
Bernard A. Nesbitt, who reads the 'Times,' the 'Wall Street Journal,' the 'Post,'
'Newsweek,' 'Time,' 'Business Week,' 'U.S. News & World Report,' 'Look,'
'Life,' and the 'Saturday Evening Post.' That's who I am!"*

Drawing by D. Fradon; © 1968 The New Yorker Magazine, Inc.

The Relative Desirability of Media

If forced to choose among media, a record number of people would keep
television. In the two most recent prior studies, 1967 and 1968, television led newspapers by a two-to-one margin. It now leads newspapers
three to one.

**"Suppose that you could continue to have only one of the following—
radio, television, newspapers or magazines—which one of the four would
you most want to keep?"**

Most want to keep	12/59 %	11/61 %	11/63 %	11/64 %	1/67 %	11/68 %	1/71 %
Television	42	42	44	49	53	50	58
Newspapers	32	28	28	27	26	24	19
Radio	19	22	19	15	14	17	17
Magazines	4	4	5	5	3	5	5
Don't know or no answer	3	4	4	4	4	4	1

Among college-educated respondents, newspapers led television through 1964. In 1967 and 1968, television and newspapers were tied. The picture changed markedly this year: among the college-educated, television now leads newspapers by almost two to one.

| | College educated | | | | | |
Most want to keep	12/59 %	11/61 %	11/64 %	1/67 %	11/68 %	1/71 %
Television	27	34	34	39	37	47
Newspapers	47	37	42	38	36	26
Radio	15	16	11	13	13	17
Magazines	9	12	10	8	12	10
Don't know or no answer	2	1	3	2	2	*

Among the upper economic groups, newspapers led in the first study, but television became the leader in the second study. Television's lead has increased and it now is slightly more than two to one.

| | Upper economic levels | | | | | |
Most want to keep	12/59 %	11/61 %	11/64 %	1/67 %	11/68 %	1/71 %
Television	35	42	45	45	45	50
Newspapers	41	33	34	33	30	24
Radio	15	17	13	13	15	18
Magazines	7	6	7	6	6	7
Don't know or no answer	2	2	1	3	4	1

Trend in Hours of Viewing

Television viewing has continued to increase steadily. Since 1961, respondents have been asked:

"On an average day, about how many hours do you personally spend watching TV?"

	11/61	11/63	11/64	1/67	11/68	1/71
Median hours of viewing	2:17	2:34	2:38	2:41	2:47	2:50

While the answers to this question are subject to respondents' reporting error, the **trend** results are meaningful, even if the absolute responses may be somewhat off the mark.

Television viewing by the college-educated and upper-income groups has consistently been below the national average every year. However, viewing by both groups has increased steadily each year—and is now greater than the average viewer's in 1961.

Median reported hours of viewing by:	11/61	11/64	1/67	11/68	1/71
College educated	1:48	2:04	2:10	2:17	2:19
Upper economic levels	2:02	2:14	2:21	2:24	2:30

The Racial Crisis in America

THE NEWS MEDIA RESPOND TO THE NEW CHALLENGE

by WOODY KLEIN

Woody Klein, newsman and journalism professor,
traces the civil rights revolution
from its beginnings in 1963
and analyzes the treatment of blacks
by the news media.

We have all heard of the police beat, the sports beat, and the political beat. But old-time reporters will tell us today they never heard of the civil rights beat when they first started reporting. The reason: It didn't exist.

It wasn't until the Supreme Court handed down its decree in 1954 calling for desegregation of the nation's schools "with all deliberate speed" that newsmen became aware of the fact that civil rights was a front-page story. Prior to that time any news about Negroes was frequently viewed as "Negro news" and given a low priority.

In recent years, however, great efforts have been made in the mass media —radio, television, magazines and newspapers—to expand and sustain coverage of race relations, often called the No. 1 domestic issue in America today. As we enter 1969, it can be said without any doubt that all members of the electronic and written press consider civil rights a top running story. The story "broke" in 1963 and it has been "good copy" in every American newsroom ever since.

Yet, the story caught the American public—and the American press— by surprise in 1963. Perhaps the most remarkable aspect of it was that so few facts about it were known. Everywhere in the United States, the Negro was suddenly on the march. But what lay behind the movement and why had it suddenly gained such momentum? Why 1963?

The Racial Crisis in America: The News Media Respond to the New Challenge: From *The Quill* (January, 1969). Reprinted by permission.

The late Dr. Martin Luther King, head of the Southern Christian Leadership Movement, gave us some reasons [in 1963] when the new revolution erupted. He reminded white America that the Supreme Court had called for school desegregation in 1954 but at the beginning of 1963—nine years after the historic decision—less than 10 per cent of southern Negro children were attending integrated schools.

Dr. King also noted that both major political parties had put forth civil rights platforms during the 1960 Presidential campaign. But 1961 and 1962 had arrived and both the Democrats and Republicans were, as Dr. King put it, "marking time in the cause of justice." There was also a direct relationship between the Negro revolution in the United States and international events. By 1963, Dr. King reminded us at the time, 34 African nations had risen from colonial bondage.

Finally, non-violence was on the rise in the early 60's. Tested earlier in Montgomery, Ala., it gradually became the major force in the greatest mass action crusade for black freedom since the Civil War. Thus in 1963, despite the popular myth held by most American whites that all was relatively good with the Negro, there was tremendous unrest, not only in the ghettos, but throughout the United States.

Whitney M. Young, Jr., executive director of the National Urban League, explained the problem this way in his book *To Be Equal:*

To most white Americans, the headlines, reporting the crescendo of victories against discriminatory practices, are clear evidence that the Negro citizen is on the threshold of equal participation in American life. This observation is unfortunately inaccurate. The reason is that the "discrimination gap" caused by more than three centuries of abuse, humiliation, segregation and bias has burdened the Negro with a handicap that will not automatically slip from his shoulders as discriminatory laws and practices are abandoned.

Massive interest by the news media in the modern civil rights revolution, as we know it today, was touched off by Dr. Martin Luther King's Birmingham sit-ins in 1963. Coverage in the national white press was negative. Dr. King was pictured at first as an irresponsible hothead who had plunged the races into a potentially violent confrontation.

Yet, the Birmingham stories of 1963 helped to establish Martin Luther King as one of the major Negro leaders of all time. The mass media, it could be said, had a direct bearing on the choice of Dr. King as the "Man of the Year" in 1964 by *Time* magazine. Birmingham had been the main battleground and Martin Luther King became to millions, black and white, in the South and the North, the symbol of the revolution.

In the six years since then, the civil rights revolution in America has become almost routine, front-page news. Every day one can find a report of the racial crisis in jobs, education, housing, politics. Every day city editors, radio and TV news directors, and wire service editors assign their staffs to cover events which now represent episodes in one of the most significant continuing stories in the history of American journalism. The headlines telling the public of the civil rights legislation of the early 1960s, the sit-ins, the riots and violence in the cities, the assassinations of America's leaders—black and white, the Report of the National Advisory Commission on Civil Disorders, the many probes into racial conflict—all these stories, and more, have been fully reported by all the media.

But has the voluminous coverage of the white press been fair? Has it been accurate? Has it reflected the mood and legitimate hopes of the black man in America? Because civil rights is a new beat in journalism, editors and reporters in the news media have only recently begun to seek answers to some of these questions.

The media first awakened to the challenge of self-analysis in Philadelphia in 1964. A local government agency, the Commission on Human Relations, held a seminar for community relations workers and 35 executives of newspapers and radio and television stations to find new ways in which the press could contribute to a better race relations in that community. The Philadelphia story is worth mentioning because it marked the first time that government officials and mass media representatives tried to hammer out a definite understanding about how to report racial news.

In 1965, the Watts riot in Los Angeles touched off a rash of public criticism of the news media. Some observers charged the media, particularly television, with exploiting racial tensions for the sake of story. Not only did TV exacerbate an already inflammatory situation, according to some critics, but it may have prolonged the riots. The possible over-coverage of the Watts riots also served to point up the bitter fact that the stories brought about polarization, rather than increased understanding, between blacks and whites.

This sensitive problem was raised by many of the nation's black leaders at a series of journalism forums sponsored by The New School in New York in 1965. Invited to give their frank opinions of the news media's coverage of the racial crisis, the group, which included black newsmen, agreed that in 1964:

(1) The news media did not fully and fairly report the civil rights movement in America; (2) Negative stories—violence and conflict—were given more space and headlines than positive achievements by Negroes; (3) The white press perpetuated a bad image of the Negro; (4) The white press "created" Negro leaders; (5) Newspapers and radio and television stations were guilty of token integration in employment; (6) Statements and events in the civil rights struggle were not adequately analyzed or interpreted; (7) The news media lacked trained specialists knowledgeable in Negro history; (8) The press generally went along with the police

in a dispute involving charges of police brutality or conflict between police and Negroes; (9) The Negro press, which is a protest press, was generally underestimated and unknown by whites; (10) Press coverage of the Negro revolution made more whites conscious of their Negro neighbors but did not bring about any real understanding between the races.

Not all the comments were negative, however. For example, Dr. Kenneth B. Clark, the nationally-known Negro psychologist and educator on whose studies the Supreme Court desegregation decision of 1954 was based, has a more positive outlook. "The press is fairly and fully reporting the civil rights revolution," he said. "It plays an important role. Television has played an extremely important part in exposing injustice. It keeps the story before the American public."

Dr. Clark's only criticism of the white news media was what he called the news media's "thirst for sensation." He cited the New York *Times'* now-famous story about the Blood Brothers gang of 400 youths in Harlem who were described as ready to attack whites all over the city. The story proved to be untrue. "The *Times,*" said Dr. Clark,

is big enough and solid enough so it didn't suffer deeply from this error. But it certainly was an embarrassing error to plaster on the front page the fact that there were 400 Negroes organized to kill whites. Those of us who work in the Harlem community know it is difficult to get 400 Negroes organized to do anything. Hiring Negro reporters, incidentally, does not immunize the white press. This particular story was written by a Negro reporter who should have known better.

Asked recently what he thought were the most significant trends in the press in recent years, Dr. Clark said: "The way the white press reports Black Power and the backlash which has resulted. Unfortunately, the media reporters still do not fully understand the tragedy of the black man."

The recent violent summer riots have brought similar indictments of the mass media and, in some instances, the criticism has come from newsmen themselves. Martin S. Hayden, editor of the Detroit *News,* for example, was recently quoted as saying he believed television was "probably the biggest instigator of the 1967 riots in Detroit." He explained that he was not blaming TV, but said it was in the nature of electronic journalism that such problems should arise. "People here watched those looters at work in Newark. They sat at home in front of their screens viewing network coverage; then when the trouble started here many thought they'd get in on similar action," he declared.

The Detroit editor was also critical of wire service reporting, stating that occasionally such reports set off a chain of action which leads to misrepresentation of the news, particularly on radio and TV. He said that because

"Lady, we don't make the news. We only peddle it."

of the competitive rush to get bulletins on the wire, such material was not always checked out as thoroughly as it deserved. "Instant journalism feeds on that sort of thing," Mr. Hayden said.

The urban riots of the past three years have been widely covered by the news media. Out of this new area of self-conscious journalism, ultra-sensitive to the coverage of racial news, came two major conferences on the topic of race and the news media by members of the news media themselves. The conferences were held in the fall of 1965 and in the fall of 1967 under the joint sponsorship of the Anti-Defamation League of B'nai B'rith and University of Missouri's Freedom of Information Center.

A book entitled *Race and the News Media,* the first of its type ever published, distilling the views of the 21 persons who participated in the conferences and offering guidelines for the media, resulted from the conferences. The book recommends that the best reporters be assigned to police news in order to insure objectivity; increasing the number of Negroes on daily newspapers—estimated recently at only 200 out of 50,000 reporters, copy editors, photographers, or deskmen on metropolitan newspapers; probing the areas of discontent and offering solutions; distinguishing between the authentic and the phony Negro leaders; exercising caution in giving advance publicity to professional bigots and hate mongers of all races; remaining objective—and calm—in reporting racial conflict.

It is very difficult, of course, to maintain dispassionate objectivity in race relations reporting. The electronic media, in particular, have been criticized as superficial, lacking insight, and even contributing to racial tensions. The late Edward R. Murrow, who accomplished more than most men in TV, was the first to admit its shortcomings. In a 1958 speech, the commentator declared:

> One of the basic troubles with radio and television news is that both instruments have grown up as an incompatible combination of show business, advertising and news. Each of the three is a rather bizarre and demanding profession. And when you get all three under one roof, the dust never settles.

After the 1967 riots, Sen. Hugh Scott of Pennsylvania said he believed "the news media, in many instances, inadvertently contributed to the turmoil." He urged the news industry to confer with specialists in civil liberties, the Justice Department, and other law enforcement agencies to draw up a code of emergency procedures to be followed in reporting riots. "The communications media," he complained in a letter to CBS television, "must meet their responsibility to report the news, but to help dampen the fires burning in our cities they must avoid inciting to further violence by the very manner in which the news is carried."

Ironically, at about the same time—during the fall of 1967—Justice Department officials were conferring in New York with a group of news executives on the subject of race and the news media. The conference was co-sponsored by the American Civil Liberties Union and Columbia University's Graduate School of Journalism. The conference participants received a report from the Justice Department which stated, in part:

> If this nation is to veer from a course toward increasing racial polarization, the media will have to view racial disorders as much more than a Memorial Day casualty toll. The challenge to the news media is whether it can do more than chronicle the fears and discomforts of whites caused by Negroes. The media should attempt to convey to both black and white the underlying causes of the dilemma of what must be done to resolve it.

The most severe criticism of American journalism was issued early [in 1968] when the Report of the President's National Commission on Civil Disorders charged that "the journalism profession has been shockingly backward in seeking out, hiring, training, and promoting Negroes." The Report also asserted: "The communications industry, ironically, have not communicated to the majority of their audience—which is white—a sense of degradation, misery, and hopelessness of living in the ghetto. They have not communicated to whites a feeling for the difficulties and frustrations of being a Negro in the United States."

The Report, released in March 1968, went on:

> The press acts and talks about Negroes as if Negroes do not read the newspapers or watch TV, give birth, marry, die and go to PTA meetings. By failing to portray the Negro as a matter of routine and in the context of society the news media have, we believe, contributed to the black-white schism in this country.

The Commission recommended: (1) Expanded coverage of the Negro community through permanent assignment of reporters familiar with urban and racial affairs; (2) Recruiting more Negroes; (3) Improving coordination with police in reporting riot news through planning, information centers, and guidelines; (4) More accurate and more responsible reporting through internal guidelines; (5) Establishing an Institute of Urban Communications to train and educate journalists in urban affairs, recruit and train Negroes, and concentrate on urban research.

After the Riot Commission broke the ice, the news media began to freely acknowledge the existence of racism in daily reporting and a willingness to do something about faulty, long-standing journalistic practices.

[In the fall of 1968] a survey of the attitudes of nearly 900 news executives was made under the auspices of Columbia University and the Anti-Defamation League of B'nai B'rith.[1] The survey revealed that (1) the media are beginning to provide better communication between whites and blacks, (2) a majority of news outlets are actively seeking more minority group personnel, (3) some news organizations are seeking to interpret and analyze stories about race relations.

Nevertheless, the poll also disclosed that only 4.2 percent of the employees in the news media today are black, that 25 percent of the newspapers and 39 percent of radio and TV stations have no black employees at all. Most of the respondents complained of great difficulties in trying to recruit Negro newsmen.

Following are a few of the comments from the poll: *Time* Magazine—"A far too limited view of Negro life in America is presented in the various news media"; *Newsweek* Magazine—"The press has made martyrs of extremists who had only small following in the Negro community"; the Washington *Post*—"Newspapers can be a vital force in opening communications between the races . . . if they report the total goings-on in their city and their nation."

The New York *Times* declared: "We believe the files of the New York *Times* will show a great awareness and sensitivity to the issues involved—

[1] EDITOR'S NOTE: see Woody Klein, "News Media and Race Relations: A Self-Portrait," *The Columbia Journalism Review,* VII, 3 (Fall, 1968).

although we would be the first to acknowledge that there is still room for improvement." The Philadelphia *Bulletin* said: "Sometimes newspapers in their anxiety to play up success stories may become patronizing and insulting. We're not doing as well as we should, but we're doing better than we were and we're trying. The one most important thing is to 'tell it like it is.' "

In addition, the *Wall Street Journal* replied: "By thoughtfully examining the problems behind the tensions and by presenting the viewpoints of all sides, the newspapers can foster better understanding"; The Miami *News*: "What primarily is wrong with coverage is that newspapers hire Negroes to cover Negroes. They send them back to the slums"; and, the Los Angeles *Times*: "The media should try and explain the causes of tension."

Among the replies from radio and TV stations were the following: WDHA, Boston—"Deep probing by the news media of the sources of racial tensions affording those afflicted an opportunity to voice their frustrations is what is needed"; WJR, Detroit, Mich.—"Until recent years, broadcast newsmen, largely because of small staffs, were unable to personally cover stories that bear on society's problems"; KATI, Casper, Wyo.—"No one who does not actually live in the ghetto can fully understand the problems. Send newsmen to live for a time in such a neighborhood"; KNTV-TV, San Jose, Calif.—"The media has over-emphasized the demi-God to the neglect of the modern Negro. We have acted as press agents for the racists"; KVII-TV, Amarillo, Tex.—"Too much of the media rushed to cover sensational stories and exploit the loud, often irresponsible spokesmen. Some degree of maturity is now evident."

Despite the news media's shortcomings, many of the executives interviewed expressed the belief that some progress has been made in the relationship between the white press and the black man in America. As newsmen themselves have admitted, many mistakes have been made. Nevertheless, the news media have taken the unusual step of holding periodic forums for the purpose of constructive self-appraisal. These sessions are bound to change—and improve—coverage of race relations in the United States in the future.

The news media's responsibility is immense, but most observers are confident that American journalism will live up to the challenge of helping to unite a divided nation.

AGNEW CHALLENGES THE NEWS MEDIA

Wetzel—Ben Roth Agency

On November 13, 1969, Vice President Spiro T. Agnew delivered a speech to the Midwest Regional Republican Committee in Des Moines, Iowa. In that speech he accused television news reporters and commentators of biased reporting and argued that too much power was concentrated in their hands. One week later, in a speech to the Montgomery, Alabama Chamber of Commerce, he extended his criticism of news coverage to the print media, especially **The New York Times** and **The Washington Post.** These criticisms set off a debate in political as well as journalistic circles. The mini–case study which follows includes the full text of the first speech and a brief excerpt from the second. The rest of the selections represent the varied reactions to the vice president's charges.

Text of Agnew Speech on TV Network News

DES MOINES, Iowa (UPI)—The text of Vice-President Spiro Agnew's speech Thursday night to the Midwest Regional Republican Committee.

Tonight I want to discuss the importance of the television news medium to the American people. No nation depends more on the intelligent judgment of its citizens. No medium has a more profound influence over public opinion. Nowhere in our system are there fewer checks on vast power. So, nowhere should there be more conscientious responsibility exercised than by the news media.

The question is . . . are we demanding enough of our television news presentations? . . . and, are the men of this medium demanding enough of themselves?

Monday night, a week ago, President Nixon delivered the most important address of his administration, one of the most important of our decade. His subject was Vietnam. His hope was to rally the American people to see the conflict through to a lasting and just peace in the Pacific. For 32 minutes, he reasoned with a nation that has suffered almost a third of a million casualties in the longest war in its history.

When the President completed his address—an address that he spent weeks in preparing—his words and policies were subjected to instant analysis and querulous criticism. The audience of 70 million Americans—gathered to hear the President of the United States—was inherited by a small band of network commentators and self-appointed analysts, the majority of whom expressed, in one way or another, their hostility to what he had to say.

Their Minds Were Made Up in Advance

It was obvious that their minds were made up in advance. Those who recall the fumbling and groping that followed President Johnson's dramatic disclosure of his intention not to seek reelection have seen these men in a genuine state of non-preparedness. This was not it.

One commentator twice contradicted the President's statement about the exchange of correspondence with Ho Chi Minh. Another challenged the President's abilities as a politician. A third asserted that the President was now "following the Pentagon line." Others, by the expressions on their faces, the tone of their

Text of Agnew Speech on TV Network News: Reprinted by permission of United Press International.

questions, and the sarcasm of their responses, made clear their sharp disapproval.

To guarantee in advance that the President's plea for national unity would be challenged, one network trotted out Averell Harriman for the occasion. Throughout the President's address he waited in the wings. When the President concluded, Mr. Harriman recited perfectly. He attacked the Thieu government as unrepresentative; he criticized the President's speech for various deficiencies; he twice issued a call to the Senate Foreign Relations Committee to debate Vietnam once again; he stated his belief that the Viet Cong or North Vietnamese did not really want a military takeover of South Vietnam; he told a little anecdote about a "very, very responsible" fellow he met in the North Vietnamese delegation.

All in all, Mr. Harriman offered a broad range of gratuitous advice—challenging and contradicting the policies outlined by the President of the United States. Where the President had issued a call for unity, Mr. Harriman was encouraging the country not to listen to him.

A word about Mr. Harriman. For 10 months he was America's chief negotiator at the Paris peace talks—a period in which the United States swapped some of the greatest military concessions in the history of warfare for an enemy agreement on the shape of a bargaining table. Like Coleridge's ancient mariner, Mr. Harriman seems to be under some heavy compulsion to justify his failures to anyone who will listen. The networks have shown themselves willing to give him all the air time he desires.

Every American has a right to disagree with the President of the United States, and to express publicly that disagreement.

The President's Right to Communicate

But the President of the United States has a right to communicate directly with the people who elected him, and the people of this country have the right to make up their own minds and form their own opinions about a presidential address without having the President's words

and thoughts characterized through the prejudices of hostile critics before they can even be digested.

When Winston Churchill rallied public opinion to stay the course against Hitler's Germany, he did not have to contend with a gaggle of commentators raising doubts about whether he was reading public opinion right, or whether Britain had the stamina to see the war through. When President Kennedy rallied the nation in the Cuban missile crisis, his address to the people was not chewed over by a round-table of critics who disparaged the course of action he had asked America to follow.

The purpose of my remarks tonight is to focus your attention on this little group of men who not only enjoy a right of instant rebuttal to every presidential address, but more importantly, wield a free hand in selecting, presenting and interpreting the great issues of our nation.

First, let us define that power. At least 40 million Americans each night, it is estimated, watch the network news. Seven million of them view ABC, the remainder being divided between NBC and CBS. According to Harris polls and other studies, for millions of Americans the networks are the sole source of national and world news.

In Will Rogers' observation, what you knew was what you read in the newspaper. Today, for growing millions of Americans, it is what they see and hear on their television sets.

How is this network news determined? A small group of men, numbering perhaps no more than a dozen "anchor men," commentators and executive producers, settle upon the 20 minutes or so of film and commentary that is to reach the public.

This selection is made from the 90 to 180 minutes that may be available. Their powers of choice are broad. They decide what 40 to 50 million Americans will learn of the day's events in the nation and the world.

These Men Can Create National Issues

We cannot measure this power and influence by traditional democratic standards for these men can create national issues overnight. They can make or break

—by their coverage and commentary—a moratorium on the war. They can elevate men from local obscurity to national prominence within a week. They can reward some politicians with national exposure and ignore others.

For millions of Americans, the network reporter who covers a continuing issue, like the antiballistic missile or civil rights, becomes in effect, the presiding judge in a national trial by jury.

It must be recognized that the networks have made important contributions to the national knowledge. Through news, documentaries and specials, they have often used their power constructively and creatively to awaken the public conscience to critical problems.

The networks made "hunger" and "black lung" disease national issues overnight. The TV networks have done what no other medium could have done in terms of dramatizing the horrors of war. The networks have tackled our most difficult social problems with a directness and immediacy that is the gift of their medium. They have focused the nation's attention on its environmental abuses . . . on pollution in the Great Lakes and the threatened ecology of the Everglades.

But it was also the networks that elevated Stokely Carmichael and George Lincoln Rockwell from obscurity to national prominence.

Nor is their power confined to the substantive. A raised eyebrow, an inflection of the voice, a caustic remark dropped in the middle of a broadcast can raise doubts in a million minds about the veracity of a public official or the wisdom of a government policy.

One federal communications commissioner considers the power of the networks to equal that of local, state and federal governments combined. Certainly, it represents a concentration of power over American public opinion unknown in history.

What do Americans know of the men who wield this power? Of the men who produce and direct the network news— the nation knows practically nothing. Of the commentators, most Americans know little, other than that they reflect an urbane and assured presence, seemingly well-informed on every important matter.

We do know that, to a man, these commentators and producers live and work in the geographical and intellectual confines of Washington, D.C., or New York City—the latter of which James Reston terms the "most unrepresentative community in the entire United States." Both communities bask in their own provincialism, their own parochialism. We can deduce that these men thus read the same newspapers, and draw their political and social views from the same sources. Worse, they talk constantly to one another, thereby providing artificial reinforcement to their shared viewpoints.

Objectivity or Fairness?

Do they allow their biases to influence the selection and presentation of the news? David Brinkley states, "Objectivity is impossible to normal human behavior." Rather, he says, we should strive for "fairness."

Another anchor man on a network news show contends: "You can't expunge all your private convictions just because you sit in a seat like this and a camera starts to stare at you. . . . I think your program has to reflect what your basic feelings are. I'll plead guilty to that."

Less than a week before the 1968 election, this same commentator charged that President Nixon's campaign commitments were no more durable than campaign balloons. He claimed that, were it not for fear of a hostile reaction, Richard Nixon would be giving in to, and I quote the commentator, "his natural instinct to smash the enemy with a club or go after him with a meat axe."

Had this slander been made by one political candidate about another, it would have been dismissed by most commentators as a partisan assault. But this attack emanated from the privileged sanctuary of a network studio and therefore had the apparent dignity of an objective statement.

The American people would rightly not tolerate this kind of concentration of power in government. Is it not fair and relevant to question its concentration in the hands of a tiny and closed fraternity of privileged men, elected by no one, and enjoying a monopoly sanctioned and licensed by government?

The views of this fraternity do not represent the views of Americans. That is why such a great gulf existed between how the nation received the President's address—and how the networks reviewed it.

As with other American institutions, perhaps it is time that the networks were made more responsive to the views of the nation and more responsible to the people they serve.

I am not asking for government censorship or any other kind of censorship. I am asking whether a form of censorship already exists when the news that 40 million Americans receive each night is determined by a handful of men responsible only to their corporate employers and filtered through a handful of commentators who admit to their own set of biases.

The questions I am raising here tonight should have been raised by others long ago. They should have been raised by those Americans who have traditionally considered the preservation of freedom of speech and freedom of the press their special provinces of responsibility and concern. They should have been raised by those Americans who share the view of the late Justice Learned Hand that "right conclusions are more likely to be gathered out of a multitude of tongues than through any kind of authoritative selection."

Newspaper, TV Situations Not Identical

Advocates for the networks have claimed a first amendment right to the same unlimited freedoms held by the great newspapers of America.

The situations are not identical. Where *The New York Times* reaches 800,000 people, NBC reaches 20 times that number with its evening news. Nor can the tremendous impact of seeing television film and hearing commentary be compared with reading the printed page.

A decade ago, before the network news acquired such dominance over public opinion, Walter Lippmann spoke on the issue: "There is an essential and radical difference," he stated,

between television and printing. . . . The three or four competing television stations control virtually all that can be received over the air by ordinary television sets. But, besides the mass-circulation dailies, there are the weeklies, the monthlies, the out-of-town newspapers, and books.

If a man does not like his newspaper, he can read another from out of town, or wait for a weekly news magazine. It is not ideal. But it is infinitely better than the situation in television. There, if a man does not like what the networks offer him, all he can do is turn them off, and listen to a phonograph.

"Networks," he stated, "which are few in number, have a virtual monopoly of a whole medium of communication." The newspapers of mass circulation have no monopoly of the medium of print.

"A virtual monopoly of a whole medium of communication" is not something a democratic people should blithely ignore.

And we are not going to cut off our television sets and listen to the phonograph because the airwaves do not belong to the networks; they belong to the people.

As Justice Byron White wrote in his landmark opinion six months ago, "It is the right of the viewers and listeners, not the right of the broadcasters, which is paramount."

It is argued that this power presents no danger in the hands of those who have used it responsibly.

But as to whether or not the networks have abused the power they enjoy, let us call as our first witnesses, former Vice-President Humphrey and the city of Chicago.

Nomination by Brutality and Violence

According to Theodore H. White, television's intercutting of the film from the streets of Chicago with the "current proceedings on the floor of the convention created the most striking and false political picture of 1968—the nomination of a man for the American presidency by the brutality and violence of merciless police."

If we are to believe a recent report of the House Commerce Committee, then television's presentation of the violence in the streets worked an injustice on the reputation of the Chicago police.

According to the committee findings, one network in particular presented "a one-sided picture which in large measure exonerates the demonstrators and protesters." Film of provocations of police that was available never saw the light of day, while the film of the police response which the protesters provoked was shown to millions.

Another network showed virtually the same scene of violence—from three separate angles—without making clear it was the same scene.

While the full report is reticent in drawing conclusions, it is not a document to inspire confidence in the fairness of the network news.

Our knowledge of the impact of network news on the national mind is far from complete. But some early returns are available. Again, we have enough information to raise serious questions about its effect on a democratic society.

Several years ago, Fred Friendly, one of the pioneers of network news, wrote that its missing ingredients were "conviction, controversy and a point of view." The networks have compensated with a vengeance.

And in the networks' endless pursuit of controversy, we should ask what is the end value . . . to enlighten or to profit? What is the end result . . . to inform or to confuse? How does the ongoing exploration for more action, more excitement, more drama, serve our national search for internal peace and stability?

Bad News Drives Out Good News

Gresham's Law seems to be operating in the network news.

Bad news drives out good news. The irrational is more controversial than the rational. Concurrence can no longer compete with dissent. One minute of Eldridge Cleaver is worth 10 minutes of Roy Wilkins. The labor crisis settled at the negotiating table is nothing compared to the confrontation that results in a strike —or, better yet, violence along the picket line. Normality has become the nemesis of the evening news.

The upshot of all this controversy is that a narrow and distorted picture of America often emerges from the televised news. A single dramatic piece of the mosaic becomes, in the minds of millions, the whole picture. The American who relies upon television for his news might conclude that the majority of American students are embittered radicals, that the majority of black Americans feel no regard for their country; that violence and lawlessness are the rule, rather than the exception, on the American campus. None of these conclusions is true.

Television may have destroyed the old stereotypes—but has it not created new ones in their place?

What has this passionate pursuit of "controversy" done to the politics of progress through logical compromise, essential to the functioning of a democratic society?

The members of Congress or the Senate who follow their principles and philosophy quietly in a spirit of compromise are unknown to many Americans—while the loudest and most extreme dissenters on every issue are known to every man in the street.

How many marches and demonstrations would we have if the marchers did not know that the ever-faithful TV cameras would be there to record their antics for the next news show?

We have heard demands that senators and congressmen and judges make known all their financial connections—so that the public will know who and what influences their decisions or votes. Strong arguments can be made for that view.

But when a single commentator or producer, night after night, determines for millions of people how much of each side of a great issue they are going to see and hear; should he not first disclose his personal views on the issue as well?

In this search for excitement and controversy, has more than equal time gone to that minority of Americans who specialize in attacking the United States, its institutions and its citizens?

Answers Must Come From the Media

Tonight, I have raised questions. I have made no attempt to suggest answers. These answers must come from the media men. They are challenged to turn their critical powers on themselves. They are challenged to direct their energy, talent, and conviction toward improving the quality and objectivity of news presentation. They are challenged to structure their own civic ethics to relate their great freedom with their great responsibility.

And the people of America are challenged too. . . . challenged to press for responsible news presentations. The people can let the networks know that they want their news straight and objective. The people can register their complaints on bias through mail to the networks and phone calls to local stations. This is one case where the people must defend themselves. . . . where the citizen—not government—must be the reformer. . . . where the consumer can be the most effective crusader.

By the way of conclusion, let me say that every elected leader in the United States depends on these men of the media.

Whether what I have said to you tonight will be heard and seen at all by the nation is not my decision; it is not your decision; it is their decision.

In tomorrow's edition of the Des Moines *Register* you will be able to read a news story detailing what I said tonight; editorial comment will be reserved for the editorial page, where it belongs. Should not the same wall of separation exist between news and comment on the nation's networks?

We would never trust such power over public opinion in the hands of an elected government—it is time we questioned it in the hands of a small and un-elected elite. The great networks have dominated America's airwaves for decades; the people are entitled to a full accounting of their stewardship.

Excerpt from

Transcript of Address by Agnew Extending Criticism of News Coverage to Press

MONTGOMERY, Alabama—The following is a transcript of Vice-President Agnew's November 20, 1969 address to the Montgomery Chamber of Commerce, as recorded by The New York Times.

Now let me repeat to you the thrust of my remarks the other night and perhaps make some new points and raise a few new issues.

I'm opposed to censorship of television, of the press in any form. I don't care whether censorship is imposed by government or whether it results from management in the choice and presentation of the news by a little fraternity having similar social and political views. I'm against, I repeat, I'm against media censorship in all forms.

But a broader spectrum of national opinion should be represented among the commentators in the network news. Men who can articulate other points of view should be brought forward and a high wall of separation should be raised between what is news and what is commentary.

And the American people should be made aware of the trend toward the monopolization of the great public information vehicles and the concentration of more and more power in fewer and fewer hands.

Should a conglomerate be formed that tied together a shoe company with a shirt company, some voice will rise up righteously to say that this is a great danger to the economy and that the conglomerate ought to be broken up.

But a single company, in the nation's capital, holds control of the largest newspaper in Washington, D.C., and one of the four major television stations, and an all-news radio station, and one of the three major national news magazines— all grinding out the same editorial line— and this is not a subject that you've seen debated on the editorial pages of *The Washington Post* or *The New York Times*.

For the purpose of clarity, before my thoughts are obliterated in the smoking typewriters of my friends in Washington and New York, let me emphasize that I'm not recommending the dismemberment of the Washington Post Company. I'm merely pointing out that the public should be aware that these four powerful voices hearken to the same master.

.   .   .

The Editorial Cartoonists Respond...

"This is my idea of a good newspaper."

Sanders in The Milwaukee Journal

"Brinkley and Bluntly"

"Your country needs you"

John Fischetti editorial cartoon, © Chicago Daily News

"I don't want to intimidate 'em—just scare hell out of 'em."

IN DEFENSE OF TV NEWS

an interview with Eric Sevareid

by NEIL HICKEY

Question   There's a conviction around the country that most TV news-men tend to be liberal and therefore more friendly to dissenters.
Answer   Yes, Mr. Agnew feels that obviously. I'm not quite so per-suaded. I think news values and judgment are something different from personal bias. If television puts a lot of protesters on, I don't think it's necessarily because a lot of editors and producers and reporters are all for the protesters, in their private, political hearts. Some may be. I think some are. It's a matter of ingrained reflexes on what is news and what isn't. I think myself we have fallen into at least some shallow ruts on this matter of what looks like news as it pours into our offices, and there's this great struggle to sort it out every day. And I've raised my private views about this inside CBS more than once. But to assume that this process gives a wildly distorted picture of what's happening in the coun-try, or that it's done out of a radical bias by a few, I really don't believe that.

I don't know what the word liberal means, except a kind of open-mindedness, a basic humanitarian view of life and concern for people. I don't know how people generally think of me. The most pointed criticism I've had in the mail has come from the left. Youth groups, protester groups, radical groups, professors, saying that I'm much too conservative, that I'm really an old square, that I don't understand the youth. And now suddenly I'm clobbered by Mr. Agnew and the right wing. So I don't know.

Question Why do you suppose so many people think they detect a large portion of bias in TV journalism?

Answer A lot of people say a lot of things. A majority of the daily newspapers in this country supported Mr. Nixon. It seemed to me the networks were right down the middle, just as fair and impartial as they could be. I will defy anybody to go through my scripts during that campaign and come out with any feeling that I was trying to push for Humphrey or for Nixon or for Wallace. I don't think you can do it.

Question In the last year or so the so-called Silent Majority has bubbled to the top like carrots in a stew. What do you make of it?

Answer It exists all right. There is a frustration with a lot of things. What Agnew did, you see, he overstepped the line of a proper democratic dialogue. He resorted to demagoguery. He gave these people to believe that there is some sort of conspiracy, an unelected elite. Well, if he means the dozen or so people who have been mentioned, of whom I am one, we rarely ever see each other, to tell you the truth.

Question You don't conspire together every night?

Answer Oh, God, I haven't had a serious conversation with Howard K. Smith, I suppose, in 10 years. I haven't run into Huntley or Brinkley in two or three years. It's ridiculous. Howard and I deeply disagree about the Vietnam War, for one thing. But you see, what Mr. Agnew did is very easy to do. I say it's demagoguery when you do that. The conspiracy theory of history, the devil theory, always finds a ready response when a lot of people are frustrated, baffled by a complexity of things. I'm not impressed with claims that a great majority of the country thinks that the war protesters are wrong. Joe McCarthy had a majority of Americans convinced that this government was crawling with Communists. It simply was not so. But a tremendous number of people believed it was, because it was an easy answer. They were disappointed and upset by many of the results of the war. The public mood of the moment is not necessarily right, nor is it necessarily going to last. A great majority believed in this Vietnam intervention, when people like me were in a minority. Mr. Agnew says we should all more closely reflect the majority feeling in the country. But majorities change. That's not **our** business. Suppose we **were** elected. You'd have an absolute shambles in communications. I think there should be some changes in the way we do various things. I've always wanted to have on the air regular programming of rebuttal—either by letters from viewers or having the people on themselves. There must be a way to do this. Well, suppose you'd had that system for the last few years on a regular basis, where all kinds of objections to what was said on television were voiced by ordinary people.

Maybe a lot of this feeling would have been dissipated. That's one of our difficulties here. People are confronted by great big organizations and they can't answer back—whether it's the press, big government, big business. I think we should have found ways to get our audience's views on the air. I think we should do it now. There must be a way to do it in an attractive, listenable form.

Question   What do you think of the idea of spectrum commentary, that is, having analysts from all across the political spectrum employed on television?

Answer   Oh, we went through that in radio days. CBS came to the conclusion it was not a good way to do it. The emphasis has to be, in a job like mine, one of exploration, of elucidation, more than advocacy. You can't keep opinions out of it entirely. But that has to be the approach. People confuse objectivity and neutrality. You may go at something very objectively but come to a conclusion about it. If you come to a conclusion, then you hold an opinion. If you hold an opinion, then you're biased, according to various people.

Question   The Violence Commission, as other commissions have suggested in the past, would like to see a national board of review to survey the performance of the news media. What do you think of that?

Answer   I don't believe in that. Television is already the most heavily monitored, scrutinized, criticized medium of communication there's ever been. Everybody is an expert on TV. Let me ask you why, when nearly every daily paper in this country gets the great bulk of its non-domestic news from two wire services—the UPI and AP—there's no running critique of their performance.

Question   And you feel, obviously, that television news is entitled to precisely the same First Amendment guarantees as are afforded the print medium.

Answer   Absolutely. Absolutely. I can't see why there should be any difference. The issue has never been resolved nor faced properly because broadcasting is in this anomalous legal position. We've always lived on this thin ice. The stations have to get approval to operate every three years. I just do not believe that the power of the press and television has been vastly increased in recent years. This statement of Mr. Agnew's quoting some FCC Commissioner that the media in this country have a power equal to the local, state and Federal governments —it's a silly statement. It's the power of **government** in my adult life that has grown far more than the power of media or business or any other big entity.

Question   I've discovered in talking to people on the left that there's a broad streak of approval among many of them for a lot of the things Mr. Agnew said. They're hostile to TV news because they feel it doesn't come to grips with the real issues, while the right wing tends to feel that TV news disseminates far too much of this, mostly bad, news.

Answer   That's right. It's just the opposite criticism. Look, FCC Commissioner Nicholas Johnson and all kinds of people on what I'd guess you'd call the left in this country, and many intellectual groups, have been hammering and hammering at television, for what? Because they say we just reflect Establishment, middle-class values. You know the litany on that. That we're not dealing enough with the poor, the blacks, the underprivileged. The Agnew criticism is the exact reverse of this. Now how do you satisfy this?

Question   The Violence Commission used the expression "crisis of confidence" between the media and the public, and said that some means should be found to make the media more responsive to the public.

Answer   More responsive to the public! What are they talking about? That's what Mr. Agnew says, in effect. I'm not about to adjust the work I do according to the waves of popular feeling that may come over the country. No responsible person can do that. They ought to be out of this business if they do.

.   .   .

THERE IS A NETWORK NEWS BIAS

by EDITH EFRON

On Nov. 12, 1969, when the liberal media were angrily aboil over Vice President Agnew's blasts at the liberal left and its frequently violent crusades, a quiet voice on ABC-TV declared:

Political cartoonists have that in common with the lemmings, that once a line is set, most of them follow it, though it lead to perdition. The current cliché shared by them and many columnists is that Spiro Agnew is putting his foot in his mouth [and] making irredeemable errors. . . . Well, . . . I doubt that party line. . . . There is a possibility it is not Mr. Agnew who is making mistakes. It is the cartoonists.

One week later, on Nov. 19, 1969, when the liberal media were even more violently aboil over the climactic Agnew speech blasting

bias in network news, that same quiet voice on ABC-TV once again was heard: "I agree with some of what Mr. Agnew said. In fact, I said some of it before he did."

The speaker was Howard K. Smith, ABC's Washington-based anchor man, ex-CBS European correspondent, and winner of a constellation of awards for foreign and domestic reporting. Mr. Smith had, indeed, said some of what Mr. Agnew said before Mr. Agnew had said it. For several years, despite his respect for network news departments and their achievements, he has been criticizing his colleagues—on the air and off—for falsifying U.S. political realities by means of biased reporting.

Mr. Smith is by no means an unqualified supporter of Mr.

Agnew, and he has reservations about The Speech. To name the two most important: "A tone of intimidation, I think, was in it, and that I can't accept. . . . Also a sense that we do things deliberately. I don't think we do them deliberately."

Mr. Smith, however, says: "I agree that we made the mistakes he says we made." And he himself levels charges at the network news departments.

In fact, according to Howard Smith, political bias in TV reporting is of such a magnitude that it fully justifies the explosion we have seen. Here is this insider's analysis of the problem.

His candor begins at the very base of the network news operation —namely, with the political composition of the staff. Networks, says Mr. Smith, are almost exclusively staffed by liberals. "It evolved from the time when liberalism was a good thing, and most intellectuals became highly liberal. Most reporters are in an intellectual occupation." Secondly, he declares that liberals, virtually by definition, have a "strong leftward bias": "Our tradition, since FDR, has been leftward."

This is not to say that Mr. Smith sees anything wrong with being a leftist—"I am left-of-center myself." But he sees everything wrong with the dissemination of an inflexible "party line"; and this, he charges, is what liberal newsmen are doing today:

Our liberal friends, today, have become dogmatic. They have a set of automatic reactions. They react the way political cartoonists do— with oversimplification. Oversimplify. Be sure you please your fellows, because that's what's "good." They're conventional, they're conformists. They're pleasing Walter Lippmann, they're pleasing the **Washington Post,**

they're pleasing the editors of **The New York Times,** and they're pleasing one another.

He says a series of cartoonlike positive and negative reflexes is determining much of the coverage.

He names a series of such negative reflexes—i.e., subjects which newsmen automatically cover by focusing on negatives. Herewith, excerpts from his comments:

Race: "During the Johnson Administration, six million people were raised above the poverty level. . . . And there is a substantial and successful Negro middle class. But the newsmen are not interested in the Negro who succeeds—they're interested in the one who fails and makes a loud noise. They have ignored the developments in the South. The South has an increasing number of integrated schools. A large part of the South has **accepted** integration. We've had a President's Cabinet with a Negro in it, a Supreme Court with a Negro on it—but more important, we have 500 Negroes elected to local offices in the deep South! This is a tremendous achievement. But that achievement isn't what we see on the screen."

Conservatives: "If Agnew says something, it's bad, regardless of what he says. If Ronald Reagan says something, it's bad, regardless of what he says. Well, I'm unwilling to condemn an idea because a particular man said it. Most of my colleagues do just that."

The Middle Class: "Newsmen are **proud** of the fact that the middle class is antagonistic to them. They're proud of being out of contact with the middle class. Joseph Kraft did a column in

which he said: Let's face it, we
reporters have very little to do with
middle America. They're not our
kind of people. . . . Well, I
resent that. **I'm** from middle
America!"

The Vietnam War: "The networks
have never given a complete
picture of the war. For example:
that terrible siege of Khe Sanh
went on for five weeks before
newsmen revealed that the South
Vietnamese were fighting at our
sides, and that they had higher
casualties. And the Viet Cong's
casualties were 100 times ours.

But we never told **that.** We just
showed pictures day after day of
Americans getting the hell kicked
out of them. That was enough to
break America apart. That's also
what it did."

The Presidency: "The negative
attitude which destroyed Lyndon
Johnson is now waiting to be
applied to Richard Nixon.
Johnson was actually politically
assassinated. And some are trying
to assassinate Nixon politically.
They hate Richard Nixon
irrationally."

"NOW LISTEN TO THIS"

an editorial from THE NEW REPUBLIC

The Vice President is having a merry time, slashing away at the Liberal-Eastern-Communications-Conspiracy, taking out after the TV networks and going on to the Washington Post Company for being too powerful and *The New York Times* for suppressing or subordinating pro-Nixon news. What he really dislikes about the *Post,* of course, is not its power but what it prints about him and his boss —those cutting Herblock cartoons, or such editorial lines as "the gaggle of bureaucratic satrapies that passes in this Administration for a government."

A reading of the network commentary to which Mr. Agnew so violently objected earlier suggests that the Administration is in a state of real paranoia. The comment that followed Mr. Nixon's November 3 Vietnam speech was feeble enough, God knows; "nothing new," the commentators chorused, as if anything was to be expected. The speech did not impress them, but their remarks were not hostile, not biased beyond the bounds of skepticism, however hastily and feebly expressed in most instances. Agnew's indignation is rendered more ridiculous by the overwhelmingly favorable response to the White House in phone calls and telegrams.

The call upon the network news presidents by the chairman of the Federal Communications Commission, Dean Burch, for transcripts was even more blatantly threatening than the fact of it makes evident. The White House already had complete tape recordings of every word spoken on the networks about the President's address—including interviews with Herbert Klein on NBC, CBS and ABC. The Army Signal Corps detail assigned to the White House Communications Branch had it all, in separate reels for each network. Nor did the members of the President's staff have to telephone TV stations, as they did, to check on editorial comment (at least 20 such calls were made the night of November 3, according to a CBS report).

Frank Shakespeare, USIA director and a CBS vice president on-the-way-out when he joined the Nixon promotional staff last year, and surely one of the most limited and least attractive characters in the present establishment, is quoted by Joe McGinnis in his *Selling of the President, 1968,* as telling how much Mr. Nixon resented NBC's treatment of him at the Miami Convention and generally. Shakespeare says:

> Now listen to this. Here's what I thought I'd do. I thought I'd go to Walter Scott, the NBC board chairman—this would be in private, of course, just the two of us in his office—and say, "Here are the instances, here are the instances where we feel you've been guilty of bias in your coverage of Nixon. We are going to monitor every minute of your broadcast news, and if this kind of bias continues, and if we are elected, then you just might find yourselves in Washington next year answering a few questions. And you just might find yourself having a little trouble getting some of your licenses renewed." . . . I'm not going to do it because I'm afraid of the reaction. The press would band together and clobber us. But Goddamit, I'd love to.

Shakespeare recently denounced the hostile "bias" of all news media, notably TV, in a speech in Detroit to a gathering of radio-TV news directors.

There is a lot that's bad about television, a point repeatedly made by FCC Commissioner Nicholas Johnson, who said the other day that "a handful of men control what the American people see of the world through their television screens." But then he added, "The answer is not to transfer this power from a handful of men in New York to a handful of men in the White House. . . . Surely less discussion, less controversy, less relevant comment are not the answer." If that is what Mr. Agnew thinks too he must make it much clearer that he isn't really asking only for more favorable treatment of Administration pronouncements.

All this goes back a long way, of course, to the press treatment of Nixon during his congressional days, his Vice Presidency, the 1962 California campaign. But it arises also from and reflects the deep resentment of conservatives of the kind who serve Nixon, that the media as a whole are oriented against them and their views, dominated by what William S. White calls "knee-jerk liberals." Agnew's attacks raise two questions—the legitimate, troubling one of a licensed and limited medium's right to constitutional speech protection; and the brutal, blatant demand by the Administration in power for friendlier treatment of its President's policies. The Vice President has spoken time and again of the outrageous effrontery of those who dare question in the streets the policy of "the President of the United States of America." That to him is the central offense, the one that he invites "the great silent majority" to rebuke and punish.

An Analysis of the News Media

by R. B. PITKIN

Vice President Spiro T. Agnew lowered the boom on some of TV's news reporting and news comment in a Des Moines, Iowa, speech [on November 13, 1969]. A few days later, in [Alabama], he fired again and included some of the newspapers, too. Naturally, that kicked up a controversy. The broadcasters attacked Mr. Agnew right back, and many newspapers joined in, though not a few newspaper columnists said he was right, even if their editors disagreed.

Better men than I at testing the public pulse believe that most of the people put themselves in the Vice President's corner.

I recall no other time when the press was held up to such open criticism. We're usually sort of immune. We have the microphone, so to speak, and can usually control how much gets out of what outsiders say about us. Many public figures are afraid to criticize the press, and would rather curry its favor. They feel with good reason that the favor or disfavor of the press will profoundly affect the impression the public gets of them. The media may knock one another—the left press versus the right press, and all that. But for outsiders to get a good stage for taking off on the weaknesses of the press is almost unheard of. Yet it has to be a good idea, and we should be the last to object to being put in the same glass house in which we put so many public and private figures.

You could write quite a list of things that the public holds against the news media, especially TV, to help explain why so many people cheered Mr. Agnew.

Political slanting that's just too obvious to be denied.

Too much emphasis on the sordid and violent.

Too little emphasis on what's good.

Encouragement of public disorder by giving it publicity that's enjoyable to its organizers.

Promotion of superficial values that give prominence to the grotesque and knock virtues.

Twisting the news by selection, emphasis, phraseology and posture to make it conform to judgments to which the media have committed themselves.

Members of the press posing as judges, prophets and experts in fields where they prove themselves to be superficial or partisan.

Hauling guests of doubtful qualifications onstage to tell us how we should run our affairs, or to satisfy their own consciences by pleading everyone but themselves guilty of what's wrong with the country.

And so on and so on.

Many viewers out there have a grudge against TV on all of these counts, and against radio, newspapers and magazines on some of them. These things are so offensive to ordinary intelligence and so tiresome to the already weary when they happen that they undo a lot of the excellent reporting and public affairs review that we also get in all the media. I actually know of a fellow who swore off TV for 1970 because he couldn't stand the tripe and the posturing. He'll miss a lot of good programs, but he says it'll make a new man of him to tune out for a year.

TV, especially, could at least turn some of this anger into better understanding if it dared admit its weaknesses a little more openly, for TV has proved to be another one of those scientific things with a built-in potential for mischief. Not like the atom bomb, but like DDT. We saw a lot of good in it at first, and there is a lot of good in it. It has more impact than any other medium. Yet it has proved to be an extremely poor news medium in many respects, and

An Analysis of the News Media: From *The American Legion Magazine* (March, 1970). Reprinted by permission of Robert B. Pitkin.

a poor medium with great impact is a social peril of sorts.

Its weaknesses have long been right in front of our eyes, and we have been reacting to them emotionally from time to time. But they've seldom been spelled out as an array of facts.

Fifteen and more years ago we said, in effect: "Now the people will get the news as never before. We will see and hear the events of the world ourselves and won't have to take a reporter's and editor's necessarily limited view and expression of it. With TV to let us judge for ourselves, we'll be on the scene of important events forever."

Consider where we are. The bulk of the average TV newscast is still a man in a studio reading out loud to us, a TV commentator interpreting events for us, a politician on one side of a question telling us how to think of his opponents.

The reader-out-loud-to-us is no part of the news. Yet his personality affects your reception of news that has nothing to do with his personality. This is inescapable, in some degree. But look how TV compares to newspapers and radio.

Three personality factors can intrude on our reception of reported news. (a) The way the words are strung together. (b) The tones of voice or inflections of speech. (c) The general appearance of the newscaster and the facial expressions with which he punctuates the news.

Newspapers offer one of these intrusions—the way the words are strung together. Radio offers two—the word structure and the inflections of speech. Television suffers all three of these naturally imposed prejudicial elements.

To the very large degree to which television still fails to show us more than the man who is reading out loud, or expressing his opinion, it is a worse medium for bringing us uncolored news than the older ones. And whenever there is a *desire* to prejudice the news, these weaknesses give television a more powerful arsenal for selling bias. This sheds light on Mr. Agnew's references to the enormous responsibilities which TV executives must accept. Their DDT is more potent than that of their press rivals, while their public responsibility is greater than the newspapers' because they are riding on the people's airwaves.

But that is only the beginning of TV's natural handicaps. The newspapers need only the attention of the eyes. Radio needs only the ears. TV needs the attention of both eyes and ears. It is thus the poorest of the three in adapting itself to ease of audience reception, and it is tempted to become more theatrical than the others in its need to get and hold your undivided attention right now. The more that theater is injected in our news, the more the news is diluted with irrelevant content, and especially with the posturing and make-believe which are at the heart of good theater.

.   .   .

DOES AGNEW TELL IT STRAIGHT?

by LESTER BERNSTEIN

The Evening News with Spiro T. Agnew, a one-shot production on all three networks, was the most disturbing performance yet by a man who may go down in a footnote of history as The Great Polarizer. What disturbed me at first was that, though it was the wrong man saying the wrong things, he was partly right. As a sometime critic of TV news, I wish he would get off my side.

Buried in Agnew's simplistic distortions and self-serving rhetoric is a nugget of truth: a relative handful of TV network newsmen wield vast influence as the stewards of the most vivid and powerful medium in the land. They are elected by no one; their qualifications are not always a matter of public examination; indeed those who function behind the camera are faceless men to a public whose view of the world they help to shape. Is there any better way to operate TV news in a free society? Do the wielders of this great power measure up to their responsibility? And if they fall short, how can they be brought up to the mark?

These are questions well worth gnawing by men of goodwill—but does Agnew qualify? Not on the basis of a speech in which the odor of sanctity is mingled with the burning tar of demagoguery. The Vice President is no mere critic but a member of the government that licenses television stations. The timing and background of his speech lend clout to the cudgel. It was crafted and approved in the White House and scheduled hastily to be given on the eve of antiwar demonstrations that TV newsmen, according to the speech itself, "can make or break." It was plainly linked with the unprecedented action of Dean Burch, chairman of the Federal Communications Commission, in telephoning the network presidents for transcripts of the comments after the President's Vietnam speech. It was the work of an Administration sophisticated in the manipulation of television as a campaign tool (and perhaps spoiled by its experience of calling the tune as a sponsor). Add all these circumstances to an inflammatory, guileful attack, and the design is appallingly obvious.

No Plot

And television news is a peculiarly vulnerable target because it is so pervasive, so visible and often so irksome that any attack upon it strikes a nerve. Since Agnew says a commentator should volunteer a disclosure of interest, I must own up that I am a former officer of NBC. I can assure him, from one ex-vice president to a sitting Vice President, that the concentration of power is there all right, but it is really not a plot. As I suspect he knows, the network system, the existence of only three commercial networks and their control of their own news programs spring from a mesh of technology, free-enterprise economics and the Bill of Rights.

Still, the network news operations are neither so monopolistic, conspiratorial, wicked nor even powerful as the speech suggests—though to misrepresent them as such is not surprising from a right-wing orator who enlists surgically removed quotations from Hubert Humphrey, Walter Lippmann, James Reston, Fred Friendly and Theodore White.

Agnew calls network news a "monopoly." The fact is, as shown by special Nielsen studies, the three network evening news shows draw a cumulative weekly audience of 75 million Americans —while the week's viewers of news programs originated by local stations total

125 million. These local shows deal with world and national events, using taped material furnished by the network news organizations (some of it not seen on the networks themselves) and film by United Press International. More to the point, each of these local shows ranging across the U.S. has its own anchor man—with his own eyebrows and inflections.

Collusion?

But even if the viewer's choice were limited to the three network news shows, he would have at least as many channels to choose among as any American now has hometown newspapers. (He would have the newspapers as well, of course, plus radio stations and newsweeklies.) And he could find diversity and disagreement in news interpretation not only among ABC, CBS and NBC but among correspondents and commentators on a single network. (Has anyone noted the bickering on those year-end wrap-up shows?) The suggestion that TV journalists are all formed by the same ideological cookie cutter is malicious nonsense. On the Vietnam issue, for example, ABC's Howard K. Smith has been an avowed hawk; for years, NBC's Chet Huntley leaned to the hawkish side while David Brinkley held dovish views. The most influential single editor in network news is the producer of the evening show; the sheer complexity of logistics compels him to delegate dozens of decisions and barely gives his vice presidential boss a look-in. Do the producers collude, as Agnew hints? Actually, they are as fiercely competitive as any professionals alive—and, incidentally, the producers of the "Huntley-Brinkley Report" and the "CBS Evening News with Walter Cronkite" have never even met.

How powerful are the "self-appointed analysts"? Agnew complains that the President's speech was subjected to "the prejudices of hostile critics" before the public could digest it. But his fear of the analysts must be greater than his faith in the people, who seemed capable of making up their own minds. A special Gallup poll showed that 77 per cent of them approved of the President's speech. Agnew feels nonetheless that the post-speech analysts failed to meet his own curious standard: they did not conform to the majority.

The Vice President harks back to the TV coverage of street rioting in Chicago —a formative event in the continuing unease over the credibility of all news media. Characteristically, he misrepresents the coverage and the effects. The fact that scenes of the rioting were interspersed in the coverage of the nominations was not by the networks' design. These went on the air as news as soon as the tapes became available—as I saw for myself in a control room at the convention. They could not be telecast live because of a telephone installers' strike that Mayor Richard Daley managed somehow to settle within the convention hall but not outside. The street coverage showed the Chicago police in an ugly light—and that impression was confirmed by the most thoroughgoing investigation of the events themselves, resulting in the celebrated Walker Report to the National Commission on the Causes and Prevention of Violence, which called the violence "a police riot." And yet, for all the vaunted power of TV, a Gallup poll after the convention showed that 56 per cent of Americans approved—and only 31 per cent disapproved—"of the way the Chicago police dealt with the young people who were registering their protest against the Vietnam war."

Failings

TV news has plenty of faults and shortfalls. Too often it lacks depth and the flexibility of media that are not such prisoners of the clock. The old sin of playing visual values instead of news values still crops up. TV cameras often distort events by their very presence on the scene; that is the nature of the beast, though news crews have learned ways to be less obtrusive. TV newsmen still "get used," as one puts it, by militants and dissidents (and by politicians). There is a premium on show-business values—on drama, suspense and good looks—and a plethora of ego. The TV coverage of the Chicago convention (on the floor, not in the streets) suffered from much of that. As elsewhere in journalism, there is human fallibility galore.

And unquestionably, though it is not the sinister cabal that Agnew sees in "provincial" New York and Washington, there is an awesome lumping of power, and where power exists, there are always abuses. That is why television sorely needs its critics and soul-searchers. Is there a better way of structuring the medium in the public interest? Can it be done without a loss of freedom? Certainly government is not a better custodian of TV news than the largely dedicated and talented professional journalists now entrusted with it.

Courage

To these problems, Agnew brings not light but the dark edge of know-nothingism. Through him the Administration seeks to exploit the slant most characteristic of TV—leaning over backward. Nothing better illustrates that slant than the decision of the three networks to bump their news shows and carry Agnew's attack live. While loftily disclaiming the role of would-be censor, the Vice President is engaging in censorship by intimidation. His tactic is calculated to sow caution and second thoughts among men who keep a nervous eye on those broadcasting licenses even as they invoke the First Amendment. So far, NBC and CBS have shown courage in meeting the issue publicly, but in small ways the tactic is already working.

Yet even the timidity of the boardroom would have to stop far short of the ultimate arrangement implied in Agnew's speech—one wherein television would become an untrammelled conduit through which the Administration line could pour, without evaluation or analysis or adverse comment of any kind. That would be to abdicate the journalistic duty of keeping our institutions, and the men who run them, under the critical scrutiny for which the Constitution guarantees freedom of expression. There is nothing sacrosanct about a speech by the President of the United States, and TV newsmen should be as free as any other journalists to analyze it. In doing so, and in covering the news with honesty and independence, they—not the politicians—are the surrogates of the people "who own the airways."

THE INFORMERS

STUDY QUESTIONS

1. What does Walter Cronkite give as some of the major problems in presenting the news on television? How would you rate television's success today in its role as informer?

2. Although Cronkite calls his article "What It's Like to Broadcast News," he also makes several statements about television's effect upon our society. What are the restrictive forces controlling television that he is concerned about?

3. Irving Fang attacks Cronkite's assertion that the news broadcaster is not responsible for the effects of his reporting. He cites riot news as one example of news which has a strong effect on viewers, including rioters. Which do you consider to be more important, the broadcaster's right to broadcast the news or his responsibility for the possible effects of that news?

4. What, according to Robert Baker, are the three primary functions of the news media today? Compare the coverage of the day's events in your daily newspaper and on television. Do you see evidence that the newspaper performs these three functions? Does television?

5. What does Baker say is the basic issue of media credibility today? Why is it important that the news media be credible?

6. Compare the way your newspaper reports a certain event with the way it is reported on television. Do the two versions differ greatly in depth of coverage? Do both report the same facts?

7. Cronkite emphasizes the need for objectivity in news reporting. Do you think the newsman should remain uninvolved? Why or why not? How would Nat Hentoff define the role of the reporter? Art Kunkin? (See pp. 71–75 and 116–22.)

8. Again compare the coverage of an event in the newspaper and its coverage on television. Does one report seem more objective than the other? Is one medium more **able** to be objective?

9. What were the chief findings of the Roper survey? What implications do the findings have for the theories of Cronkite, Fang, and Baker?

10. Woody Klein focuses on the treatment of blacks by the information media. Like Hentoff, he questions the coverage given to minority groups. Does the "white establishment press" seem to adequately cover news of specific interest to blacks? Is any one medium more effective than the others? If a concerted effort were to be made to improve minority-group coverage, do you think the effort should be concentrated in local, regional, or national media? Might the underground press which Art Kunkin describes (pp. 116–22) be suited to this?

11. In his November 13, 1969, speech, Spiro Agnew is critical of television reporters and commentators, who, he says, "wield a free hand in selecting, presenting and interpreting the great issues of our nation." Why does Agnew feel this is undesirable? From your own observations, do you feel that the media commentators are or are not accurate reporters and constructive interpreters? Give evidence to support your viewpoint.

12. What are the differences between televised and printed news coverage that Agnew points out? Do you agree that the public should be more wary of televised information? Why or why not?

13. The criticisms which followed Agnew's speeches were numerous and varied. In the few selections included here, do you find any media critics supporting the vice president? Does the media's role as "watchdog of the government" seem to be threatened by intimidation?

BIBLIOGRAPHY FOR FURTHER STUDY

Agnew, Spiro T. "Another Challenge to the Television Industry." *TV Guide* (May 16, 1970), 6–8, 10.

"Analyses That Touched It All Off, The." *Broadcasting,* LXXVII (November 24, 1969), 50–52.

Arnold, Mark R. "The News Media—Besieged by Critics." *National Observer* (July 6, 1970), 1, 12.

Boldt, David R. "TV News and Not-So-Candid Cameras." *Wall Street Journal* (December 20, 1967), 16.

Brucker, Herbert. "Can Printed News Save a Free Society?" *Saturday Review,* LIII (October 10, 1970), 52–55, 64.

Buckley, William F., Jr. "Agnew on TV." *National Review,* XXI (December 2, 1969), 1235.

Crawford, Kenneth. "Government and the Press." *Newsweek,* LXXIV (December 1, 1969), 33.

Daly, Charles U. *The Media and the Cities.* Chicago: The University of Chicago Press, 1968.

Daly, John Charles. "The News Media: The Public Right to Know." *Vital Speeches,* XXXIV (April 15, 1968), 407–10.

Duscha, Julius. "The President and the Press." *Progressive,* XXXIII (May, 1969), 25–28.

Friendly, Fred W. "Some Sober Second Thoughts on Vice President Agnew." *Saturday Review,* LII (December 13, 1969), 61–62 ff.

Gilmor, Donald M. *Free Press and Fair Trial.* Washington, D.C.: Public Affairs Press, 1966.

Gould, Jack. "TV: Reporting News or Making It?" *Current* (October, 1968), 19–21.

Grannis, Chandler B. "Threat to the Climate of Free Opinion." *Publishers' Weekly,* CXCVI (November 24, 1969), 29.

Hentoff, Nat. "Uncovering News Uncoverage." *Evergreen Review,* XIV (March, 1970), 16, 18.

Hohenberg, John. "The World's Press: Just How Free Is It?" *Saturday Review,* LII (December 13, 1969), 70–72.

James, Howard A. "The Crisis in Our Courts." *Nieman Reports,* XXII (December, 1968), 19–22.

Lyle, Jack. *The News in Megalopolis.* San Francisco: Chandler Publishing Co., 1967.

McCombs, Maxwell E. "Negro Use of Television and Newspapers for Political Information, 1952–1964." *Journal of Broadcasting,* XII (Summer, 1968), 261–66.

"Moon Hours: Watching Apollo 11 in New York." *The New Yorker,* XLV (July 26, 1969), 25–30.

Reston, James. "Washington: Mr. Agnew and the Commentators." *The New York Times* (November 21, 1969), 46.

Stanton, Frank. "Pressures on the Press." *Nieman Reports,* XXII (December, 1968), 3–6.

Tullock, Gordon. "A Note on Censorship." *American Political Science Review,* LXII (December, 1968), 1265–67.

"TV Was Fair in Chicago, FCC Allows." *Editor and Publisher,* CII (March 8, 1969), 59.

Whiteside, Thomas. "Corridor of Mirrors: The Television Editorial Process, Chicago." *Columbia Journalism Review,* VII (Winter, 1968–69), 35–54.

Witcover, Jules. "Washington: The News Explosion." *Columbia Journalism Review,* VIII (Spring, 1969), 23–27.

the entertainers

POP SEX AMONG THE SQUARES

by DESMOND SMITH

Smith, a frequent contributor to **The Nation** and a member of the CBS news staff, deals with some of the sociological implications of the current preoccupation with sex in the print media and films. He is especially concerned with commercial exploitation—with the way pop pornographers cater to "the national sex hang-ups" by flooding the entertainment media with destructive and debasing representations of sexual matters.

Not long ago, Russ Meyer, who likes to think of himself as America's top "nudie" film maker, produced *Good Morning . . . and Goodbye!* The *New York Post* called it "a smutty sex show" and complained that the dialogue "would embarrass a third-rate burlesque comic." But weep no tears for Russ. Every one of his more than twenty movies has grossed at least four times its cost. And his early masterpiece, *The Immortal Mr. Teas*—made on a G-string budget of $24,000—has returned well over $1 million.

Al Goldstein and Jim Buckley put up $175 apiece to start *Screw,* a 50c-a-copy tabloid that promised in its first issue to "uncover the entire world of sex. We will be the *Consumer's Report* of sex, testing new products such as dildoes, rubbers, and artificial vaginas." Two months ago the editors flatly rejected a $50,000 offer to buy them out. "It sounds silly," Jim Buckley told Claudia Dreifus of *New York Scenes,* "but one day I'd like to see a giant skyscraper. 'The Screw Building'—it would be penis-shaped, of course. One of these days, you'll see, we'll be so big that the building will be called Time, Life and Screw!"

Jacqueline Susann, who told *The Wall Street Journal* that she is a "conservative moralist," made her fame and fortune typing *Valley of the Dolls,*

Pop Sex Among the Squares: From *The Nation* (August 25, 1969). Reprinted by permission.

a book that sold 10 million copies and is now in its fifty-third paperback printing. Miss Susann's latest stint at the typewriter begat *The Love Machine,* a novel which deals with the sadistic love affairs of a TV mogul named Robin Stone. Wrote Nora Ephron in a favorable *New York Times Book Review* article: "Sweaters are always being ripped open in Miss Susann's books. Pants are always being frantically unzipped. And everyone is always *wanting* everyone else." Sold to Columbia Pictures for $1.5 million and number one on the best-seller charts, Miss Susann's only rival is *Portnoy's Complaint.* "It's wild," Michael Korda, editor in chief at Simon & Schuster, told the *Times.*

You have these two giant books out at the same time and their merits aside, one of them is about masturbation and the other is about successful heterosexual love. If there's any justice in the world, *The Love Machine* ought to knock *Portnoy* off the top simply because it's a step in the right direction.

Meyer, Goldstein, Buckley and Susann are in the "if you got it, so flaunt it, baby" tradition. Each has found the big dollar in catering to what Russ Meyer calls "the pant-and-drool crowd." One might guess that in the waning 1960s—the "Late Sensate" period, Herman Kahn calls it—spectator sex is the opiate of the people. One might also suppose by studying the thematic material—wife-swapping, flagellation, sadism, autoeroticism, nymphomania, homosexuality, Lesbianism, masochism—that the private sex life of America is completely wrecked. Only partly true. The pop pornographers don't have the complete file yet, but they're working on it.

A decade ago, the Granahan committee of the House denounced the billion-dollar-a-year mail-order commerce in salacious materials; today it appears to have mushroomed into one of the most competitive of the new "growth" industries. Pop pornography, which is the slick version of what once was called "smut," has become the bluest of the blue chips. What has happened is what always happens to any industry that enjoys extraordinary profit margins: unless it is enjoined by statute or possesses an ability to control the market, it must make elbow room for sharp-eyed competitors lusting to share those juicy profits. For reasons that will be explained later, it is above and beyond all else a peculiarly middle-class phenomenon. Pop pornography is the new white-collar obsession. Lingerie manufacturers and Sunday newspapers revel in it. The *Ladies' Home Journal* abandons faithful Princess Grace and the Duchess of Windsor in favor of serializing Jacqueline Susann. Kenneth Tynan approves. *Time* profiles it. Broadway musicals extol it. Suburban housewives pant and lust for it. And, since the United States is a consumer society that thrives on satisfying wants and desires, what is pop pornography if not the ingenious one-handed icing on the manufacturers' cake? In short, sex has become very big business indeed.

In the 1930s D. H. Lawrence wrote:

The plain and simple excitement, quite open and wholesome, which
you find in some Boccaccio stories is not for a minute to be confused with the furtive excitement aroused by rubbing the dirty little
secret in all secrecy in modern best-sellers. This furtive, sneaky,
cunning rubbing of an inflamed spot in the imagination is the very
quick of modern pornography, and it is a beastly and very dangerous thing.

Thirty years later he would almost certainly feel the same way if he could
walk the aisles of the drugstores of America and examine the latest selection of paperbacks and magazines.

When our mass magazines, to name but a single source, tell us we are
"liberated" and enjoying the "sexual revolution," why are some of us
suspicious? A large part of the answer is that this so-called "new permis-
siveness" has the ring of the cash register about it. It is a liberalization of
sexual morality within prescribed institutional limits. The kind of true
sexual freedom that must evolve out of continuing social change, *pace*
Fromm and Marcuse, is still light years away from any kind of reality.

What we are now observing is a commerical happening, like Father's
Day or National Shoe Week. As a merchandising technique it has added
untold points to the Dow Jones average. Sex sells. So what is now taking
place is an industrialization of our ideas and our dreams. In case you
haven't been paying attention, your subconscious has become part of the

"The sex isn't so much, but the violence is marvellous!"

Drawing by Koren, © 1971 The New Yorker Magazine, Inc.

Gross National Product. To latch onto the head-over-pillow profits in sex the pop pornographers—writers, movie makers, advertising men, journalists and manufacturers—have had to package the erotic element in sex, and to package sex they have had to restructure the national psyche. Tougher to remove than any household stain has been that bugaboo, the Puritan ethic. In recent months, as you have no doubt read, it looks as though the big breakthrough has finally occurred—the orgasm has finally replaced the old rugged cross as the joyous symbol of what we are all about. "The 60's," says Dr. William Masters (*Human Sexual Response*) "will be called the decade of orgasmic preoccupation."

The mirror image of that phallic symbol of America's technological prowess—Saturn V with its *2 million* functional parts—is the "Love Machine," the pneumatically endowed Playmate who implores us to "take it all off" in TV commercials, examine her unshaved genitalia (next to a whisky advertisement in *Playboy*), live the good bad life in best-seller novels, and join her in the Dodge "rebellion" down at the nearest automobile showroom. ("Mother warned me that there would be men like you, driving cars like that. Do you really think you can get to me with that long, low, tough machine you just rolled up in?") The programming that supports this decaying morality is grounded largely on a syntax of manipulation. Women, says Roxanne Dunbar in *A Journal of Female Liberation,*

are particularly the victims of the machination, programmed as we are to be wife, mother, childbirth expert, sex object, career woman, stay-at-home, mechanic, chauffeur, and yet offered as the stylistic model a mod, free jet-setter. What this does is keep her buying things which symbolize those roles, since playing all of them is impossible, and buying things that symbolize freedom like bright-colored clothes, jewelry, etc. . . .

Like the astronauts we are becoming extensions of the market technology. And as the moon shot was reduced to a blatant sales pitch for American free enterprise, albeit subsidized by the taxpayer ("The soles of the boots you saw are made of GE silicone rubber. . . . NASA has been launching a missile the size of a building. If some time soon, they launch a building, it will be a Hilton—the Lunar Hilton," and so on), so too is the sexual sphere reduced to a commodity—a cluster image that possesses neither humanity nor grace but simply another merchandising lever. Much of this new attitude and most of pop pornography's expansion has come in the last twelve years.

It was the Supreme Court's decision in *Roth vs. United States* (1957), with its ambiguous definition of obscenity, that gave the pop pornographers the impetus to expansion, rather than any sudden erotic renaissance. In that decision, involving a California bookseller, the Court measured obscenity by "whether, to the average person, applying contemporary community standards, the dominant theme of the material taken as a whole appeals to prurient interests." The grotesque notion that Sam Roth, with a twenty-six-count indictment covering the mailing of obscene pictures, photographs, magazines and books, could pose as the champion of literary freedom had important consequences. As far as pop pornographers were concerned, the Roth decision prepared the way for other departures from the claim of community conscience. It was like the first visit of a respectable citizen to the town brothel. As he sneaks along in the half-light he hopes his neighbors will not observe him; if they do see him and say nothing, the next time he takes courage, until he is as indifferent to being observed on his way to the brothel as on his way to church. The Roth decision has of course touched everyone, but it has had its biggest impact on middle-class America. Twenty years ago the white-collar class was already the willing victim of an exploitative society. The cheery suburban American way of life illustrated by Norman Rockwell, the strong happy-go-lucky Western families who settled a Big Valley or a Ponderosa were all magazine or prime TV time mythology by 1950. The absence of any order of belief "makes him [the average citizen] excellent material for synthetic moulding at the hands of popular culture—print, film, radio, and television," wrote C. Wright Mills in the early fifties. "As a metropolitan dweller, he is especially open to the focused onslaught of all the manufactured loyalties and distractions that are contrived and urgently pressed upon those who live in worlds they never made."

The commercial exploitation of the Roth decision can now be found—a decade later—in a massive take-over of our fantasy life. So the sexual sphere becomes the new marketing mode; it is what consumers have in common with one another; it is the steady destruction of the ultimate human freedom in commercial bondage to the sexual. The mentality of pop pornographers can be studied by examining the kind of movies they produce, the magazines they edit, the newspapers they print, the advertisements they write. The really astonishing thing common to all such material is its generally sex-negative attitude. The mirror they hold up reflects a middle-class America in which there is a great deal of sexual misery. Characteristically, the new sex vendors fail to provide the clues to understanding the national sex hang-up. The profit side of the ledger is to be found in merchandising the debasing, dehumanizing, degrading aspects of sexuality; it is sexual adventurism rather than sexual love that is the true grit of this trade.

Despite the popular belief to the contrary—a belief created by confusing the availability of pornographic material (no matter how vicious) with sexual health—the pornographic racketeers have never shown the slightest enthusiasm for a social morality that might precondition man for genuine sexual freedom. So in sex education. Its grace is what it means to be a man or a woman, a subject long under the interdict of the common bigot. In the elementary and secondary schools of Houston, otherwise known as the base camp for the moon, the children of space-age technicians learn that plants and animals have reproductive systems, but when it comes to

people their teachers stand silent. Sex education is not allowed in the schools of Harris County, nor, for that matter, in more than half the schools of this nation. So because the franchise of sexual health is at the mercy of religious fundamentalists, minor political aspirants, and bumper-sticker conservatives, sex in most communities is still taught as it was when President Lincoln was in the White House—behind the candy store or in the dark. Now for the answering results. One in three brides pregnant at time of marriage; a national divorce rate that is rising half again as fast as the marriage rate; venereal disease among teen-agers: more than 90,000 cases reported in 1968, an increase of 80 per cent since 1956; about a quarter of all military draftees unfit for duty due to neuroses of familial or sexual origin. It is, pointedly, one of the horrors of growing up—and growing up, especially for a middle-class kid, is nowadays a genuine horror —that the young are confronted by so much hypocrisy at home. What you behold, sweeping a glance over suburbia, is the end result of this bogus, commercially inspired "pleasure ethic." It is there, out among the Big Boy power mowers, Sears drapes, and the Sentinel burglar alarms where the porn is really green.

Pop pornography is aimed at the widest possible market—the groin of suburbia. Here are the avid consumers of the breathy novels of Jacqueline Susann, Irving Wallace, Harold Robbins and the rest of the rich and prospering school of one-handed fiction; of movies such as *The Fox, Prudence and the Pill* and *Three into Two Won't Go;* of the women's magazines that have followed *Cosmopolitan*'s market break into the New Sex ("Adultery for Adults: Probably the Farthest-Out Advice You'll Ever Read on Marriage!") and *Mademoiselle* ("Sex: The New Status Symbol. What, Why, and Where It Is Sexy. The All-Time Like-It-Is Roundup"). Here on the coffee table is the interior fantasy world outside PTA, Laundromats, office squabbles and school lunches. Meanwhile for Dad's brief case and bathroom reading is *Playboy*. Embraced by *Business Week* recently as the magazine totally right for the late 1960s, *Playboy* (5.5 million copies a month, read by 12 million men) has reached the point where, from its wholly owned 37-story headquarters (topped by a "Bunny Beacon") chief stockholder and publisher Hugh Marston Hefner can look out on an empire that includes *Playboy* ($25 million in ad revenues last year) *and* a nineteen-unit chain of Playboy clubs and resorts, *and* a motion picture division, *and* a syndicated TV series, *Playboy After Dark*. "Ten years ago," says a media buyer at J. Walter Thompson, the world's largest advertising agency, "none of our clients would have dared use *Playboy*. Today it's a routine buy."

Sex sells. And by any yardstick this commercial takeover of the middle-class subconscious must be reckoned a prodigious financial success. Giving pop pornography respectability has been a fantastic challenge, and a challenge that has involved jettisoning the Gospel of Work for the fun ethic. A far tougher nut the pleasure merchandisers have had to crack is organized religion in America. At the heart of things, beyond all the slippery arguments for a healthy hedonistic society, the question curls: hedonism for what? Hefner has chosen to meet the religious question head-on, recognizing that his main job is not to sell *Playboy* but to give moral permission to have fun without guilt. "By stressing self-denial and heavenly reward," argues Hefner, "[religion] has kept man from enjoying, without guilt, the fruits of his earthly labors and to that extent is incompatible with the free enterprise system." Given the kind of demand the pop pornographers have created there is no reason why sales and earnings will not continue rising in the years ahead. Pornography, in a few brief years, has moved from an under-the-counter item to an open-market commodity, a part of the capitalist system.

Scenting the sweet smell of success, Maurice Girodias, once the supreme pornographic publisher of Paris, has immigrated to these shores. In an interview with *The New York Times* (that's the kind of press pornographers receive these days) the reporter noted: "He is looking forward to making his first million dollars within the next six months, thanks to such recent titles as *Curtain of Flesh* and *A Sea of Thighs*. As he smilingly acknowledged, 'There seems to be an endless demand for the stuff.' " And Mr. Girodias is going to do his best to make sure the supply does not dry up. That's in the American free enterprise tradition: in 1969, just about everyone is reaching out for a share of the "Sexual Revolution." As for the future, Rabbi Jacob J. Hecht recently observed: "The home of the future will consider pornography as commonplace and necessary as a color TV or dishwasher."

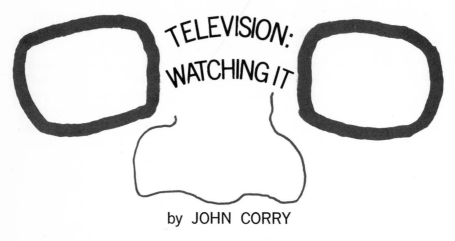

by JOHN CORRY

John Corry, a contributing editor of **Harper's** and author of **The Manchester Affair,** evaluates television's attempts to deal with current social issues. Citing some especially "relevant" episodes from popular television programs, Corry discusses the liberal's tendency to oversimplify and supply easy answers.

We are deep into a new television season, and the most striking thing about it is the wonderful way the writers and producers and advertising men have shown they have with liberal concerns, and the wonderful way they want to be *relevant,* and the wonderful way they have established once and for all that the networks truly are in the hands of a liberal cabal, which, of course, is what the Vice President and the Governor of Alabama have been insisting on all along.

On the relevant television shows, a great many young men, most of whom appear to be from Southern California, wear earnest expressions and $35 razor haircuts, and they hustle about, and they ease problems like race, poverty, and addiction. On television, the great questions of life, death, and politics are simple, which they all should be, but hardly ever really are, and on television virtue is always rewarded, which occasionally in life it should be, and sometimes even is. There is nothing wrong with the television people laying things out this way if we remember that television is show business, and that show business is meant to entertain. Now, ours is an age where life tries to imitate art, and indeed there are a great many young guys hustling about with earnest expressions and $35 razor haircuts, and they are offering not much more than themselves as the solution to great problems. This is circular, however, and at some point in the past ten years or so it got to be impossible any longer to tell with the politicians when art was imitating life, or life was imitating art.

The relevant television shows reaffirm the liberal's old faith in good works and good intentions, and the television heroes find goodness all about them. *Matt Lincoln,* played by Vince Edwards, who once was Ben Casey, is a community psychiatrist, and a more relevant thing to be it is hard to imagine. Psychiatry is an art, and seldom a science, and this allows Matt Lincoln great license. When a sniper called Charlie was terrorizing the town in which Matt Lincoln practiced, he told Matt Lincoln on the phone that he was lonely, and that all he was really doing when he shot people was punishing them for rebuffing him. In the climactic episode, Matt got Charlie to drop his gun, and to release the pretty girl he was holding hostage, simply by telling him that he wanted to be his friend, and that he really wanted to *listen* to him. Summing it all up later, Matt said that wickedness could be explained, and that all that Charlie needed was a friend. "We know that people who are deprived and neglected can get to be like Charlie," he said, and when a colleague earnestly asked Matt whose fault Charlie was, Matt said, "I'd say that someone who had a chance to help him . . . a parent, a teacher, dropped the ball."

Matt was saying, in fact, that it was everyone's fault but Charlie's. This is reasonably liberal thinking, denying the possibility of anyone choosing to be wicked, and denying the possibility of wickedness itself. Liberals do this quite often, taking away much of the stuff and substance of life, and in the name of goodness they set limits on what a man can be. Charlie is denied the dignity of even a decent psychosis, and his problem is only that no one was ever nice to him. The other thing about Charlie was that he was young and attractive, and his teeth were capped, and Matt Lincoln said he was alienated. As a general rule on television, alienation is something practiced by the sensitive young, and it has to do with their living in a world they never made, and it is an attractive quality. Among the older folks on the television shows, alienation is more likely to show up as simple surliness. The kids get all the better of it.

Now, being nice to Charlie, the sniper, is not much in the way of therapy, and in fact it is a way of pandering to him. Nonetheless, it is easier to be nice to someone than to come to grips with him, and it makes whoever is being nice feel good, too. This is more or less the way that liberals handle militants and issues of one sort or another, and sometimes they do it as innocuously as to wear a button saying "Give a Damn," and sometimes they do it by paying serious attention to some of the age's screwier ideologists. This is the kind of outlook that puts great faith in the goodness that comes only from being oppressed.

In *Storefront Lawyers,* a white construction worker was accused of
blowing up a building and killing a man, apparently because he objected to
the presence of a black on the job. A storefront lawyer defended him, and
he put a black construction worker on the stand. The black construction
worker, who had a natural hairstyle, a pretty wife, and a full load of
hostility, finally admitted that he was to blame for the explosion, although
it was really just an accident. The storefront lawyer, recoiling, asked him
why he hadn't said so before. "I've been keeping quiet for the black man,"
he said. But the white construction worker might have been put to death,
the storefront lawyer said. "If a thousand of them went, you think we'd
be even?" the black man said, showing he was boiling with rage, and that
he was oppressed. We already had seen that he was attractive, which was
enough to make us mighty sympathetic, anyway, and now we were ready
to love him. "It ain't you personally," he said later to the white construction worker, who would have been hanged, and then he walked off, full
of pride and nobility.

The trick on the relevant shows is to keep the issues simple, and the people
fuzzy. Ideally, on television, no one is ever quite what he seems. On
Bracken's World, which is about what really goes on in and about a Hollywood studio, a couple of hippies were suspected of murdering a fancy
writer's wife. The hippies were offensive creations, both empty *and* dumb,
but they didn't murder the wife, and the message was that they were just
a couple of free spirits, getting persecuted because of their life-style. ("The
slow poison called the life-style," said the writer, indicating his own, which
was a pretty damn attractive one. On television, you can have it both
ways.) In an episode of *Dan August,* who is a detective, the Chicano farm
workers were striking, and they were led by a man who was supposed to
be like Cesar Chavez. The word "spic" was hurled about freely, a Mexican-American child died in a school-busing accident (allowing the introduction of two relevant social concerns), and you might have thought that
the big farmer in the area, who was blocking the settlement of the strike,
was a bit of a bigot. Not at all; it was mentioned that his dead wife, whom
he loved very much, was a Chicano, and so he was all right, after all.

Given time, nobility will win out in every case on relevant television. In
Marcus Welby, M.D., a champion civil-rights lawyer, a hero of the oppressed, was simultaneously battling cancer and a tough case. (He was also
long in the tooth, and his marital adventures got you thinking pretty
quickly about Justice Douglas.) The lawyer was willing to let his young
assistant risk his own life to develop cancer antibodies, but then in a
mysterious fit of goodness he chose not to. Then he went on to win the
case, and presumably face a lingering death. On *The Young Lawyers,* a
couple of law students reopened the murder trial of an imprisoned black.
They said that his lawyer had been incompetent, even though he was a
famous civil-rights guy, who lately had been elevated to the bench. He, of

course, was snippy when he learned what the students wanted to do, but ultimately he stood up in court and said he had been incompetent, and that the students were absolutely right. (The other notable thing about *The Young Lawyers* is that one of the students is a black girl, so put together and appealing that any right-thinking man instantly would want to bundle her off to bed. There is just badinage between her and her colleagues, however, which is the least fruitful way of ever easing the tensions between black and white.)

Relevant television teaches us that we are all God's children, and that there are no real bastards among us. If there are no real bastards, then nobody has to pay because nobody deserves to. It is all very unclear who is ever to blame for anything, and a show called *The Bold Ones* once managed to quote Cardinal Spellman and Cardinal Cushing as being agreeable to a reform in the abortion laws. The liberals, having bought the left theology that the fault is all in society, and not in ourselves, become stricken when they have to apply the theology, and that is why nothing much ever seems to happen in American politics. Like the relevant television shows, they depend on good intentions.

Finally, what television does to important things is to reduce them, and to make them less than what they are—which is also a standard liberal failing. Television can do it by a tone of voice; so can a liberal. It is another way of dehumanizing us, and of taking away a part of our freedom. We buy anything these days, and everything is merchandised, and solemn things become part of the popular culture. Some of them have no business being there.

Music: The Silent Stepchild

by PETER HERMAN ADLER

Peter Herman Adler, music consultant for National
Educational Television and former artistic and musical
director of the NBC Opera Company, recalls the place
that music occupied in earlier radio and television
entertainment and traces its gradual decline in
importance. He sees commercial pressures (in the form
of the rating system) as the chief cause of this decline
and argues for the return of dance, opera, and symphonic
music to television.

To most Americans, the very notion that they should look to television for
opera, dance, and symphony music must seem foreign—almost as foreign
as my native Czechoslovakia seemed to Neville Chamberlain at the time
of Munich ("a country . . . about which we know nothing"). But those
of us who have experienced what radio and television are doing for serious
music in the rest of the civilized world—from London to Tokyo, from
Moscow to Melbourne—cannot be content with the present state of broadcast music in this country.

Commercial television makes one small but meaningful contribution:
Leonard Bernstein's extraordinary "Young People's Concerts." During the
rest of the year it may proudly present "Hurok Presents" or, equally daring, take its cameras into Carnegie Hall to tape an eminently salable attraction such as Vladimir Horowitz. Radio—which has yielded its place in
the sun to its glamorous offspring but still manages to live comfortably in
its shadow—presents serious music essentially by playing commercial recordings, only occasionally hanging its microphones in the concert halls of
major symphony orchestras or (most important) at the Metropolitan
Opera on Saturday afternoons.

Few of our younger generation are aware that it was not always thus. Some may know there was an NBC Symphony Orchestra, performing under the greatest of them all, Arturo Toscanini, and that these concerts were broadcast live from coast to coast. How many know that there was also an excellent CBS Orchestra, led by Bernard Herrmann and employing the young Eileen Farrell as a staff artist, which presented weekly programs different in style and content from the subscription audience programs of the New York Philharmonic, also carried live on the same network? How many have heard of the weekly programs under Alfred Wallenstein's direction, sponsored by New York's WOR in the 1940s, including in one year a cycle of studio productions of Mozart operas at a time when works such as *Abduction from the Seraglio* or the now almost popular *Così fan tutte* were practically unknown in the United States?

How many know that supporting a studio orchestra was once considered a mark of respectability and achievement for our large radio stations? The Sarnoffs, the Paleys, and the others who brought radio to the center of American life were struck by the excitement of musical broadcasts; when challenged to show that radio could enlighten as well as entertain, they thought immediately of music.

That, of course, was before television pushed radio into the background. The almost hypnotic attraction of the new medium led American broadcasting leaders to chop off in a hurry some of the best things radio had been doing.

Early in the television era, however, NBC, much to its credit, started and maintained an opera program. It was not a once-in-a-blue-moon spectacular, used as a vehicle for Metropolitan Opera stars, but a regular program produced by a small permanent team, cast exclusively by largely unknown young American singers who were trained on the premises for the new and demanding task of direct broadcasts, all done live, without the crutch of prerecorded "playback." The NBC Opera Company, in which I served as musical and artistic director, got its start at a time when television was not yet obsessed with the rating monster, when the music-loving Sarnoffs were prepared to do in television what they had done in radio, when the daring Pat Weaver was network president and Toscanini was still available as an interested observer and constructive critic. With the late Samuel Chotzinoff as producer and liaison to the top brass, we were given a moderate budget and left to work without being subjected to the medium's insane pressures.

At the outset, no one—not even the producing staff—thought that such a venture could make a large or lasting impression in a medium so dominated by the "star" psychology. But the result exceeded our most optimistic expectations, and made itself felt not only in television but also in the world of music. As a matter of policy, the NBC Opera commissioned or gave first performances of new operas by American composers such as Gian Carlo Menotti, Lukas Foss, and Norman della Joio, as well as American premieres of works by Prokofiev, Martinu, and Benjamin Britten. All foreign language works were produced in newly commissioned English translations, with poets such as W. H. Auden leading the list of collaborators. Leontyne Price was featured as Tosca—the first time, I believe, that a Negro artist was cast in a romantic "white" role on any American opera stage, let alone on a network with its sensitive outlets in the South. If one remembers for a moment that I am talking of the year A.D. 1954, you might agree that to take such a risk was an act of true network pioneering.

Menotti's little masterpiece *Amahl and the Night Visitors*—the first opera commissioned for television anywhere—did more than land on the front page of *The New York Times:* It was an immediate international success. Kinescopes of the original production were shown abroad and studied as an example of how effective the television screen can be when it leaves grand opera to the grand opera houses and concentrates instead on intimacy and direct emotional appeal. Other productions such as Prokofiev's *War and Peace* were acquired by central European networks. *Don Giovanni,* with Price singing her first Donna Anna, was broadcast in Auden's new English version in Austria—a remarkable "first" for Mozart's homeland. Countries that had long looked down on America as a cultural nouveau riche openly recognized the NBC Opera as a leader. Today, specialists from Tokyo or Moscow, not to mention London, Hamburg, and Vienna, still remember the NBC Opera as a trail blazer.

The early 1950s undoubtedly saw much in American television that was shoddy; but those who refer to that era as television's "Golden Age" are not nostalgic dreamers. Because it was still awkward and experimental, television could find room for an NBC Opera—just as it found room for newly commissioned dramas such as *Marty,* intimate and wholly adapted to the television screen.

We soon learned, however, that the fullest exploitation of TV's commercial potential called for a different approach. The growing emphasis on ratings made opera's status as a "minority taste" more and more apparent. Viewer figures of 5,000,000, occasionally reaching as high as 10,000,000, were no match for action-adventures or situation comedies. At the same time, the rising budget for television opera was a continual reminder to the network that it was making an expensive gesture for culture. But money was not the only consideration. Even more important was the fact that no other network had followed NBC's lead. With by now typical network psychology, NBC concluded that a format not copied by its competitors was not worth retaining.

The death of the NBC Symphony without any uprising by the public or murmur from Washington showed such a thing could be done. And so, while the name NBC Opera was still used for a time, the permanent team which gave the name meaning was gradually disbanded.

There have been, of course, a few subsequent ventures in the production of music for television. For example, Igor Stravinsky and George Balanchine were persuaded by CBS to collaborate on a newly commissioned ballet-pantomine, *The Flood;* despite immense publicity for the world premiere of a work by two artists of the highest rank, the broadcast was generally regarded as a failure and has not been repeated.

Whether the work or the production or both were at fault may remain open to discussion. Not to be doubted, however, was the artistic director's reaction to the way the production was handled by an organization unfamiliar with this type of work. At a recent exploratory conference on cultural programing for television, Balanchine revealed that a seventeen-minute ballet had been written before it was learned that the network had scheduled and sold a full hour. In a hurried, last-minute process, with an overall studio time of about two days, those seventeen minutes were padded out to one hour, with little or no opportunity for general review and artistic coordination. Balanchine's experience with *The Flood* left the leading choreographer of our time with the feeling that television is not for ballet and ballet is not for television—an attitude obviously directed at the manner in which the medium is used in this country, rather than at the medium itself.

Similarly, Gian Carlo Menotti, considered a safe investment after his television success with *Amahl,* was commissioned to write another children's opera with holiday appeal by the same network. It was no secret that practically everybody was dissatisfied with the end result, to such a degree that after a number of delays the tape was buried in an unpopular time-slot and forgotten.

In both cases, the network certainly desired to do something creative. CBS must at least be credited with trying at a time when others had given up. But the truth is that production of serious musical television shows is an infinitely complicated process, which cannot be carried through successfully on a haphazard basis, no matter how eminent the participants. It requires long-range planning, extensive rehearsal time, and, even more important, a production team whose members understand each other as well as they understand the medium in which they work.

On the one hand, few television technicians have the musical experience to find the right balance between ear and eye—a particularly delicate judgment in a medium full of visual temptations. On the other hand, singers whose schooling is aimed at the cavernous areas of halls such as the Met (and what young artist is not aiming at this hall?) need fundamental retraining if they are to project before the "cruel" eye and ear of the TV camera. And this means that achievement can only come from slow, quiet growth, together with a budget designed to foster such growth rather than to lure big names and support huge advance publicity.

More than once it has been proved that without such preparation big names plus big publicity cannot even produce a *succès d'estime,* much less an audience reaction that the rating-watchers will regard as less than disastrous. Why then should commercial broadcasters bother?

How different the situation is in other countries! BBC radio, for example, did not diminish its output of live music when television became the dominant medium. All these years it has employed seven orchestras, spread all over Great Britain, led by the famous BBC Symphony. Two years ago, it added another unit, a training orchestra for young musicians, which performs on radio and television and in public concerts as well. BBC's efforts in television opera are on a similar scale. Since 1948, it has produced an average of ten operas a year, including an occasional relay from Covent Garden or the Glyndebourne Festival, and since 1956 it has commissioned eleven new works.

And BBC is not alone. From the Scandinavian countries in the north to Rome and Naples in the south some thirty major European radio and television organizations, within and outside the Iron Curtain, have their own orchestras and musical staffs, produce ballets and operas (aside from concerts of all kinds), apply the latest film techniques to the presentation of music on television, and commission new works.

.   .   .

In opera and symphony, quite unlike modern ballet, we are still very much tied to European apron strings. And the effect is far from healthy. A young and talented composer looking at the enormous Metropolitan Opera House, its repertoire, and its audience can hardly be other than discouraged. Only the most striking physical production, with a name cast, can hope to command attention. On the other side, the price of failure must make the opera managers cautious in the extreme. Consequently, the commissioning of new operas has trickled down to a bare minimum. More and more, one hears composers say, "What sense does it make for an American to attempt opera?"

The opportunities for young opera singers are still very much limited. The 400 plus American singers working in European opera houses reflect a famine of musical opportunities in this country that is just as severe as the potato famines, which in the past brought so many immigrants to America's shores.

And finally, while the young instrumentalist can at least look forward to a year-round job in a symphony orchestra, if his youthful dream of taking up where Heifetz left off evaporates, the chaining of our orchestras to a standard repertoire must increasingly make that job just a job.

It is no answer to point to the widespread distribution of phonograph records. True, their phenomenal technical development has made a surfeit of nonstandard music available to the public, but without creating any ongoing relationship between composer, performer, and audience; and their near-monopoly on radio spreads everywhere an ideal of technical perfection and brilliance as the final aim of musical performance rather than a means to an end.

It is here that radio and television make their contribution in other countries, as they once made in the United States and as they could do again. Radio can again supply live concert performances that are not tied to subscription audiences and the standard repertoire; television can supply a wide range of other concerts, exposing through informal conversation during rehearsals the way in which music is put together. It is in this area that Leonard Bernstein and his "Young People's Concerts" have created a format as popular in London, Tokyo, and Prague (where you can hear them dubbed in in Czech!) as they are in Surinam, Paraguay, and Iceland. While it is true that without the specific genius of its creator the program would never have gotten on the air, particularly not on a commercial network, it has such lasting value that continuing development of its basic formula seems necessary and possible—to be sure, without the rather hopeless attempt of aping "Lenny."

Imaginative television treatment can give a new focus to chamber music and ballet. But most important, it can dispel the lie of those who say that America is not an "opera country." Indeed, the way has already been indicated. The most significant fact about Menotti's *Amahl* is not its worldwide success on TV or its rebroadcast Christmas after Christmas; it is the staggering number of stage productions mounted in the United States since its television premiere in 1952. By Christmas 1967, according to Menotti's publishers, G. Schirmer, rights for 3,461 legitimate productions had been granted in this country. (Let it be understood we are talking about 3,461 productions, not performances.)

More significant than the full professional stagings are those in small high schools and colleges, in churches and community playhouses, often accompanied only by piano or organ. They are the ones that could point the way out of the blind alley where grand opera has obviously lost the momentum of a living art form.

What is the explanation for this success, unparalleled in operatic history? In the first place, as the television medium absolutely demands, the libretto for *Amahl* was written in the language of the country for which it was created. Perhaps decisive for its initial impact on TV was the producer's insistence that nearly every word should be easily understood—something rarely expected and still more rarely achieved in operatic stage performances.

Second, conforming to the small television screen, *Amahl* is not grand opera; no elaborate spectacles are involved, and no expensive production is required. Instead, like the best of television drama, *Amahl* capitalizes on the intimate, the warm, and the human. Third, *Amahl* was not written over the head of the audience as an experiment, but specifically for a mass medium where even minority audiences are counted in the millions. Without a hint of condescension, *Amahl* speaks directly to that audience.

The right kind of opera, produced by a team that knows its medium as well as its music, can repeat this success. And it can do more to make opera live in this country than any alternative of which I am aware. When NBC, encouraged by its opera company's success on TV, sent a young road company on tour, the two-year effort came close to breaking even, despite deliberately restricted publicity and promotion. This convinced the originally skeptical NBC officials that a third year could have been self-sustaining—a phenomenon unheard of before or since as, among others, the unhappy fate of the Metropolitan Opera's National Touring Company demonstrates.

Is it so surprising that the most powerful advertising medium in the world should turn out to be the best possible base for a touring opera company? While television opera cannot hope to match the popularity of ordinary commercial programing, the audience it can reach even on educational stations is overwhelming by comparison to the audiences available by other means.

But all of this, once again, needs money and a willingness to invest it over a long period of time—probably more money and more time than other cultural uses of TV demand. Musicians who have tried know that this requirement is inescapable. They know that broadcast music cannot live without a major financial commitment, and they have a corresponding concern with the question of who is to make it. This is precisely the reason why a musician, more than his colleagues in the other arts, may be excused if he raises the question: Who is to do the job?

Our commercial networks and stations have abandoned the field. Any notion that the FCC can or will require them to return seems a forlorn hope. Even the supposedly literate and highbrow segment of the public—more ignorant of what other countries do in this sphere than in any other area of the arts and sciences, not to mention sports, politics, or public affairs—has been conditioned step by step to accept the concept of radio as a playback gadget for records, and television as a medium that may once or twice a year relay a concert from Tanglewood or an attraction from the Hurok stable for the benefit of a humbly grateful minority audience.

And so we come to public broadcasting. Having touched on the musical "vast wasteland" of those affluent organizations that have all the money to equal or better what the rest of the civilized world is doing, it is doubly remarkable to remember what the National Education Television Network and some individual educational stations have been able to produce from time to time. Unfortunately NET's painfully inadequate budget has up to now forced it to rely, to a considerable extent, on purchases from foreign organizations. It stands to reason that these foreign productions, usually artistically valid, occasionally brilliant, cannot always reflect the particular requirements of the American musical scene; much less frequently do they offer opportunities to our own creative and re-creative forces.

Public broadcasting cannot, the way it has been financed up to this point, hope to perform for music the service abandoned by industry, and this fact has been recognized for some time by the two powers best qualified to do something about it: the Ford Foundation and the Corporation for Public Broadcasting. Happily, an encouraging move was announced during the first week of [April, 1969]. Grants have been made to NET by the Ford Foundation for the formation of a semi-autonomous opera company and for a Sunday night series devoted to summer festivals of music and other cultural events. Beginning June 1, this series will replace the Public Broadcast Laboratory series, which has often been criticized for being top-heavy with public affairs.

Does this mean that the pendulum is swinging back toward the area where American television is furthest behind the rest of the world? Will public television at last become the kind of "cultural force" which the BBC is credited with being?

It is, of course, much too early to tell. To reach the goal of $200,000,000 a year for public television (the figure suggested by the report of the Carnegie Commission for Public Broadcasting), the treasury of the ever-caring Ford Foundation and the so-far very meager Congressional appropriation for the Corporation are not nearly enough. Public broadcasting cannot achieve its aims until government (and perhaps commercial television?) can be persuaded to open its heart—and especially its hand—more generously.

Culture has no high-powered lobbyist in Washington, and a musician is hardly well cast in the role. But an adopted American, in whose life broadcast music, both here and abroad, has played a central role, can surely be forgiven for feeling that the richest country in the world must find an answer.

the   recollected:
an incisive report

by CHRIS HODENFIELD

Chris Hodenfield, a contributing editor of the rock magazine **Circus,** gives
an impressionistic history of rock
music and, almost incidentally, of
cultural changes in the sixties.

Rock & Roll Music is a big sociological phenomenon, on one hand, y'know,
and it's made a lot of capitalizing fatback executives rich on the other.
From 1960 to 1970, music went in cycles, (from sludge to sludge in the
pop sense), and went on careful lines of just how society was at the same
time. Figure then, yeah, that all them kids snatching up records and listening for the big Social Push in life, would all be doing it for a reason.

Back in the late 50's, parents said rock & roll was leading our children
off to the mouths of hell, sin, degradation, illicit nookie, and hot legs. And
innocent Levittown girlhood was being ruined in the back seats of
souped-up jalopies, while Rock & Roll Played Loud And Loose On The
Radios! Shame!

And they were right. Elvis Presley didn't rattle and thrust his way into
the heartloins of America's budding youth because he successfuly amalga-
mated the WASP dream of Southern black music and mannerism and
pelvic thrusts with the necessary white face. No, not only that, but also
there was some stud up there on the Ed Sullivan screen that, in one flash
of his curled lips, said: *sexharleydavidsonsmidniterumblesloosefreeandgo
fugyourmom   & dad*   Those kids, then, with their black tennis shoes

and their way-out chicks, said yeah and yep and that was the James Dean way to go and the times were repressive and gangs were sprawling out, *Blackboard Jungle,* gangs and rumbles, Wayne Morse filibustering for your parents, mannnnn.

But . . .

. . . by the time the year 1960 came around, we were again back in the carmel sludge racket. Allen Freed done shot his load and took payola. Scandal with Jerry Lee Lewis and Chuck Berry. Purity Drives. Elvis Presley went into the Army. Cold wars getting down to brass tacks. What did 1960 give us? "Teen Angel," that's what. Mark Dinning's *lategreat oldieclassic,* along with other such hard and fast hitters as "Theme From A Summer Place" and "Running Bear." Bobby Rydel singing "Volare" through his hamburger stand dimples and getting away with it. Eisenhower's years finished off with a huge belch of sedentation. Rolls of fat on America's hide. John Kennedy was taking reign of our country. And youth was being looked on by some good majorities of people as having, well, clear blue eyes, crew cuts, and baggy pants. Forget those gaudy nightmares about J. D. hysteria; America's children were okay. And they were watched, too.

1961. Homogenized versions of gone Elvis. Del Shannon. Rick Nelson. Bobby Lewis. Real sterling examples of young American boyhood. If you think rock stars are being hounded today, (facts? money? contracts? color guitar? five dozen groupies? length of genitalia?), think of it back then. Fanzines, glorious Sunday spreads on Frankie Avalon and why he likes french fries while sitting in his brand-clean sharp Chevy convertible.

Next year we had The Twist, the Peppermint Twist, Don't Knock The Twist, Son of the Twist Returns. The President's first lady was rumored to have *done it,* and there was Killer Joe Piro, and Wop Rock was showing its head, and it was very boring indeed.

Up until the time of the assassination of John Kennedy, music was popsie cutsie marvelsie gooie. "Hey Paula" by Paul and Paula. A rash of girl groups and soloists, (the black of which were great, the white of which were half-baked and spoiled-sounding), the Chiffons, Peggy March, Leslie Gore ("It's my party and I'll cry if I want to . . ." ". . . and now it's Judy's turn to cry . . ."), the Angels, the Crystals.

The death of the young president took America straight down and then back again bouncing even more cerebral. The civil rights movement that had been floundering around was gone, it seemed, and now—well, there was to be something more. The following weeks saw the likes of "Dominique" by a Belgian nun and Bobby Vinton with his hushed puppy-lap "There I've Said It Again." BUT THEN!

On Walter Cronkite's news program one night, they report on these four lovable moptop lads who are charming girlie-fans right out of their collective pants and wheezings and screamings with their new Chuck Berry music and this is really *it,* let me tell you. "I Want To Hold Your Hand" went to the top of the charts for seven weeks, then "She Loves You" for a couple more, then "Can't Buy Me Love" for another five weeks, and the only thing that could ever stop the charge was Louis Armstrong singing "Hello Dolly." But that didn't matter because suddenly we had Peter & Gordon, the Animals, Manfred Mann, Herman's Hermits, the Dave Clark Five. We had Liverpudlian boots, oatmeal-bowl haircuts, *gearfabohmostmarvy* expressions, fanzine revivals, *Shindig* and *Hullabaloo,* new fervor. There were songs like "Leader of the Pack" and "The Ballad of Ringo" sure, but we also had the birth of American blue-eyed soul, like the Righteous Brothers, and the most important movement of the decade, almost: Hot Rod Music. "I Get Around" by the Beach Boys, "Hey Little Cobra" by the Rip Chords. America rolled its own.

Kids out there putting the mobile phase of America's history to good use, driving around in potential quarter-miler bombs with duals and four-barrel carburetors and stick shifts and traction masters and Big Daddy Roth exclamations on the side, like "Mother's Worry" or "Shutdown King." Glorious hot rod music, Jan & Dean, Dick Dale, surfs-up Fender guitar music on the radio dial while belting down the freeway at impossible speeds, holding the plush automatic transmission of your daddy's Caddy in second gear all the while for that all-important *whine* and boost of power and hot rod music on the radio dial and America's youth had no reason to jack off. . . .

. . . and besides America was going through a Dylan phase, and the first vague traces of an actual "underground" were started as some cats whined and said "Man, turn that Dylan guy off . . . he sounds . . . well, man, *weird,* y'know, un-American." The Byrds, anyway, sang "Mr. Tambourine Man" and the Beatles turned out the likes of "Yesterday." Introspective? Barry McGuire singing "The Eve of Destruction" on America's precious AM radio dial. (It was safe to protest in those days, eventually hip . . . and Protest Rock, later to be called Folk Rock, was born.) Simon & Garfunkel were getting started. Donovan showed up with his scuffed boots and Woody Guthrie trappings all original and the Turtles sang "It Ain't Me Babe" on channel seven.

The folk boom, which had been laying around gathering strength with the button-down-sport-shirt mob, hashed forth and beheld young white boys who played like old black men. Tom Rush. John Hammond. Dave Van Ronk. Down in the urban cool-crawl; havin' a mind ramble, yes indeedy; gonna leave mah woman; gonna put on my walkin' shoes; and that letter ya left me woman done broke my heart.

And the Rolling Stones sang "Satisfaction" and the American summer air was rent with the sound of clattering hot lust.

Those were, you could say, the Good Old Days to this decade. Music was taken very seriously, but it was also free. It was a matter of the artist and his sincerity. In fact, Sincerity was the word. Come in long-haired, clear-eyed folk girls, Joan Baez, Judy Collins, Buffy Ste.-Marie. We also had LBJ in office. Cold, ego-maniac, Texas six-shooting, aloof LBJ and then we had . . .

"The Ballad of the Green Berets," by Sgt. Barry Sadler. And then we had big money in the music game. We had two months of "I'm A Believer" by this new group, the Monkees, on the charts. Lovable moptop lads. The Buckinghams. The Turtles even softer. The Beatles did "Strawberry Fields" and people were actually *disturbed.* ACID! *Sgt. Pepper* and all the fluky things. (Is this the answer? Is this . . . or . . .?) Came the monumental summer of 1967 and America's lovely children rose up in response to the chilled government, pushed their thumbs through their second and third fingers, wore flowers in their hair and hitch-hiked out to San Francisco, while Scott MacKenzie urged them over the car radio and Eric Burdon did his warm San Francisco nights and Monterey Popped all over. Musically, we were at our heights: "Light My Fire," "Whiter Shade of Pale," "Ode to Billy Joe," "All You Need Is Love." Kids taking drugs, expanding their milk-fed minds, that's what. Soul music was also at its best and the Real Hits were established, "Respect," "Groovin'," "Soul Man," and Little Stevie Wonder's immortal "I Was Made To Love Her." The blues revival was kicking up; Paul Butterfield organized hisself a white blues band with a big black drummer with the name of Sam Lay and Chicago was some hot bed. . . .

. . . and meanwhile, as has been said of this here *up yours* charge made by the fresh-faces, America countered with the well-thought-of obscenity charge. (I forgot who first said that.) Reactions! Berkeley peace marches suddenly turned dead serious. SDS. Guerrilla yahoo. Grim looks. Radicals. Institutional magazines writing up big exposés on Drugs, Free Sex, Dropping Out, and Other Things That Looked Like Fun . . . but . . . just weren't right.

Harrumph, yes, 1968 saw "Hey Jude" and "Jumpin' Jack Flash," (the first sign of rock going simple and straight), but it also saw "Yummy Yummy Yummy" by the Ohio Express and "Simon Says" by the inimitable 1910 Fruitgum Company. Sports fans, it looks as if we grew too fast for the audience, they're leaving us here to wallow in our own expanded-mind juices.

Understand of course, we'd just been through the Psychedelic Eyewash Cycle, what with everybody doing their own version of *Sgt. Pepper,* and every album having a long cut, and Bill Graham discovering that tribes gathering for rock shows and be-ins and cosmic-consciousness euphoria meetings could make money and cause whole cults of Socially Rampant & Bulldozing American Youth, and take the night by storm. Well, we got the Fillmore Auditorium, and the Electric Circus. And the Electric Kitchen. And the Electric Toilet, for chrissakes, as people thought cosmic-commercial and the nights grew cold and ice-blue on acid whisperings and . . .

. . . bodies trundled off to war and Youth Turned Inward. And frustrated beyond belief, both sexually and socially. Which is why today, rock music is such a chrome-steel piece of pinball-machine-goliath searing business. If you took some candy store dude from back in the days of the Crew Cuts and "Sh-boom Shaa-boom, ya dadadadada dadadada Sh-boom Sha-boom" and placed him in an "underground ballroom," while Jimi Hendrix had his Chinese-nightmare Wall of Amplifiers all the way up and his fuzz-tones and his wah-wah buttons and guitar implanted in his crotch in a show-off frenzy while the fans are just eyes-glazed *diggin' on it* . . . well, I bet you that good old boy would really think something.

Music is power, today. Half-a-million English bands have taken Jimi's premise to the next steps, à la Jeff Beck, Led Zeppelin, & That Mob, while another half-million did the Cream scream and the American bands muddled around trying to get an authentic sound: country? doo-wop again? mountain music? revolutionary music? Moog synthesizers? The San Francisco bands in their raga/blues/kozmic days seemed to make more sense than a dozen blues groups. Grateful Dead, Quicksilver Messenger Service, Big Brother, Country Joe, music for the body and the spirit. On the other hand, English bands sort of fell naturally to the occasional first-esoteric-then-imitable-fad. Traffic was "jazz" before, say, a good number of these "rock-jazz fusions" that are making the rounds today.

The developments since 1963 made the music of today. Only so many Kennedy & Kings can get shot. Only so many body counts on the radio for Viet-Dominican-Berkeley World Wars, before 1969 gives us the MC5. Those amplifiers up on the stage like mountains aren't necessarily for loudness, but for balls. Understand now, civilization (as we know it today) would have us castrated so as to, 1.) don't reproduce; 2.) don't even ball; 3.) don't listen to that rock & roll music that makes us wanna ball.

What Tony Glover called "psychedelic backlash" on *CIRCUS* pages a while back, still exists. That's what all this "going back to my roots" bit is all about. (Guy comes out on stage with his custom–Los Angeles–made leather pants and his flowing silk shirt with genuine western fringe, and plays the blues with a feelin'. Thing is, he might be good with his axe, and that's what counts.)

That Bob Dylan is now singing "redneck music," is something akin to Richard Nixon being in office. That the vogue for the good old rock from the Fabulous Fifties now, can't be too far removed from the amount of acts you see today on stage who *reeeeeally* don't give a damn what goes on in the audience. All these complications, understand, lead to simplicity. You don't go fruggin' around with the body's music, with Madison Avenue approaches of greed, sensationalism, and curried vice.

The effects of rock on clothing are obvious. Neil Young used to show up in a fringed buckskin jacket back in the days of Buffalo Springfield. After a while, half of Sunset Strip thought it was Buffalo Bill Cody. And now, good Christ, Rock stars have to stay one notch above propriety if their music is to be spiced by theatre–show biz attentions and pretensions. Remember when the Rolling Stones came on the *Ed Sullivan Show* to sing

"Let's Spend the Night Together" (which, yes, came out sounding like "Let's Spend Some Time Together"). Army uniforms, they wore. And in a year, smart shoppes had their rafters loaded with any old American Legion rag they could find.

In the first days of the English arrivals, the most prominent stand-out piece of freakness was the *hair*. "Boy," some of us staunch cats muttered, "they must be some kinda pansy guys, you bet." Then we started to grow our hair long. Not that we were pansies, but that was the way, and man, we had to keep up with the times.

(As a note for the future, Mick Jagger first appeared at the Hyde Park concert wearing a little girl's dress over his t-shirt and jeans.)

It's no accident that rock has brought the sexes together. Identification with the sex symbols on both sides leads to what would appear to be, (people harrumph), bi-sexuality.

Girls swoon over a cat, who, say, doesn't come on like a burly, hairy lumberjack, but rather a silky dude. With a scream, in the corridors of Alvin Lee and James Morrison, of a bitch in heat . . . but is in firm reality, the howl of the Real Man, a man of a dozen facets and capabilities being both lion and butterfly for his woman. A girl who wants to submit herself totally to this is correct. A guy who gets furiously-swimming nightmares about rolling with an impassioned tigress like Janis Joplin or Tina Turner is also normal. Where the catch comes in, is when they deposit their own sexual abilities into the stars on stage. "I wish I could do it like Lance Silverbush up there," they say, when, of course, they probably *could*. What this amounts to is a merging of the rock culture and the television culture. Just watch. Somebody will do it for you. Get your rocks off on the people who jive on stage.

What happens next is a pain in the axe, to say. We could have *CIRCUS Magazine Takes A Look Into The Future* or else a star-studded *Chris Hodenfield Predicts*. Shucks.

Rock & Roll when it first appeared in the Fifties was a combination of gospel, dixieland, spiritual, jazz, rhythm and blues, and a whole lotta shakin'. Then it gradually channelled out. Now the supergroups, (which are, after all, necessary for establishing a hot group in the middle of the competition of a thousand others), are saying now, Right! Here's some jazz, here's some country-diddling. Or here's some good-ol' happiness music. Blendings of everyone's and everybody's music, such as is done by the Beatles, NRBQ, or even Blood, Sweat & Tears in their own kind of balls-less way, is a stiff and sudden harkening to Real Music.

THE ROCK PILE

by HENRY S. RESNIK

In this article, which appeared in the **Saturday Review's** first Multi Media monthly supplement, Henry S. Resnik also considers the impact of the rock culture. He notes the emergence of a new genre, the rock film.

Rock is the backbone of the counter-culture. Movies and cameras are almost as important. Naturally enough, this has led to a vital art form: rock movies. Although the festival scene and the movie industry have soured, and you keep hearing that nobody will make rock movies again, we're likely to see a great deal more of rock on film—or on videotape and cassette.

Movies with rock scores aren't necessarily rock movies. *Easy Rider* is a counter-culture movie of a sort, but the music is merely decorative. And in the world of Russ Meyer, notably in *Beyond the Valley of the Dolls,* the music is a vapid fume in the general air of cheap titillation. Meyer has little real sympathy with rock or the counter-culture; for him rock is nothing more than the rhythm of sex.

Help!, A Hard Day's Night, and *Yellow Submarine* make the music a much more intimate part of the whole than *Easy Rider,* but these aren't what one would readily call rock movies either. The best rock movies are documentaries. Among the earliest to reach a wide audience were *Don't Look Back,* a portrait of Bob Dylan on tour in England in May 1965, and *Monterey Pop,* which covered the three-day Monterey International Pop Festival in June 1967.

There are all kinds of rock movies, and any talk of categories is artificial at best. Nevertheless, an acquaintance with the form leads to at least one broad distinction: Some rock movies are principally vehicles for music; if they're well done, the music comes across in ways that are unique to the film medium. Other films examine the culture of rock more than they present the music itself; in this kind of movie, the music is always there, but it's somehow incidental. *Monterey Pop* shows us a great deal about the festival-goers, but the real thrust of the film is musical. Even when we're watching the peripheral action of the crowd, the sound track continues with music. *Don't Look Back,* on the other hand, is a film about Bob Dylan; only a few songs are presented in their entirety, and even these are indifferently sung—Dylan is a tired, irritable, snotty little prince and musically way below par throughout the film. (It's nearly impossible to make a musically interesting movie about an event where the music wasn't very good; good music can easily be distorted, however, by sloppy filmmaking.)

Metro-Goldwyn-Mayer's recently released *Elvis—That's the Way It Is* embodies some of the worst aspects of bad rock movies. The film is little more than an elaborate advertisement for Elvis and MGM, but it's stupidly done. Like Elvis's fans, so many of whom in their appearances on camera seem afflicted with serious cases of spiritual malnutrition, all the film can do is gape. In the opening scene, which takes place in an MGM rehearsal studio, Elvis flashes a benignly cute smile and says, "Hello, Hollywood camera"—and there can be no question of who is in control. Later the film reaches the apex, or nadir, of its technical expertise when the camera locks in on Elvis during his appearance at the International Hotel in Las Vegas, then zooms in and out in a dull suggestion of sexual intercourse that leaves one with a headache.

The cheapest moment in this monumentally cheap film occurs when Elvis descends from the stage during his Las Vegas show and plows through the throngs who have been allowed to charge him. The whole thing is a setup for the film, of course; Elvis struggles the length of the proscenium and mounts the stage with a few spangles trailing seductively from his costume—sweating, triumphant, a mighty survivor of sexual combat. The only good thing about *Elvis—That's the Way It Is,* which was directed by Denis Sanders, is Elvis. And Elvis is magnificent, more powerful than ever as he sings twenty-seven numbers, still one of the most compelling of all rock performers.

The staged non-event, the absence of a critical sensibility, the bemused awe of the superstar, and finally unmotivated technical tricks are earmarks of badly made rock movies, and *Let It Be*—which shows the Beatles in a couple of rehearsal sessions, then in a sluggish concert on the roof of their Apple headquarters in London that was obviously planned as a way of rescuing the film from total dreariness—has all these qualities without the virtue of an interesting performance. It even has consistently poor color. The film's only plus is that it affords an occasional glimpse of the Beatles themselves, then so close to breaking up that they all seem to be hiding from the camera.

The Elvis film and *Let It Be* are both essentially musical, but neither one makes the slightest move toward enhancing the musical performance it records. *Monterey Pop* represents a distinct rock movie genre—the festival film—but it's also a landmark in the transference of live musical performance to the screen. How does D. A. Pennebaker get such amazing results? Perhaps most important, Pennebaker has an unfailing sense of himself as an artist; superstar egos don't faze him. He has a knack, too, for filming what he finds, rather than trying to impose a preconceived sense of what he wants to see. Filming the 1965 Dylan tour as a musical event would have been a disaster; Pennebaker realized that the music was less important than Dylan, and he didn't hesitate to show Dylan at his worst. The Monterey festival, on the other hand, was one of the great moments in the history of rock—the public debut, in a way, of the San Francisco sound. The music, the weather, and the vibrations were right, and the film is completely in harmony with them.

Pennebaker improves on *Monterey Pop* in the soon-to-be-released *Sweet Toronto,* made during the twelve-hour Toronto Rock 'n' Roll Festival of September 1970. Here Pennebaker has scrapped the familiar one-or-two-songs-to-a-group approach, selected a limited number of performers, and focused on whole sets. He's been even more selective in his choice of musicians; although the festival included a wide variety of styles, Pennebaker presented the roots of rock embodied in Bo Diddley, Jerry Lee Lewis, Chuck Berry, and Little Richard—all of them in top form—but then juxtaposed this with an unusual blues set by John Lennon, who made a surprise appearance, backed up by Eric Clapton, and a fantastically weird, yet interesting, moaning and wailing number by Yoko Ono. The result is dazzling.

The singular triumph of *Sweet Toronto* is the perfection of what Pennebaker calls the "line" of music and film—a continuing visual and musical image that becomes a unique musical composition itself. Interestingly, though, this can have an almost enervating effect, an immediate consequence of the principal difference between live and filmed rock performance. Filmed rock presents a unique vision of the live performance that one could never have at the performance itself, but it's didactic and intense. Live concerts are mitigated by the distractions of the crowd, the amplification system, and other environmental factors excluded from filmed versions, and when they're performed outdoors, at least they're likely to be much less exhausting. In the case of *Sweet Toronto,* the difference seems to be between an emotional catharsis and a good high. Partly because the film concludes with Yoko's extraordinary "thing," one leaves it numbed and mystified; this can't have been true of those who heard the live concert.

Another festival film, Michael Wadleigh's much-touted *Woodstock,* suffers terribly in comparison with Pennebaker's films, for *Woodstock* rarely makes real contact with the music. This is partly a reflection of the performances—Hendrix's "Wild Thing" at Monterey was infinitely better than even the double-barreled "Star-Spangled Banner" of Woodstock. But *Woodstock* tries to make up with technical flashiness what it lacks in art. The split-screen technique in *Woodstock* actually detracts from the music, and the best moments are the most straightforward—Sha-na-na's frenzied "At the Hop" and the shot of Richie Havens's foot during "Handsome Johnny."

Woodstock is essentially a film about an event, however, and on this level it's more successful. Its scope is huge, and it conveys the sense people had of being together—much more attention is paid to life-style, community, and dope than in any of the Pennebaker films, and the film exudes a benevolent euphoria. To a great extent, of course, this euphoria is the result of distortion.

Gimme Shelter is also about an event, the Rolling Stones' free concert at the Altamont Speedway near San Francisco on December 6, 1969, four months after Woodstock. Some say that Altamont, an epic disaster in which all the beautiful groovy people turned ugly and mean and at least one was murdered, marked the end of the peaceful and loving "Woodstock Nation." This may be an inflated interpretation, just as the Woodstock Nation was an inflated myth, but there can be no doubt that Altamont was brutal and violent and that the Maysles brothers and Charlotte Zwerin have managed brilliantly to capture this mood on film.

The murder of a young black man by one of the Hell's Angels whom Jagger had hired to be the concert's security guard has been widely reported, and at first one wouldn't expect any real suspense in *Gimme Shelter*. We know at the beginning that we're going to see a murder; we know that Altamont was ugly; we know that the Maysleses caught the murder on film and that the film was subpoenaed as evidence in court. Yet Maysles/Zwerin have focused the entire film on this climactic moment, and their masterful editing has created the jarring and surprising impression of a headlong rush into satanic darkness.

But there is something terribly wrong with *Gimme Shelter* despite its technical brilliance. As many critics have already argued, this is an amoral film that lacks critical judgment in a situation that demands a moral response. Everything is sacrificed to editing, pace, and structure—the film's implicit purpose is to dramatize the murder as effectively as possible. No one ever questions why the Angels were hired—doubtless to satisfy Mick Jagger's cynically vaunted impression of himself as a street-fighting revolutionary. Nor is it ever mentioned that the film-makers themselves were hired partly in order to make the free concert profitable through the proceeds of the film. Part of the problem is the Maysleses' fawning acceptance of the Stones. More than anything else, the film is a humble tribute.

Relatively few rock movies have set out to explore specific aspects of the rock culture, but *Groupies* was inevitable, and it may well be unique. No one need bother, at any rate, to make another film about the sex-crazed rock fans whose sole purpose in life is the ultimate unity of musician and audience—*Groupies* is perfect. There is plenty of music in the film—by Alvin Lee and Ten Years After, by Joe Cocker, Spooky Tooth, Dry Creek Road, and Terry Reid—but it's somehow peripheral, though capably filmed. The groupies themselves, a dozen or so, including a few male homosexuals, are much more vivid than the music.

The photography and direction by Ron Dorfman and Peter Nevard focus constantly, and in highly inventive ways, on a dozen or so groupies, but this isn't the mindless acceptance that one finds in lesser rock movies. Rather, Dorfman and Nevard have created a series of endearing caricatures. In one scene the camera watches a groupie putting on her makeup from a distance of about an inch—throughout the film, close-up is used in a tremendously witty manner. Another scene allows a totally stoned homosexual groupie to ramble on and on to various rock singers in a backstage room where he is trying to find a partner for the night, and the result is an intensely intimate sense of character. One of the funniest scenes in this hilarious film shows a groupie named Cynthia P. Caster combing a huge mass of frizzy hair, totally deadpan, and explaining in detail how she makes plaster casts of the rock stars' genitalia.

Groupies doesn't judge, although it suggests that groupies are pathetic; the film offers some broad insights into the rock culture, however, and for this reason alone it's an important document. "Wherever I go there's music," says a California baby-groupie as she embarks on a new "trip" in an airplane. "Everybody in America is bi-sexual," announces one of the groupie males matter-of-factly. And, most trenchant of all, from a girl in New York: "You get to screw the prettiest boys; you get to smoke the best dope; you get to meet the most far-out people. I don't know—it's magic, it's really magic."

by BARTON MIDWOOD

FICTION

In an **Esquire** review of Mario Puzo's **The Godfather** and Joseph Arleo's **The Grand Street Collector,** Barton Midwood explores the factors that made one book a bestseller and the other a relative failure commercially. His criticisms of **The Godfather** are typical of those often aimed at the entertainment media in general.

The Godfather by Mario Puzo has been advertised as the fastest selling book in publishing history. It has sold more than seven and a half million copies in a year and the publisher predicts that twenty million copies may be sold before the book goes out of print.

My friend Wilson, who has cultivated a taste for high-class literature, said, "I know that *The Godfather* is a kitsch book, but I couldn't put it down."

When I asked him why, he said: "Because this Godfather character is really fantastic. I kept thinking how great it would be to have someone like him to take care of me. I wouldn't have any more trouble from my boss, my landlord, or anybody else." He laughed self-consciously and confessed that he knew that this was not a legitimate reason for liking a book.

I protested, however, reassuring him of the legitimacy of the reason, and then asked him to tell me more about the character of the Godfather.

Fiction: From *Esquire* (February, 1971). Reprinted by permission *Esquire* magazine. © 1971 by Esquire, Inc.

"Well," he said, "he is a man who helps people who are oppressed by one thing or another. Sometimes his methods are violent—but before he uses violence, he usually tries persuasion and reason. Besides, the people he hurts usually deserve what is coming to them. He is not a bad man, really."

He then proceeded to tell me about some of the murders perpetrated by the Godfather, and I began to feel pity for Wilson. It is very sad, I thought, that he feels he needs such a monster to protect him. And yet surely he assesses his condition correctly. A few appropriate murders *would* make life easier for him. Even simply being under the protection of a murderer would be quite beneficial.

I said, "Do you think, then, that every one of us could do with the protection of this Godfather of yours?"

"Definitely," he said. "Every one of us."

"That's terrible," I said. "And I'm afraid that you are speaking in earnest."

"I am."

"But what then do you suppose is at the bottom of this terrible state of affairs?"

"Money is at the bottom of it. The poor man needs murderers to protect him from the rich, and the rich man needs murderers to protect him from the poor."

"I don't like it but I think you're right," I said. "What do you propose to do, then?"

"Well, there are, as I see it, only two alternatives. Either I've got to find myself a very ruthless Godfather, or the wealth has to be redistributed."

"How do you mean 'redistributed'?"

"I mean an equal share of the pot for everyone. I mean no more rich and no more poor."

"Well then, which do you prefer? The Godfather or a redistribution of the wealth?"

"A redistribution of the wealth. But how am I going to redistribute the wealth? I mean, it's ridiculous. A lot of people would have to cooperate to do it."

"You're right about that. As an individual you are impotent in this matter."

"On the other hand, if I put my mind to getting myself a Godfather, I think I could manage it. With a little education, practice and luck, I might even become a sort of Godfather myself—though I don't think I'd be inclined to." He laughed.

Later I bought a copy of *The Godfather* myself and read it out of a sense of obligation to Wilson. As I had suspected, it is bad. The very first chapter, which is a strenuous attempt to reinforce the popular but wildly erroneous prejudice that the courts have become "too lenient," announces at the outset like a fanfare the charlatanism and stupidity of the book's intentions. The prose has a moronic sound, and the whole affair is calculated to play on the uglier prejudices and pathetic longings of an impotent public. The character of the Godfather is, however, as Wilson says, "fantastic." It is a character that illustrates convincingly just how much murder one has to do in order to seize and maintain power in the American economy. Unfortunately, however, the author has chosen to portray all the Godfather's victims as vermin and his henchmen as fairly sympathetic, and in this way the book manages to glamourize both the murderer himself and the economy in which he operates.

The Grand Street Collector by Joseph Arleo is a novel which uses the technique of flashbacks in the way it was frequently used in movies in the Forties. The book is well written, makes certain literary gestures, usually in the direction of Hemingway, contains only one murder, and is fundamentally an affair of the conscience. It has sold about ten thousand copies.

Pietro Sbagliato, a young university instructor, travels to Masinalto, Italy, to visit his father, whom he has not seen in more than twenty years. Pietro was motherless since infancy and was cared for by an aunt. He has heard rumors throughout his childhood that his father was an assassin who had betrayed his own people. Pietro has come to Italy to demand a reckoning with his father. But he arrives early in the day and Don Natale Sbagliato is not yet at home. Therefore Pietro talks with his uncle. The uncle tells the story of Don Natale's life—of the assassination and so on. This story is presented to the reader in the form of flashbacks told from a third-person point of view and constitutes the major portion of the novel. In the last chapter the Don arrives, there is a brief confrontation between him and his son, and the book ends on a note of existential horror.

In 1936, in New York City's Little Italy, Don Natale had assassinated the editor of a socialist newspaper, Guido Sempione. He had assassinated Sempione under compulsion: either you kill him, he was told, or we will get somebody else to kill him and then we will also kill both you and your son. It was the administrators of the Mussolini regime who compelled Don Natale to become a murderer. Sempione was a thorn in their side and had to be eliminated.

After the murder Don Natale flees to Italy, leaving his son Pietro in the care of an aunt in New York, and degenerates into a broken and despised man. The fact that Don Natale was a fascist sympathizer, who "ordinarily" would have approved of the murder of an outspoken socialist but was hardly prepared to commit such a murder with his own hands, makes the story a political fable, expressing a general truth about how a man's ideological allegiances may compromise him into committing an act for which he is psychologically unfit.

Advertising copy for *The Grand Street Collector* compares it to *The Godfather,* but the two books have nothing in common, except that they are both about Italian immigrants in New York in the Thirties. Moreover, the intentions of the two books are diametrically opposed. *The Godfather* is essentially exhibitionist and makes its appeal to ignorance and fear, while *The Grand Street Collector* is essentially introspective and makes its appeal to reason.

I gave *The Grand Street Collector* to my friend Wilson. He read it but wasn't moved. "It's too thin," he said. "There's no sex in it, hardly enough violence. Also the characters aren't fat enough, if you know what I mean. Frankly the whole business is too anemic to suit my taste. I liked that Sempione character though—the socialist. He had some passion, an ideal. I liked the way he shouted in the streets at the fascist politicians, and the way he told off the cops in the police station. But he was killed off too quickly. I could have gone on reading for a thousand pages about this Sempione character. But what happens? He appears on five or six pages and then gets his head blown off. I just lost interest after that."

Poor Wilson, I understand him. I would have liked to see more of Sempione myself.

CURRENT SOCIAL ISSUES and the ENTERTAINMENT MEDIA

Certainly entertainment does not exist in a vacuum; it must deal with the times. And, as evidenced by John Corry's article earlier in this section, the social issues of the day are finding their way into the entertainment media more and more often. In our era of changing values, this can pose problems. Until a social issue becomes popular the media are not apt to treat it in an entertainment format, and any entertainer who attempts to lead the way may find the media doors closed to him. Once the issue is popular, the media may merely exploit it or treat it superficially. Commercial success is usually uppermost in the mind of the entertainer—and while some people prefer a serious exploration of reality, most seem to want light, escapist entertainment.

The following selections deal with the media's attempts to treat current social problems in an entertainment format. As will be seen from the criticisms of these attempts, they have been only partially successful.

FROM

the new

by PAUL D. ZIMMERMAN

· · ·

At the same time that they are examining prevailing values, the new wave of American films is also destroying or discarding the myths on which a generation of films was founded. For one thing, the morality of the traditional Western is under attack in such films as *Doc* and Dennis Hopper's *The Last Movie,* in which an Indian tribe, after watching a conventional Western being made, produces its own real-life Western, killing the white men. "The Western moral code is wrong," says the 34-year-old Hopper. "You don't have the right to take up a gun if someone wrongs you. That's the job of the police." Agrees actor Jon Voight, "We're breaking down those old myths about killing faceless people with no moral questions raised."

Arthur Penn's *Little Big Man,* in which Dustin Hoffman as a 120-year-old survivor of Custer's last stand tells the story of how the West was won, redefines American history. "It challenges the notion that the heroes of America are the ones you read about in the history books," says Penn. "It challenges the glorification of the gunfighter and the simple proposition that the cavalry was the good guys and the Indians the bad guys. It exposes the rotten morality of commercialism."

Redford's films attack other shibboleths: the value of winning and obsessive competition that informs American life. Frank Perry, in *Diary of a Mad Housewife,* implicitly assaults the cheery connubial comedies of the 1940s.

But, at the same time, American movies are minting fresh myths of their own that are often as naïve as those that shaped the films of the 1940s. "Some movies are creating the myths of the young," says Penn.

They promote the notion that freedom from all authority is an unqualified good, that mobility as a life-style is superior to permanence, that the older generation is totally corrupt, that cool is the only legitimate emotional response. And what's worse about these films is that they patronize young people. They reduce them to their accouterments—their grass, their bikes, their music—all their labels.

"I haven't seen a lead character in a movie who is young and still three-dimensional," agrees Dustin Hoffman. But he feels that the young are confederates in the creation of false myths. "These kids were raised in affluence and they

movies

have a legitimate feeling of guilt about their privileged position," says Hoffman.

Out of this comes a feeling of sympathy for the outcast—the black, the alienated, the down-and-outer. But that's all crap, because all they're getting at the movies is entertainment that alleviates their guilt. It's an easy way out for them without having to work in a ghetto or fight for what they believe.

"The romance of rootlessness put forward in *Easy Rider*," adds Alan Pakula,

is the essence of the American Western with its fantasy of the vagabond life. This myth of rootlessness that today's youth is aching for is the same ache that their fathers sought to answer in going to John Wayne movies and their grandfathers did when they watched William S. Hart. Hollywood is merely exploiting the same naïve myth of male adventure, only dressing it up in more sophisticated clothing. After all, what is *Butch Cassidy and the Sundance Kid* but the story of the Rover Boys shooting it up?

Pakula's indictment, however, does not apply to all American films. Many, like *Five Easy Pieces* and *Little Murders,* are striving to come to grips with American society and, in the process, are acting out a search for a better way to live. Screenwriter Charles Eastman talks of the need for films to "remind man of what is positive in his nature." Jeff Young notes the "nonspecific sense of anxiety" in today's films and talks of a search in movies for "a way to live in American society that is not built on selfish consumerism or clogged with soot or chained to suburbia." Alan Arkin speaks of his films hopefully "helping the human race to survive."

A new seriousness among today's moviemakers is undeniable and it promises at its best to produce in the months and years ahead the kind of intelligent, personal and relevant cinema Americans have admired in European filmmaking for decades. Hopefully, it will be a film industry grounded in the traditional humanism of John Ford and George Stevens, just as in France, Truffaut has carried through and updated the humanism of Jean Renoir. At least the conditions are ripe for such a flourishing. And the need is clear. "We have so many strident voices on every side," says Arthur Penn, "from the hate rhetoric of an Agnew to the wild cries of the radicals. The best we can hope for from our films is that they will talk to us about how we can live decently. People are looking for a way of coming together, and perhaps movies can aid in this search for mercy and goodwill."

329

SOCIAL

COMMENT

and

TV

CENSORSHIP

by DAVID DEMPSEY

When the Smothers Brothers gave their farewell show [in the spring of 1969] Tom Smothers told their fans that three-fourths of the program had been censored to some degree by the Columbia Broadcasting System. Ever since the show went on the air in January 1967, the elder of the brothers (Tommy the Militant, as his friends call him) had engaged in a running battle with the network's Department of Program Practices, headed by William H. Tankersley (or Tankersley the Timid, as he is known to many writers and producers in Hollywood). A sketch written and performed by Elaine May dealing with censorship was censored. Ditto Harry Belafonte singing a medley of calypso songs before a newsreel backdrop of the Democratic convention (with scenes of Mayor Daley and the Chicago police). Ditto again when Dr. Benjamin Spock made a guest appearance. Joan Baez could say that her husband had gone to jail, but she wasn't allowed to say why (for refusing draft induction).

The show had seemingly committed the unpardonable sin of making social comment within an entertainment format. Dan Rowan, of *Laugh-In,* points out that Tom and Dick Smothers used comedy as a platform for doctrine, whereas he uses doctrine as a platform for comedy. The Smothers Brothers work from a youthful, anti-Establishment, often sophomoric point of view. Rowan and Martin tell jokes about the Establishment from a neutral position. ("Let's make peace in Vietnam and not tell Martha Raye" isn't the same as Tom Smothers getting off a crack at the very idea of the war.) Moreover, *Laugh-In's* humor flies by so fast that half the audience gets the joke but not the message. Watching the Smothers show, viewers got the message—and sometimes a little smut—but frequently wondered what happened to the joke. The brothers' transgressions, moreover, were simply not offset by a high enough rating in competition with NBC's popular *Bonanza* in the same time slot.

For whatever reasons, public sympathy was with the network. Forty-seven per cent of those questioned by Lou Harris pollsters agreed that CBS was right in canceling the show; 19 per cent disagreed. (The remaining 34 per cent had no opinion.) By 55 per cent to 32 per cent, the same group expressed a negative view of the program's contents.

Yet, when the smoke had cleared, millions of Americans had, perhaps for the first time, become aware of the pervasive infrastructure of television's tastemakers; the men, day in and day out, in New York, Washington, Hollywood, and London who decide what shall be shown and what shall not. Thanks to their efforts, viewers are protected from dirty jokes, crooked prize shows, commercials for unworkable toys, racial slurs, nudity, vulgarity, and the three great taboos of television—sin, sex, and sacrilege.

As an entertainment medium with the largest single audience in history (45 million persons at one sitting for some prime-time shows), television is under constant pressure to exercise "good taste," and is at the mercy of its sponsors if it strays into unpopular or controversial territory. For its lapses, it is recurrently threatened with punitive action by Congress. Last winter, Senator John A. Pastore, chairman of the Commerce Committee's Communications Sub-committee, cranked up a new investigation of "sex and violence" in TV programing. As a result, networks have tightened up their standards. CBS announced that it has "achieved a 30 per cent reduction over the preceding season in the number of violent incidents in our prime-time programs." NBC has dropped all of its "action adventure" shows, and ABC is currently planning to do only one next season.

ABC also cut out a bikini contest in its *Wide World of Sports,* officially because of the poor quality of the film—and who knows, maybe that was the reason. The line between censorship and editorial acceptability in TV, as in other media, is a thin one. In any case, there will be no bikini contest sharing footage with Alpine skiers and log-rolling demonstrations on *Wide World of Sports.*

The new mood of caution comes at a time when American society is groping toward a more permissive, less hypocritical set of moral standards. In the arts, pornography is gaining an accepted place as a bedfellow of rectitude. The sex act is described freely in books, and the theater of nudity flourishes under the protection of the First Amendment. Almost anything goes in the movies; profane—even obscene —language is tolerated as a literary right. Shock has become a catalyst for artistic and social change.

In this disturbing context, millions of Americans find prime-time entertainment a nostalgic sanctuary—perhaps the only one left—where few men swear, everyone is politically neutral, the church is never criticized, men and women do not live together out of wedlock, the happy ending is assured, the criminal brought to trial, and the little disturbances of life are usually resolved in favor of the status quo. Critics of television, including many of its own creative personnel, point out that the fallacy of playing to these "accepted moral standards" is that they are not the true standards of most communities, but rather those which the community wants to think are true. By eliminating the unpleasant, the controversial, and the "immoral," TV helps to sustain a mass illusion that is false to the society which gives the medium its franchise.

Yet, no one expects television to emulate the printed page or the theater in matters of frankness. The question isn't whether there should or should not be censorship, but rather how much and to what end. "It's a rare entertainer," writes Steve Allen, "who will willingly eliminate the funniest parts of his act when working a television show, if instructed only by his own conscience."

The conscience of television, on the working level, is embodied in some eighty-five network representatives who must have a thorough knowledge of the National Association of Broadcasters Code—seventy-three do's and don'ts (mostly don'ts) that comprise the parameters of acceptable programing—a high degree of tact, and the ability to delete objectionable material without making their cuts seem too obvious. "We are—to use that harsh and emotive term—censors," Bill Tankersley told a Midwest broadcast group recently. "The inescapable fact is that broadcasters are fully and finally responsible for everything that is broadcast over their facilities, and that responsibility cannot be delegated to anyone."

With this in mind, the censor almost always has the last word in any dispute with a producer. The code itself is a product of the industry's self-regulation, and although adopted in 1952, most of its provisions have gone unchanged over the years. Many of these are common-sense reflections of social decency involving ethnic prejudice, respect for the law, and demeaning references to the handicapped. More inhibiting is what constitutes "anti-social behavior"—illicit sex relations ("not to be treated as commendable") and drunkenness ("should never be presented as desirable or prevalent").

.   .   .

"OUR STRUGGLE IS NOT TO BE WHITE MEN IN BLACK SKIN"

by
JOHN
OLIVER
KILLENS

There was a time not many years ago when 25 million Black Americans were invisible in the media of mass communications. A Black child could go to school and look into his school books and children's books and come home and stare at television and go to an occasional movie, and go through this routine from day to day, month to month and year to year, and hardly (if ever) see himself reflected in the "cultural" media. It was as if he had no real existence, as if he were a figment of his own imagination, or at best, if he had an existence it wasn't worth reflecting or reflection.

It was a time when my family and I lived in the Bedford-Stuyvesant section of Brooklyn, N.Y., in a brownstone, on the parlor floor and basement. Our television was in the living room on the parlor floor. At that time my daughter Barbara, who was 7 or 8 years old, was an incorrigible TV watcher. She stared at the little box hour upon hour, from program to program; she did not discriminate. She appeared to watch the commercials with as much interest as she did the programs, which was just as well when you think about it. We finally came to the conclusion that Barbara was looking for some reflection of her own identity, someone who looked like her or her mother or her brother or her father on the TV screen. When once in a month of Sundays she saw a Black man on television, she would run downstairs where we usually were, shouting: "Daddy! Mommy! Negro on TV!" And by the time we'd get upstairs, he would have done his little old thing and gone.

But Black men and women fought back, protested, demonstrated, wrote letters, threatened boycotts, played upon the White established conscience. P. J. Sidney walked a million miles in protest. And what have we to show for it? Progress, right? No more invisibility.

"What do you think of the progress we have made in TV?" I asked a lady.

"Just fabulous," Mrs. B. replied. "Tremendous. I mean we've really got it made." Mrs. B. is a middle-aged, middle-class, brown-skinned, pleasant-faced, exuberant woman. Her husband works in New York's transit system. Mrs. B. teaches school.

"What do you mean tremendous?" I asked her.

"I mean tremendous," she answered. "It's not like it used to be, when you could stare at TV all day and all night long and hardly ever see a Black face except in an athletic contest or clowning in the kitchen. But it's different now. You have to admit it's different now."

"Yes," I said. "I'll have to admit it's different. But I'm not sure about tremendous."

"Why," she said, "you can hardly look at a TV show without seeing a Black man or woman, and they're not domestic servants either. And if they are, they speak good English."

"Yes," I said reluctantly. "But—"

"Even the commercials got us in them."

"What is your favorite colored show?"

"I like **Julia** best of all. Diahann Carroll is such a lovely, charming lady, and that little boy just steals your heart away. What I like about **Julia,** it's a show that isn't about Negroes at all. It's universal. It doesn't stereotype the Negro. It's got no 'dis here' and 'dat dare' in it."

"That is apparently true," I had to admit reluctantly.

"I also like **Room 222** and **Sesame Street.** They're nice and easy—especially **Sesame Street**—and they're integrated. **Sesame Street** is especially good for children."

I posed the same question to Mrs. X., middle-class, middle-aged, nurse, socially-conscious, active in Black women's organizations. Her husband is a postal employee. Mrs. X. said she didn't watch much television. She usually listened to the talk programs over radio. "They're more informative." As to television, she shrugged it off with, "It's all right. **Julia** is OK and **Sesame Street.** Once in a while I watch **Mission: Impossible** and **Mod Squad** and **Julia.** My favorite show on television is **Sesame Street.** It's the best children's show they ever had." She said she liked to watch the variety shows in which Black people appear. She liked **Black Journal.** "On second thought," Mrs. X. said, "my favorite Black show is **Soul!** Did you see that wonderful show Ossie and Ruby did on Langston Hughes? That was truly soul. That's the kind of thing I'd like to see more of. And the one with LeRoi Jones and Abbey and Max and the Muslims. That was out of sight!"

"That was **Black Journal,**" I suggested.

"Yes, of course," Mrs. X. agreed.

Mr. A. is a working man on the waterfront. He stated matter-of-factly, "My favorite show is **The Name of the Game.**"

"I mean Black TV shows."

Working man said, "Ain't no Black shows. They're just shows with Black people acting like they White. Excepting **Soul!** and **Like It Is** and **Black Journal.** They the only truly Black shows. I liked that Belafonte show a few years ago. Pigmeat Markham and Godfrey Cambridge and Diana Sands and the rest of them people. That was a Black show. One of the best shows

I used to like was **The Outcasts,** and it wasn't long before they cast it out and off the air. It had a feeling of truth to it somehow or other. I especially liked that time when Roscoe Browne was on that show and killed that **White** man. That was beautiful! I also like to watch the basketball games and stuff like that. The Black man really runs them games. It makes me feel so good to watch them."

I have a class in Black Culture at Columbia University. I asked the students what they thought about the strides Black folk were making in the television media. The response was almost unanimous.

Miss L. said, "Ain't nothing happening."

Mr. K. said, "All of them—**Julia,** Leslie Uggams, Della Reese, all those shows—are just White folks masquerading in Black skin."

Mr. F. said, "That cat in **Mission: Impossible** is the natural end. He's the White folk's handy man. They should call that show 'I was a Stooge for the CIA.' I mean, like what you're always talking about, Brother Killens, he puts you in the mind of good old Gunga Din."

From various and varied samplings of Black opinion, one gets a picture that only a very few people believe the millennium has come for colored people in television. There are some who believe that things are getting better, decidedly improving. Others agree, believing that it would **have** to be getting better, since it couldn't get any worse. "There is no way but up," they say. "Which is not saying very much."

How do I see it? I think that progress **has** been made, in that there are more actors employed in the medium,

and that is good. The Black man is no longer invisible in the medium, and that is good. I mean a Black kid can see an image of himself on television, even though it is a false image. Is that good? The problem is that the television establishment is attempting to give to the world the image of an integrated society in all facets of American life, even in advertising and commercials, which is all well and good except that it is a colossal lie, because America is not an integrated society. It is a segregated society. A society in which the Black psyche and the White psyche are different altogether. So that the image is at the very best a false image, which is what some Blacks are realizing.

We also know that wishing or pretending will not make it so. The basic problem is, of course, that with all that "Black" exposure on television, there are damn few Black writers participating and the proof of the pudding is not only in eating but fundamentally in the ingredients. The play is the fundamental thing, not the players (as important as they certainly are). White writers, intentions notwithstanding, cannot write about the Black experience, cannot conjure up a true Black image, cannot evoke the wonderful—sometimes terrible—beauty of our Blackness. I have said it before and I say it again: only club members can sing the blues because we're the ones who have paid the dues—of membership in the Brotherhood of Blackness.

I am not one to attack Black actors like Diahann Carroll and Clarence Williams (in the first place, they are valued friends of mine) for appearing in **Julia, The Mod Squad,** etc. They are the **victims** of the establishment, not the culprits. They do not call the shots in television. It was clear in an interview in **TV Guide** that Diahann has no illusions about **Julia;** and, having spoken to Clarence, I know that he has none about **The Mod Squad.** It's a job. For Clarence it means employment and piling up some experience in the medium. For Diahann, and according to her, it is a means of getting into a position in which she **will** be able to do something truly of Black value. I hope her aspirations are realized, for all our sakes.

I would not be concerned with television at all but for the fact that millions of Blacks watch the damn thing every day. It is the great uncontested mass medium.

So what do I think Black people should work for in TV? The kind of television that reflects the Black experience and our special hopes and aspirations. I want to see some stories and programs on the screen that speak of the Black family, its trials and tribulations, its triumphs and defeats.

Life is a great, throbbing, dramatic thing in the Black community. Everything is there—life, death, laughter, tears, irony and paradox, tragic figures, heroes and heroines, living out their days in the Great American Tragedy. For, after all, the Great American Tragedy is the Black Experience. (The other Great American Tragedy is, of course, the experience of the Red men, the original Americans.) But what we see on TV is a very anemic imitation, acted out in pallid blackface.

For example, **Room 222** is a nice, liberal-oriented, interracial, innocuous show with handsome Lloyd Haynes and his beautiful love Denise Nicholas and Mike Constantine, all nice, wonderful people. The Black folk here are full of understanding and wisdom, sympathetic all the way. No basic problems between the races. All men are brothers. Right? An undramatic, middle-classish situation that hardly has anything to do with the Black experience.

I'm saying that Black people have an existence, a life's experience and a life style all their own in this segregated society. We did not segregate the society. The Whites did. We have an identity all our own. We have a peoplehood that shouts out for reflection and dramatization. As I have said before, our struggle is not to be White men in Black skin, but to be our own Black selves. This means, first of all, Black writers. But it also means Black producers, Black directors, Black cameramen, Black grips, Black set designers, all along the line. In a word, Black conceptualization.

But I try very hard to steer clear of illusions, so as not to become disillusioned. So I don't imagine that such Black television exposure will come to pass till we achieve some Black control.

Letters from Listeners:

KSJR/KSJN FM Radio, Collegeville, Minnesota

KSJR and KSJN are subscription radio stations (operated by Minnesota Educational Radio, Inc.) which broadcast classical music and public affairs programing. The following letters appeared in **Preview,** the stations' monthly program guide.

—*Our public affairs programming policy has come under criticism, and received praise during the last few months. On May 9 [1970] we broadcast live from Washington, D.C. part of the anti-war rally which was being held there. We received many telephone calls and letters about that broadcast, both angry and pleased. Other programs have touched off similar controversy. Compare the two following letters, the first in response to the anti-war rally broadcast, the second in response to a program on American students working in Cuban sugar cane fields.*

Gentlemen:

Finally there is a radio station that is not afraid to present the views of the revolutionaries of our country! Your program today is excellent.

Keep up the good work!

All power to the people—

Linda and Dale Viehoff
Rick Meinz

Radio KSJR/KSJN;

I have just heard your Pacifica broadcast which disturbs me deeply. I have a sealed envelope which I thought I had already mailed to you with $25 enclosed. I am not sending it after hearing that broadcast.

Why should your otherwise excellent station stoop to voicing Communistic propaganda? Surely this is not required by the FCC, nor is it required in the search for free speech.

These "student" sugar-cane harvesters are nothing less than communistic indoctrinaries with only one consuming passion—the destruction of our "imperialistic" society and government.

Tonight was not the first time such misleading views were presented on

Letters from Listeners: KSJR/KSJN FM Radio, Collegeville, Minnesota: Reprinted by permission of KSJR and KSJN FM Radio, Collegeville, Minnesota.

your station. A few weeks ago a broadcast dealing with the killing of Black Panthers was, in my view, equally bad. It seemed to favor the Panther cause. If your management is aware of the goals of the Black Panthers, I feel sure their views would not be given valuable air time.

In your defense, your news broadcasts are very good and your music is also very enjoyable—but please don't air things that will give aid and comfort to those who would so readily destroy our country.

Sincerely yours,
Dolan Toth

—Our management sent a reply to Mr. Toth. The letter represents a preliminary statement of policy, equally applicable to the writers of the first and the second letters. In essence, we take no sides. We devote ourselves to providing alternative ideas, unavailable elsewhere.

I am sorry to hear of your decision to withhold support of KSJR and KSJN. Were you to make a contribution, it would not necessarily indicate that you agreed with everything that was broadcast. By the same token, our broadcasting of the Pacifica programs is in no way an endorsement of the views contained in those programs. This is true of all our public affairs programs, not just those from Pacifica.

If we are controversial, so be it. Our feeling is that our listeners are capable of judging for themselves the value—or lack of it—in the views presented on certain programs. We feel that beyond the reporting of news as events in which a listener is interested, there are situations which a listener must be aware of and upon which he must form a judgment. Our function is to present these situations to the listener as an aid to his awareness. We do not endorse the opinions presented in programs apt to be controversial. It is the listener who must make his own judgment.

We do not air these programs to "aid and comfort" anyone who wishes to destroy this country. Their goal would be easily attained if they could proceed silently and without opposition; but when they openly espouse their views, the presentation of these views on public radio serves a valuable function of alerting people to the fact of their existence. If you disagree with their goals, then you are armed with the knowledge necessary to combat them.

Since you do enjoy our news and musical presentations, I urge you to seriously reconsider supporting KSJR and KSJN. We do need your support. Thank you for writing.

Sincerely,
Michael W. Obler
Director of Broadcasting

KING HENRY

by PETE SEEGER

In the sixties, music became another medium for expressing dissatisfaction
with social conditions. No longer content with romantic ballads and love songs,
rock and folk singers have been attacking social ills ranging from racial
discrimination to pollution to materialism. The folk song below, which Pete
Seeger wrote in 1965, is an example of antiwar protest presented through the
medium of music. (The title refers to former president Lyndon Johnson.)

King Henry marched forth, a sword in his hand,
Two thousand horsemen all at his command;
In a fortnight the rivers ran red through the land,
The year fifteen hundred and twenty.

The year it is now much later, it seems,
It's easier far in the land of our dreams;
Just keep your mouth shut and don't hear the screams,
Ten thousand miles over the ocean.

Simon was drafted in 'sixty-three,
In 'sixty-four, sent over the sea;
Last month this letter he sent to me,
He said, "You won't like what I'm saying."

He said, "We've no friends here, not hardly a one,
We've got a few generals who just want our guns;
But it'll take more than them if we're ever to win,
Why, we'll have to flatten the country."

"It's my own troops I have to watch out for," he said,
"I sleep with a pistol right under my head;"
He wrote this last month, last week he was dead,
His body shipped home in a casket.

I mind my own business, I watch my TV,
Complain about taxes, but pay anyway;
In a civilized manner my forefathers betray,
Who long ago struggled for freedom.

But each day a new headline screams at my bluff,
On TV some general says we must be tough;
In my dreams I stare at this family I love,
All gutted and spattered with napalm.

King Henry marched forth, a sword in his hand,
Two thousand horsemen all at his command;
In a fortnight the rivers ran red through the land,
Ten thousand miles over the ocean.

Comics Go Relevant

Comic books, which were first regarded as "trashy" and then as "camp" (during the pop-art movement of the sixties), now seem to be getting some consideration as a respectable art medium. The formation of the Academy of Comic Book Artists in 1970 is evidence that the industry is beginning to take itself seriously. Comics have had to change their tactics to survive; in the 1950s they lost a dangerously high proportion of their audience to television, and comic-book editors began to question the premises on which they were operating. In 1961 Marvel comics came out with a new magazine, "The Fantastic Four," in which the heroes acted like real people rather than behaving woodenly and predictably in the tradition of such superheroes as Superman and Batman. In the 1970s the new type of comic-book hero was followed by a new type of comic-book plot. The hero's problems became more complex and his enemies less villainous; he was often faced with social issues such as discrimination, poverty, and even women's liberation, and third-world members began to appear more frequently in his environment. The two comic-book covers shown here illustrate the new direction comics have taken since the beginning of the decade.

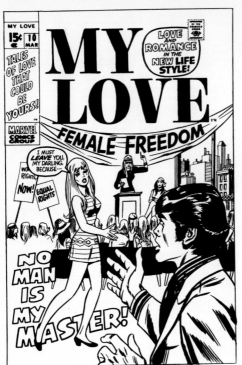

THE ENTERTAINERS

STUDY QUESTIONS

1. Do you agree with Desmond Smith that sex sells entertainment as well as products? Examine the use of sex as content in a variety of media entertainment offerings. Also examine its use as an advertising technique (that is, in a persuasive role).

2. John Corry seems to feel that the television industry's recent preoccupation with liberal concerns is frivolous. Why does he think this? What characteristics of entertainment shows and of television in general might hinder a serious treatment of relevant ideas?

3. Peter Herman Adler is concerned about television's failure to provide serious music. Should the television industry attempt to satisfy an interest held by a very small segment of its audience? What practical problems would be involved in the presentation of serious music on television? Consider the present musical offerings of the other media. Are there any good alternatives to commercial television?

4. Chris Hodenfield says the rock music of today was made by events since 1963. He also claims that rock music is responsible for styles in clothing and personal appearance. Does there seem to be a cause and effect relationship between world events and music? between music and cultural mores?

5. Henry S. Resnik, like Hodenfield, feels that rock music has had a tremendous impact on our culture. Resnik describes a new art form, the rock movie, which is basically a documentary (a filming of a real event rather than a fabricated one) and strongly emphasizes another medium, music. What value can you see in this type of multimedia composition?

6. What criticisms does Barton Midwood make of fiction which could just as easily apply to magazines, television, and films?

7. Paul Zimmerman says, "The best we can hope for from our films is that they will talk to us about how we can live decently. People are looking for a way of coming together, and perhaps movies can aid in this search . . . ." John Corry claimed that television fails when it tries to present relevant issues. Is television more limited than film in its capabilities in this direction?

8. David Dempsey says that the question is not whether there should be censorship of television, but how **much** censorship there should be. Why does it seem more acceptable to censor television than other media? Should any medium be censored today?

9. John Oliver Killens makes a charge of tokenism against the media's attempts to include minority groups. How visible are minority-group members in media entertainment? How honestly are they presented? Are they exploited? Can any fictional portrayal of a character be honest if it has not been conceived and presented by people who have personally experienced the life that is being portrayed?

BIBLIOGRAPHY FOR FURTHER STUDY

Agee, James. *Agee on Film: Reviews and Comments.* Boston: Beacon, 1964.

Alpert, Hollis. "The Film of Social Reality." *Saturday Review,* LII (September 6, 1969), 43–44.

Bluestone, George. *Novels into Film.* Berkeley: University of California, 1966.

Brown, Roger I. "Creative Process in the Popular Arts." *International Social Science Journal,* XX (1968), 613–24.

Burgheim, Richard. "Television Reviewing." *Harper's,* CCXXXIX (August, 1969), 98–101.

Cohen, Larry. "The New Audience: From Andy Hardy to Arlo Guthrie." *Saturday Review,* LII (December 27, 1969), 8–11, 36.

Crist, Judith. "Movies: Morals, Violence, Sex—Anything Goes." *The Private Eye, the Cowboy and the Very Naked Girl.* New York: Holt, Rinehart and Winston, 1967, pp. 262–71.

Dolan, Robert Emmett. *Music in Modern Media.* New York: G. Schirmer, 1967.

Ewen, David. *Great Men of American Popular Songs.* Englewood Cliffs, New Jersey: Prentice-Hall, 1970.

Houston, Penelope. *The Contemporary Cinema.* Baltimore: Penguin, 1968.

Huss, Roy and Norman Silverstein. *The Film Experience: Elements of Motion Picture Art.* New York: Harper & Row, 1966.

Jacobs, Lewis. *The Emergence of Film Art.* New York: Hopkinson and Blake, 1969.

Johnson, Nicholas. "Silent Screen." *TV Guide,* XVII (July 5, 1969), 6–13.

Kael, Pauline. "Trash, Art, and the Movies." *Harper's,* CCXXXVIII (February, 1969), 65–68, 73–83.

Karp, David. "TV Shows Are Not Supposed to Be Good." *The New York Times Magazine* (January 23, 1966), 6–7, 40, 42–43.

Kauffmann, Stanley. *Figures of Light.* New York: Harper & Row, 1971.

Koch, Stephen. "Fiction and Film: A Search for New Sources." *Saturday Review,* LII (December 27, 1969), 12–14, 38.

MacDonald, Dwight. *Dwight MacDonald on Movies.* Englewood Cliffs, New Jersey: Prentice-Hall, 1969.

Randall, Richard S. *Censorship of the Movies: The Social and Political Control of a Mass Medium.* Madison, Wisconsin: Wisconsin University, 1968.

Renan, Sheldon. *An Introduction to the American Underground Film.* New York: E. P. Dutton, 1967.

Ross, T. J. *Film and the Liberal Arts.* New York: Holt, Rinehart and Winston, 1970.

Salant, Richard S. "He Has Exercised His Right—to Be Wrong." *TV Guide,* XVII (September 20, 1969), 10–11 ff.

Stephenson, Ralph and J. R. Debrix. *The Cinema as Art.* Rev. ed. Baltimore: Penguin Books, 1969.

Wakefield, Dan. "New Styles of Storytelling." *Atlantic,* CCXXIV (November, 1969), 170–72.

Walker, Alexander. *Sex in the Movies.* Baltimore: Penguin Books, 1968.

THE PERSUADERS

Basic Research in Persuasion and Motivation: The Capability of Communications Media to Influence Opinions on New Issues

by JOSEPH T. KLAPPER

Joseph T. Klapper, Director of Social Research for the Columbia Broadcasting System, has studied mass communication for twenty years. The following is part of Klapper's testimony to the Subcommittee on International Organizations and Movements of the House Committee on Foreign Affairs on February 8, 1967. He discusses mass communication's tendency to reinforce already-held views and to create opinions on new issues, noting that people in developing countries are particularly susceptible to influence by the media.

.　　　.　　　.

I will devote myself for these few minutes to saying a few words about what research reveals about the effects of communication, particularly mass communication, here in the United States, and what this implies regarding the effects of mass communication in international persuasion. I would like to emphasize also that I am talking about effects on attitudes which are important to the individual; what I say cannot, therefore, be assumed to be true also of the effects of advertising, which is aimed at less basic attitudes.

Basic Research in Persuasion and Motivation: The Capability of Communications Media to Influence Opinions on New Issues. Testimony given at the Hearings before the Subcommittee on International Organizations and Movements of the Committee on Foreign Affairs, House of Representatives, 90th Congress (Washington, D.C.; U.S. Government Printing Office, 1967).

Here in the United States the effects of persuasive mass communication have been found to be in the main reinforcing. This is to say that mass communication seems in the main to buttress or reinforce the views already held by its audience. Rarely does it convert people from one point of view to another.

There are many factors which serve to produce this situation. In the first place, people tend to watch and listen to those mass communications which espouse views to which they are sympathetic and to avoid communications which preach opposing views. They remember material with which they are sympathetic better than they remember material with which they are unsympathetic. Other psychological factors, too complex to mention in these few minutes, are also at work.

People's social contacts, and the way they obtain information, also contribute to the tendency of mass communication to be reinforcive. For example, virtually all people belong to groups—family groups, peer groups, play groups, clubs, church groups, and the like. These groups are characterized by certain opinions, and are often the source, and also the guardian, of the individual's opinions. And these groups, through both formal and informal processes, serve to mediate the effects of mass communication on their members. For example, group discussion makes the member aware of communications with which both he and the group agree; the need for his being able to talk with the group prompts him to watch or listen to those communications; and if any communication threatens opinions which the group values, discussion among group members tends to find fault with and discount that communication. Thus groups are potent strainers in reference to mass communication, and they strain in such a way as to intensify the tendency of mass communication to serve as an agent of reinforcement.

This tendency of mass communication to reinforce is seen in many areas. In political campaigns, for example, people who are reinforced in their original vote intention have been found to outnumber those converted by about 10 to 1. Similar tendencies have been documented by research in reference to other important attitudes, and also in reference to less solemn modes of behavior.

Indeed, even conversion may be a kind of indirect reinforcement. We have noted in our research that in many cases of conversion, the convertee had become dissatisfied with his previous point of view before the communication converted him. He was already predisposed to some sort of change, and mass communication both reinforced that predisposition and pointed out a particular road of change. . . . I can give you many examples of this, if you desire them, and point out how the same factors that ordinarily make for reinforcement in these instances made for conversion.

But I have been talking up to now only about reinforcement or change of existing attitudes. There is another area in which mass communication is extremely effective, and that is in the creation of opinion on new issues.

By "new issues" I mean issues on which the individual has no opinion and on which his friends and fellow group members have no opinion. The reason for the effectiveness of mass communication in creating opinions on new issues is pretty obvious: The individual has no predisposition to defend, and so the communication falls, as it were, on defenseless soil. And once the opinion is created, then it is this new opinion which becomes easy to reinforce and hard to change. This process of opinion creation is strongest, by the way, when the person has no other source of information on the topic to use as a touchstone. He is therefore the more wholly dependent on the communication in question.

Now, what I have been saying is true in the United States and in Canada and in England and in other highly developed countries where mass communication reaches the masses and in sufficient variety for them to pick and choose which communications they will listen to and which they won't listen to. And I want to point out as my last point, that in many developing countries these conditions don't obtain in anything resembling the same degree. Where few people are literate, few can read the papers. Where there are few radios, few can hear them, and still fewer can choose what programs they want to hear. In such situations, mass communication reaches many individuals through intermediaries, that is, by word of mouth from those people who do have access to the media. These intermediaries therefore become particularly important in the communication process. Communication researchers call them gatekeepers or opinion leaders. . . .

Let me also point out, in closing, that in developing countries there is a far higher incidence of people who are unaware of various issues, who therefore have no opinions upon them, and who are thus, at least in theory, particularly susceptible to the influence of mass communication, whether from the media or through the intervening gatekeepers. In conclusion, then, the potential influence of mass communication in developing countries is vast, but the nature and limits of that potential must be clearly understood if the potential is to be realized.

.   .   .

AMERICAN NOTES

Mr. Nixon Meets the Language

by DAVID HALBERSTAM

Pulitzer Prize–winning reporter David Halberstam analyzes
the content and style of several speeches by Richard
Nixon, concluding that Nixon's language is "repressing
rather than expressing." The logical gaps and impreci-
sions pointed out by Halberstam are typical of those found
in the persuasive medium of political speech.

He has, of course, never been known for his rhetoric. It has always bor-
dered on the banal, a little spongy, a few interlocking clichés, not even
quite commonplace. Even in the golden days when he was the semi-hatchet
man of the Grand Old Party his phrases were curiously weak; perhaps he
cared too much about respectability, and good hatchet men must never
desire respectability. Now he is President, and we are informed of his minor
doings with infinite detail. Indeed, we are informed of his doings in inverse
proportion to their import, the smaller the action, the greater the detail on
how he accomplished it; the greater the import, the more scarce the information. When he writes a major speech we are with him, the long hours
at Montauk Point or San Clemente, scribbling on those large yellow pads,
casting aside draft after draft. We wait with bated breath for the final product, only, in its mediocrity, to wonder what the first drafts were like. One
speculated, reading his speeches, why there was so little feeling for the
country or for the language. We remembered that he came to us in his
political life not so much as a young man attached to causes, issues, ideas,

but propelled simply as a vintage product of an era, another good clean young American who wanted nothing more than to get ahead. Young men who want to get ahead are not likely to value language. Indeed, a sense of language might be interpreted as a weakness. Adlai Stevenson, after all, cared about language, and look where it got him.

Yet finally language, like style, is important as a reflection of what we are; it can be overemphasized, it is not an end in itself, and good style and a sense of rhetoric do not substitute entirely for toughness of mind and generosity of spirit. But they are in fact brief outer glimpses of the inner man, so little revealed in our public figures. Take, for instance, that basic staple of the Nixon diet, *Let me make one thing perfectly clear.* One associates this phrase somehow with the lawyers in the Perry Mason show. But what kind of a phrase is it for a President of the United States? Men who are sure of what they are saying, of the force and clarity of their language and their vision, do not need to say, Let me make one thing perfectly clear ("I would like to make perfectly clear that we are now testing whether that nation or any nation so conceived and so dedicated can long endure . . ."). Here I think one finds the most basic clue to the public Nixon, the essential falseness; he says he is being perfectly clear and he is not.

The second part of the basic Nixon diet is the Whittier Debating Society Exposition. Why are we in the Pacific? Well, first, the Pacific Ocean is a large body of water. Point one, point two, point three, point four. Again it is not particularly becoming to the President of the United States. In style it reeks of someone underestimating his audience, and in substance, or lack

"And now let me make one thing perfectly clear to you."

Drawing by Carl Rose; © 1971 The New Yorker Magazine, Inc.

of substance, of a man projecting a false clarity. The idea, of course, is that if he spells it out that carefully he is being candid, he is telling all, whereas more often than not the reverse is true. (The style reminds me of how *Time* and *Newsweek,* when doing cover stories and failing to penetrate their subjects with any real substance or insight, would give us the breakfast treatment, how many eggs, what style, how long they were cooked, how many strips of bacon, crisp or not. Thus if you are intimate with the subject at breakfast, you must be intimate period: the journalism of illusion.)

So there is a key to Nixon to be found in formal language: a certain falseness, more than likely involuntary, in that language which claims to bring frankness and clarity but which inevitably reflects a certain subterfuge and murkiness. It was not, after all, critics of the Administration who defined Nixonian language for us—Don't watch what we say, watch what we do— it was the Administration spokesmen themselves. If the slogan is *Bring us together,* the politics, slowly unfolding, the Cambodian War Games coming on the eve of the Yale Panther Rally, is to drive us apart, split the already shaky Democratic Party coalition on racial and class lines. If the speech talks about a just peace it will almost surely mean a longer war; if the President, as he did in April, congratulates Americans on how they have suffered and borne their burdens during this war, then the truth is that, except for a very few homes, this country has borne no burden at all, at least not in the sense that Mr. Nixon means. When it comes to placement of the burden, it has in fact been a particularly unfair war. If Mr. Nixon talks about sacrificing his political career and becoming a one-term President in order to destroy the base camps in Cambodia, it is a sure sign that by his political reckoning of what he feels the new political majority to be, he is not thinking of himself as a one-term President but indeed trying to set himself up as a two-term officeholder (yet the very raising and injecting of such considerations into a speech which is allegedly about a crisis in national security is the kind of unseemly and demeaning action one has come to expect with Nixon). If he talks as he did with the Pentagon secretaries about his war record and his fears when he was "there," then it is almost a sure thing that his war service was on the periphery of combat, for one cannot imagine anyone with a distinguished combat record needing to remind a faithful public of it at a time like that. If he talks as he did during the 1968 campaign of a "plan" to end the war, then it is a sure sign that there is no plan at all, but simply an excuse for a front-runner not to discuss an issue which plagues the country, since if he did tell how he felt, if his chauvinistic post-election speeches had been given during the campaign, it might well have cost him the election.

In formal speech there is a particular imprecision when he refers to history. At best it is something to be plucked off a page, hopefully in support of some point, and in general his sense of it is shady ("My fellow

Americans, we live in an age of anarchy, both abroad and at home. We see mindless attacks on all the great institutions[1] which have been created by free civilizations in the last five hundred years. Even here in the United States great universities are being systematically destroyed"). Worse, he seems to be surrounded by men who do not correct his mistakes and his imprecision. His November 3, 1969 speech abounded in factual mistakes (such as doubling the accepted number of refugees who came down from the North). It is Henry Kissinger's job to correct this sort of thing. Does Kissinger not know any better? Or worse, does he know better, but is just too weak in his relationship with the President to suggest corrections?

Or even worse? . . . The White House seems to be particularly weak on its facts about the 1954 period. In the April 30 [1970] Forward-to-Cambodia speech, we are fighting in order not "to expose them [the eighteen million freedom-loving South Vietnamese] to the same slaughter and savagery which the leaders of North Vietnam inflicted on hundreds of thousands of North Vietnamese who chose freedom when the Communists took over North Vietnam in 1954."[2] Did the North Vietnamese inflict slaughter and savagery on those who stayed behind, or those who opted—at American urging—to go south? Did they really slaughter those going south? Does this mean that in addition to the 800,000 who finally made it below the 17th parallel that hundreds of thousands of others were slaughtered on their way down the trails? Would Henry Kissinger of Harvard accept a sentence like that from a Harvard graduate student? Most assuredly not. Would Henry Kissinger of the White House accept a sentence like that from the President of the United States? Most assuredly he would, and has. Just two years ago, Henry Kissinger, the professor and aide to Nelson Rockefeller, used to give reporters devastating critiques of the many flaws of Richard Nixon. Is it Nixon who has changed, or Kissinger? And if it is Kissinger, why are the college students so restless?

Beyond the formal, there is of course the extemporaneous Nixon, most recently contrasting good Americans with bad Americans for the benefit of Pentagon secretaries:

You see these bums, you know, blowing up the campuses. Listen, the boys that are on the college campuses today are the luckiest people in the world, going to the greatest universities, and here they are burning up the books, storming around about this issue. You name it. Get rid of the war there will be another one.

Then out there we have the kids who are just doing their duty. They stand tall and they are proud. I am sure they are scared. I was when I was there. But when it really comes down to it, they

[1] He includes, one assumes, his own recent attacks upon the Senate of the United States and his party's attacks upon the Supreme Court.

[2] Department of Further Escalations: in his post–Kent State press conference, the number of Vietnamese who will be slaughtered if we leave precipitously has become "millions."

stand up and, boy, you have to talk to those men. They are going
to do fine and we have to stand in back of them.

The description is so imprecise that the poor *New York Times,* in trying
to present it the next day, had to refine for Nixon what he failed to do
himself; it did its own qualifying. Though the attack is a blanket one, the
Times headline read: "Nixon Puts 'Bums' Label On Some College Radicals," and the story itself claimed that Nixon had attacked *some* campus
radicals. Bums? If they are bombers actually destroying the universities
they are a good deal worse than bums. It seems above all, in this painful
turmoil, when a sense of language, of nuance, is so terribly important, a
singularly inappropriate word, revealing more of the viewpoint of the accuser than of the actions of the accused.

But it is his support of the troops which is even more extraordinary.
Were his motive genuinely that of wanting to praise the poor grunts in
Vietnam, even according to the prevailing mythology of heroism (a mythology to which the grunts themselves no longer subscribe), it would be a
motive worthy and deserving of worthy language. His words are somehow
so spiritually and intellectually bankrupt as to be virtually illiterate. Can
a man have the education Richard Nixon has, know the things he must
know, suffer the defeats he has suffered, run the political campaigns he
has run, read the books he is said to have read, and speak like that? Has
nothing rubbed off? (Feeling that he had to communicate with the youth,
he went one night to the Ellipse to talk to the young people. Where are you
from? he asked a young girl. Syracuse, she said. So of course he began to
talk about the Syracuse football team. Then he turned to the boy next to
her. Where was he from? California. Boy, he said, the surfing out
there . . .) Has something so terrible to the mental processes happened
that he has finally perfected the art of using language for repressing rather
than expressing? Should we be surprised, then, that when he hears of Kent
State, there is no sign of outrage, pain, or sadness?

Even Lyndon Johnson, who was not a reader of books (he was a reader
of memos, which is a form of non-language rather than language) and who
was extremely and falsely pious in formal speech, has a kind of primal
force and strength in his extemporaneous talks. We are told of the last
two Presidents that we must respect their decision in Asia because they
have more "facts" than we do. The decade has sadly proven that to be an
illusion; we are less isolated than they, and we are given less self-serving
information. Similarly, we are told about Nixon that we do not know the
real man, that the real man in small private conversation is intelligent,
forceful, even brilliant, but I think the judgment is finally that we poor un-
initiates on the outside know more about him than those so privileged as to
be on the inside. He is what we always thought he was.

Enticers, 1970; on TV,

WHO DO THEY THINK YOU ARE?

by STEPHANIE HARRINGTON

In this article from Vogue magazine, Stephanie Harrington sees our television commercials as enticing people to buy products through the exploitation of certain typically American fantasies and fears.

Television commercials may be many things to many people, but two things are obvious—they're an index to our anxieties and a boon to anthropology. What better crash course in the values, mores, fantasies—and particularly the fears—of Americans?

How do Americans feel about sex? Consult your network television commercial. Consider the teaser about "Lovestick," a lipstick "men can look at but they can't taste." Are we overly concerned with surface appearances? Just try adding up the amount of television time spent on pushing make-up, hair spray, perfume, hair tonic, hair rinses, fashions, foundations, and the other products under which we seem determined to bury any part of us that's more than skin deep—not to mention the skin itself. Are we obsessed with cleanliness? If you have any doubts, they'll be quickly drowned in the flood of suds spilling out of the commercials for detergents, floor cleaners, soap flakes, shampoos, bath soaps, facial soaps, baby soaps, scented soaps, unscented soaps, hypoallergenic soaps, deodorant soaps.

What's the state of our collective nerves? Evidently, bad enough to support the headache remedies, tension relievers, and sleeping pills that are a staple of television advertising. In fact, we seem positively to enjoy our headaches. After all, two of the funniest commercials ever broadcast have been for Alka Seltzer and Excedrin.

On the other hand, the absence of commercials for certain items offers

Enticers, 1970; on TV, Who Do They Think You Are? From *Vogue* (January 15, 1970). Reprinted by permission of Stephanie Harrington.

some indication of what does not particularly concern the mass of Americans. For instance, have you ever stopped to think why one of the few things not advertised on television is books?

But getting back to the question about sex. Just how do we see our attitude as it is bounced back to us through the television tube? Well, in addition to the look-but-don't-touch message, there is the gamesmanship pitch: "A woman can taunt you, tease you . . . should you give her another tactic? Should you give her Ambush [perfume] by Dana?" And, of course, the big television tease of all time was the Noxzema Shave Cream commercial with a sultry blond Swede whispering over her bare shoulder, "Take it off, take it all off." It's all in the double entendre.

On the other hand, there's the sado-masochism of the misogynous message from Silva Thins (cigarettes) in which beautiful women get pushed out of cars or into descending elevators by a slick-looking stud in shades. And then there's the straightforward conquest by virile male of passive female implied in the Black Belt After Shave and Cologne [ad]. In that one, a fine figure of a karate expert brings his hand down on a pile of boards or bricks or something equally resistant and, as filmed in slow motion, gracefully, effortlessly—lovingly?—slices right through it.

Sex, then, as projected by the American mind for the American mind (to persuade it to keep the American dollar in motion) is a game, a tease, a test of wiles versus brawn, of ego against ego. Or just plain conquest and submission.

If we can believe what our commercials tell us (and can all those psychologists, sociologists, market researchers, and pollsters be wrong?), the basic attraction that sets this *mano a mano* in motion is not the attraction of one human being for another, but of one product for another. It's really a case of Aqua Velva After Shave falling madly in love with Wind Song Perfume. "I can't seem to forget you," whispers the lithe, luscious man in the Wind Song (by Prince Matchabelli) commercial. "Your Wind Song stays on my mind." "There's something about an Aqua Velva man," croons the kittenish female in a pitch for "the after-shave girls can't forget." Love at first sniff. Indeed, Aqua Velva is presented not merely as the key ingredient of a man's surface charm, but as the definition of the man himself. Use it, advises the commercial, "to bring out the Aqua Velva man in you." Or, the essence is the essence. Essence of Aqua Velva, that is.

Of course, commercials indicate not only that there is a growing male market for cosmetics, but also that there is still considerable resistance among men to using sissy stuff like cologne and hair spray, for fear of calling their masculinity into question. The angst of this particular American dilemma is reflected in reassuring he-man commercials showing one rocky-looking male after another doing a real *man's* work—like running a pile driver or driving a truck—and telling you that he uses hair spray. And if hair spray is manly enough for a two-hundred-pound truck driver, it's manly enough, isn't it? This trans-sexual operation on the image of formerly women-only cosmetics involves christening the products with strong, virile names like Black Belt or Command. Command hair spray and Command Tahitian Lime anti-perspirant are "for men only," an aggressive male voice informs us, adding almost threateningly, *"And I mean for men only."*

The American romance with superficiality as documented in our commercials does, however, have occasional moments of deeper meaning. As in the ad for Alton Ames men's clothes, in which another of those Swedish sex kittens practically blows in our ears on the subject of her man's (their relationship is naughtily but safely ambiguous) Alton Ames suits, fondling them as she purrs. It's clear that it's the suit she loves, not the man. Indeed, she would probably love any man who put it on (even you, Mr. Average Television Viewer). But at least in this case the relationship is not between two products but between a person and a product.

Flesh-and-blood people lead very precarious lives on television commercials. They are in constant danger of being rubbed, scrubbed, slimmed, trimmed, and deodorized out of existence, leaving no traces. There are certainly no clues remaining in our clothes, which can be purified with detergents like Dash, which not only gets out easily removable "outside dirt," but tough "ground-in body dirt" as well.

Body dirt! Under the influence of the staggering number of soap commercials on television, we were so busy using detergents, pre-soaks, bleaches, and enzyme-active stain removers to get out soil, grease, paint, blood, grass stains, food stains, and goodness knows what else, that we might have forgotten all about body dirt, if Dash hadn't come along with its anti–body dirt ingredient. (And if your husband cleans a lot of fish, you might like to know that, according to another commercial, a fisherman's wife washed his apron in Procter and Gamble's Gain and lo! the "set-in, dried-in blood stains were virtually gone, gone!" Which is the next best thing to bloodless fish.)

"To Keep Our Dark, Physical Secrets"

Of course, if we would only be provident enough to use a good anti-perspirant in the first place, we wouldn't have to worry so much about something like body dirt. There are certainly enough preventive products to choose from. Like Dial Soap "with AT7" (it always helps to throw in some scientific-sounding ingredient like AT7). Or "ice-blue Secret." The name itself promises to keep our dark, physical secrets.

The amount of television time taken up by commercials for products that clean, deodorize, disguise, and sometimes almost threaten to dissolve our bodies and whatever touches them seems to indicate that there is something about bodies that makes us nervous. True descendants of our Puritan forebears, we spend an impressive amount of time and energy—and pass a lot of money over the counter—trying to deny the animal in us. It scares us. And the American mind, both fashioner and product of the consumer society par excellence, has developed the notion that our fears and insecurities, like everything else, can be bought off. After all, as long as we have them, we might as well make a profit.

Scared of sex? Buy Ambush and turn it into a game. Do you worry about being drab, uninteresting? Afraid that beneath your surface there's just more surface? Terrified that your body odour will make you a wallflower at the PTA or get you read out of the Rotary?

Afraid of being rejected by the opposite sex? Write to good ole Fran, paradigm of advice-to-the-wretched columnists. Sympathetic, motherly, solid. Fran knows best and Fran will tell you to buy Lavoris. Or, if you're a go-go type who hasn't the time to stop and gargle, chew Dentyne and, like the girl in the commercial, have "the freshest mouth in town." And, so the implication goes, like the girl in the commercial, look smashing in a bikini and get kissed by the dreamiest guy on the beach. So what if you have a mouth full of gum?

We seem to have convinced ourselves that there's no end to the relief that can be bought. Even political relief. When the kids complain about the System trying to co-opt the revolution, they know what they're talking about. When it became clear that youth was in revolt, that the black ghettos were organizing their own resistance, retaliation came with the Dodge Rebellion. If you can't lick 'em, join 'em. Join the Dodge Rebellion. Buy a Dodge. Feel like Che Guevara just driving to the country club.

Feel stranded on the far side of the generation gap? Relax. Buy a beer. A Ballantine. According to the commercial, the three-ring sign is "a happy sign" because "both the generations go for Ballantine." And to prove it, a neatly dressed young man, with hair just long enough to qualify as an under-thirty growth but not long enough to make anyone really nervous, is shown clinking glasses with someone definitely over thirty.

The ad men are even trying to buy off women's liberation by selling the resurgent female militants a cigarette: Virginia Slims. "You've come a long way, baby," says the commercial, as it traces the emancipation of the woman smoker who starts out sneaking a puff in the basement and ends up in a smashing sexy mod outfit, dangling a cigarette designed just for her.

The cigarette commercials in general have been rather subtle in their way. They seem to be selling fantasies. Smoke a Marlboro and be what you always wanted to be when you grew up—a cowboy. Or smoke a Salem and feel like you're in the country even when you're in the city. Smoke a Winston and find contentment by yourself in some secluded spot.

In Selling Fantasies, They, Too, are Buying Off a Fear

Fear of contaminated lungs. Of cancer. Of heart disease. For, you notice, almost all these fantasies take place in the great outdoors where the air is fresh and clean. Smoking, they seem to be saying—turning the threat into an asset—is good for you, as well as a way to find fun, romance, and *machismo*.

But two can play at the commercial game; and, ironically, some of the cleverest and most effective television advertisements now running are the anti-smoking commercials. And when it comes to working on a fear, they have the most obvious target. So until the cigarette commercials are finally off the air, the anti-commercials may provide a reasonably potent antidote.

There will always be other commercials to fill the breach. We start them young, after all. Probably the loudest, shrillest, densest concentration of commercials is to be found on children's programs, which hustle whole families of dolls and wardrobes of clothes to buy for them. There are miniature race tracks and garages and dozens of miniature cars to fill them with. There are miniature appliances, miniature pots, pans, dishes, plastic food to cook, dolls that crawl, walk, dance, clap, drink, grow teeth. Anything to make a little girl feel that the doll she has is passé and simply has to be replaced.

But with all this emphasis on spending money to buy a sense of security, one of the things we seem most insecure about is spending money. For one thing, we're afraid we'll be taken advantage of. Like the poor schnook in the Volvo commercial who can't even trade in his old car at the place where he bought it. After some quick calculations, the very salesman who sold him the car tells him its trade-in value is zero. Now he tells him. Taken again. (The point is, of course, that this doesn't happen with Volvos. They last.)

The fear of being conned, however, is secondary. The soothing commercials that comfort us with the assurance that we'll find a friend at Chase Manhattan or Irving at Irving Trust suggest that what we are really terrified about is that one day we may run out of money. And then how could we buy, buy, buy our anxieties away?

With worries like that, no wonder we get Excedrin headaches.

Visual Persuasion in the Media

The following advertisements demonstrate various persuasive appeals used in advertising. The first ads illustrate the methods advertisers use in attempting to reach minority and ethnic groups. The Greyhound Corporation's soft-sell ad, which appeared in Ebony magazine, emphasizes human rights. Of course, underlying the message is the hope that blacks will go Greyhound. The Milk Foundation's billboard makes a more direct verbal appeal for its product while visually suggesting the theme of integration.

Philip Morris, in advertising its Virginia Slims brand of cigarettes, uses two basic ad campaigns, both of which are aimed exclusively at a female audience. One campaign, illustrated by the first ad shown here, emphasizes the progress that women have made in achieving equal rights with men. The other campaign, illustrated by the second ad, is fashion-oriented and stresses the point that Virginia Slims are made "especially for women."

Finally, in 1970 the fashion industry made an all-out attempt to dictate fashion, as illustrated in the collage. For many months bibles of the fashion industry, such as Women's Wear Daily and Vogue, waged a sometimes not-so-subtle campaign to lower hemlines. They featured the "longuette" look on covers and front pages, playing up the midi length in an attempt to set fashion standards.

The Milk Foundation

"It is of no consequence of what parents a man is born, so he be a man of merit."

Horace (65-8 B.C.)

The common sense of this old quotation must be recognized. Why has it taken so long for so many?

The Greyhound Corporation 10 South Riverside Plaza Chicago, Illinois 60606

You've come a
long way, baby.

VIRGINIA SLIMS

VIRGINIA SLIMS.

Regular & Menthol: 18 mg."tar," 1.2 mg. nicotine av. per cigarette, FTC Report Nov.'70

Philip Morris

"The woman is neither sufficiently sensible nor sufficiently responsible to vote. Of politics and issues, she is, by nature, ignorant. Give a woman the right to vote and, by heavens, next thing you know, she'll want to smoke like a man." —Robt. D. Nolan

By heavens, Nolan was right. First, you got the vote, and now you've got a cigarette all your own.

Virginia Slims.

Slimmer than the fat cigarettes men smoke. They're tailored slim to fit your hands, your lips, your purse. And blended with the full, mild Virginia flavor women like. Extra long. Light one up. Regular or Menthol.

You've come a long way, baby.

Philip Morris

363

A Toddle Down "Sesame Street"

from EBONY MAGAZINE

**Television's ability to educate has been demonstrated by
Sesame Street, a program for preschoolers produced by
the Children's Television Workshop. This Ebony article
describes the theory behind the program—its goal of
educating disadvantaged children persuasively rather
than dogmatically, using techniques that young children
find truly entertaining.**

It is, as they say, a captive audience. Of the nation's nearly 12 million
preschoolers, virtually all of them watch television. Children of this group,
according to estimates, spend some 60 hours a week in front of the Tube.

So why, television reasoned, give them Cronkite?

Why not help them discover the world—using techniques common in
adult TV to enhance their receptiveness to knowledge and ideas?

This is the purpose of *Sesame Street*—a program, seen over 160 National Educational Television stations, designed to utilize what, in the
opinion of many, are the most crucial years in intellectual development—
those from three to five. The show's plaudits, in the first two months, have
been many. But none quite compares with those of the kids. Said a little
Cleveland girl, as a program came to an end: "Is that all? I hope there's
more."

Preschoolers, as any parent will tell you, have definite preferences concerning the Tube. A commercial is remembered with uncanny accuracy—
while a movie or a talk show may go unrecorded. A comedian is funny
when he trips on his shoelaces. But he will lay an egg if he tells a joke.

Intrigued by all this, probers launched a special study to determine what
children, in fact, do enjoy. These results were obtained:

Youngsters strangely are fond of commercials—the shorter, more zest-
fully animated the better. Puppets, too, will hold their attention, as will
animated cartoons and even star personalities. Comedy-wise, the rule is

A Toddle Down "Sesame Street": From *Ebony* (January, 1970). Reprinted by permission.

slapstick; while songs and games, to no one's surprise, are an ageless favorite with the nursery set.

Edified by this, Children's Television Workshop was then developed. Supported by a fund of $8 million (from the federal government and related agencies; plus the Ford, Carnegie and other foundations), the program was conceived, through National Educational Television, as an "open sesame" to the world of information.

Sesame Street, the first of its efforts, is, as a consequence, thoroughly researched. Says Joan Ganz Cooney, its executive director: "We weren't concerned with what we *thought* the kids should be watching. We wanted to find out what television programs they were in fact watching."

Hence the program's unusual format—a scientific study in the form of a commercial; a lesson in logic that is filled with laughs.

But for all their success, some staffers at least have been less than satisfied. Matt Robinson ("Gordon" on the show) believes the program's format may be too "diluted"—that in attempting to reach every American preschooler, it fails to attract a large number of them. "This aim to reach the disadvantaged child just won't be realized, I'm afraid. These kids need less fantasy and . . . more realism in black-oriented problems."

Yet a striking feature of *Sesame Street* is the "catholicity" of its setting and cast. Blacks and their culture are much in evidence on the show.

It is a circumstance which will benefit all, but particularly blacks in encouraging them to identify.

Says the Chicago *Daily News:* "One of the problems will be getting [them] to watch. *Sesame Street* could open doors . . . that have too long remained closed."

TV
The Greatest Educational Tool

by HUBERT H. HUMPHREY

In this syndicated column, which is itself a persuasive medium, former Vice President Hubert H. Humphrey discusses television's potential for educating and the need for governmental support of public television.

America was founded on a base of public education; and we now spend $60 billion a year on such education.

We have done little, however, to develop the most powerful educational tool yet created by man, television. Many children now learn more from television than from school.

During the most critical learning period—ages 3 to 5—the average child watches 25 hours of television per week. Television teaches these children, and the rest of us, but we need to ask ourselves what is being taught. Does television bring a balanced view of the world in which we live?

In our current system of commercial television, the networks can and do present some excellent public service programming, but such programs do not get the highest ratings, and each network understandably tries to put together a schedule of the highest-rated shows.

What sells best to a mass audience is entertainment and excitement—comedies, games, westerns, crime and spy stories. Even on news programs, things have to be kept moving fast, with conflict more important than a balanced view of the world.

TV: The Greatest Educational Tool: From *The Minneapolis Tribune* (May 16, 1970). Reprinted by permission of Hubert H. Humphrey.

Commercial networks are caught in a ratings rat race, and it means that the most important educational tool we have does not teach us enough about the real world. I think it is time to invest enough money in public television to take advantage of its full educational potential.

Four hours of network westerns per week matches all the programming money for all 190 public television stations.

Even on a starvation budget, public television has proved it can serve the people. Programs such as *Misterogers, The Advocates* and *Black Journal,* plus local programs on everything from how to find a job to coverage of city council meetings, have helped to educate and inform over half the TV viewers in America.

And then there is *Sesame Street,* an hour-long program of education and entertainment which reaches about 12 million pre-schoolers each morning. One of the few public TV programs adequately funded, it is without a doubt the best TV series ever shown for children. Children are learning from *Sesame Street.* They are learning, and not about a false world of escapism and conflict and violence.

We are far behind other countries in the development of public television. England and Japan both have two public TV networks that compete with commercial networks.

Both spend 100 times more on public television than we are prepared to spend in the next several years. Mexico is developing most of its secondary school system on a base of public television. On a recent visit to Mexico City, I observed the educational television programming—the preparation of materials and the reception of the program at the community level.

The government produces the television programs, furnishes workbooks, and trains monitors. Each community builds TV classrooms—many are built as a public service by business or by volunteers. The largest TV network in Mexico contributes five hours each day during the week and two hours on Saturday.

An entire generation of Mexican children is being educated with a very low public investment, and Mexico now is working with the international Latin American Communication and Education Agency, which is funded by UNESCO and by Latin American governments, to expand the program to other countries.

What public television we have in the United States is more the result of Ford Foundation grants than any investment by the federal government. It was not until 1967 that Congress created the Public Broadcasting Corp. It invested $5 million in public television [in 1969], and $15 million [in 1970].

The Nixon administration proposes interim financing of $22.5 million in 1970–71, $38 million in 1971–72, and $58.5 million in 1972–73; but it says it is not prepared to recommend any permanent system of financing public television. The Public Broadcasting Financing Acts of 1970 are still in House and Senate committees, and have yet to come to the floor for action.

A stronger, permanently funded system of public TV is overdue. It is time for Congress, the administration, the FCC and the Corporation for Public Broadcasting to work together and set a deadline for permanent financing. A small excise tax on new TV sets could bring in $60 million a year, or there could be a small tax on the receipts or profits of commercial television.

At a time when the basic assumptions of our society are being questioned, television can help us to understand and participate in an increasingly complex world. Television may turn out to be the most important social invention in the history of mankind. It is what we make of it.

RADICAL CHIC IS DEAD

by STEWART ALSOP

The following are two versions of a column by Stewart Alsop. Originally appearing in **Newsweek,** the column was later condensed for the **Reader's Digest.** The two versions are presented together to illustrate how changes in diction, style, and supporting detail can amount to a subtle form of persuasion.

FROM **Newsweek**

Something has happened that is hard to define precisely or to prove conclusively, but that is important all the same, politically and in other ways. What has happened is that radical chic suddenly isn't chic any more. Instead, it has become a bore, and because it has become a bore, it is dying.

Watch the faces at some more-or-less politically sophisticated gathering the next time the "rage and alienation" of "the kids" is mentioned. Is there not a certain glazing of the eyeballs? Or when Eldridge Cleaver, say, or the Black Panthers, or Dr. Timothy Leary, or the youth culture, or Ti-Grace Atkinson, or women's lib, or the Gay Liberation Front, or some other icon of radical chic is introduced. Is there not a faintly embarrassed haste to change the subject?

The fact is that radical chic—or the New Left, or call it what you will—was essentially a fad, and all fads die. This is the world's most faddish nation, but our fads die very suddenly. Mah-jongg, Joe McCarthy, flagpole sitting, the Hiss trial, Communist-baiting, dirty jokes about Eleanor Roosevelt—they were all fads, in their different ways, and they all occupied the obsessive attention of the nation. Then they became a bore, and they died, utterly, overnight.

Crossover

The reason seems to be that a sort of crossover point is reached with our fads. The promoters of the fads go from excess to greater excess, to hold the attention of the faddists, until appetite sickens on the surfeit, and so dies. When this crossover point is reached, the fad suddenly comes to seem a bit silly, or a little sickening, or very boring, or all three together.

Take the case of Dr. Timothy Leary, the original guru of the drug culture, who was once taken entirely seriously. He is now wandering woozily about North Africa, stoned to the eyeballs as always, and issuing such pronouncements as this:

"Resist lovingly . . . Resist spiritually, stay high . . . praise god . . . love life . . . blow the mechanical mind with Holy Acid . . . Arm yourselves and shoot to live . . . Life is never violent. To shoot a genocidal robot policeman in the defense of life is a sacred act."

The "literature" of radical chic is full of this sort of silly-sickening-boring stuff. For example, this syllogism from Chicago's "underground" paper, *Rising Up Angry:* "Kill a pig—satisfaction. Kill more pigs—more satisfaction. Kill all pigs—complete satisfaction."

This sort of thing has rather suddenly ceased to be chic, and its un-chicness is reflected in the liberal-intellectual press. The phrase "radical chic" first appeared in *New York* magazine, no reactionary journal, in a brilliantly funny piece by Tom Wolfe, describing Leonard Bernstein's famous party for the Black Panthers. The rapid decline of radical chic may have started with that article.

Infra Dig

More recently, *New York* has published a two-part series by Gail Sheehy on the Black Panther trial in New Haven. The Panthers emerge as more pathetic than heroic, and Sheehy points out that the appeal of the Panthers to many young Negroes lies in the fact that "those cats do more travelin' than rich folks do."

This is a far cry from the recent past, when the Panthers were so radically chic that Yale University was plastered with "Free the Panthers" signs, and president Brewster had announced that he was "appalled and ashamed" to discover that he was "skeptical of the ability of black revolutionaries to get a fair trial anywhere in the United States." In those days, in the academic community, it was considered hideously *infra dig* to mention a fact that seemed to leave no one appalled and ashamed—that, as Sheehy points out, a "whimpering, dull-witted black" had been subjected to prolonged torture, and then brutally murdered.

There is plenty of other evidence of the sudden unchicness of radical chic. For example, *The Wall Street Journal* thus summarizes the thrust of four recent lead articles in *Commentary,* the New York liberal-intellectual magazine: "This talk of political repression is nonsense. The Black Panthers are a menace. Women's liberation is silly . . . The New York *Review of Books,* chief intellectual organ of the New Left, is 'anti-American.' "

For another example, there was the recent witty article by John Corry in *Harper's,* reprinted in *The Washington Post*—neither being reactionary journals. Corry takes hard swipes at many targets—women's lib, *The Village Voice,* the fashionable radicalism of the ladies' fashion magazines. But his hardest swipes are reserved for the radical young—"stupefyingly dull when they are not being simply unpleasant"—and the Panthers. He makes the case that the Panthers, in their role of "furnishing entertainment for the white radicals" are simply "the natural sons of Stepin Fetchit."

SDS is already moribund, and it seems a good bet that, as radical chic becomes more and more obviously a bore, the Panthers and women's lib and the rest will fade away too. What has killed radical chic?

The elections, for one thing, in which the liberal Democrats scuttled toward the center to save their skins, defying the thunderbolts of *The Village Voice* and J. K. Galbraith. The winding down of the war, obviously. And perhaps also the winding down of the U.S. economy, which has had the sobering effect on the fashionably radical that the sight of the gallows is supposed to have on the condemned man. But above all there is the curious crossover process that makes all fads fade, by making them silly, or sickening, or boring.

Poor-Boying It

For wonderful silliness, consider the pants a good many of the revolutionary young now wear. To bestow on a pair of bell-bottomed blue jeans the correct poor-boy-Woodstock look, it used to be necessary to "tie-dye" them with Clorox, to make them look messy, and to unravel the bottom seams, to make them look ragged. It costs a bit more, of course, but the more affluent young revolutionaries can now buy their pants pre-tie-dyed and pre-raggedized.

These pre-poor-boyed pants—and much else besides—make it a little difficult to take the famous youth revolution quite so solemnly as it once was taken. It is now even possible to suggest, without being labeled a horrid old reactionary, that the revolution springs as much from an entirely natural desire not to get drafted or shot at as from a burning idealism. Now that radical chic is dying, it should also be possible for serious people to get on with the serious business of dealing with poverty, the war, the draft, discrimination against women and Negroes, and the other serious problems that the faddish posturings of radical chic have served to obscure.

FROM R eader's Digest

Something has happened that is hard to define precisely, or to prove conclusively, but that is important all the same. Suddenly, radical chic isn't chic any more.

Watch the faces the next time the "rage and alienation" of "the kids" is mentioned at some more or less "politically sophisticated" gathering. Or when the talk turns to Eldridge Cleaver, say, or the Black Panthers, or Dr. Timothy Leary, or the youth culture, or Ti-Grace Atkinson, or women's lib or the Gay Liberation Front. Is there not a certain glazing of the eyeballs?

The fact is that radical chic—call it the New Left, or what you will—was essentially a fad, and all fads die. They occupy the obsessive attention of the nation for a time. Then they become a bore, and they die, utterly, overnight.

Take the case of Dr. Timothy Leary, the original guru of the drug culture, who was once taken entirely seriously. He is now wandering about North Africa, issuing such pronouncements as: "Resist lovingly. . . . Resist spiritually, stay high. . . . Blow the mechanical mind with Holy Acid. . . . Arm yourselves and shoot to live. . . . To shoot a genocidal robot policeman in the defense of life is a sacred act."

It has all come to seem silly or sickening or boring, or all three together. And the literature of radical chic is full of such stuff. For example, this from Chicago's underground paper, *Rising Up Angry:* "Kill a pig—satisfaction. Kill more pigs—more satisfaction. Kill all pigs—complete satisfaction."

This sort of thing has suddenly ceased to be chic.

The phrase "radical chic" first appeared in *New York* magazine, no reactionary journal, in a brilliantly funny piece by Tom Wolfe, describing

Leonard Bernstein's famous party for the Black Panthers. The rapid decline of radical chic may have started with that article.

More recently, *New York* ran a series by Gail Sheehy on the Black Panther trial in New Haven, in which the Panthers emerge as more pathetic than heroic. Their appeal to many young Negroes, Sheehy says, lies in the fact that "those cats do more travelin' than rich folks do." This is a far cry from the recent past, when the Panthers were so radically chic that Yale University was plastered with FREE THE PANTHERS signs. In those days, in the academic community, it was considered tactless to mention that, as Sheehy points out, a "whimpering, dull-witted black" had been subjected to torture, then brutally murdered.

Consider also *The Wall Street Journal's* summary of the thrust of four recent lead articles in *Commentary,* a liberal-intellectual magazine: "This talk of political repression is nonsense. The Black Panthers are a menace. Women's liberation is silly. The New York *Review of Books,* chief intellectual organ of the New Left, is 'anti-American.' "

For other evidence, there was the recent witty article in *Harper's,* reprinted in the Washington *Post*—neither being reactionary journals—in which John Corry takes hard swipes at such targets as women's lib, *The Village Voice,* and the fashionable radicalism of ladies' fashion magazines. But his hardest swipes are reserved for the radical young—"stupefyingly dull when they are not being simply unpleasant"—and the Panthers. He makes the case that the Panthers, in their role of "furnishing entertainment for the white radicals," are simply "the natural sons of Stepin Fetchit."

SDS is already moribund. And it seems a good bet that the Panthers and women's lib and the rest will fade away too. What has killed radical chic?

The elections, for one thing, in which the liberal Democrats scuttled toward the center to save their skins. And the winding down of the war, obviously. But above all there is the curious process that makes all fads silly.

For wonderful silliness, consider the pants many of the revolutionary young now wear. To bestow on a pair of bell-bottomed blue jeans the correct poor-boy-Woodstock look, it used to be necessary to "tie-dye" them with Clorox and to unravel the bottom seams. It costs a bit more, of course, but the more affluent young revolutionaries can now buy their pants *pre*-tie-dyed and *pre*-raggedized. These pants—and much else besides—make it a little difficult to take the youth revolution quite so solemnly as it once was taken.

It is now even possible to suggest that the revolution springs as much from an entirely natural desire not to get drafted or shot at as from a burning idealism. Now it should also be possible to get on with the serious business of dealing with poverty, the war, the draft, discrimination against women and blacks, and the other serious problems that the faddish posturings of radical chic have served to obscure.

COSMO GOES

by LIZ SMITH

This review and the one which follows illustrate another form of persuasion: film criticism. These brief criticisms of **Five Easy Pieces,** a significant film of 1970, show how two reviewers attempted to influence their readers in their magazine columns. Liz Smith writes for **Cosmopolitan** magazine, which is aimed at career women, and Christopher Flinders writes for **Circus** magazine, which is aimed at rock fans. Thus they are addressing their reviews to very different segments of the movie-going public.

Five Easy Pieces is serendipitous—the kind of "little" film you stumble on, an absolute delight because it sticks with you even though you never expected anything from it. We get a chance to see Jack Nicholson of *Easy Rider* fame in a starring role where he displays much more than charm. For the very charm of this movie is its unstarriness, its reality, and its unusual story plus quality. The film juxtaposes far-apart worlds—handling the country-Western oil fields of the Southwest as deftly as it does the Chopin-dominated, sensitive Northwest retreat of some dedicated classical musicians. To which world does Jack belong? To both and yet to neither. We open with his corny bowling-alley–rowdy-drunk–motel–mobile-home phase. Jack is coping with his girl, a heart-of-gold waitress whose sex appetites, childish narcissism, and demanding pouts and love-talk get on his strung-out nerves. Little by little, we discover he isn't just another of those tough *machismo* males who like being mean to women, but a serious

From *Cosmo Goes to the Movies:* From *Cosmopolitan* (November, 1970). Reprinted by permission of Liz Smith.

TO THE

MOVIES

pianist who has deserted his art for "real" life and is in a consequent conflict. Here is a man searching, running, grabbing at life-styles, escaping, showing his heels. He is hunting and haunted. He goes to Washington (state) to see his ailing father, chubby, lovable sister, patronizing brother —all immersed in their Victorian and yellowing self-sufficient world of music. Next he tries to take away his brother's mistress-protégée; the waitress follows him. Worlds collide. The film is beautifully photographed and well-directed by Bob Rafelson. Karen Black will get attention for her "good old girl" waitress, though frankly all that teary ignorance in the picture got on my nerves almost as much as it did on Jack's. (I guess that's good acting, Karen.) I liked the brother's girl, Susan Anspach, who looks like a coltish young Betsy von Furstenberg and has a smolderingly intelligent sex appeal. There are funny slice-of-life inserts—two tough Women's Lib types hitchhiking to Alaska to escape pollution; the appealing Fannie Flagg as a gum-chewing Texan watching TV; the sister, Lois Smith, ruining her recording session by humming tonelessly over her keyboard. Nicholson himself is totally fascinating.

FROM *CIRCUS*

by CHRISTOPHER FLINDERS

Another story of the New American Road, *Five Easy Pieces* (Columbia), has drawn all sorts of comparisons with *Easy Rider,* and for good reason. It stars Jack Nicholson, and was produced by the same fellow, Bert Schneider, who obviously is developing quite an eye for films on contemporary Americana.

That is to say, not *America,* but Ameri*cana.* While *Pieces* is not a film about any particular year in the past twenty or the next ten, it is surely involved with the current emotional folkways and lifestyles of our country.

Nicholson uses many of the same fine talents which won him acclaim in *Easy Rider* in this, his first lead role. And while you are convinced that you are watching a completely new and distinct character, you can't help but think that he is at least *related* to the affable Southerner we met on our way to New Orleans with Peter Fonda.

This new character is Robert Eroica Dupea, a child prodigy pianist who has forsaken a musical career for a life on the road. We meet him in fine, dusty scenes as a worker in the oilfields of the South, but we quickly realize that he has probably been working in all sorts of odd jobs: the dishwasher, the handyman, the arm behind a jackhammer, the face beneath a hard hat on a thousand construction sites.

We live his life. Make love to the waitress with whom he lives. Go bowling with her. And spend a boy's night out with the girls. And work the grueling, repetitive, brawny life of a field hand.

But Dupea quickly becomes bored with this job, this lifestyle—as quickly as he must have decimated hundreds of previous ones. He heads for his family's ancestral home in Washington.

His family runs a veritable music colony on an island off the coast, and he finds them as stilted, overly-intellectual and as devoid of life as he did when he first left them.

MOVIE

REVIEWS

He visits them for a while, creating a marvelously satirical and flip scene as he seduces his brother's girlfriend, Katherine. There's a good squirmy scene when his waitress girlfriend is brought into the midst of his family's stodgy friends, and another, sublime and poignant, as he tries to communicate with his father, struck mute by a coronary.

In the end, Dupea leaves for a life where we will presumably find him climbing trees as a lumberjack, but once again free and unencumbered by a life where he will have to commit himself.

For *Five Easy Pieces* is more than a film about life on the road. It is a story of an enormously talented individual who is terrified of yielding or commiting himself to a person or a talent. His life is lonely because he has denied himself the openness to love anyone. His career is unfulfilled because he will not give himself nor his emotions to his music. As we see in the haunting scene where he plays for Katherine, he is excellent without feeling, but he fears how well he might do if he put himself into his gift.

In all, *Five Easy Pieces* explains a great deal about the people who, although quite talented, choose a life of drifting; and perhaps the film is more contemporary than ever, because it deals with the passivity of a talented, youthful segment of our society which is afraid to commit itself to classical quests for fulfillment.

The cast in the film is altogether excellent. Each role has been filled with a stunning precision. Karen Black is excellent as the waitress. Lois Smith is unforgettably pathetic as Dupea's sister, who *has* sacrificed herself to her art. And Susan Anspach as Katherine is superb as the frosty, dryly brilliant musician whose breeding and articulation has given him all the answers, and quite a few of the correct ones.

Five Easy Pieces is a richly evocative mood film. Not that much happens, but [it] remains an often wistful, always romantic look at the children of America, and how they are burning to give relevance and realization to their talents. A lively welcome is due to writer-director Bob Rafelson for this, his first venture as a true author of the cinema.

PERSUASION IN POLITICS

This mini–case study deals with an event that obviously involved persuasion: the 1968 presidential campaign. Roger E. Ailes and Joe McGinniss present different views of Richard Nixon's use of television during the campaign. The selections by Paul Sigmund and Murray Kempton, which offer the liberal different solutions to his election-day dilemma, illustrate the role of the political columnist. To conclude the mini–case study we have selected **Mad** magazine's "Guaranteed Effective All-Occasion Non-Slanderous Political Smear Speech," an example of persuasion by satire. This speech, written by Bill Garvin, does not specifically treat the 1968 campaign; it offers a humorous comment on the entire political process, criticizing the intelligence of the electorate as well as the ethics of the typical candidate.

HOW NIXON CHANGED
HIS TV IMAGE

INTERVIEW with ROGER E. AILES,
PRESIDENT'S TV ADVISER

.　　.　　.

Question　What was your role in the 1968 campaign?

Answer　I came in as a general television adviser and then I took over as executive producer and eventually director of the television programs for Richard Nixon. We knew that Mr. Nixon liked the question-and-answer format and that he was not afraid of going on live television. I set the style for the "Man in the Arena" programs in which the candidate faced panels of questioners—at least half of whom were not pro-Nixon.

It seemed to me that any man who could go out and face such panels and field questions on live television would demonstrate a certain amount of ability to stand up under pressure.

Question　You are aware, of course, of contentions that Mr. Nixon was "packaged and sold" in the 1968 campaign. Do you think he was?

Answer　No. Certain columnists and others argue that because there are advertising people involved in a presidential campaign, the candidates are "packaged" much like a box of soap. That's what they are trying to plant in the public's mind. Frankly, that is the only reason that I decided to speak out on this subject. I think it's wrong to create doubt or confusion about our leadership in this country by insinuating that somehow some mysterious men on Madison Avenue or somewhere are controlling or influencing candidates—selling the public a bill of goods, so to speak. I think the public should know what a TV producer can and, more importantly, cannot do in politics.

How Nixon Changed His TV Image: From a copyrighted interview in *U.S. News and World Report* (February 2, 1970).

Question   What is it, exactly, that you and other television experts can do for Mr. Nixon or any other political figure?

Answer   First of all, we tend to approach it in a way that may seem more negative than positive. A man who has reached a mature age—has been elected to office—has already set a style for himself. To try to change that style, I think, would cause confusion and make him insecure.

But if there is something in his performance—and I use the term "performance" to describe a speaker on a platform or in an interview situation on camera—that is annoying or detracting, we can eliminate it.

Question   For example?

Answer   For example, a man may clear his throat at the end of every sentence and not even be aware of it. Or perhaps he has a hissing "s" sound in his speech. Or he does not have particularly good eye contact with the camera.

So you can eliminate certain negative qualities that you know will be magnified by television. Television is like an X-ray. I contend that it's neutral, that it photographs what is there. The camera does not lie.

Question   What is the President's attitude about going before millions of people on television? Is he a little apprehensive?

Answer   I think he is mildly apprehensive, as we all are, but I don't think he's frightened of it at all. He does his homework very well. He knows the facts and he is prepared for emergencies. He's very cool and very withdrawn just before going on camera.

From a producer's standpoint, I have found that the President's reaction is good. If anyone were to appear on a television show I was producing or in some way involved in, and he was not nervous, then I would be terribly nervous. As long as he is slightly nervous, I'm pretty comfortable, because I know his responses will be natural.

Question   Does the President have any particular problem with television that you have to keep reminding him about?

Answer   No, I don't think that he has. There have been suggestions that when he ad-libs he perhaps uses phrases rather repetitiously.

Question   Commentators have talked about his habit of saying, "Let me make one thing perfectly clear"—

Answer   I've put that in a memo.

Question   But you haven't been able to stop him?

Answer   No, and, frankly, I haven't pressed it very hard, because I don't think it's worth it—to start him worrying about one phrase and perhaps blowing something else he might say.

I don't think it's that negative. It has become a characteristic now that people interpret, I think, pretty neutrally. Some may joke about it; many don't even notice it. It doesn't reflect on his ability to get his message across. So I don't think it's important.

Question   The President seems to handle himself well in ad-lib appearances, such as news conferences. Why, then, does he read his speeches?

Answer   There are just too many facts in speeches that can't be ad-libbed. In a news conference, an answer may take a maximum of three minutes. A speech may be a minimum of 25 minutes and he has to cover many specific points—names, dates, places, figures that would be impossible to remember.

Question   What is the advantage to Mr. Nixon in reading from a text on a desk in front of him, compared with Mr. Johnson's use of a TelePrompTer?

Answer   Purely and simply personal comfort. I believe very strongly that you should use whatever makes you comfortable. Anyone in television knows that if you are not comfortable with a TelePrompTer, you shouldn't use it.

Question   Does Mr. Nixon use the TelePrompTer at all?

Answer   Mr. Nixon does not use the TelePrompTer. There are a couple of reasons. One is, I think, that the fewer mechanical things there are around to be concerned with, the happier he is. The second reason is that the Tele-PrompTer can be used well only if its use is rehearsed. And Mr. Nixon does not rehearse.

It was my understanding that Mr. Johnson did set up cameras, rehearse before them, tape his rehearsals and play back the tapes before he went on the air, so he could correct whatever he thought might need correction. Mr. Nixon doesn't do that. He doesn't look at himself on monitors when he is on camera. He doesn't, to my knowledge, even watch playbacks of his appearances on TV.

Question   Why not? That would seem to be a good way for him to spot any errors and polish his style—

Answer   I think it's a point in his favor that he's not concerned about style particularly. I remember one time when we were traveling and I suggested that he might want to view a playback of a speech he had made.

"Well, look," he said. "We've done that speech. I've said what I had to say. Let's worry about tomorrow."

And I think that is pretty much his thinking about it.

Question   It has been suggested that President Nixon, at least in the past, looked on television as a form of "gimmickry" that he didn't like. Does he feel that way?

Answer   When I first talked with him, I was producing a major national entertainment show. He was in my office, about to go on the program, and we were talking. Mr. Nixon very offhandedly said something to this effect: "Well, I guess a man has to rely on a gimmick to get elected." I think he said it humorously, putting me on because I was a television producer.

I got a little angry about it, and I told him: "I'm sorry, sir, but I disagree with you. Television is certainly not a gimmick. It's here to stay, a major means of communication, instant sight and sound around the world, and you should understand how to use it, how to appear on it and how to be comfortable with it, because it's part of our life."

Mr. Nixon stopped for a minute and looked at me. I thought maybe I'd lost him. But he shut his briefcase and said, "Explain that to me." For the better part of the next hour he asked me questions about television. I gave him my opinions. He thanked me and went on the program.

A couple of days later I got a call from one of his people, who asked me about working with them in the campaign and said that Mr. Nixon had found it interesting to talk with me about television.

Question   Does Mr. Nixon still have much to learn about television?

Answer   No, I don't think he has much to learn. I think he knows as much as he needs to know, which is how to be comfortable on it—what he can do, what he can't do, what he does well and what he doesn't do so well.

.   .   .

Question   What importance do you attach to the role of television in politics in the future, from the Presidency to the office of mayor?

Answer   I don't think any man will be elected to major office again—including mayors of large cities—without going on television to do it. And therefore, it seems to me, television will play a critical role in the future of politics and the future of our lives, really.

Question   Do you believe that TV experts can create misleadingly favorable images of politicians, who, in reality, might lack qualifications for high office?

Answer   No, in general. No—not in a free society. Television doesn't have that much control. The candidate must stand on his own feet, do his own homework, face grilling in question-and-answer format, make clear his grasp of the issues. Even if we tried to make something out of nothing, we couldn't get away with it. If a man is a phony, he will come through on TV as a phony.

I think that one of the things that have to be understood about what we do in political television is that we try to approach reality. The closer we can get to achieving reality, the better job we've done, in my opinion.

Question   What about men without access to big bankrolls? Doesn't the importance of television add enormously to the costs of running for public office?

Answer   Yes, it does. Some measures are being brought into effect to correct this, including cutbacks by many stations on rates for political telecasts, expanded news coverage during campaigns, the institution of National Educational Television, and so on. But at the present moment, it's terribly expensive —and perhaps too expensive.

from

The Selling of the President 1968

by JOE McGINNISS

One of the valuable things about this idea [the idea of having television programs in which Nixon appears "live" before regional audiences and answers questions put to him by a panel], from a political standpoint, was that each show would be seen only by the people who lived in that particular state or region. This meant it made no difference if Nixon's statements —for they were not really answers—were exactly the same, phrase for phrase, gesture for gesture, from state to state. Only the press would be bored and the press had been written off already. So Nixon could get through the campaign with a dozen or so carefully worded responses that would cover all the problems of America in 1968.

And, to carry it one step sideways, it made no difference either if the answer varied—in nuance—from state to state. No one, unless he traveled a lot, would hear any statement but the one designed for him. So, a question about law and order might evoke one response in New England and a slightly different one in the South. Nothing big enough to make headlines, just a subtle twist of inflection, or the presence or absence of a frown or gesture as a certain phrase was spoken. This was what the new politics was to Frank Shakespeare. And he did all he could to make sure Richard Nixon's definition would be the same.

Roger Ailes, the executive producer of the Mike Douglas Show, was hired to produce the one-hour programs. Ailes was twenty-eight years old. He had started as a prop boy on the Douglas show in 1965 and was running it within three years. He was good. When he left, Douglas' ratings collapsed. But not everyone he passed on his way up remained his friend. Not even Douglas.

Richard Nixon had been a guest on the show in the fall of 1967. While waiting to go on, he fell into conversation with Roger Ailes.

"It's a shame a man has to use gimmicks like this to get elected," Nixon said.

"Television is not a gimmick," Ailes said.

Richard Nixon liked that kind of thinking. He told Len Garment to hire the man.

Ailes had been sent to Chicago three days before Nixon opened the fall campaign. His instructions were to select a panel of questioners and design a set. But now, on the day of the program, only six hours, in fact, before it was to begin, Ailes was having problems.

"Those stupid bastards on the set designing crew put turquoise curtains in the background. Nixon wouldn't look right unless he was carrying a pocketbook." Ailes ordered the curtains removed and three plain, almost stark wooden panels to replace them. "The wood has clean, solid, masculine lines," he said.

His biggest problem was with the panel. Shakespeare, Treleaven and Garment had felt it essential to have a "balanced" group. First, this meant a Negro. One Negro. Not two. Two would be offensive to whites, perhaps to Negroes as well. Two would be trying too hard. One was necessary and safe. Fourteen percent of the population applied to a six- or seven-member panel, equaled one. Texas would be tricky, though. Do you have a Negro *and* a Mexican-American, or if not, then which?

Besides the Negro, the panel for the first show included a Jewish attorney, the president of a Polish-Hungarian group, a suburban housewife, a businessman, a representative of the white lower middle class, and, for authenticity, two newsmen: one from Chicago, one from Moline.

That was all right, Roger Ailes said. But then someone had called from New York and insisted that he add a farmer. A farmer, for Christ's sake. Roger Ailes had been born in Ohio, but even so he knew you did not want a farmer on a television show. All they did was ask complicated questions

"In answer to that question—and here I speak off the
cuff without notes or teleprompters, and with
the minimum of makeup . . ."

about things like parities, which nobody else understood or cared about. Including Richard Nixon. He would appoint a secretary of agriculture when he won, yes, but why did he have to talk to farmers on live television in the campaign?

Besides, the farmer brought the panel size to eight, which Ailes said was too big. It would be impossible for Nixon to establish interpersonal relationships with eight different people in one hour. And interpersonal relationships were the key to success.

"This is the trouble with all these political people horning in," Ailes said. "Fine, they all get their lousy little groups represented but we wind up with a horseshit show."

There was to be a studio audience—three hundred people—recruited by the local Republican organization. Just enough Negroes so the press could not write "all-white" stories but not enough so it would look like a ballpark. The audience, of course, would applaud every answer Richard Nixon gave, boosting his confidence and giving the impression to a viewer that Nixon certainly did have charisma, and whatever other qualities he wanted his President to have.

Treleaven and his assistant, Al Scott, came to the studio late in the afternoon. They were getting nervous. "Nixon's throat is scratchy," Treleaven said, "and that's making him upset." Al Scott did not like the lighting in the studio.

"The lights are too high," he said. "They'll show the bags under R.N.'s eyes."

Then there was a crisis about whether the press should be allowed in the studio during the show. Shakespeare had given an order that they be kept out. Now they were complaining to Herb Klein, the press relations man, that if three hundred shills could be bussed in to cheer, a pool of two or three reporters could be allowed to sit in the stands.

Shakespeare still said no. No *newspapermen* were going to interfere with his TV show. Klein kept arguing, saying that if this was how it was going to start, on the very first day of the campaign, it was going to be 1960 again within a week.

Treleaven and Ailes went upstairs, to the WBBM cafeteria, and drank vending machine coffee from paper cups.

"I agree with Frank," Ailes said. "Fuck 'em. It's not a press conference."

"But if you let the audience in . . ."

"Doesn't matter. The audience is part of the show. And that's the whole point. It's a television show. Our television show. And the press has no business on the set. And goddammit, Harry, the problem is that this is an electronic election. The first there's ever been. TV has the power now. Some of the guys get arrogant and rub the reporters' faces in it and then the reporters get pissed and go out of their way to rap anything they consider staged for TV. And you know damn well that's what they'd do if they saw this from the studio. You let them in with the regular audience and they see the warmup. They see Jack Rourke out there telling the audience to applaud and to mob Nixon at the end, and that's all they'd write about. You know damn well it is." Jack Rourke was Roger Ailes's assistant.

"I'm still afraid we'll create a big incident if we lock them out entirely," Treleaven said. "I'm going to call Frank and suggest he reconsider."

But Shakespeare would not. He arranged for monitors in an adjacent studio and said the press could watch from there, seeing no more, no less, than what they would see from any living room in Illinois.

It was five o'clock now; the show was to start at nine. Ray Voege, the makeup man, borrowed from the Johnny Carson Show, had arrived.

"Oh, Ray," Roger Ailes said, "with Wilkinson, watch that perspiration problem on the top of his forehead."

"Yes, he went a little red in Portland," Ray Voege said.

"And when he's off camera, I'd give him a treated towel, just like Mr. Nixon uses."

"Right."

Ailes turned to Jack Rourke, the assistant. "Also, I'd like to have Wilkinson in the room with Nixon before the show to kibitz around, get Nixon loose."

"Okay, I'll bring him in."

Then Treleaven and Scott went back to the Sheraton Hotel for dinner. Ailes stayed in the studio to rehearse the opening with the cameramen one more time. There was nothing he could do about what Nixon would say or would not say, but he did not want anyone turning off before the hour was over because the program was dull to watch.

The set, now that it was finished, was impressive. There was a round blue-carpeted platform, six feet in diameter and eight inches high. Richard Nixon would stand on this and face the panel, which would be seated in a semicircle around him. Bleachers for the audience ranged out behind the panel chairs. Later, Roger Ailes would think to call the whole effect "the arena concept" and bill Nixon as "the man in the arena." He got this from a Theodore Roosevelt quote which hung, framed, from a wall of his office in Philadelphia. It said something about how one man in the arena was worth ten, or a hundred, or a thousand carping critics.

At nine o'clock, Central Daylight Time, Richard Nixon, freshly powdered, left his dressing room, walked down a corridor deserted save for secret service, and went through a carefully guarded doorway that opened onto the rear of the set.

Harry Treleaven had selected tape from WBBM's coverage of the noon-time motorcade for the opening of the show. Tape that showed Richard Nixon riding, arms outstretched, beaming, atop an open car. Hundreds of thousands of citizens, some who had come on their own, some who had been recruited by Republican organizations, cheered, waved balloons, and tossed confetti in the air. One week before, at the Democratic convention, it had been Humphrey, blood, and tear gas. Today it was Nixon, the unifying hero, the man to heal all wounds. No disorder in his crowds, just dignified Republican enthusiasm, heightened a notch or two by knowledge of the inevitable comparisons between this event and those of the previous week. If the whole world had been watching then, at least a fair portion would see this on the network news. Chicago Republicans showed a warm, assured, united front. And Harry Treleaven picked only the most magical of moments for the opening of his show.

Then the director hit a button and Bud Wilkinson appeared on the screen. And what a placid, composed, substantial, reassuring figure he was: introducing his close personal friend, a man whose intelligence and judgment had won the respect of the world's leaders and the admiration of millions of his countrymen, this very same man who had been seen entering Jerusalem moments ago on tape: Richard Nixon.

And the carefully cued audience (for Jack Rourke, the warmup man, had done his job well) stood to render an ovation. Richard Nixon, grinning, waving, *thrusting,* walked to the blue riser to receive the tribute.

It was warmly given. Genuine. For Nixon suddenly represented a true alternative: peace, prosperity, an end to discord, a return to the stable values that had come under such rude and unwarranted attack. Nixon was fortification, reaffirmation of much that needed to be reaffirmed. They needed him now, these Republicans, much more than they had in 1960. Then they were smug; and they did not especially like him. They toyed with him, as a small boy would poke a frog with a stick. They made him suffer needlessly, and, in the end, their apathy had dragged a nation down. Now, on this night, this first night of his campaign to restore decency and honor to American life, they wanted to let him know they cared. To let him know 1960 would not happen again.

He looked toward his wife; the two daughters; Ed Brooke, the most useful Negro he had found; Charles Percy, the organization man; and Thruston Morton, resigned if not enthusiastic. They sat in the first row together.

Then, eagerly, forcefully, strong, confident, alive, he turned toward the panel to begin.

He was alone, with not even a chair on the platform for company; ready to face, if not the nation, at least Illinois. To communicate, man to man, eye to eye, with that mass of the ordinary whose concerns he so deeply shared; whose values were so totally his own. All the subliminal effects sank in. Nixon stood alone, ringed by forces which, if not hostile, were at least—to the viewer—unpredictable.

There was a rush of sympathy; a desire—a need, even—to root. Richard Nixon was suddenly human: facing a new and dangerous situation, alone, armed only with his wits. In image terms, he had won before he began. All the old concepts had been destroyed. He had achieved a new level of communication.

.   .   .

THE CASE FOR

by PAUL E. SIGMUND

.　　.　　.

It is argued that it is necessary to punish the Democratic Party for its past sins by assuring its defeat in 1968 so that a new liberalized reform party may come back to power in 1972. This assumes of course that there is or will be a liberal majority which will opt for change in four years, which is not at all certain. In fact the lesson that is likely to be drawn from a Nixon victory will be the need to move the party further to the right to win future elections.

It also assumes that the Democrats will not follow the time-honored custom of opposition parties in America and break down into a number of squabbling factions. To argue that they are more likely to follow the example of the Republicans after 1964 and emerge stronger and more united after a cataclysmic defeat is to ignore the fact that the new-found Republican strength emerged from precisely the opposite starting point. The Republicans derive their present strength from emphasizing party unity as the highest value and ignoring ideological differences. The dissident Democrats by contrast wish to refashion the party along ideological lines similar to those which were the very reason for the Republican debacle in 1964. Has everyone forgotten "a choice, not an echo"?

Finally, the war. The evidence at the moment points clearly in the direction of another bombing halt and renewed efforts at a political settle-

The Case for Humphrey: From *Commonweal* (November 1, 1968). Reprinted by permission.

HUMPHREY

ment if Humphrey is elected. He has said so on television and if that promise was qualified so as to prevent the North Vietnamese from exploiting his position in Paris, does this make Humphrey a warmonger or a Johnson puppet, as the press has implied? It is significant that two of those who are best known for their disagreement with Johnson on the bombing issue, Arthur Goldberg and George Ball, are actively campaigning for Humphrey. If the opponents of the war are concerned with saving lives and ending hostilities, they will vote for the candidate who is most likely by instinct, experience, ideology, and associations to end it as quickly as possible. Now that the Nixon secret plan for ending the war has been revealed to be a fiction, and his only new approach appears to rely on a nuclear threat, it should be clearer than ever that there is a certain lack of proportion in punishing the Democrats by destroying the country, if not the world.

Politics is the art of the possible. It is not possible this year to vote for Eugene McCarthy despite his TV sex appeal and his position on the war. He was opposed by the Party professionals as much for his too-casual personality and eighteenth-century conception of the presidency as for his independence and opposition to Lyndon Johnson. It is not possible to vote for Ted Kennedy this year. A vote for Nixon or an abstention will not secure Kennedy the nomination in 1972, and could bring the country to disaster well before that date. It *is* possible to vote for a man who has shown his openness to change, breadth of interest, and capacity for imaginative and creative response to the needs of the country. That man is Hubert Humphrey.

AN HONORABLE CHOICE

by MURRAY KEMPTON

.   .   .

It is often said that if you do not vote for one candidate you may be responsible for the election of another. Why is it never said that when you vote for a candidate you may be responsible for his election, which can be a heavy burden on the conscience? There must be millions of Americans who are ashamed of having voted for President Johnson; is there anyone who can tell a voter that, if he votes for the Vice President, he will not again be ashamed?

What was most interesting about Mr. Humphrey's Vietnam speech was not so much the desperation of its attempt to suggest by grimace that he had differences with the President, but his warning us that Mr. Nixon will get us in a wider war in just the same tones as the President used in warning us against Senator Goldwater four years ago. That dreadful reminder is what this election is about; we could trust President Johnson talking about Senator Goldwater, but we could not trust him talking about himself. We have lost all pride and common sense if we trust Hubert Humphrey talking about himself now.

An Honorable Choice: From *The New Republic* (November 2, 1968). Reprinted by Permission of THE NEW REPUBLIC, © 1968, Harrison-Blaine of New Jersey, Inc.

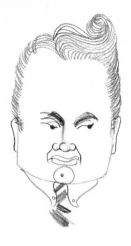 

Humphrey, Nixon and Wallace seem, each in different degrees, to have made the calculation that America has turned fearful and repressive. I don't think this is true; the people are confused, certainly, but I don't think them malignant. They are confused for two primary reasons: (1) our history has been made for five years by the consequences of political assassination, and (2) the institutions which are supposed to represent us are either decayed or distorted. The wonder is that the public temper is not more malignant than it is.

Still this nation's preservation and recovery depend now on those persons who stood up against Mr. Johnson in the Democratic primaries and at the convention. These people have a great charge; upon them rests the future of whatever resistance is raised against 'President Johnson's successor. The politics of revenge should have no place in considerations of how that tedious effort is to be conducted. Our part is not to punish the Vice President for what he has done; it is rather to reward those men who have refused to do the same thing, and to do our best for O'Dwyer and Allard Lowenstein in New York, for Governor Hughes in Iowa, for James Gilligan in Ohio and for countless others. The politics of conscience will have to be fought for. We must struggle for every candidate who fought against this time when there is nothing to vote for at the top of the line; that alone gives us a chance for another time when there will be a face there again.

Guaranteed Effective All-Occasion
Non-Slanderous Political Smear Speech

by BILL GARVIN

My fellow citizens, it is an honor and a pleasure to be here today. My opponent has openly admitted he feels an affinity toward your city, but I happen to **like** this area. It might be a salubrious place to him, but to me it is one of the nation's most delightful garden spots.

When I embarked upon this political campaign I hoped that it could be conducted on a high level and that my opponent would be willing to stick to the issues. Unfortunately, he has decided to be tractable instead—to indulge in unequivocal language, to eschew the use of outright lies in his speeches, and even to make repeated veracious statements about me.

At first I tried to ignore these scrupulous, unvarnished fidelities. Now I will do so no longer. **If my opponent wants a fight, he's going to get one!**

It might be instructive to start with his background. My friends, have you ever accidentally dislodged a rock on the ground and seen what was underneath? Well, exploring my opponent's background is dissimilar. All the slime and filth and corruption you can possibly imagine, even in your wildest dreams, are glaringly nonexistent in this man's life. And even during his childhood!

Let us take a very quick look at that childhood: It is a known fact that, on a number of occasions, he emulated older boys at a certain playground. It is also known that his parents not only permitted him to masticate excessively in their presence, but even urged him to do so. Most explicable of all, this man who poses as a paragon of virtue exacerbated his own sister when they were both teenagers!

I ask you, my fellow Americans: is this the kind of person we want in public office to set an example for our youth?

Of course, it's not surprising that he should have such a typically pristine background—no, not when you consider the other members of his family:

His female relatives put on a constant pose of purity and innocence, and claim they are inscrutable, yet every one of them has taken part in hortatory activities.

The men in the family are likewise completely amenable to moral suasion. My opponent's second cousin is a Mormon.

His uncle was a flagrant heterosexual.

His sister, who has always been obsessed by sects, once worked as a proselyte outside a church.

His father was secretly chagrined at least a dozen times by matters of a pecuniary nature.

His youngest brother wrote an essay extolling the virtues of being a homo sapiens.

His great-aunt expired from a degenerative disease.

His nephew subscribes to a phonographic magazine.

His wife was a thespian before their marriage and even performed the act in front of paying customers.

And his own mother had to resign from a woman's organization in her later years because she was an admitted sexagenarian.

Now what shall we say of the man himself?

I can tell you in solemn truth that he is the very antithesis of political radicalism, economic irresponsibility and personal depravity. His own record **proves** that he has frequently discountenanced treasonable, un-American philosophies and has perpetrated many overt acts as well.

He perambulated his infant son on the street.

He practiced nepotism with his uncle and first cousin.

He attempted to interest a 13-year-old girl in philately.

He participated in a seance at a private residence where, among other odd goings-on, there was incense.

He has declared himself in favor of more homogeneity on college campuses.

He has advocated social intercourse in mixed company—and has taken part in such gatherings himself.

He has been deliberately averse to crime in our streets.

He has urged our Protestant and Jewish citizens to develop more catholic tastes.

Last summer he committed a piscatorial act on a boat that was flying the American flag.

Finally, at a time when we must be on our guard against all foreign isms, he has coolly announced his belief in altruism—and his fervent hope that some day this entire nation will be altruistic!

I beg you, my friends, to oppose this man whose life and work and ideas are so openly and avowedly compatible with our American way of life. A vote for him would be a vote for the perpetuation of everything we hold dear.

The facts are clear; the record speaks for itself.

Do your duty.

THE PERSUADERS

STUDY QUESTIONS

1. What implications do Joseph Klapper's theories have for educational television? for advertisers? for the possibility of media helping to bring about social changes?

2. In criticizing Nixon's means of persuasion, David Halberstam has himself written a persuasive article which he hopes will bring the reader to share his thoughts about Nixon. Why does he feel that Nixon is not communicating honestly? Does Halberstam himself communicate his ideas honestly and effectively?

3. Basing your opinions solely upon television commercials, as Stephanie Harrington did, what subjects would you say are of most concern to Americans today? Do you feel it is valid to draw such conclusions merely from advertising content? Would you reach the same conclusions from a study of printed advertisements?

4. The goal of **Sesame Street** is to educate through persuasion. Analyze some other children's television programs. Do they also seek to persuade children in some way, or are they purely for entertainment? Do some children's programs seem to be built around the commercials?

5. In the entertainment section, Peter Herman Adler made a case for government support of the arts on television. In this section Hubert H. Humphrey pleads for government support of educational television. In view of Klapper's theories on the influence of mass communication, does public broadcasting seem to have a substantial potential for educating viewers?

6. Make a point-by-point comparison of the two Alsop articles. What details have been omitted in the **Reader's Digest** version? What other kinds of changes have been made? Do connotations change when the vocabulary changes? Do the two versions have the same overall effect?

7. In a preface to her review of **Five Easy Pieces,** Liz Smith said, "Deep reflective film criticism abounds in other periodicals, and you don't need us for that. Here, wanting you to enjoy, enjoy, we recommend, with never enough space to do our enthusiasms justice." What methods does she use to achieve her stated purpose? Do you think she succeeds in enticing the reader? Is Flinders' purpose different? How do you think his audience differs from Smith's? Might he be persuading the reader to do more than see the film?

8. After reading the selections about President Nixon's use of television for image building, does it seem to you that political broadcasts in the medium are doing an adequate job of informing voters about the issues in a presidential campaign? From looking at Sigmund's and Kempton's columns on the 1968 campaign, and from studying other political columns, do you think columnists concern themselves more with issues or with images?

BIBLIOGRAPHY FOR FURTHER STUDY

Baker, Stephen. *Visual Persuasion*. New York: McGraw-Hill, 1961.

"Bias—The Human Side of Media Buying." *Media/Scope,* XIII (May, 1969), 32–41.

Brickman, William W. "Mass Media as Educators." *School and Society,* XCVIII (February, 1970), 78–79.

"Brown is Beautiful." *Newsweek,* LXXV (March 23, 1970), 92.

Browne, Don R. "The American Image as Presented Abroad by U.S. Television." *Journalism Quarterly,* XLV (Summer, 1968), 307–16.

Court, Catherine. "Fashion Fascism: An Interview with Marshall McLuhan." *Rags* (October, 1970), 23.

Doan, Richard K. "Kindergarten May Never Be the Same Again." *TV Guide* (July 11, 1970), 6–9.

Freberg, Stan. "The Freberg Part-time Television Plan." *Mass Media in a Free Society*. Ed. by Warren K. Agee. Lawrence, Kansas: The University Press of Kansas, 1969, pp. 63–78.

Gerbner, George. *Mass Communications and Popular Conceptions of Education: A Cross-Cultural Study*. 2 vols. Urbana, Illinois: Institute of Communications Research (ERIC), 1964.

Henninger, Daniel. "The One-Eyed Slicker: TV's Long Lasting, Super Strength Half-Truths." *New Republic,* CLXII (May 2, 1970), 17–19.

"Little Magazines in the Big Cities." *Media/Scope,* XIII (February, 1969), 26–28.

Mendelsohn, Harold and Irving Crespi. *Polls, Television, and the New Politics*. Scranton: Chandler Publishing Co., 1970.

Sedulus. "Slouching Toward Bethlehem." *New Republic,* CLXIII (December 12, 1970), 29–30.

Staab, Walter. "Radio's New Reach." *Media/Scope,* XI (September, 1967), 121–22.

Steiner, Shari. "Europe and America: A Question of Self-Image." *Saturday Review,* LII (December 27, 1969), 18–20.

Tebbel, John. "Broadcasting's Hidden Power: The TV–Radio Reps." *Saturday Review,* LII (December 13, 1969), 68–69.

Tobin, Richard L. "Spots Before Our Eyes." *Saturday Review,* LIII (February 14, 1970), 67–68.

A 1
B 2
C 3
D 4
E 5
F 6
G 7
H 8
I 9
J 0